1,000,000 Books

are available to read at

ISBN 978-1-331-28673-8
PIBN 10169199

This book is a reproduction of an important historical work. Forgotten Books uses
state-of-the-art technology to digitally reconstruct the work, preserving the original format
whilst repairing imperfections present in the aged copy. In rare cases, an imperfection in
the original, such as a blemish or missing page, may be replicated in our edition. We do,
however, repair the vast majority of imperfections successfully; any imperfections that
remain are intentionally left to preserve the state of such historical works.

1 MONTH OF
FREE
READING

at

www.ForgottenBooks.com

By purchasing this book you are eligible for one month membership to ForgottenBooks.com, giving you unlimited access to our entire collection of over 1,000,000 titles via our web site and mobile apps.

To claim your free month visit:

www.forgottenbooks.com/free169199

English
Français
Deutsche
Italiano
Español
Português

www.forgottenbooks.com

Mythology Photography **Fiction**
Fishing Christianity **Art** Cooking
Essays Buddhism Freemasonry
Medicine **Biology** Music **Ancient**
Egypt Evolution Carpentry Physics
Dance Geology **Mathematics** Fitness
Shakespeare **Folklore** Yoga Marketing
Confidence Immortality Biographies
Poetry **Psychology** Witchcraft
Electronics Chemistry History **Law**
Accounting **Philosophy** Anthropology
Alchemy Drama Quantum Mechanics
Atheism Sexual Health **Ancient History**
Entrepreneurship Languages Sport
Paleontology Needlework Islam
Metaphysics Investment Archaeology
Parenting Statistics Criminology
Motivational

THE GOSPEL

ACCORDING TO

MARK,

TRANSLATED FROM THE ORIGINAL GREEK,

AND ILLUSTRATED BY

EXTRACTS

FROM THE THEOLOGICAL WRITINGS

OF

EMANUEL SWEDENBORG,

TOGETHER WITH
NOTES AND OBSERVATIONS OF THE TRANSLATOR
ANNEXED TO EACH CHAPTER.

BY THE LATE REV. J. CLOWES, M.A.,
RECTOR OF ST. JOHN'S CHURCH, MANCHESTER, AND FELLOW OF
TRINITY COLLEGE, CAMBRIDGE.

SECOND EDITION,
THOROUGHLY REVISED, WITH MANY ADDITIONAL EXTRACTS.

"WHOSO READETH, LET HIM UNDERSTAND."—MATT. xxiv. 15.

LONDON:
W. WHITE, 36, BLOOMSBURY STREET;
J. S. HODSON, PORTUGAL STREET, LINCOLN'S INN.
SOLD IN MANCHESTER, BY L. KENWORTHY,
CATEATON STREET.
1858.

MANCHESTER:
CAVE AND SEVER, PRINTERS, PALATINE BUILDINGS, HUNT'S BANK.

PREFACE.

ALTHOUGH the Translator of the following Gospel is decidedly of opinion that he has already, in the Prefaces to his translations of the other three Gospels, made a *sufficient* apology to the public for his *Extracts* from the Theological Writings of EMANUEL SWEDENBORG, yet he is still willing to add to that apology, by suggesting some further considerations tending to confirm the credibility of that Writer's testimony, and thus proving him to be, what thousands are now convinced he is, "a Scribe instructed unto the kingdom of heaven." Having already, then, in the above Prefaces, endeavoured to establish the credit of this *Heaven-instructed Scribe,* so far as it is grounded in the sublime and edifying views presented in his various Writings, respecting,—first, the Divinity and Plenary Inspiration of the Sacred Scriptures; secondly, respecting the Divine Character of the GREAT SAVIOUR, and His Oneness with the ETERNAL FATHER; and thirdly, respecting the truly Christian Life, as being the result of *Charity, Faith, and Good Works united;*—the Translator is now eager to add to all this splendid testimony the doctrine inculcated by the same Writer concerning a future state, or that invisible world of *certainties* and *realities,* to which every human being is introduced on the removal of those material bonds which at present detain him in a world of shadows and uncertainties.

This doctrine may be viewed under three distinct aspects, all of which are in its favour, as indicative of its origin, its excellence, and its blessed tendency.

First, As to its full agreement with the documents of Revealed
  Wisdom, and the persuasions of the most enlightened men,
  on the interesting subject;

Secondly, As to the elucidation which it receives from the light
  of *metaphysical investigation*, made and pursued by the
  enlightened Author; and

Thirdly, As to the highly conclusive and confirming evidence
  resulting to it from the Author's *own experience*, during the
  protracted period of twenty-seven years.

To begin with the *first* of these aspects.

I. It is impossible for any intelligent reader to peruse, with any
degree of serious attention, the edifying pages of the Old and
New Testament, without being forcibly struck with the conviction
that they inculcate, both by implication and positive assertion, the
doctrine of a future state of rewards and punishments, in which
all good men are admitted to the full enjoyment of the good
which, during their abode here below, they have made the object
of their supreme love, thus of their deliberate choice and practical
pursuit; and all wicked men are left to experience the frightful but
necessary effects of that evil which they also, whilst in the body,
have made the ruling principle of their affections, thoughts, and
actions. In the *Old* Testament, indeed, this doctrine is not taught
so expressly as in the *New*, probably because the people to whom
the Old Testament was first delivered, were not in a state to
admit the doctrine in all its brightness and purity; and therefore,
as in the law respecting marriage, an abatement was made to that
people of its full requirements, "because of the hardness of their
hearts," (Matt. xix. 8; Mark x. 5.) so likewise, and for the same
reason, a veil of obscurity might possibly be thrown over the
doctrine of a future state, both as to the certainties and the
characteristics of such a state. But in the *New* Testament this
veil, we find, like the veil of the temple at the crucifixion of the
GREAT REDEEMER, was "rent in twain," (Matt. xxvii. 51.) and
when a New Church was to be established here on earth, in the
place of that corrupt one which had "filled up the measure of
its inquities," a new and eternal world was presented more clearly

to the view of mortals, marked with its distinct characters of consolation to the penitent believer, and of woe to the impenitent.
For thus we find it written on the interesting occasion,—"When
the Son of Man shall come in His glory, and all His holy angels
with Him, then shall He sit on the throne of His glory; and
before Him shall be gathered all nations: and He shall separate
them one from another, as a shepherd divideth his sheep from the
goats; and He shall set the sheep on His right hand, and the
goats on the left. Then shall the King say to those on His right
hand, Come, ye blessed of My Father, inherit the kingdom prepared
for you from the beginning of the world. Then shall He say also
to them on the left hand, Depart from Me, ye cursed, into everlasting fire, prepared for the devil and his angels. And these shall
go away into everlasting punishment: but the righteous into life
eternal." (Matt. xxv. 31—34, 41—46.) In the parable too of the
rich man and Lazarus, we behold a still more particular display
both of the comforts and miseries of this new and eternal world,
whilst we read how "Lazarus died, and was carried by the angels
into Abraham's bosom; and how the rich man also died, and was
buried, and in hell he lifted up his eyes, being in torments, and
seeth Abraham afar off, and Lazarus in his bosom." (Luke xvi.
19, to the end of the chapter.) Here, then, we find all doubt
dissipated respecting the eternal destination of the human race,
whilst a final seal is set by the Almighty Himself to the certainty
of a future state, involving in it a fulness of joy to all His
penitent and obedient children, and of misery to the impenitent
and disobedient.

But if such be the important document of Revealed Wisdom, as
we find it written in the Book of God Himself, the impression
made by that same Wisdom on the tablet of every human heart
is in exact agreement with it. For how else shall we give any
rational explanation of the general assent of mankind to the interesting doctrine under consideration, or how else shall we account
for the persuasions which, in all ages of the world, and amongst
all nations, have led pious and enlightened men to assert this full
belief,—that "this corruptible must put on incorruption, and this
mortal must put on immortality," though possibly not in the same

precise language, nor in the same fulness of conviction, with the Apostle?

Comparing now the above testimony of the Sacred Scriptures, and the persuasions of good men in all ages of the world, with the doctrine concerning a future state, as taught in the Theological Writings of the enlightened SWEDENBORG, we discover an agreement and coincidence greatly in favour of the character of the Author of those Writings. For, do the Sacred Scriptures assert that the impenitent and unbelieving, after death, "shall go away into everlasting punishment, and the righteous into life eternal"? So does SWEDENBORG. Is there an impression too on the minds of all good men, that, under the covering of a material body, man possesses an immaterial and immortal soul, or spirit, which survives the dissolution of its earthly shell, and when liberated from its shackles of clay, becomes the inhabitant of a world better suited to the spirituality of its being? SWEDENBORG concurs exactly in the same sentiment. But he is not content only in concurring. To the *general* acknowledgment of a future state of existence, he superadds a thousand *interesting particulars*, all tending to confirm the general idea, and by particularising, to complete and substantiate it. The *future* world thus becomes to the believer a *present* world, by convincing him not only *that it is*, but *what it is*, and especially that it is *near* to him, and he to it, in agreement with the Divine declaration,—"The kingdom of GOD is come nigh unto you." (Luke x. 9.) The *visionary* and *empty* world too (as *another world* is commonly supposed to be), acquires, from the views presented of it in the Writings of SWEDENBORG, both *reality* and *fulness*, whilst by the indefinite variety of its inhabitants, its objects, its laws, its customs, &c., it is seen to be a world infinitely surpassing the world of matter in the multiplicity and grandeur of its external manifestations, as well as in the superior activity of the living principles from which they are derived. But what, above all other considerations, tends to remove all doubt, and thus to establish the well-disposed reader in a satisfactory conviction of the certainty of the existence, not only of another world, but of its inhabitants, is the edifying Scripture doctrine continually insisted on and confirmed in the Writings of SWEDENBORG, that all man's inclinations, purposes, thoughts, delights, &c., whether good or evil, originate in that world,—the *good*, in the world of Divine order and bliss, called *heaven*, and the *evil* in the world of infernal disorder and misery, called *hell*. Mankind, therefore, have only to look into the little kingdom of their own minds, and to explore there, with due attention, the original sources of their love, intelligence, ends of life, &c., and they will then see the great realities of another world, and at the same time the testimony of SWEDENBORG respecting it, unfolded and confirmed to them by the most satisfactory, as well as by the most edifying of all evidence.

II. But the doctrine of SWEDENBORG respecting a future state is recommended, not only by its full agreement with the testimony of the Sacred Scriptures, and the persuasions of all good men on the subject, but by the elucidation which it receives from the light of *metaphysical investigation*, as that investigation has been made and pursued by the illustrious Author of the doctrine.

The result of this investigation may be comprised in the following summary, collected from the Author's voluminous Writings, both philosophical and theological, all tending to prove the following propositions :—

First,—That the body of man is an organized material form, deriving both its organization and its form from its parent soul, as an *instrumental* cause, and from the life originating in GOD, as a *supreme* cause, operating by and through the *instrumental* cause.

Secondly,—That the human soul and body are thus perfectly distinct from each other, as *cause* and *effect*, or as *mind* and *matter* are distinct, both in *essence* and in the *degree* of their component principles, by virtue of which distinctness no purity of matter can possibly approximate to *soul*, neither can any grossness of soul be convertible into *matter*.

Thirdly,—That the *soul* of man is the *real* man, whether existing in the present world or in the future, and that the *material body* is only an *appendix* or a *covering*, which is discarded and put off at death, as a man puts off his clothes, whilst the *soul*, or *real man*, remains and lives as before, either in the world of order and of bliss, which he has made the object of his voluntary choice, or in the world of disorder and of misery, into which his voluntary choice has plunged him, in opposition to that Divine Mercy which was always in the endeavour to elevate him to heaven and its happiness.

Fourthly,—That therefore what is commonly called *death*, is nothing but the liberation of man from the shackles of matter, on which occasion the soul of every good man enters immediately, with kindred souls, into the enjoyment of the blessings of good, grounded in the love of GOD and neighbourly love; and the soul of every wicked man descends, by its own gravitation, not by any arbitrary vengeance of the ALMIGHTY, into the miserable abodes of wicked spirits like unto itself.

Fifthly,—That a future state is thus both the *continuation* and *completion* of the present state, without which the present state is involved in inextricable perplexity, utterly irreconcileable with the goodness, wisdom, and power of the BENEVOLENT FATHER of the universe, since it may reasonably be asked,—Why did this GREAT and GOOD CREATOR gift His creature man with a *desire of immortality*, if He never intended that this desire should be gratified? Why did He endow this creature, in distinction from all the inferior creatures, with a capacity of knowing and of loving the DIVINE AUTHOR of his being, and of tasting the delights of that knowledge and love, if those delights were to be limited to the short period of his present life? Why too is temporal joy and prosperity, in many instances, the lot of the wicked in this life, whilst temporal sorrow and adversity is the lot of the righteous, supposing that no other life is to follow, in which the Divine Providence of the MOST HIGH is to be justified by the inversion of these lots? Why, in short, was an *idea* of a future world ever communicated to man, if no such world exists? or indeed, *how* could it, in such case, be communicated, since an *idea* of a thing necessarily implies its *existence*, it being absolutely impossible that man should have a notion, or impression on his mind, of what *is not*, consequently impossible that he should have a notion of GOD, if there be *no* GOD; or a notion of heaven and its angels, if there be *no* heaven and *no* angels; or a notion of hell and its devils, if there be *no* such place, and *no* such inhabitants.

Such are the results of *metaphysical investigation* on the interest-ing subject of a future state, which are to be found in the voluminous Writings, both philosophical and theological, of SWEDENBORG. Who then will ever refuse to that Author the credit so justly due to him for his researches, by which he not only asserts the doctrine of the Sacred Scriptures respecting the soul's immortality and a life after death, but also illustrates and confirms it by such a light and force of rational argument, as to secure it against the sceptical reasonings of the infidel, the doubts of the half-convinced believer, and the denial of the impious and profane.

III. But if agreement with the testimony of Divine Revelation and the persuasions of all good men, on the doctrine of a future state, and a confirmation of that testimony and of those persuasions by *metaphysical investigation*, must be allowed to have due weight in favour of our Author's character as an expositor of truth, the Author's *own experience* on the subject, especially when continued to the protracted period of twenty-seven years, cannot surely be denied its share of importance, particularly when it is in perfect harmony both with the declarations of HOLY WRIT, the surmises of good men, and the conclusions of rational inquiry.

And here the Translator wishes to observe that it cannot, and indeed ought not to be concealed, that the Author of the following Extracts (quoted from his voluminous works to explain the true and spiritual meaning of the Gospel of ST. MARK), made no scruple of confessing that, during the last twenty-seven years of his life, the interiors of his mind or spirit were opened by the ALMIGHTY, so as to enable him to have communication with angels and spirits in the spiritual world, and at the same time with men in the natural world, and thus to acquire an indefinite variety of informa-tion respecting both the heavenly and infernal world, such as was never before vouchsafed to any human being. This information too he has thought proper to publish at large, especially in his interesting Work on "Heaven and Hell," and also occasionally in his other Writings, from the whole of which the reader is supplied with important documents, not only confirming the *existence* of another world and its various inhabitants, but likewise unfolding the *quality* of the *heavenly principles* necessary to introduce man into the kingdom of eternal bliss, and the *quality* too of the *infernal principles* which have a tendency to plunge him into the opposite regions of everlasting sorrow.

It is accordingly an important article in the enlightened Author's testimony respecting both the ᵢjoys and miseries of the other life, that they are not grounded in any *arbitrary appointments* either of Divine Mercy or Divine Judgment, but in the *ruling disposition* of the parties concerned, inasmuch as it is an eternal law of Divine Order that, without *heavenly love*, which is the love of GOD and of our neighbour, there can be no admission into heaven, since heaven is heaven by virtue of that love. From the same eternal law too (according to our Author) it follows, that *infernal love*, which is the inordinate love of self and of the world, *necessarily* precipitates man into the kingdom of misery and darkness, in spite of all the will and endeavour of the MERCIFUL CREATOR to elevate him into light and joy, inasmuch as infernal love is directly opposed to heavenly love, and consequently the subjects of the *former* love cannot possibly dwell together with the subjects of the *latter*, but shun them as *tormentors*, comparatively as a wicked man on earth feels interior pain in the society of the good and well-disposed.

Having established then this fact—that the principle of heavenly love and charity is the sole qualification for admittance hereafter into the kingdom of bliss, and that the want of such love and charity has a necessary tendency to shut the doors of heaven against the thoughtless and impenitent—the enlightened Author next proceeds to unfold the *operation* both of this principle, and of the want of it, by pointing out its *two-fold* effects,—first, on the *internal* man; and secondly, on the *external*. He teaches, therefore, that in whatsoever mind this principle has been made the ruling principle, it produces hereafter, in the *internal* man, a sensation of *joy*, grounded in divine innocence and peace, and in the *external* man an exquisite *delight*, arising from a variety of gratifications adapted to that man, such as result from the enjoy-ment of social intercourse, of useful employment, of recreating scenery, of garments, habitations, gardens, &c., exactly adapted to the peculiar temper and taste of each heavenly inhabitant. For thus the Author writes on the interesting subject from his own experience :—" The things which exist in the heavens do not exist in like manner with those which exist in the earths, all things in the heavens existing from the LORD, according to their correspondence with the interiors of the angels; for the angels have both interiors and exteriors, and the things which are in the interiors have all of them reference to love and faith, thus to will and understanding as their receptacles. But the exteriors correspond to the interiors, as may be illustrated by what was said above concerning the heat and light of heaven, viz., that the angels have heat according to the quality of their love, and light according to the quality of their wisdom. The case is similar in regard to all other things which appear before the senses of the angels."— (Treatise on *Heaven and Hell*, n. 173.)

And again :—" Inasmuch as the angels are men, and live one amongst another as men on earth live, therefore they have garments, habitations, and several other like things; yet, with a difference, that all things with them are more perfect, because in a more perfect state." (n. 177.) And as the principle of heavenly love and charity, in the interiors of the angels, is thus productive of corresponding delightful things in the exteriors, so likewise the want of this principle, in the interiors of the infernals, is shewn by the Author's experience to give birth to correspondent effects in the exteriors, and of course to produce an external manifestation of objects the most deformed, filthy, and disgusting.

It is plain to see (and no one saw it plainer than the Author himself) how all this information was likely to be received by a world immersed in all the pollution and darkness of scepticism respecting the great realities of another life. The testimony was accordingly rejected by some as visionary, ridiculed by others as nonsensical, and doubted by almost all as groundless, so that the pious and enlightened Author, instead of receiving from his fellow-mortals the tribute of the praise and thanks due to him for being the favoured messenger of *glad tidings* from above, was exposed to all that virulence of censure and accusation with which the GREAT SAVIOUR Himself had before been assailed by the thoughtless multitude, when they exclaimed in their folly and perverseness,— " He hath a devil, and is mad; why hear ye Him?" (John x. 20.)

But ought not this example of hasty and unjust judgment in the Jews of old to have operated as an everlasting caution to *Christians*, to secure them against the impiety and delusion of becoming the miserable dupes of a similar infatuation? For do not all Christians profess their full belief in the testimony of the Sacred Scriptures, or WORD OF GOD? And yet, in that testimony, how many instances are recorded of holy men who have been admitted to the sacred privilege and distinguished honour of having their spiritual eyes opened to behold the great realities of the eternal world, and their spiritual ears to hear the edifying language of its inhabitants! For to say nothing of what is related concerning PETER, (Acts x.) and also concerning PAUL, (2 Cor. xii.) of the Prophets too in the Old Testament, particularly EZEKIEL, DANIEL, and ZECHARIAH, who were, each of them, favoured with views of various objects in the spiritual world, what shall we think, or say, of the blessed JOHN in the Apocalypse, who himself testifies in the most solemn manner, that he "saw the SON OF MAN in the midst of seven candlesticks;" that he also saw "a tabernacle, a temple, an ark, and an altar in heaven; a book, too, sealed with seven seals, the book opened, and the consequent going forth of four horses; four animals around the throne; twelve thousand chosen out of each of the tribes of Israel; locusts ascending from the bottomless pit; a woman bringing forth a man-child, and flying into a wilderness by reason of a dragon; two beasts, one ascending out of the sea, the other from the earth; an angel flying in the midst of heaven, having the everlasting Gospel; a glassy sea mixed with fire; seven angels having seven plagues; vials poured out by them on the earth, on the sea, on the rivers, on the sun, on the throne of the beast, on Euphrates, and on the air; a woman sitting on a scarlet beast; a dragon cast out into a lake of fire and sulphur; a white horse; a great supper; a new heaven and a new earth; the holy Jerusalem coming down from heaven, described as to its gates, its walls, and foundations; also a river of the water of life, and trees of life bearing fruit every month," with many things besides, which were all seen by the Apostle, whilst as to his spirit he was in the spiritual world, or heaven. (See the Apocalypse throughout.)

It is evident, then, that in former ages it has pleased the ALMIGHTY, in His adorable mercy, and in agreement with His gracious purposes of blessing to His people, to appoint some of His chosen servants here below, to be the favoured spectators and delegated witnesses of what is passing in His kingdom, and amongst its blessed inhabitants above. Who, then will have the boldness to say that this day of holy revelation is for ever past, or that the hand of the ALMIGHTY is now shortened that He *cannot*, or His mercy so gone that He *will not*, open the door of His invisible kingdom to His children of the present generation, as He is acknowledged to have done to His children of the past? Shall a Christian, more especially, be chargeable with this boldness? With the BOOK OF GOD in his hand, testifying the Divine willingness and ability to unveil to mortals such things as "eye hath not seen," unless opened by HIM of whom it is written—"He openeth, and no man shutteth; and shutteth, and no man openeth," (Rev. iii. 7.) will he venture to set a limit in his heart to this *opening* power of the GOD of heaven? For is it not possible that this GREAT AND MERCIFUL FATHER may discover, in His children of the present generation, some peculiar necessity, or at least expediency, for a more particular manifestation of the certainties and comforts of His heavenly kingdom, than has been heretofore vouchsafed? Is it not possible that a belief in a future state may, at this day, have become so weak and unsettled in men's minds, and at the same time so obscure and confused, as no longer to be sufficient to stem the torrent of modern Sadducism, and thus to elevate man above its destructive waves, by convincing him of his immortality? Shall a professor of Christianity, then, denying those possibilities, take upon him to decide on necessities and expediencies known only to the OMNISCIENT? Or rather, would it not better become him on an occasion of such vast importance, to distrust his own judgment, and in the spirit of fervent prayer and Christian humility to examine attentively the nature and tendency of the testimony concerning another world, as delivered by the honourable Author, and if he finds that its grand object is to elevate the love and affections of man to an

ETERNAL END, thus to GOD and Heaven, then to adopt it accordingly for the regulation of his life and conduct?

The Translator of the following Gospel has now only to observe, in reference to his Translation, that he has endeavoured, as in the other Gospels, "to make it as correct as possible, by consulting the best and most approved commentators, and that whensoever he has felt himself under the obligation to adopt a sense differing from what is expressed in the authorised version, it has always been with regret, on account of the commendation so justly due to that version for its general accuracy and correctness. He has accordingly thought it right to give his reasons for his occasional deviations from that version, which reasons may be found in the *notes* and *observations* annexed to each chapter."

It only remains, then, that both the Gospel itself, and also the accompanying extracts, notes, and observations, may be perused by the reader in that spirit of humility, prayer, and the sincere love of Truth for its own sake, which led the Psalmist of old to address himself to his HEAVENLY FATHER in these interesting words,—"Open Thou mine eyes, that I may behold wondrous things out of Thy law." (Psalm cxix. 18.)

That such may be the mind and temper of the reader, and such the blessed end of his reading, is the devout prayer of

J. CLOWES.

PREFACE TO THE SECOND EDITION.

THE GOSPELS, it is well known, form so important a portion of GOD's Word, that the entire system of Christianity is founded upon the divine Truths revealed by the LORD Himself in these most holy Records. A right understanding of the Gospels is consequently of infinite moment to a right understanding of the Doctrines of Christianity. If these doctrines, by a false or fallacious interpretation of the Gospels, are misunderstood, the entire system of Christian doctrine founded on such a misinterpretation will be fallacious and false, and by no means *Evangelical*, or in agreement with the pure Truth revealed in the Gospels.

Again, it may be affirmed that the more truly and spiritually the Gospels are interpreted and understood, the more will the church, founded on such an interpretation, partake of the "*spirit and the life of the* LORD's *word*," (John vi. 63.) and the more effectual will it become as the medium of enlightening and saving the human race. But to adduce only one, out of innumerable instances that might be quoted, of the uncertainty and contradiction with which the prevailing theology interprets the LORD's sayings, we will refer to chapter ix. verse 49, of this Gospel,— "*Every one shall be salted with fire.*"

WHITBY supposes this to mean that—

"Every man shall be seasoned with fire itself, so as to become inconsumable, and shall endure for ever to be tormented, and therefore may be said to be 'salted with fire,' in allusion to that property of salt which is to preserve things from corruption."

This is the interpretation of this celebrated commentator.

We will now adduce the interpretation of the equally celebrated commentators, LIGHTFOOT and DODDRIDGE, who say that the "man salted with fire" means—

"That he who is a true sacrifice to GOD shall be seasoned with the salt of grace to the incorruption of glory."

Here the meaning of being "salted with fire" is supposed to be that of being "seasoned with the salt of grace," quite opposed to WHITBY's interpretation, which is that of "being salted with the fire of hell."

Lastly, we will quote the celebrated commentators, BEZA and GILPIN, who suppose that this passage means—

"That every Christian is purified by the difficult and fiery trials of life, in the same manner as every sacrifice was purified with salt."*

Now, what can deliver us from such a conflict of opinions founded on misinterpretations of the LORD's words, but a true system of Scriptural Interpretation according to the Doctrine of Correspondences between things spiritual and natural? This system SWEDENBORG was, of the LORD's mercy, the means of making known to mankind, and it requires but little study and attention to see how uniform and beautiful the meaning of the Gospels becomes when interpreted according to the doctrine of correspondences, and how impossible it is to come to any luminous and satisfactory interpretation without this "key of knowledge."

Everything relating to GOD's Word, and especially to the Divine Gospels, will grow in the esteem and love of mankind as generations come on in uninterrupted succession. This is not the case with most other books; they become antiquated, obsolete, and are replaced by others better adapted to the more developed state of the human mind. But it is not so with the WORD OF GOD; this must, as ages roll on, be held in a constantly increasing veneration. The great condition indeed of true mental progress, is the degree in which the Truths of the Divine Word are understood, loved, and practised. This progress is synonymous with regeneration, which is the only true progress of man. The more interiorly, spiritually, clearly, and rationally the Word is understood, the greater will be the elevation and power of the human mind, and the more exalted its wisdom and happiness.

With this object in view, the Editors of the new editions of the Gospels of MATTHEW, LUKE, and JOHN, published within these

* These statements are taken from Bagster's *Comprehensive Bible*. See the notes on the passage in question.

last few years, have thought it worthy of every effort not only to supply a translation as correct as possible, but to furnish every illustration they could find in the voluminous works of SWEDENBORG of the divine Text of the Gospels.

The present edition of the Gospel of MARK has for some time past been expected and desired by the public, but owing to the illness and subsequent infirmities of one of the Editors, the late Rev. D. HOWARTH, the work was unavoidably delayed. The present Editor, after the decease of his beloved friend and coadjutor in the editing of these Gospels, devoted his time and study to the work, taking into consideration the references of his late friend as far as available for the purpose.

The version has been carefully collated with the Greek, and has been brought more closely to the original, expressing in some instances more correctly the inspired words, so that the correspondences may be more clearly and readily perceived. Thus in chap. iv. 39, instead of "Peace, be still!" it is rendered "Be silent, be dumb!" from which expressions, taken from the human frame, the correspondence to the subjugation of the infernal powers denoted by the tempestuous sea is distinctly seen, but not so from the common version, nor from the former edition of this work. Other instances of this kind might be adduced. The rendering also of the *aorist* participles has been attended to, and their peculiar force conveyed in English, as far as the genius of the two languages will admit.

The explanation of the Text has been enriched with about 180 additional and copious Extracts from the Works of SWEDENBORG, which render this new edition, as to the spiritual exposition of this Divine Gospel, so complete as to leave but little to be desired.

J. H. SMITHSON.

MANCHESTER, *April*, 1858.

EXPLANATION

Of the Abbreviated Titles of the Works of Emanuel Swedenborg,
referred to in the foregoing pages.

A. C.—Arcana Cœlestia.
A. E.—Apocalypse Explained.
A. R.—Apocalypse Revealed.
C. L. or *C. S. L.*—The Delights of Wisdom concerning Conjugial Love, and the Pleasures of Insanity concerning Scortatory Love.
D. Influx.—The Doctrine of Influx.
D. Life.—Doctrine of Life for the New Jerusalem.
D. L. or *D. Lord.*—Doctrine of the New Jerusalem concerning the Lord.
D. P.—Angelic Wisdom concerning Divine Providence.
Div. Wisdom.—On the Divine Wisdom, at the end of *A. E.*
H. D. or *H. D. N. J.*—The Heavenly Doctrine of the New Jerusalem.
H. H.—Treatise concerning Heaven and Hell.
L. J.—Treatise concerning the Last Judgment.
S. S.—Doctrine of the New Jerusalem concerning the Sacred Scriptures.
Spir. Diary.—Swedenborg's Spiritual Diary.
T. C. R.—True Christian Religion.

ERRATA.

Page 84, line 4 from bottom, for 1940 read 1941.
" 87, " 9 " read γινωσκω for γινοσκω.
" 169, " 18 " dele *s* in principles.
" 312, Internal Sense, at verse 1 dele 2, and in the next verse for 3 read 2.

Cave & Sever, Printers, Palatine Buildings, Hunt's Bank, Manchester.

THE GOSPEL ACCORDING TO

MARK.

CHAPTER I.

THE WORD.

THE INTERNAL SENSE.

1. THE Beginning of the Gospel of Jesus Christ, the Son of God.

2. As it is written in the Prophets, Behold, I send My Messenger [Angel] before Thy face, who shall prepare Thy way before Thee.

3. The voice of one crying in the wilderness, Prepare ye the way of the Lord, make His paths straight.

4. John was baptizing in the wilderness, and preaching the baptism of repentance for the remission of sins.

5. And all the country of Judea went out to him, and they of Jerusalem, and were all baptized by him in the river Jordan, confessing their sins.

THAT JEHOVAH, according to prediction, was manifested in the flesh, and under that manifestation was called JESUS CHRIST, and the SON OF GOD. (Verses 1, 2.)

That the Jewish Church was in a state of vastation at that time, so that there remained in it no longer any good or any truth, and in this state was instructed from the Word to shun all evils as sins against God, and to believe in the Lord's Divine Human principle, since otherwise the evil of sin can never be removed. (Verses 3, 4.)

That this instruction was received by the humble and the penitent, who were thus admitted into the Church, being made sensible that of themselves they are nothing but evil. (Verse 5.)

1

6. And John was clothed with camel's hair, and with a girdle of a skin about his loins, and he did eat locusts and wild honey;

7. And preached, saying, There cometh one mightier than I after me, the latchet of whose shoes I am not worthy to stoop down and unloose.

8. I indeed have baptized you in water, but He shall baptize you in the Holy Spirit.

9. And it came to pass in those days, [that] Jesus came from Nazareth of Galilee, and was baptized by John in Jordan.

10. And straightway coming up out of the water, He saw the heavens rent, and the Spirit like a dove descending upon Him.

11. And there was a voice from the heavens, [saying] Thou art My beloved Son, in Whom I am well pleased.

12. And immediately the Spirit sendeth Him forth into the wilderness.

13. And He was there in the wilderness forty days, tempted by Satan; and was with the wild beasts; and the Angels ministered unto Him.

The ultimates of the Word, which are natural, are figuratively described. (Verse 6.)

Which ultimates testify that they can only effect external purification, whereas the Word itself, by and through its internal sense, is effective of internal purification, which is regeneration, by Divine Truth and Good. (Verses 7, 8.)

That the LORD as to His Human essence, submits to be initiated into the external truths of the Word, because He thus became the Word in its ultimates, as He was the Word in its first principles, and because also He glorified His Humanity, or made it Divine, as He regenerates man, and makes him spiritual. (Verse 9.)

Yet ascending rapidly out of external truths, He enters into the interior truths and goods of the Word, even to the Divine Truth and Good in Himself. (Verses 10, 11.)

And is thus admitted, as to His Humanity, into temptations, which are nothing else but the assaults of infernal spirits, seeking to destroy what is true by what is false, and what is good by what is evil. (Verses 12, 13.)

But these assaults are succeeded by victory, attended with divine peace and consolation. (Latter part of verse 13.)

14. Now after John was delivered to custody, Jesus came into Galilee, preaching the Gospel of the Kingdom of God;

15. And saying, That the time is fulfilled, and the Kingdom of God is near; Repent ye, and believe the Gospel.

Whence a greater measure of Divine power was communicated to the LORD's Humanity to announce the descent and nearness of Divine Truth and Good, calling man to forsake all evil as sin against God, and to believe in the manifestation of GOD in the flesh. (Verses 14, 15.)

16. But walking near the sea of Galilee, He saw Simon, and Andrew his brother, casting a net into the sea; for they were fishers.

17. And Jesus said to them, Come ye after Me, and I will make you to become fishers of men.

Which annunciation was first received by those who were in the investigation of scientific and rational truth, and who were thus led to the pursuit and acquirement of spiritual and celestial truth. (Verses 16—20.)

18. And immediately leaving their nets, they followed Him.

19. And going a little further thence, He saw James [the son] of Zebedee, and John his brother, who also were in the ship, mending the nets.

20. And immediately He called them, and leaving their father Zebedee in the ship with the hired servants, they went after Him.

Renouncing the concupiscences of self-love, and adoring the LORD as the Divine source of all that is good and wise and blessed. (Verses 18—20.)

21. And they went to Capernaum, and immediately on the Sabbaths He went into the Synagogue, and taught.

22. And they were astonished at His doctrine, for He taught them as one that had power, and not as the Scribes.

Who teacheth Truth from the Divine Good of the Divine Love, in which all Truth originates, and not from any end of worldly reputation and gain. (Verses 21, 22.)

23. And there was in their Synagogue a man with an unclean spirit; and he cried out,

24. Saying, Ah! What have we to do with Thee, Jesus of Nazareth! Art Thou come to destroy us? I know Thee who Thou art, the Holy One of God.

25. And Jesus rebuked him, saying, Be silent, and come out of him.

26. And the unclean spirit having torn him, and cried with a great voice, came out of him.

27. And they were all amazed, so that they questioned among themselves, saying, What thing is this? What new doctrine is this? For with power He commandeth even the unclean spirits, and they obey Him.

28. And the fame of Him went forth immediately into all the region round about Galilee.

29. And straightway when they had come out of the Synagogue, they entered into the house of Simon and Andrew, together with James and John.

30. But Simon's wife's mother lay sick of a fever, and immediately they tell Him of her.

31. And He came and raised her up, having taken hold of her hand, and the fever instantly left her, and she ministered unto them.

And who by that truth cleanseth man from his natural evils, and thus casteth out the infernal spirits who are in connection with those evils, and who yet are principled in heavenly knowledge, but not in the life of such knowledge. (Verses 23—27.)

So that inquiry is hence excited respecting the LORD's Humanity, which thus proves its Divinity by the subjugation of the powers of darkness, and by the brightness of the Divine Truth which it teaches. (Verses 27, 28.)

And also by its omnipotence in delivering the affection of truth in the Church from the infestation of the love of evil. (Verses 29—32.)

32. But in the evening, when the sun did set, they brought unto Him all that were diseased, and them that were possessed with devils.

33. And all the city was gathered together at the door.

34. And He healed many that were sick of divers diseases, and cast out many devils; and suffered not the devils to speak, because they knew Him.

35. And in the morning, when the night was far advanced, rising up He went out, and departed into a desert place, and there prayed.

36. And Simon and they that were with him followed Him.

37. And when they had found Him, they say unto Him, All [men] seek Thee.

38. And He saith unto them, Let us go into the neighbouring towns, that I may preach there also, for therefore came I forth.

39. And He preached in their Synagogues throughout all Galilee, and cast out devils.

40. And there came a leper to Him, beseeching Him, and kneeling down to Him, and saying unto Him, If Thou wilt, Thou canst make me clean.

41. And Jesus, moved with compassion, put forth His hand, touched him, and saith to him, I will, be thou clean.

42. And having spoken, immediately the leprosy departed from him, and he was cleansed.

And in likewise liberating those who were infested with evil and false persuasions, and who, in consequence of such liberation, became receptive of Truth and Good. (Verses 32—35.)

But the Humanity of the LORD can of itself do nothing but through union with its Divinity, and therefore it is occasionally let into temptation, that by the labour of combat it may attain a fuller union, and thus a greater measure of power to impart instruction, and to deliver mankind from infernal influence. (Verses 35—40.)

And especially to check the profanation of truth in all those who, through prayer and humiliation, and the acknowledgment of the LORD's DIVINITY, sought to be cleansed from their sins. (Verses 40—43.)

43. And He strictly charged him, and forthwith sent him away.

44. And saith to him, See thou say nothing to any man, but go, shew thyself to the priest, and offer' for thy cleansing those things which Moses commanded for a testimony unto them.

45. But he, having gone out, began to preach many things, and to publish the saying, insomuch that He [Jesus] could no more openly enter into the city, but was without in desert places; and they came to Him from every quarter.

To whom instruction is given, that truth, when rescued from profanation, ought to open itself to the reception of the heavenly good of love and charity, by acknowledging that it thence derives its life and quality. (Verses 43, 44.)

In which case truth acquires a greater power of making itself known, yet not in connection with its Divine Good, which is still in a state of persecution. (Verse 45.)

EXPOSITION;

BEING EXTRACTS

From the Theological Writings of EMANUEL SWEDENBORG.

CHAPTER I.

VERSE 1. *The beginning of the Gospel of Jesus Christ.*
Gospel *(evangelium)* signifies *glad tidings;* wherefore by
preaching the Gospel, or glad tidings, is signified to announce
the Lord's advent; hence by the Gospel, in this supreme
sense, is signified the Lord Himself as to His advent, as to
Judgment, and as to the Salvation of the faithful. This is
evident from various passages, see Mark viii. 3; ix. 29, 30;
xvi. 15. *A. E.* 612. See also Exposition, verse 14.

Jesus Christ.—When these names are pronounced, few have
any other idea than that they are proper names, and almost
like the names of another man, but more holy. The learned
indeed know that JESUS signifies SAVIOUR, and CHRIST the
ANOINTED, and hence they conceive some more interior idea.
But still this is not what the angels in heaven perceive from
those names, their perceptions extending to things still more
divine; for by JESUS, when the name is pronounced by a man
in reading the Word, they perceive the Divine Good, and by
CHRIST the Divine Truth; and by both the divine marriage
of Good and Truth, and of Truth and Good, consequently of
all that is Divine in the heavenly marriage, which is heaven.
That JESUS in the internal sense denotes Divine Good, and
that CHRIST denotes Divine Truth, may be evident from many
passages in the Word. The ground and reason why Jesus
denotes Divine Good is, because it signifies safety, salvation,
and Saviour; and, in consequence of such signification, it signifies Divine Good, inasmuch as all salvation is from Divine
Good, which is of the Lord's love and mercy, and thus by the
reception thereof. The ground and reason why Christ denotes
Divine Truth is, because it signifies Messiah, Anointed, and
King, for that these terms denote Divine Truth, will appear
from what follows. *A. C.* 3004—3006.

The Lord is called a Priest from Divine Good, and a King from Divine Truth; the latter, viz., Divine Truth, is involved in the name Christ, and Divine Good in the name Jesus. *A. C.* 8625.

Son of God.—No other opinion is held by the church than that the "Son of God" is a separate Person of the Godhead, perfectly distinct from the Person of the Father; which has given rise to the belief that the Son of God was born from eternity. In consequence of the general prevalence of this notion, and because it relates to God, no liberty is allowed, in thinking about it, to make use of the understanding, not even upon the meaning of the expression, "born from eternity." And indeed were any one intellectually to reflect upon it, all that he could say would be—"It transcends my powers of comprehension, but still I affirm and believe it, because others do the same." Let it however be well noted, that there is no Son from eternity, yet that the Lord is from eternity. When an accurate knowledge of the Lord and of the Son is obtained, then, and not before, can we think intellectually of the Triune God. That the Human principle of the Lord, conceived of Jehovah the Father, and born of the Virgin Mary, is the "Son of God," is very manifest from the following passages, as in Luke:—"The angel Gabriel was sent from God to a city of Galilee, named Nazareth, to a virgin betrothed to a man whose name was Joseph, &c., and said unto her, Thou shalt conceive in thy womb, and shalt bring forth a Son, and shalt call his name Jesus. He shall be great, and shall be called the Son of the Highest. But Mary said to the angel, How shall this thing be, seeing I know not a man? And the angel answering said to her, THE HOLY SPIRIT SHALL COME UPON THEE, AND THE POWER OF THE HIGHEST SHALL OVERSHADOW THEE; therefore also THE HOLY THING which shall be born of thee shall be called the SON OF GOD." (i. 26—35.) It is here said, "Thou shalt conceive and bring forth a Son, He shall be great, and shall be called the *Son of the Highest;*" and again, "The Holy Thing which shall be born of thee shall be called the *Son of God,*" whence it is evident that the Human principle, conceived of God, and born of the Virgin Mary, is what is called the *Son of God.* So in Isaiah, "The Lord Himself gives a sign, behold a virgin shall conceive and bring forth *a Son,* and shall call His name, GOD WITH US." (vii. 14.) That the Son born of the virgin, and conceived of God, is He who shall be called "God with us," thus who is the Son of God, is evident. So again in the same prophet,—"A Child is born unto us, a SON is given unto us; upon whose shoulder is the

government; and He shall call His name Wonderful, Counsellor, God, Hero, the FATHER OF ETERNITY, the Prince of
Peace;" (ix. 5, 6.) where the same thing is asserted, for it is
said, "A Child is born unto us, a Son is given unto us," who
is not a Son from eternity, but the Son born in the world,
which is also evident from the words of the prophet at verse 6,
and from the words of the angel Gabriel to Mary, (Luke i.
32, 33.) which are of like import. So in David, "I will
announce concerning the statute, Jehovah hath said, THOU
ART MY SON, to-day have I begotten Thee. Kiss ye the Son,
lest He be angry, and ye perish in the way." (Psalm ii. 7, 12.)
In which passage is not meant a Son from eternity, but the
Son born in time, for it is a prophecy concerning the Lord
who was about to come, wherefore it is called "a statute,"
concerning which Jehovah announced to David; "to-day" does
not denote from eternity, but in time. From these passages
it is manifest that Jesus was conceived of Jehovah God, and
born of the Virgin Mary; so that the Divinity was in Him, and
was HIS SOUL. Since, then, His soul was the very Divinity
of the Father, it follows that His body or Humanity must
have been made Divine also; for where the one is Divine, the
other must necessarily be so too: thus, and no otherwise, can
the passages be true which say that the "Father and the Son
are ONE." D. L. 19 and 29. See also A. C. 2798.

Verse 2. *As it is written in the Prophets, &c.—By the
Testimony of Jesus being the spirit of Prophecy*, (Rev. xix. 10.)
is signified that it is the all of the Word and of Doctrine
deduced from it. For the Word in a universal sense treats
only of the Lord, and of a life according to His commandments. Hence it is that the Lord is the Word, (John i. 14.)
because the Word is from Him, and, in the supreme sense,
treats of Him alone. A. R. 819.

Verse 3. *The voice of one crying in the wilderness, &c.—*
By these words is signified that the church, at that time, was
altogether vastated, so that there was no longer any thing good,
nor any thing true, which is manifest from this consideration,
that no one knew, at that time, that man hath any internal
principle, nor that there is any internal principle in the Word;
thus neither that the Messiah, or Christ, was about to come to
save them for ever. Hence also it is evident what is signified
by John being in the "deserts" till the day of his appearing
to Israel, (Luke i. 80.) and by preaching in the "wilderness of
Judea," (Matt. iii. 1, and following verses.) and by baptizing
"in the wilderness," (Mark i. 4.) for thereby he also represented the state of the church. From the signification of a
2

wilderness it may also be manifest why the Lord so frequently retired into a "wilderness," as Matt. iv. 1; xv. 32, to the end. Mark i. 12, 13, 35—40, 45; vi. 31—36.   Luke iv. 1; v. 16; ix. 10, and following verses.   John xi. 54.   *A. C.* 2708·

Prepare ye the way of the Lord, &c.—That the church, which acknowledges faith alone, hath extinguished the essential truths respecting the Divine Human of the Lord, is a known thing, for what member of that church believes the Lord's Human to be Divine? Doth he not rather hold such a tenet in aversion? When yet in the ancient churches it was believed that the Lord, who was to come into the world, was a Divine Man, and He likewise, when seen by them, was called Jehovah, as is evident from several passages in the Word. For the present, however, let the following passage from Isaiah suffice:—" The voice of one crying in the wilderness, Prepare ye the way of [or for] *Jehovah*, make smooth in the desert a path for *our* God." (xl. 3.) That these things were said concerning the Lord, and that a way was prepared, and a path smoothed for Him by John the Baptist, is manifest from the Evangelists, Matt. iii. 3; Mark i. 3; Luke iii. 4; John i. 2, 3; and moreover from the Lord's words themselves, that " He was One with the Father," and that " the Father was in Him, and He in the Father;" also that " all power was given to Him in the heavens and on earth;" and likewise that " judgment is committed to Him;" for a very slight knowledge concerning power in heaven and on earth, and concerning judgment, may be sufficient to convince any one that they are nothing, unless He was Divine even as to His Human. *A. C.* 4727.   See also *D. L.* 30.

Verse 4. *John was baptizing in the wilderness, and preaching the doctrine of repentance*, &c.—Inasmuch as with the Jewish nation all things of the Word were adulterated, and there was no longer any Truth amongst them, because there was no longer any Good, therefore John the Baptist was in the wilderness, by which was represented the state of that church, concerning which it is thus written in the Evangelists, " John the Baptist was in the *deserts* until the days of his appearing to Israel;" (Luke i. 80.) that " he preached in the *wilderness of Judea;*" (Matt. iii. 1—3; Mark i. 2—4; Luke iii. 2, 4, 5.) and in Isaiah, " The voice of one crying in the *wilderness*, Prepare a way for Jehovah, make smooth in the *desert* a path for our God." (xl. 3.)   On which account the Lord said concerning Jerusalem, " Your house shall be left desolate," [or desert] (Luke xiii. 35.) where a desert house signifies a church without truths, because without goods. *A. E.* 730.

From what is said in the Word of the Old Testament concerning *washing*, it is evident what was signified by John's
"baptizing in Jordan;" (Matt. iii.; Mark i. 4—13.) and what
by the following words of John concerning the Lord—"He
shall *baptize* with the Holy Spirit and with fire;" (Luke iii.
16; John i. 33.) and concerning himself, that "he *baptizeth*
with water;" (John i. 26.) by which is to be understood, that
the Lord washeth or purifieth man by Divine Truth and
Divine Good, and that John by his baptism represented those
things; for the Holy Spirit is Divine Truth; fire is Divine
Good; and water is a representative of those principles; for
water signifies the truth of the Word, which truth is made
good by a life according to it. *A. R.* 378.

John the Baptist being sent before to prepare a people for
the reception of the Lord, was by baptism, for baptism represented and signified purification from evils and falses, and
likewise regeneration by the Word from the Lord, and unless
this representation had preceded, the Lord could not have
manifested Himself, taught, and tarried in Judea and Jerusalem; because the Lord was the God of heaven and the God
of earth under a human form, who could not dwell together
with a nation which was in mere falses as to doctrine, and
in mere evils as to life; wherefore unless a representative of
purification from evils and falses by baptism had prepared
that nation for the reception of the Lord, the nation would
have perished by diseases of every kind at the presence of the
Divine Being Himself; this, therefore, is what is signified by,
"Lest I come and smite the earth with a curse;" (Mal. iv. 6.)
that this would have been the case, is very well known in the
spiritual world, for in that world all who are in falses and evils
are dreadfully tormented, and spiritually die, at the Lord's
presence. The reason why the baptism of John could produce
that effect was, because the Jewish church was a representative
church, and all conjunction of heaven with members of that
church was by representatives, as may likewise be manifest
from the washings enjoined in that church, as that all who were
made unclean should wash themselves and their garments, and
hence they were reckoned as clean; in like manner that the
Priests and Levites should wash themselves before they entered
the tent of assembly, and afterwards, when they entered into
the temple to perform holy duties; in like manner that Naaman
was cleansed of his leprosy by washing in Jordan; the washing
itself and the baptism did not indeed purify them from falses
and evils, but only represented and thence signified purification
from them, which yet was accepted in heaven, as if themselves

were purified; thus heaven was conjoined with the people of
that church by the baptism of John, and when heaven was so
conjoined with them, the Lord, who was the God of heaven,
could there manifest Himself, teach, and abide. *A. E.* 724.

Verse 4. *And preaching the baptism of repentance for the
remission of sins.*—As to the necessity of *repentance*, it is
received as a doctrine in all Christian churches, that a man,
before he approaches the Holy Supper, should examine himself, should see and acknowledge his own sins, and should
perform repentance, desisting from his sins, and rejecting
them, because they are from the devil, or from hell, and that
no otherwise can his sins be remitted, and that unless he does
this, he is in a state of damnation. The English, although in
the doctrine of Faith only, do, nevertheless, in their address at
the Holy Communion, openly teach the necessity of examination, and the acknowledgment and confession of their sins, also
of repentance and newness of life; and they threaten those who
do not do this, in these words, that otherwise the devil will
enter into them as he entered into Judas, and fill them with
all iniquity, and destroy both their body and their soul. The
Germans, Swedes, and Danes, who are also in the doctrine of
Faith only, in their address at the Holy Communion, teach
similar things, threatening also that otherwise they will make
themselves guilty of infernal punishments, and of eternal
damnation, because of mixing together what is holy and
profane. These things are read by the clergyman with a loud
voice before all those who come to the Holy Supper, and are
heard by them in the full acknowledgment that it is so.
Notwithstanding all this true plain declaration, the very same
persons when, on the same day, they hear a sermon on
Salvation by Faith only, and that the Law doth not condemn
them, because the Lord hath fulfilled it for them, and that of
themselves they can do no good except what is meritorious,
and that works have consequently nothing of salvation within
them, but faith only, they return home with an entire forget-
fulness of their former confession, and reject it in so far as
they think from the sermon on Faith only. Which now is
true, this or that? Two things contrary to each other cannot
be true, as that without examination, knowledge, acknowledgment, confession, and rejection of sins, thus without
repentance, there can be no remission of sins, consequently
no salvation, but eternal damnation; or that such things contribute nothing to salvation, because a plenary satisfaction for
all the sins of mankind has been made by the Lord through
the passion of the cross, for those who are in the faith, and

that those who are in the firm belief that it is so, and in
confidence respecting the Lord's merit, are without sin, and
that they appear before God as being washed and their faces
shining.　From this it is evident that the common religion of
all churches in the Christian world is—that a man should
examine himself, should see and acknowledge his sins, and
afterwards should desist from them, and that otherwise there
can be no salvation, but damnation.　That this is also the
Divine Truth itself, is evident from those passages in the
Word where man is commanded to repent, as from the following:—Jesus said, "*Bring forth fruit worthy of repentance;*
and now also the axe is laid to the root of the trees, every
tree therefore which bringeth not forth good fruit is hewn
down and cast into the fire." (Luke iii. 8, 9.)　"Jesus said,
Except ye repent, ye shall all likewise perish." (Luke xiii.
3, 5.)　"Jesus preached the Gospel of the kingdom of God,
saying, *Repent ye,* and believe the Gospel." (Mark i. 14, 15.)
"Jesus sent forth His disciples, who went forth and preached
that men *should repent.*" (Mark vi. 12.)　Jesus said unto the
apostles that they should "preach *repentance and remission of
sins* in His name, among all nations." (Luke xxiv. 47.)　John
preached the "baptism of *repentance* for the remission of sins."
(Mark i. 4; Luke iii. 3.)　Think (my reader) of this from some
degree of intellect, and if you have any religion, you will see
that repentance from sins is the way to heaven, and that faith
separate from repentance is no faith, and that those who are
in no faith from no repentance, are on the way to hell.
D. P. 114.

　The sins which man commits are inscribed on his very
life, and constitute it; on which account no one is delivered
from them unless he receives new life from the Lord, which
is effected by regeneration.　That man from himself cannot
do what is good, nor think what is true, but from the Lord,
is manifest from these words—"A man cannot receive any
thing unless it be given him from heaven;" (John iii. 27.)
"He that abideth in Me, and I in him, the same beareth
much fruit, since without Me ye cannot do any thing." (John
xv. 5.)　Hence it is evident that no one can withdraw a
man from sins, thus remit them, but the Lord alone.　The
Lord continually flows in with man with the good of love and
with the truths of faith, but they are received differently by
different persons; by those who are regenerated, well, but
otherwise by those who do not suffer themselves to be regenerated.　They who are regenerated, are held continually by
the Lord in the good of faith and of love, and in this case are

withheld from evils and falses; but they who do not suffer
themselves to be regenerated by the Lord, are withheld also
from evil, and held in good, for from the Lord there is a
continual influx of good and truth with every one; but the
infernal loves, which are the loves of self and of the world,
in which the unregenerate are principled, oppose and turn the
influx of good into evil, and of truth into the false. From
these considerations it is manifest, that remission of sins consists in the ability of being held by the Lord in the good of
love and the truths of faith, and of being withheld from evils
and falses; and that to shun, on this occasion, what is evil
and false, and to hold it in aversion, is repentance. But such
remission and repentance are not given, except with those
who by regeneration have received new life from the Lord.
A. C. 9444—9449.

Verse 5. *Judea.*—That *Judea*, in the internal sense of the
Word, does not signify Judea, may appear from many passages
in the Word. In the Word it is not so often named *Judea*,
as the land of Judah, and by the "land of Judah," as by the
"land of Canaan," is signified the Lord's kingdom, consequently also the church, for the church is the Lord's kingdom
in the earth. *A. C.* 3654.

In the opposite sense, as in Matt. xxiv. 16, *Judea* signifies
the church devastated. *A. C.* 795.

Jerusalem.—By *Jerusalem* is understood the church with
respect to doctrine, inasmuch as at Jerusalem in the land of
Canaan, and in no other place, there was the temple, the altar,
the sacrifices, and of consequence all divine worship. Wherefore those festivals were likewise celebrated there every year,
to which every male throughout the land was commanded to
go. This then is the reason why by "Jerusalem," in the spiritual sense, is signified the church with respect to worship, or,
what is the same thing, with respect to doctrine; for worship
is prescribed by doctrine, and is performed according to it.
H. D. N. J. 6.

Verse 5. *And were all baptized by him in Jordan,* &c.—By
"Jordan" is signified initiation into the knowledges of truth
and good, the ground of which signification is, because it was
a boundary of the land of Canaan; and that all the boundaries
of that land signified those principles which are the first and
last of the Lord's kingdom, also which are the first and last of
the church, thus which are the first and last of things celestial
and spritual, which constitute the Lord's kingdom and church,
may be seen, n. 1585, 1866, 4116, 4240; hence "Jordan," as
being a boundary, signified initiation into the knowledges of

good and truth, these being the first principles, and at length, when man becomes a church or kingdom of the Lord, they become the last. That "Jordan" hath this signification, may be manifest also from other passages in the Word, as from David—"My God, my soul boweth itself upon me, therefore I will remember Thee from *the land of Jordan*, and from the little mountain of Hermon;" (Psalm xlii. 7.) where to "remember from the land of Jordan" denotes from what is last, or ultimate, thus from what is lowly. So again, "Judah was made his sanctuary, Israel his dominion; the sea saw and fled, *Jordan turned itself backwards;*" (Psalm cxiv. 2, 3, 5.) where "Judah" denotes the good of celestial love, and "Israel" the good of spiritual love, n. 3634; "the sea" denotes the knowledges of truth, n. 28; "Jordan" denotes the knowledges of good, which are said to turn themselves backwards when the good of love obtains the dominion, for in such case knowledges are viewed from that good, but not good from them, as hath been often shewn above. So in the Book of Judges, "Gilead abode *in the passage of Jordan,* and why shall Dan sojourn in ships?" (v. 17.) where "Gilead" denotes sensual good, or what is pleasant, by which man is first initiated when he is regenerating, n. 4117, 4124; to "abide in the passage of Jordan" denotes in those things which are initiaments, thus which are the first and last of the Lord's church and kingdom. These things were also represented by Jordan, when the sons of Israel entered into the land of Canaan; (Joshua iii. 14, to the end; iv. 1, to the end;) for by "the land of Canaan" was represented the Lord's kingdom, and by "Jordan being divided, and the sons of Israel passing through on the dry [ground]," was signified the removal of evils and falses, and the admission of those who are principled in goods and truths. The like was signified by the waters of Jordan being divided by Elijah, when he was taken up into heaven, (2 Kings ii. 8.) and by Elisha, when he entered upon the prophetic office in the place of Elijah. (v. 14.) Naaman being cured of his leprosy, by "washing seven times in Jordan according to the command of Elisha," (2 Kings v. 1—14.) represented baptism, for baptism signifies initiation into the church, and into those things which are of the church, thus regeneration and the things of regeneration; not that any one is regenerated by baptism, but that it is a sign of regeneration which ought to be remembered. And whereas those things which relate to the church are signified by "baptism," and the like by "Jordan," as was said above, therefore John baptized in Jordan, (Matt. iii. 6; Mark i. 5.) and the Lord also was willing that Himself should be baptized there by John. (Matt. iii. 13—17.) Inasmuch as "Jordan" signifies those things which are the first and last of the Lord's kingdom and church, such as are the knowledges of good and truth, for by them man is introduced; therefore also "Jordan" is mentioned as the boundary of the new earth, or holy land, in Ezek. xlvii. 18. *A. C.* 4255.

Verse 5. *Confessing their sins.*—To "confess sins" is to become acquainted with evils, to see them in one's self, to acknowledge them, to make one's self guilty, and to condemn one's self on account of evils; when this is done before God, confession of sins is made. *A. C.* 8388.

It is not sufficient therefore for any one to say in general, " I am a sinner, I was born in sins; there is nothing sound in me from head to foot; I am nothing but evil; O good God! be merciful to me, pardon me, purify me, save me; make me to walk in purity, and in the way of what is just," and the like; since if he doth not explore himself, and consequently doth not know any evil, he is still in his sins, inasmuch as no one can shun, still less fight against, what he doth not know; thus, howsoever he believes himself after confession to be clean and washed, he is still unclean and unwashed from the crown of the head to the soles of the feet; for general confession is general drowsiness, which terminates in blindness, being like a whole destitute of parts, which hath no existence. *D. P.* 278.   See also *T. C. R.* 510.

Verse 6. *But John was clothed with camel's hair, and with a girdle of a skin about his loins, and he did eat locusts and wild honey.*—Inasmuch as John the Baptist represented the Lord as to the Word, which is Divine Truth in the earth, in like manner as Elias, n. 2762, 5247, therefore he was the Elias who was to come before the Lord; (Mal. iv. 5; Matt. xvii. 10—12; Mark ix. 11—13; John i. 17.) on which account his raiment and food were significative. "Raiment of camel's hair" signified the Word, such as is its literal sense as to truth, which sense is a clothing for the internal sense, as being natural, for what is natural is signified by "hair," also by "camels;" and the food, which was "locusts and wild honey," signified the Word, such as is its literal sense as to good; its delight is signified by "wild honey." *A. C.* 5620.

By "clothing," or "garment," when predicated of the Word, is signified Truth Divine therein in the ultimate form; by a "leathern girdle" is signified an external bond connecting and holding in order all interior things; by "food" is signified spiritual nourishment derived from the knowledges of truth and of good from the Word; by "locusts" are signified ultimate or most general truths, and by "wild honey" their pleasantness. *A. C.* 9372. See also n. 7643.

John the Baptist represented the like with Elias, wherefore also it is said that "Elias was come," by whom is meant John. Elias represented the Lord as to the Word, or the Word which is from the Lord, in like manner John; and whereas the Word teacheth that Messiah, or the Lord, was to come, therefore John was sent before, to preach concerning the coming of the Lord, according to the predictions in the Word. And whereas John represented the Word, therefore the ultimates of the Word, which are natural, were represented by John by his raiment, and also by his food, viz., by raiment of camel's hair, and by a leathern girdle about his loins; "camel's hair" signifying the ultimates of the natural man, such as are the exteriors of the Word, and "a leathern girdle about the loins" signifying their external bond and connection with the interiors of the Word, which are spiritual. Similar things are signified by "locusts" and "wild honey;" by *locusts* the truth of the natural man, and by *wild honey* the good thereof; whether we say the truth and good of the natural man, or natural truth and good, such as the Word is in its ultimate sense, which is called the sense of the letter, or natural sense, it is the same thing, for John represented it by his raiment and food. *A. E.* 619.

Verse 7. *And preached, saying, There cometh one mightier than I after me, the latchet of whose shoes I am not worthy to stoop down and unloose.*—In the Word, the "sole of the foot" and "the heel" signify the ultimate natural principle, as was shewn above, n. 259; the shoe is what invests the sole of the foot and the heel, wherefore the "shoe" signifies the natural principle still lower, thus the very corporeal principle, and this being the signification of a *shoe*, it was hence adopted in common language to express the least and vilest of all things [or principles], since the ultimate, natural, and corporeal principle is the vilest of all things appertaining to man, which was meant by John the Baptist, when he said, "There cometh one mightier than I, the latchet of whose shoes I am not worthy to unloose." *A. C.* 1748.

Verse 8. *I indeed have baptized you in water, but He shall baptize you in the Holy Spirit.*—That the Lord regenerates man by means of faith and charity, is signified by these words of John the Baptist, "I baptize you in water unto repentance, but He that cometh after me shall baptize you in the Holy Spirit and with fire." (Matt. iii. 11; Mark i. 8; Luke iii. 16.) To "baptize in the Holy Spirit and with fire," is to regenerate by Divine Truth which is of faith, and by Divine Good which is of charity. The same is signified by these words of the Lord—"Except a man be born of water and of the spirit, he cannot enter into the kingdom of God." (John iii. 5.) By "water" here, as in other parts of the Word, is signified truth in the natural or external man, and by "spirit," truth derived from good in the spiritual or internal man. *T. C. R.* 144.

By the above words is meant, that John only inaugurated them into knowledges derived from the Word concerning the Lord, and thereby prepared them to receive the Lord, but that the Lord Himself regenerates man by the Divine Truth and the Divine Good proceeding from Him; for John represented the like as Elias, viz., the Word; the "waters with which John baptized," signified truths introducing, which are knowledges concerning the Lord derived from the Word; the "Holy Spirit" signifies the Divine Truth proceeding from the Lord, and "fire" signifies the Divine Good proceeding from Him, and "baptism" signifies regeneration effected of the Lord, by Divine Truths derived from the Word. He who believes that baptism contributes any thing to the salvation of man, unless he be, at the same time, principled in the truths of the church, and in a life according to them, is much mistaken; for baptism is an external ceremony, which, without an internal principle, is of no effect to salvation, but is of effect where what is external is conjoined with what is internal. The internal of baptism is, that by truths derived from the Word of the Lord, and by a life according to them, falses and evils may be removed by the Lord, and thereby man may be regenerated, as the Lord also teaches, Matt. xxiii. 26, 27. *A. E.* 475.

To "baptize" is to regenerate; "with the Holy Spirit" is by Divine Truth; and "with fire" is from the Divine Good of the Divine Love. *A. C.* 9818.

Verse 9. *And it came to pass in those days,* [that] *Jesus came from Nazareth of Galilee, and was baptized by John in Jordan.*—The reason why the Lord Himself was baptized by John was, that He might not only institute baptism as a future rite, and establish it by His own example, but also because He glorified His Humanity and made it Divine, as He regenerates man, and makes him spiritual. *T. C. R.* 684.

Verse 10. *And straightway coming out of the water, He saw the Heavens rent, and the Spirit like a dove descending upon Him.*—The reason of this was, because "baptism" signifies regeneration and purification, as doth also a "dove." Who cannot perceive that the Dove was not the Holy Spirit, nor was the Holy Spirit in the Dove? Doves often appear in heaven, and the angels know, when they observe them, that they are correspondences of the affections and thoughts relating to regeneration and purification in some persons not afar off. Wherefore when they approach those persons, and converse with them on a subject foreign to what was in their thoughts when that appearance was presented, the doves instantly vanish. The case was the same with respect to many things which appeared to the prophets, as when John saw a lamb on Mount Sion, (Rev. xiv.) and in other places. How plain is it to see that the Lord was not that lamb, nor was He in the lamb, but the lamb was a representative of His innocence. Hence the error of those is manifest, who, from the appearance of the Dove, when the Lord was baptized, and from the voice then heard from heaven, "This is my beloved Son," conclude that the Trinity consists of three Persons. *T. C. R.* 144.

That by a "dove" are signified the truths and goods of faith appertaining to a person about to be regenerated, is manifest from the signification of a dove in the Word, especially from the dove which appeared over Jesus when He was baptized, on which occasion the "dove" signified nothing else but the holy principle of faith, "baptism" itself denoting regeneration. Hence in the New Church, which was to be established, it signified the truth and good of faith, which was to be received by regeneration from the Lord. Similar things were represented by and involved in the young doves or turtles, which were offered in sacrifice, and for burnt-offerings, in the Jewish church, concerning which see Lev. i. 14, to the end; v. 7—10; xii. 6; xiv. 21, 22; xv. 15, 29, 30; Numb. vi. 10, 11; Luke ii. 22—24; which may be manifest from each of those passages. That such things were significative, may be obvious to every one from this single consideration, that they must of necessity be representative of something, since otherwise, they would have no meaning, still less any divine meaning: the external of the church is somewhat inanimate, but it derives life from what is internal, and what is internal derives life from the Lord. That a "dove" in general signifies the intellectual things of faith, is also manifest from the prophets, as in Hosea, "Ephraim shall be as a foolish *dove*, without heart; they call to Egypt, they go to Assyria;" (vii. 11.) again in the same prophet, "Ephraim shall be afraid, as a bird out of Egypt, and a *dove* from the land of Assyria;" (xi. 11.) where "Ephraim" denotes one who is intelligent, "Egypt" one who is scientific, "Assyria" one who is rational; "dove" denotes those things which regard the intellectuals of faith; where, also, the

regeneration of the spiritual church is treated of. So in David,
" Oh Jehovah, give not the soul of thy *turtle dove* to the wild
beast;" (Psalm lxxv. 19.) where " wild beast" denotes those
who have no charity; the " soul of a turtle dove" denotes the
life of faith. *A. C.* 870.

Verse 11. *And there was a voice from the Heavens,* [saying]
Thou art my beloved Son, in whom I am well pleased.—In the
Jewish church, by the Son of God was meant the Messiah,
whom they expected, and of whom they knew that He was
to be born in Bethlehem. That by the " Son of God" they
understood the Messiah, is evident from the following passages:
" Peter said, we believe and acknowledge that Thou art the
Christ, the Son of the living God;" (John vi. 69.) again, in
the same Evangelist, " Thou art the *Christ the Son of God,*
who was to come into the world;" (xi. 27.) and in Matthew,
" The high Priest asked Jesus, whether He was the *Christ
the Son of God?* Jesus said, I am." (xxvi. 63; Mark xi. 27.)
And in John, " These things are written, that ye may believe
that Jesus is the *Christ the Son of God.*" (xx. 31; also Mark
i. 1.) Christ is a Greek word, and signifies anointed; in like
manner Messiah in the Hebrew tongue; wherefore John saith,
" We have found the Messiah, which is, being interpreted,
the *Christ;*" (i. 41.) and in another place, " The woman said,
I know that Messias cometh, who is called *Christ.*" (iv. 25.)
That the law and the prophets, or the whole Word of the
Old Testament, treats of the Lord, was shewn in the first
article, wherefore no other can be meant by the " Son of God
who was to come," than the Human [principle] which the Lord
assumed in the world. Hence it follows, that this principle was
meant by Him who was called Son by Jehovah out of heaven,
at the time of the Lord's baptism, when it is said, " This is
my beloved Son, in whom I am well pleased;" (Matt. iii. 17;
Mark i. 11; Luke iii. 22.) for His Human [principle] was
baptized; and when He was transfigured, "This is *my beloved
Son,* in whom I am well pleased, hear ye Him." (Matt. xvii.
5; Mark ix. 7; Luke ix. 35; see also other passages, as Matt.
viii. 29; xiv. 33; xxvii. 43, 54; Mark iii. 11; xv. 39; John
i. 18, 34, 50; iii. 18; v. 25; x. 36; xi. 4.)

Inasmuch as by the " Son of God" is meant the Lord as to
the Human which He assumed in the world, which is the
Divine Human, it is evident what is meant by what the Lord
so often said, that He was " sent of the Father into the
world," and that He " came forth from the Father." By
being " sent of the Father into the world," is meant, that He
was conceived of Jehovah the Father. That nothing else is

meant by being "sent of the Father," is manifest from all the passages, where also it is said, that He did the will of the Father and His works, which will and works were, that He overcame the hells, glorified His Humanity, taught the Word, and established a New Church; which things could not have been done but by the Humanity conceived of Jehovah, and born of a Virgin, that is, unless God had been made a Man.

Many at this day entertain no other thought concerning the Lord, than as of a common man, like unto themselves, because they think only of His Human and not of His Divine [principle] at the same time, when yet His Divine and Human [principles] cannot be separated; for the Lord is God and Man, and God and Man in the Lord are not two, but one Person, *so altogether one as soul and body are one man,* according to the doctrine received throughout the Christian world, which is derived from councils, and is called the Athanasian Creed. Lest therefore man, henceforth, should separate in thought what is Divine and Human in the Lord, let him read, I pray, the passages above adduced from Luke, also these words from Matthew—"The birth of Jesus Christ was on this wise: when His mother Mary was betrothed to Joseph, before they came together, she was found with Child of the *Holy Spirit.* Then Joseph, her husband, being a just man, and not willing to make her a public example, was minded to put her away privily. But while he thought on these things, behold, the Angel of the Lord appeared unto him in a dream, saying, Joseph, son of David, fear not to take unto thee Mary, thy wife, for that which is begotten in her is of the *Holy Spirit:* and she shall bring forth a Son, and thou shalt call His name Jesus, for He shall save His people from their sins. And Joseph, being raised from sleep, did as the angel had bidden him, and took unto him his wife: and knew her not until she had brought forth her first-born Son, and he called His name Jesus." (i. 18—25.) From these words, and from what is written in Luke concerning the Lord's Nativity, it is manifest, that the "Son of God" is Jesus conceived of Jehovah the Father, and born of the Virgin Mary, of whom the prophets and the law prophesied even to John. *D. L.* 19—22.

Verses 12 and 13. *And immediately the spirit sendeth Him forth into the wilderness: and He was there in the wilderness forty days, tempted of Satan, and was with the wild beasts, and the Angels ministered unto Him.*—By a "wilderness" is signified a place uninhabited and uncultivated; in a spiritual sense, a mind destitute of Good and of Truth, also a mind in which Truth is not yet conjoined with Good; thus, by a "wilderness" is signified the state of those with whom conjunction will be effected; and whereas conjunction is not effected except by temptations, these are also signified, but only when the number *forty* is added, whether they be forty years, or forty months, or forty days; for "forty" signifies temptations, and their duration howsoever long. These things are signified by the journeys of the sons of Israel in the wilderness forty years; the temptations also which they underwent, are described. That they were led into the wilderness, to the intent that they might undergo those temptations, and might thus represent them, is evident from these words of Moses—"Thou shalt remember all the way in which Jehovah thy God led thee *these forty years in the wilderness*, that *He might afflict thee*, that *He might try thee*, that He might know what was in thine heart. He fed thee with manna in the wilderness, which thy fathers knew not, that *He might afflict thee*, that *He might try thee*, to do thee good in thy latter end." (Deut. viii. 2, 16.)

Inasmuch as by *forty* were signified temptations and their durations, and by a *wilderness* the state of those who undergo them, therefore also the Lord when He was tempted, "went out into a wilderness, and was there *forty days*." (Matt. iv. 1, 2, and following verses; Luke iv. 1, 2, and following verses; Mark i. 12, 13.) *A. C. 8098.*

The Lord, by being in the wilderness *forty days*, represented the duration of all the temptations which He Himself underwent, and sustained to a degree of intensity far surpassing the temptations of all men in the universal earth; for by "forty days" is signified the entire period and duration of temptations, thus, not that He was tempted only at that particular time, but that He was tempted from childhood, even to the last period of His life in the world. *A. E. 650.*

And He was with the wild beasts.—The last temptation which He underwent was in Gethsemane, for by temptations He subdued all the bells, and also glorified His Human [principle]; and whereas temptations exist by evil spirits and genii who are from hell, thus, by the hells, whence arise evils and false principles, with their lusts and concupiscences, therefore by the *wild beasts in the wilderness*, with whom He was, are not meant "wild beasts," but the hells and evils thence arising. *A. E. 650.*

Tempted of Satan.—Hell is called the devil and Satan, and by the hell which is called the "devil," are meant those who are in evils, properly those who are principled in self-love;

and by the hell which is called "Satan," are meant those who are in false principles, properly those who are in the pride of their own intelligence. *A. R.* 97.

Those who are in evil by derivation from the understanding, are called *Satans,* but those who are in evil by derivation from the will, are called *devils;* it is on account of this universal distinction that mention is made in the Word of *Satan* and the *devil.* *C. L.* 492.

And Angels came and ministered unto Him.—By the "Angels who ministered unto Him" are not meant Angels, but Divine Truths, by which, from His own proper power, He conquered and subdued the hells. That by "Angels" in the Word are signified Divine Truths, may be seen above, n. 130, 200, 502, 593. *A. E.* 650.

After every spiritual temptation come illustration and affection, thus pleasantness and delight; pleasantness by illustration of Truth, and delight by the affection of Good; the reason is, because by temptations, Truths and Goods are implanted and conjoined; hence man, as to his spirit, is introduced more interiorly into heaven, and to the heavenly societies with which he had before been associated. When temptation is finished, communication with heaven is opened, which before had been in part closed; hence come illustration and affection, consequently pleasantness and delight, for on such occasions the Angels, with whom communication is given, enter in by the influx of Truth and of Good. *A. C.* 8367.

The Lord's combat with hell may be compared, but yet imperfectly, with a combat against all the wild beasts throughout the whole world, and with their slaughter and complete subjugation, so that not one of them dares to stir out of his den, and attack any man that is in the Lord : the consequence is, they are afraid to shew their teeth, and suddenly check in themselves every hostile attempt, as if they felt a vulture at their bosom, endeavouring to eat his way to their hearts. Infernal spirits are also described in the Word by *wild beasts,* and are signified particularly by those amongst which the Lord is said to have been forty days. (Mark i. 13.) It may be compared also with an opposition to the whole body of the ocean, when it defies all restraint, and deluges whole countries and cities with its waves. The reducing of hell to subjection by the Lord, is also signified by His power over the sea, when He said—"Peace, be still;" (Mark iv. 38, 39; Matt. viii. 26; Luke viii. 23, 24.) for by the *sea* there, as in other passages, is signified hell.

The Lord, by the same divine power, fights at this day against hell, in every particular person who is made regenerate; for hell rises up against every such person, with all its diabolical fury, and unless the Lord opposed and subdued it, man must of necessity fall an easy prey to its tyranny. For hell is like a single gigantic monster, or like a huge lion, with which it is also compared in the Word; and consequently, unless the Lord kept that lion, or that monster, bound hand and foot, it must of necessity come to pass that man, though rescued from one evil, would of himself fall into another, and so on into an infinity, without end or number. *T. C. R.* 123.

Verses 14 and 15. *But after that John was delivered to custody, Jesus came into Galilee, preaching the Gospel of the Kingdom of God; and saying, That the time is fulfilled, and the Kingdom of God is near; Repent ye, and believe the Gospel.*—That redemption and the passion of the cross are two distinct things, which ought by no means to be confounded together, and that the Lord, by both, acquired the power of regenerating and saving mankind, was shewn in the chapter on Redemption. From the prevailing faith of the present church concerning the passion of the cross, as constituting the sum and substance of redemption, have arisen legions of horrible falsities, respecting God, Faith, Charity, and other subjects connected with those three in a regular chain, and dependent upon them; as for instance, respecting God, that He passed the sentence of condemnation on all the human race, and was willing to become again merciful and propitious towards them, in consequence of that sentence being laid on His Son, or received by the Son, in Himself, and that they alone are saved who are gifted with the merit of Christ, either by the Divine Providence, or predestination. This fallacy has also given birth to another tenet belonging to that faith, that all such as are gifted with that faith, are instantly regenerated, without any regard to their own coöperation, yea, that they are thus delivered from the curse of the law, and are no longer under the law, but under grace, notwithstanding what the Lord declared, that "He would not take away one jot or tittle from the law;" (Matt. v. 18, 19; Luke xvi. 17.) and also that He commanded His disciples to "preach repentance for the remission of sins;" (Luke xxiv. 47; Mark vi. 12.) and likewise Himself said,— "The Kingdom of God is at hand; repent ye, and believe the Gospel." (Mark i. 15.) By the *Gospel* is meant, that they had the power to be regenerated, and thereby saved, which power they could not have had, unless the Lord had wrought redemption, that is, unless He had deprived hell of its power, by His combats against it, and victories over it; and unless He had glorified His Human [principle], that is, had made it Divine.

Consult your own reason, and tell me what sort of creatures, in your opinion, would men become, supposing the faith of the present church were to continue, which teaches that they were redeemed solely by the passion of the cross, and that such as are gifted with the merit of Christ, are not under the curse of the law; and further, that this faith, of whose abiding in him, man is altogether ignorant, remits sins, and regenerates, and that man's coöperation in its act, that is, whilst it is given, and entereth into him, would destroy that faith, and make salvation void, inasmuch as man, in such case, would mix his own merit with the merit of Christ. Consult, I say, your own reason, and tell me whether the whole Word must not of necessity be thus rejected, which insists principally on regeneration, by a spiritual cleansing from evils, and by exercises of charity. Supposing this faith alone to regenerate man, without any regard to repentance and charity, what then is the internal man, which is his spirit that liveth after death, but like a city reduced to ashes, the rubbish of which forms the external man? Or like a field or a garden, eaten up by canker-worms and locusts? Such a man appears in the sight of the angels like a person who cherishes a serpent in his bosom, whilst he covers it with his garments to prevent its being seen; or like a person who lies down to rest under a fine wrought coverlid, in a garment wrought of spider's webs. *T. C. R.* 581, 582.

The time is fulfilled.—The "fulness" [or fulfilling] of the states and times of the church signifies their end; the church resembling, in this respect, the ages of man, the first of which is infancy, the second is youth, the third is adult age, the fourth is old age, which last is called the fulness or end. It resembles also the times and states of the year, the first of which is spring, the second is summer, the third is autumn, and the fourth is winter, which last is the end of the year; it resembles also the times and states of the day, the first of which is morning, the second is mid-day, the third is evening, and the fourth is night, and when this last comes it is the fulness or end. In the Word, the states of the church are compared both to the former and the latter, and are signified by the same, because by "times" are signified states, n. 2625, 2788, 2837. The principles of goodness and truth, appertaining to those who are of the church, are thus wont to

4

decrease, and when there is no longer any Good and Truth, or as it is said, any faith, that is, any charity, then the church comes to its old age, or to its winter, or to its night; and its time and state, in such case, is called [in the Word] *decision*, *consummation*, and *fulfilling*: see n. 1857. When it is said of the Lord, that He came into the world in the "*fulness of time*," or when there was fulness, the same thing is signified, for then there was no longer any Good, not even natural Good, consequently not any Truth. *A. C.* 2905.

The providence of the Lord is principally exercised in preventing the profanation of Divine Good and Truth, and this prevention is especially effected by this, that the man who is of such a quality that he cannot be withheld from profanation, is withheld, as far as possible, from the acknowledgment and belief of what is True and Good; for, as was said, no one can profane what he hath not first acknowledged and believed. This was the reason why internal truths were not discovered to the posterity of Jacob, the Israelites and Jews, nor was it even openly said that there was any internal principle in man, thus that there was any internal worship, and scarcely any thing concerning a life after death, and concerning the heavenly kingdom of the Lord, or of the Messiah whom they expected. The reason was, because they were of such a quality that it was foreseen, in case those things had been discovered to them, they could not have been restrained from profaning them, since earthly things were the sole objects of their affection. This likewise was the reason why the Lord did not come into the world, and reveal the internal things of the Word, until no Good whatsoever, not even natural Good, remained amongst them, for, in this case, they could no longer receive any Truth, even to internal acknowledgment, since the principle of Good is what receives: thus they could no longer profane. Such was the state which is meant by the *fulness of times*, and by the *consummation of the age*, also by the *last day*, so frequently spoken of by the prophets; the same also is the reason why the Arcana of the internal sense of the Word are now revealed, because at this day there is scarcely any faith, in consequence of there being no charity, thus in consequence of its being the "consummation of the age," on which occasion those Arcana may be revealed without danger of profanation, because they are not interiorly acknowledged. *A. C.* 3398.

There have existed on this earth several churches, all of which, in process of time, have come to their consummation, and then have been succeeded by new ones, and so on to the present time. The consummation of the church comes to pass when there remains no Divine Truth but what is falsified and rejected, in which case there cannot remain any genuine Good, inasmuch as the whole quality of good is formed by truths, *good* being the essence of truth, and *truth* being the form of good, and no quality can exist without a form. Good and truth can no more be separated than will and understanding, or what is the same thing, than affection of love and thought thence originating; wherefore whensoever truth comes to its consummation in the church, good also comes to its consummation at the same time, and when this is the case, the church is at an end, that is, comes to its consummation. *T. C. R.* 753.

And the Kingdom of God is near.—By the "Kingdom of God," in the universal sense, is meant the universal heaven; in a sense less universal, the true church of the Lord; in a particular sense, every one who is of a true faith, or who is regenerated by the life of faith, wherefore he also is called *heaven* because heaven is in him; he is called also a *kingdom of God*, because the kingdom of God is in him, as the Lord Himself teaches in Luke:—"Jesus being asked by the Pharisees when the Kingdom of God cometh, answered them and said, The Kingdom of God cometh not with observation: neither shall they say, Lo here! or, Lo there! *for, behold, the Kingdom of God is within you.*" (xvii. 20, 21.) *A. C.* 29.

Every regenerate man is a kind of little heaven, or an effigy or image of the universal heaven, wherefore also, in the Word, his internal man is called heaven; such is the order in heaven, that the Lord, by things celestial ruleth things spiritual, and by these, things natural, and thus the universal heaven, as one man, wherefore heaven is also called the Grand Man. Such order also has place with every one who is in heaven; when man likewise is in such a quality, then in like manner he is a little heaven, or what is the same thing, is a kingdom of the Lord, because the kingdom of the Lord is in him. *A. C.* 911.

Repent ye.—To repent [or to do the work of repentance] is to desist from sins, and to lead a new life, according to the precepts of faith, when confession has been made respecting sins, and supplication has been offered up from an humble heart for their remission. He who only acknowledges in general that he is a sinner, and makes himself guilty of all evils, and does not explore himself, that is, discover his sins, makes confession, but not the confession of repentance, for he lives afterwards as before. He who leads an active life of faith, doeth daily the work of repentance, for he reflects on the evils appertaining to himself, he acknowledges them, he is

watchful against them, he supplicates the Lord for help; for
man, of himself, is continually falling, but is continually raised
up by the Lord; of himself he falls, when his will inclines
him to think what is evil, and he is raised up by the Lord,
when he resists evils, and in consequence of such resistance
does not commit evil: such is the state of all who are principled in good.   But they who are principled in evil, are
continually falling, and likewise are continually elevated by
the Lord, but the elevation is only into a milder hell, and
thus to prevent their falling into the deepest hell, into which,
of themselves, they are continually plunging with all their
might.   Repentance of the lips, and not of the life, is not
repentance; by repentance of the lips, sins are not remitted,
but by repentance of the life.   Sins are continually remitted
to man by the Lord, for He is mercy itself; but sins adhere
to man, howsoever he thinks they are remitted, nor are they
removed from him, except by a life according to the precepts
of faith; so far as he lives according to those precepts, so
far sins are removed; and so far as they are removed, so far
they are remitted.   For man is withheld from evil by the
Lord, and is held in good; and he is so far capable of being
withheld from evil in the other life, as he had resisted evil
in the life of the body; and he is so far capable of being
held in good at that time, as, during his life in the body,
he had done good from affection; hence it may be manifest
what the remission of sins is, and what is its source.   He is
much mistaken who believes that sins are remitted in any
other way.   When a man has explored himself, and acknowledged his sins, and done the work of repentance, he must
remain steady in good even to the end of life; for if he
relapses thence to his former life of evil, and cherishes it,
in such case he is guilty of profanation, for in such case he
conjoins evil with good; hence his latter state becomes worse
than his first, according to the Lord's words,—" When the
unclean spirit is gone out of a man, he walketh through dry
places, seeking rest, but doth not find; then he saith, I will
return to mine house whence I came out; and when he is
come, and findeth it empty, swept, and garnished, then goeth
he and adjoineth to himself seven other spirits more wicked
than himself, and entering in they dwell there: *and the latter
things of that man are worse than the first.*" (Matt. xii. 43—45.)
A. C. 8389—8394.   See above, verse 4, Exposition.

And believe the Gospel.—By " preaching the Gospel" is
meant the preaching of all things which in the Word treat
of the Lord, and all things which represented Him in worship;

for preaching the Gospel is annunciation concerning the Lord, concerning His Advent, and concerning those things from Him which relate to salvation and eternal life. And since all things of the Word in its inmost sense, treat of the Lord alone, and also things of worship represented Him, therefore the whole Word is the Gospel, in like manner all worship which was performed according to those things which are commanded in the Word. *A. C.* 9925.

And I heard a great voice saying in heaven, Now is come salvation and power, and the kingdom of our God, and the power of His Christ.—By these words is signified that mankind are now saved by the Divine power of the Lord, because the Lord alone reigneth in heaven and in the church. This is meant by the *Gospel of the Kingdom,* and by the *Kingdom of God. A. R.* 553.

Mention is made of believing *in* God, and of believing those things which are *from* God. To believe *in* God is the faith which is saving, but to believe the things which are *from* God is a faith which, without the former, is not saving; for to believe *in* God, is to know and to do; but to believe the things which are *from* God, is to know and yet not to do. They who are true Christians both know and do, thus they believe *in* God; but they who are not true Christians, know and do not; the latter are called by the Lord *foolish,* but the former *prudent.* (Matt. vii. 24, 26.) The faith [or belief], which is meant by believing those things which are from God, that is, the truths which are derived from the Word, has no place with those who are in evils grounded in the love of self or of the world; for the love of self or of the world either rejects, or extinguishes, or perverts the truths of faith. *A. C.* 9239—9244.

Verses 16—21. *But walking near the sea of Galilee, He saw Simon and Andrew his brother, casting a net into the sea, for they were fishers. And Jesus said to them, Come ye after Me, and I will make you to become fishers of men,* &c.—When it is known that there is an internal man and an external, and that truths and goods from the Lord flow in from the internal man, or through the internal man to the external man, although it does not so appear, then those truths and goods, or the knowledges of truth and good which appertain to man, are stored up in his memory, and have their place among scientifics; for whatsoever is insinuated into the memory of the external man, whether it be natural, or spiritual, or celestial, remains there as a scientific, and is thence called forth by the Lord; those knowledges are the waters gathered together to one place, and are called *seas.* That "waters" signify knowledges and scientifics, is an idea most generally prevalent in the Word, and hence that "seas" signify their gathering together, as in Isaiah:—"The earth shall be full of the knowledge of Jehovah, as the waters which cover the sea;" (xi. 9.) and in the same prophet, speaking of the defect of knowledges and scientifics,— "Waters from the sea shall fail, the river shall be dried up and wasted, and the streams shall recede. (xix. 5, 6.) *A.C.* 27, 28.

The reason why the creatures of the sea, or "fishes," signify scientifics, is, because the "sea" signifies the natural man; hence "fishes in the sea" signify the scientifics themselves, which are in the natural man. The reason why "fishes" have this signification, is grounded in correspondence; for spirits who are not principled in spiritual truths, but only in natural truths, which are scientifics, appear in the spiritual world to be in seas, whilst they are viewed by those who are above them, thus they appear as fishes, since the thoughts which proceed from the scientifics appertaining to them, present such an aspect. For all the ideas of thought, both of angels and spirits, are turned into various representatives of objects out of them. When they are turned into objects of the vegetable kingdom, they assume the aspect of trees and fruits of various kinds; but when into objects of the animal kingdom, they assume the aspect of animals of the earth, and fowls of various kinds, thus the aspect of lambs, of sheep, of goats, of heifers, of horses, of doves, and of several species of beautiful birds; but the ideas of the thought of those who are natural, and who think from mere scientifics, are turned into the forms of fishes; hence also in the seas there appear several species of fishes, which it has frequently been given me to see. It is from this ground that by "fishes" in the Word are signified scientifics, as in the following passages:—"At my rebuke I dry up the sea, I make the rivers a wilderness: their *fish* stinketh, because there is no water, and dieth for thirst;" (Isaiah l. 2.) where by the "rebuke of Jehovah" is meant the destruction of the church, which takes place when there is no longer any knowledge of Truth and of Good, or no longer any living knowledge, because no perception. By "drying the sea," is signified to deprive the natural man of scientific truths, and hence of natural life, grounded in spiritual life. By "making the rivers a wilderness," is signified to deprive the rational man in like manner, whence there is no longer any intelligence. By "their fish stinking because there is no water, and dying of thirst," is signified that there is no longer any living scientific, because there is no truth; "fish" denotes what is scientific; "water" denotes truth; to "stink" denotes to die as to spiritual life. So in Ezekiel,—"Thus saith the Lord God, Behold, I am against thee, Pharaoh, king of Egypt, the great whale that lieth in the midst of his rivers, which hath said, My river is mine own, and I have made myself; therefore I will put hooks in thy jaws, and I will cause the fish of thy rivers to stick unto thy scales, and I will bring thee up out of the midst of thy rivers, and all the fish of thy rivers shall stick unto thy scales; and I will leave thee in the wilderness, thee and all the fish of thy rivers." (xxix. 3—5.) By "Pharaoh" is here signified the same thing as by "Egypt," since king and people have a similar signification, denoting the natural man and the scientific principle in that man; wherefore also he is called a "great whale," for by a "whale," or a large sea-fish, is signified the scientific principle in general, on which account it is said that he "should be drawn out of the river," and in such case "the fish shall stick to his scales," by which is signified that all intelligence will perish, and that science, which shall succeed in its place, will be in the sensual man without life; for in the sensual man, which is the lowest natural man, most nearly connected with the world, there are fallacies, and consequently false principles, which is signified by "the fish sticking to the scales of the whale." That the natural man, and the scientific principle therein, will be without life derived from any intelligence, is signified by the words, "I will leave thee in the wilderness, and all the fish of thy rivers;" and that such effects will come to pass because the natural man attributes to himself all intelligence, is signified by the words, "Because he said, My river is my own, I have made myself;" where the "river" denotes intelligence. Again in Isaiah,—"The fishes shall mourn, and all they that cast a hook into the river shall lament, and they that spread nets upon the waters shall languish;" (xix. 8.) in which passage by "fishers casting a hook into the river, and spreading out a net," are meant those who are willing to procure to themselves knowledges, and by them intelligence, denoting in this case that they are not able to procure them, because the knowledges of truth are not any where to be found. So in Habakkuk,—"Why makest thou a man like the fishes of the sea, as the creeping thing which hath no ruler? Let every man draw it out, and gather it into his net. Shall he therefore empty his net, and not spare continually to slay the nations?" (i. 14, 15, 17.) These words were spoken of the nation of Chaldea, wasting and destroying the church; by which nation is signified the profanation of truth and the vastation of the church. To "make men as the fishes of the sea, and as the creeping thing which hath no ruler," signifies to make man so natural that his scientifics are without spiritual truths, and his delights without spiritual good; for in the natural man there are scientifics which are the materials of thought, and delights which give birth to affections, over which, if there be no spiritual principle to rule, both the thoughts and affections are vague, and thus man is without intelligence to guide and rule him; that in such case every false and evil principle may draw them aside, and thus altogether destroy them, is signified by the words, "Let every one draw and gather them into his net, and afterwards let him slay;" where "to draw," is to draw away from good and truth; "into his net," denotes into what is false and evil; and "to slay," is to destroy. And in Amos,—"The day shall come in which they shall draw you out with prickles, and your posterity with fish-hooks;" (iv. 2.) by which is signified, that by acute reasonings grounded in false principles and fallacies, they will be led away and alienated from truths; those words are spoken of those who abound in knowledges, because they have the Word and the prophets. *A. E.* 513.

From the above passages it may now be manifest what is meant by *fishers*, by *fishes*, and by *nets*, which are so often mentioned in the New Testament, as in the following passages:— "Jesus seeing two brethren, Simon called Peter, and Andrew his brother, casting a net into the sea, for they were fishers, said unto them, Come after Me, and I will make you fishers of men;" (Matt. iv. 18, 19; Mark i. 16, 17.) and in another place,—"Jesus entered into the ship of Simon, and taught the multitude; and after said to Simon, that he should let down his nets for a draught, and they enclosed a great number of fishes, and they were ready to sink: and all were astonished at the draught of the fishes; and Jesus said to Simon, Fear not, from henceforth thou shalt catch men." (Luke v. 3—10.) In these words also there is a spiritual sense, similar to that which is in the other parts of the Word; for by the Lord choosing those fishers, and saying that they should "become fishers of men," was signified that they should gather men together to the church; by the "nets which they spread out, and in which they enclosed a great number of fishes, so that the ships were ready to sink," was signified the reformation of the church by them; for by "fishes" are there signified the knowledges of truth and good by which reformation was effected, also the multitude of men who were to be reformed. Similar things are also signified by the *fishes* caught by the disciples after the Lord's resurrection, on which subject it is thus written in John:—"Jesus said, on manifesting Himself to the disciples who were fishing, that they should cast their net on the right side of the ship, and they cast it, so that they were not able to draw the net for the multitude of fishes. Afterwards they went to land, where they saw a fire of coals and a little fish lying upon it, and bread; and Jesus gave them the bread and also the little fish." (xxi. 2—13.) The reason why the Lord manifested Himself to the disciples when they were *fishing*, was, because "to fish" signified to teach the knowledges of Truth and of Good, and thus to reform. By His commanding them to "cast their net out on the right side of the ship," was signified that they should do all from the good of love and charity, for the "right side" signified that good under the influence of which they were to act; for in proportion as knowledges are grounded in good, in the same proportion they live and are multiplied. The disciples also said that "they had laboured all the night and taken nothing," by which was signified that nothing can be effected by man himself, or by what is proper to himself, but all from the Lord; the like was also signified by the "fire of coals, on which was a little fish," and by "bread;" for by "bread" was signified the Lord, and the good of love from Him; and by the "little fish on the fire of coals," the knowledge of truth grounded in good; by a "little fish" the knowledge of truth; by "fire" the principle of good. *A. E.* 514.

Verse 21. *And they went to Capernaum, and immediately on the Sabbaths He went into the synagogue, and taught.*—The "Sabbath" amongst the children of Israel was the Holy of Holies, because it represented the Lord, six days being significative of His labours and combats with the hells, and the seventh of His victory over them, and of the *rest* which He thereby attained; and whereas that day was representative of the close and period of the whole act of redemption which the Lord accomplished, therefore it was esteemed very and essential holiness. But when the Lord came into the world, and in consequence thereof made all representations of Himself to cease, that day was then made a day of instruction in Divine things, and thus also a day of rest from labours, and of meditation on subjects which concern salvation and eternal life, and also a day for the exercise of love towards our neighbour. That it was made a day of instruction in Divine things, is evident from this circumstance, that the Lord on that day taught in the temple and in the synagogues; (Mark i. 21; vi. 2; Luke iv. 16, 31, 32; xiii. 10.) and that He said to the man that was

5

healed—"Take up thy bed and walk;" and to the Pharisees, that "it was lawful for His disciples on the Sabbath day to gather the ears of corn and eat;" (Matt. xii. 1—9; Mark ii. 23, to the end; Luke vi. 1—6; John v. 9—19.) by which particulars are signified, in a spiritual sense, to be instructed in doctrinals. That that day was also made a day for the exercise of love towards our neighbour, is evident from what the Lord both did and taught on the Sabbath day. (Matt. xii. 10—14; Mark iii. 1—9; Luke vi. 6—12; xiii. 10—18; xiv. 1—7; John v. 9—19; vii. 22, 23; ix. 14, 16.) From these and the foregoing passages it is evident why the Lord said that He is "Lord also of the Sabbath;" (Matt. xii. 8; Mark ii. 28; Luke vi. 5.) and from this His declaration it follows, that the Sabbath day was representative of Him. *T. C. R.* 301.

Synagogues.—By a "synagogue" is signified doctrine, because doctrine was taught in the synagogues, and also because differences in doctrinal subjects were there decided. *A. E.* 120.

Verse 22. *And they were astonished at His doctrine, for He taught them as one that had power, and not as the Scribes.*— By "power" is signified salvation, inasmuch as all Divine Power hath respect unto salvation as an end; for man, by virtue of Divine Power, is reformed, and is afterwards introduced into heaven, and is there withheld from what is evil and false, and kept in what is good and true, which cannot be effected by any one but by the Lord alone. They who claim to themselves that power, are altogether ignorant of what salvation means, for they do not know what reformation is, nor what heaven is, as appertaining to man: to claim to themselves the power of the Lord, is to claim power over the Lord Himself, which power is called the "power of darkness." (Luke xxii. 53.) That power, when predicated of the Lord, principally respects salvation, is manifest from the following passages:—"Jesus said, Father, Thou hast given to the Son *power* over all flesh, that He may give eternal life to those whom Thou hast given Him." (John xvii. 2.) Again in the same Evangelist,—"As many as received, to them gave He *power* to become the sons of God, believing in His name." (i. 12.) Again,—"I am the vine, ye are the branches: he that abideth in Me, and I in him, the same beareth much fruit, since without Me ye cannot do any thing." (xv. 5.) And in Mark,—"They were astonished at His doctrine, for He taught them as one that had *power*." (i. 22.) And in Luke,—"With *power and authority* He commandeth the unclean spirits, and they come out;" (iv. 36.) besides other passages. The Lord also has *power* over all things, because He is the only God; but the salvation of the human race is the chief power, since on that account the heavens and the worlds were created, and salvation is the reception of the Divine proceeding [principle]. *A. E.* 293.

Verse 23. *And there was in their synagogue a man with an unclean spirit,* &c.—An "unclean spirit" denotes the uncleanness of life appertaining to man, and it likewise denotes the unclean spirits attendant on him, for unclean spirits dwell in the uncleanness of the life of man. *A. C.* 4744.

Verse 24. *Jesus of Nazareth.*—The Nazarites represented the Lord as to the divine natural principle, which is the external divine Human. The *Nazariteship,* in Hebrew, is hair; hence it was that the Nazarites had this representation. *A. C.* 6437. [Hence also it was that the Lord dwelt in *Nazareth,* and was called a Nazarene. Matt. ii. 23.]

Verse 24. *The Holy One of God.*—As Divine Truth proceeding from the Lord is understood by the term *Holy,* therefore in the Word the Lord is called the " Holy One," the " Holy One of God," the " Holy One of Israel," the " Holy One of Jacob." *A. C.* 204.

Verse 30. *Sick of a fever.*—A "burning fever" denotes the lust of evil. *A. C.* 8364.

All the infernals induce diseases, but with a difference, by reason that all the hells are in the lusts and concupiscences of evil, which was thus confirmed by experience :—There exhaled from hell a molesting heat, arising from lusts of various kinds, as from haughtiness, lasciviousness, adulteries, hatreds, revenges, and contentions; when this heat acted into my body, it occasioned in a moment a disease like that of a *burning fever,* but when it ceased to flow in, instantly the disease ceased. There are also spirits who infuse unclean colds, such as are those of a cold fever [or ague], which it has been granted also to know by experience. *A. C.* 5713, 5715, 5716.

Verses 32 and 34. *And when it was evening, when the sun did set, they brought unto Him all that were diseased, and them that were possessed with demons; and He healed many that were sick of divers diseases,* &c.—By "disease" is signified evil, and the reason is, because "diseases," in the internal sense, signify such things as affect spiritual life, which things are evils, and are called lusts and concupiscences. Faith and charity constitute spiritual life, which life sickens when what is false takes place of the truth which is of faith, and when evil takes place of the good which is of charity; for what is false and evil brings that life to death, which is called spiritual death, and is damnation, as diseases bring natural life to its death ; hence it is, that by " disease," in the internal sense, is signified evil.

Inasmuch as diseases represented the iniquities and evils of spiritual life, therefore by the "diseases which the Lord healed," is signified deliverance from the various kinds of evil and false principles which infested the church and the human race, and which were about to produce spiritual death; for divine miracles are distinguished from other miracles by this, that they involve and have respect to states of the church and of the kingdom of heaven. On this account the Lord's miracles consisted principally in the healings of diseases; this is what is meant by the Lord's words to the disciples sent by John,—"Tell John the things which ye hear and see; the blind see, and the lame walk; the lepers are cleansed, and the deaf hear; the dead are raised up, and the poor hear the Gospel." (Matt. xi. 4, 5.) Hence it is, that it is so often said that the Lord "healed every disease and sickness." (Matt. iv. 23; ix. 35; xiv. 14, 35, 36; Luke iv. 40; v. 15; vi. 17; vii. 21; Mark i. 32, 34; iii. 10.) *A. C.* 8364.

Verses 40—43. *And there came a leper to Him, beseeching Him, and kneeling down to Him, and saying unto Him, If Thou wilt, Thou canst make me clean,* &c.—In the historical Word, much mention is made of the leprosy, of its various appearance in the skin, of the judgment thence to be formed of its quality, of the leper, that he was either to be shut up, or excluded from communion, or to be liberated, and of the leprosy in garments, in vessels, and in the very houses. The reason why so much mention is made of the "leprosy," is not on account of the leprosy, as a disease, but because it signified the profanation of truth, thus on account of the spiritual sense, and because the Jews and Israelites were capable of profaning truth more than other people; for if they had been acquainted with the internal things of the Word, and with the essential truths, represented by the rituals of the church appertaining to them, and had believed therein, and yet had lived according to their own inclinations, viz., in the love of self and the world, in hatred and revenge one amongst another, and in cruelty towards other nations, they must of necessity have profaned the truths in which they had once believed. For to believe truths, and to live contrary to them, is to profane them; wherefore also they were withheld, as far as was possible, from the knowledges of internal truth, insomuch that they did not know that they were to live after death; neither did they believe that the Messiah was to come to save souls to eternity, but only to exalt that nation above all others in the universe; and whereas that nation was of such a quality, and likewise is of such a quality at this day, they are therefore still withheld

CHAP. I.]　　　　TO MARK.　　　　**37**

from a true faith, although they live in the midst of Christendom: hence now it is, that the leprosy was so particularly
described as to its quality. That the "leprosy" signifies the
profanation of truth, is evident from the statutes respecting
the leprosy in Leviticus xiii. 1, to the end, in which description
is contained, in the internal sense, every quality of the profanation of truth; as, what its quality is, if it be recent, what,
if it be old, what, if it be interiorly in man, what, if it be also
exteriorly, what, if it is capable of being healed, what, if it
cannot be healed, what are the means of healing, and several
things besides, none of which can be known to any one except
by the internal sense of the Word. *A. C.* 6963.

　　Verse 41. *And Jesus, moved with compassion, putting forth
His hand, touched him,* &c.—By "touching with the hand,"
is signified to communicate and to transfer to another what
appertains to a man himself, and likewise to receive from
another; and when it relates to the Lord, as in the present
case, it denotes to communicate and transfer to another the
life, such as they enjoy, who are in illustration, and see and
hear such things as are in heaven. The reason why "touching with the hand" denotes to communicate and transfer to
another, is, because all the power of man is transferred from
the body to the hands, wherefore what the mind willeth that
the body should do, the arms and hands do it; hence it is,
that by "arms" and "hands" in the Word, is signified power,
but this power is a natural power, and communication by it is
the exertion of bodily strength; but spiritual power consists
in willing the good of another, and in willing to transfer, as
far as possible, to another what a man possesses in himself;
this power is what is signified by "hand" in the spiritual sense,
and its communication and translation by "touching with the
hand." From these considerations it may be manifest what is
signified by the Lord *touching,* and *touching with the hand,* in
several passages of the Word. *A. E.* 79.

TRANSLATOR'S NOTES AND OBSERVATIONS.

CHAPTER I.

Verses 2 and 3. *As it is written in the Prophets, Behold,
I send My messenger before Thy face, who shall prepare Thy
way before Thee. The voice of one crying in the wilderness,*

Prepare ye the way of the Lord.—It is remarkable in these words that two different expressions are employed, in the original Greek, to denote what is here rendered alike by the English term *prepare*, the former expression being derived from κατασκευασω, and the latter from ετοιμασω, but it is difficult to say what is the distinct and precise idea intended to be suggested by each expression.

Verse 10. *And straightway coming up out of the water, He saw the heavens rent.*—In the common English Version of the New Testament, what is here rendered "rent" is expressed by "opened," but the original Greek is σχιζομενους, which properly signifies *rent* or *split*, and not improbably has reference to the *three heavens*, which, on this occasion, were seen in a state of distinction from each other, and thus more ready to descend by their operation into the souls of men.

Verse 35. *And in the morning, when the night was far advanced*, &c.—What is here rendered, "when the night was far advanced," is expressed in the common English Version of the New Testament by "a great while before day," but the original Greek is Εννυχον λιαν, which literally means *far in the night*, or, as it is here rendered, "when the night was far advanced," having respect, no doubt, to the *night of spiritual darkness* which was then passing away.

MARK.

CHAPTER II.

1. AND again He entered into Capernaum, after [some] days; and it was heard that He was in the house.

2. And immediately many were gathered together, insomuch that there was no room, not even about the door; and He spake the Word unto them.

THAT the LORD, as to His Humanity, again consults the doctrine of Truth and Good, and thence instructs in the interiors of the Word. (Verses 1, 2.)

3. And they came unto Him, bringing one sick of the palsy, borne of four.

4. And when they could not come nigh unto Him because of the crowd, they uncovered the roof where He was, and breaking it up they let down the couch on which the sick of the palsy lay.

So that they in whom truth and good are not fully conjoined, and who are yet in integrity of life, seek by that doctrine to attain the conjunction of those principles, which yet cannot be effected but by the removal of evil and false persuasions, and an elevation to the interior things of love and charity. (Verses 3, 4.)

5. But Jesus seeing their faith, saith to the sick of the palsy, Son, thy sins are remitted to thee.

Since the removal of what is evil and false is one and the same thing with the conjunction of what is good and true. (Verse 5.)

6. But there were certain of the Scribes sitting there, and reasoning in their hearts,

But the perverse church is not willing to allow that the LORD, in His Humanity, has

7. Why doth this [Man] thus speak blasphemies? Who can remit sins but God only?

8. And Jesus immediately knowing in His spirit that they so reasoned within themselves, said unto them, Why reason ye these things in your hearts?

9. Whether is it easier to say to the sick of the palsy, Thy sins are remitted to thee, or to say, Arise, and take up thy couch, and walk?

10. But that ye may know that the Son of Man hath power to remit sins on the earth, (He saith to the sick of the palsy,)

11. I say unto thee, Arise, and take up thy couch, and go to thy house.

12. And immediately he arose, and taking up the couch, went forth before them all; insomuch that they were all amazed, and glorified God, saying, We never saw it thus.

13. And He went forth again by the sea-side, and all the multitude came to Him, and He taught them.

14. And as He passed, He saw Levi the [son] of Alpheus, sitting at the place where custom is received, and said unto him, Follow Me; and rising up he followed Him.

15. And it came to pass, that, as He sat in his house, many publicans and sinners sat also together with Jesus and His disciples; for there were many, and they followed Him.

any power to remove what is evil and false, insomuch as this power belongs only to Divinity. (Verses 6, 7.)

Therefore they are instructed that the LORD'S Humanity is not like the humanity of other men, but is a DIVINE HUMANITY, since it has the power both of conjoining what is good and true in the human mind, and of removing what is evil and false, and thus of elevating the doctrine of Truth to conjunction with the life of Truth. (Verses 6—13.)

That rational good, being required to obey the LORD, obeys, and that thus the affections and thoughts which had been perverted by evils and falses, are restored to communication with goods and truths from the LORD. (Verses 14, 15.)

16. And the Scribes and Pharisees seeing Him eating with publicans and sinners, said unto His disciples, How is it that He eateth and drinketh with publicans and sinners?

17. And Jesus having heard, saith to them, They that are whole have no need of a physician, but they that are sick: I came not to call the just, but sinners, to repentance.

18. And the disciples of John and of the Pharisees used to fast, and they come and say to Him, Why do the disciples of John and of the Pharisees fast, but Thy disciples do not fast?

19. And Jesus said unto them, Can the sons of the bridechamber fast while the Bridegroom is with them? So long as they have the Bridegroom with them they cannot fast.

20. But the days will come when the Bridegroom shall be taken away from them, and then shall they fast in those days.

21. And no one seweth a piece of unwrought cloth on an old garment: else the new piece that filled it up taketh away from the old, and the rent is made worse.

22. And no one putteth new wine into old bottles: else the new wine doth burst the bottles, and the wine is spilled, and the bottles will be marred; but new wine must be put into new bottles.

Which communication is offensive to such as are in hypocritical good, but this without cause, since the end of the LORD's coming in the flesh, was not to save the celestial, or those who were in orderly love, but the spiritual, or those who were in disorderly love, with whom there nevertheless remained the affection of truth. (Verses 16, 17.)

And who, by receiving the internal truths of the church in that affection, were blessed and happy so long as good was conjoined to their truths, but unblessed and unhappy when they are in truths without good. (Verses 18—21.)

That these things were unknown in the Jewish church, which was a church representative of spiritual things, and therefore the truths of that church do not accord with the truths of the Christian church, which are spiritual truths themselves. (Verses 21, 22.)

23. And it came to pass, that He went through the corn fields on the Sabbath day; and His disciples began, as they went, to pluck the ears of corn.

24. And the Pharisees said unto Him, Behold, why do they on the Sabbath day that which is not lawful?

25. And He said unto them, Have ye never read what David did, when he had need, and hungered, he, and they that were with him?

26. How he went into the house of God in the days of Abiathar the high priest, and did eat the shewbread, which is not lawful to eat but for the priests, and gave also to them that were with him?

27. And He said unto them, The Sabbath was made for man, not man for the Sabbath.

28. Therefore the Son of Man is Lord also of the Sabbath.

The LORD teacheth by representatives, that when spiritual good and truth are conjoined, which conjunction is the true Sabbath, then the church may enter into the appropriation and enjoyment of all natural goods and truths. (Verse 23.)

Which liberty is condemned as contrary to order by those who are in the mere representative church, and thus only in the literal sense of the word Sabbath. (Verse 24.)

But the LORD teacheth that it is agreeable to the internal sense of the word Sabbath, which sense teaches that by the Sabbath is meant the union of the LORD's Divinity and Humanity, also His conjunction with heaven and the church, and lastly, every conjunction of heavenly good and truth, and thus that the LORD Himself is the Sabbath in the supreme sense. (Verse 25, to the end of the chapter.)

EXPOSITION.

CHAPTER II.

VERSE 3. *Sick of the palsy.*—For the meaning of *diseases,* see above, chap. i. 30, 32, 34.

Verses 5, 9, 11, 12. *Jesus said to the sick of the palsy, Son, thy sins are remitted to thee. And He said to the Scribes,*

*Which is easier to say, Thy sins are remitted to thee, or to
say, Take up thy couch [or bed] and walk?* &c.—That in this
passage the term "couch" is significative, is evident, because
Jesus said—" Which is easier to say, Thy sins are remitted to
thee, or to say, Take up thy couch and walk?" By a "couch"
is signified doctrine, and the ground of this signification is
from correspondence, since, as the body lies down in its couch
[or bed], so the mind, in its doctrine; but by a "couch" is
signified the doctrine which every one procures to himself,
either from the Word or from his own intelligence, for in that
doctrine his mind rests, and as it were sleeps. The couches
[or beds] which are slept in, in the spiritual world, are from
no other origin, every one having a couch [or bed] there
according to the quality of his science or intelligence; the
wise sleeping in magnificent beds, the unwise in worthless
beds, and they who are in false principles in filthy beds.
Hence by "carrying a couch and walking," is signified to
meditate in doctrine. So it is understood in heaven. *A. R.*
137. See also *A. E.* 163.

Verse 10. *The Son of Man hath power to remit sins,* &c.—
It should be well known that man, in doing the work of
repentance, ought to look up to the Lord alone. If he looks
up to God the Father only, he cannot be purified; nor if to
the Father for the sake of the Son; nor if to the Son as a
man only; for there is one God who is the Lord, for His
Divine and Human Essence constitutes one Person, as is shewn
in "The Doctrine of the New Jerusalem concerning the Lord."
In order that every one in the work of repentance might look
to the Lord alone, He instituted the Holy Supper, which
confirms, to those who repent, the remission of sins; and it
confirms it because in that Supper or Communion every one
is kept looking to the Lord only. *D. P.* 122.

Verses 15, 16. *And it came to pass, as He sat in his house,
many publicans and sinners sat also together with Jesus and
His disciples. And the Scribes and Pharisees seeing Him
eating with publicans and sinners, said unto His disciples,
How is it that He eateth and drinketh with publicans and
sinners?*—The reason why the Lord did "eat with publicans
and sinners," at which the Jews murmured and were offended,
is, because the Gentiles, who were meant by *publicans and
sinners,* received the Lord, imbibed His precepts, and lived
according to them, by virtue of which the Lord appropriated
to them the good things of heaven, which is signified in the
spiritual sense by "eating with them." That by "eating and
drinking" in the Word is also signified spiritually to eat and
drink, which is, to be instructed, and by instruction and life

to imbue and appropriate what is good and true, consequently intelligence and wisdom, may be manifest from the Word throughout, where mention is made of eating and drinking. *A. E.* 617.

Verse 17. *I came not to call the just, but sinners, to repentance.*—The "just" are the celestial, and the "sinners" are the spiritual, who could not be raised to heaven until the Lord's advent.

In the things contained in this verse, namely, "I am come down to deliver them out of the hand of the Egyptians," (Exodus iii. 8.) there is a great mystery which has never as yet been known in the church, wherefore it shall be made known. They are called spiritual, who are such as cannot be regenerated except only as to the intellectual-part, but not as to the will-part; in whose intellectual-part therefore a new will is implanted by the Lord, which will is according to the doctrinals of faith peculiar to their church,—these, viz., such spiritual persons, were only saved by the Lord's coming into the world. The reason is, because the Divine [principle] passing through heaven, which was the Divine Human [principle] before the Lord's coming, could not reach to them, inasmuch as the doctrinals of their church were for the most part not true, and hence the good which is of the will was not good, n. 6427. Because these could only be saved by the coming of the Lord, and thus were incapable of before being elevated into heaven; therefore in the mean time they were kept in the lower earth, in places there which in the Word are called pits, which earth was obsessed around by the hells abounding with falses, by which at that time they were much infested; nevertheless they were still guarded by the Lord. But after the Lord came into the world, and made the Human in Himself Divine, then He delivered those who were there in *pits*, and elevated them to heaven; and out of them He also formed a spiritual heaven, which is the second heaven: this is what is meant by the descent of the Lord to those that are beneath, and by the deliverance of those who were bound. This is the mystery which in the internal sense is also described in this verse, and in the following. See what was shewn above concerning those spiritual persons, viz., that the spiritual are in obscurity as to the truth and good of faith, n. 2708, 2715. That their obscurity is illuminated by the Lord's Divine Human [principle], n. 2716, 4402; whereas they are in obscurity as to the truth and good of faith, they are greatly assaulted by the hells, but that the Lord con. tinually protects them, n. 6419. That the spiritual cannot be regenerated as to the will-part, but only as to the intellectual-part, and that a new will is there formed by the Lord, n. 863, 875. That the spiritual were saved by the coming of the Lord into the world, n. 2833, 2834, 3969. In the prophetic Word throughout, mention is made of the bound, and of those that are bound in a pit, and that they were delivered by the Lord; by which bound are specifically meant those who are here spoken of, as in Isaiah,—" I Jehovah have called thee in justice, and will take hold of thy hand, for I will guard thee, and will give thee for a covenant to the people, for a light of the Gentiles; to open the blind eyes, *to bring forth out of prison him that is bound, out of the house of inclosure them that sit in darkness.*" (xlii. 6, 7.) Again in the same prophet,— "I have kept thee, and given thee for a covenant of the people, to restore the earth, to divide the wasted inheritances, *to say to the bound, Go ye forth; to them who are in darkness, Be ye revealed.* They shall feed on the ways, and in all hills shall be their pasture;" (xlix. 8, 9.) speaking manifestly of the Lord; where the " bound" specifically denote those who were detained in the lower earth, even to the Lord's coming, and who were then elevated into heaven; and in general all those who are in good, and are kept as it were bound by falses, from which nevertheless they are desirous to be delivered. And in Zechariah,—" By the blood of thy covenant, *I will send forth thy bound out of the pit.*" (ix. 11.) And in Isaiah,—"Gathering they shall be gathered together, *the bound in a pit, and shall be closed in an inclosure;* after a multitude of days they shall be visited;" (xxiv. 22.) where the " bound in a pit" has the same signification. *A. C.* 6854.

Verses 18, 19, 20. *And the disciples of John and of the Pharisees were fasting, and they come and say to Him, Why do the disciples of John and of the Pharisees fast, but Thy disciples do not fast? and Jesus said unto them, Can the sons of the bridechamber fast while the Bridegroom is with them?* &c.—They are called the *sons of the bridechamber,* who are in the truths of the church, and receive good, for the good which is from the Lord is the *bridegroom.* The reason why the sons of the bridechamber do not mourn so long as the bridegroom is with them is, because they are in a blessed and happy state, thus are with the Lord when they are in truths conjoined to good. Their *fasting* when the bridegroom is taken from them, denotes that they are in an unhappy state when good is no longer conjoined to truths. *A. C.* 9182.

The Lord here calls Himself *the Bridegroom,* and the men of the church He calls *the sons of the bridechamber;* by "fasting" is signified to mourn on account of the defect of truth and good. *A. E.* 1180. *B. E.* 101. *C. L.* 117.

Verse 21. *And no one seweth a piece of unwrought* [*or new*] *cloth on an old garment*, &c.—Inasmuch as a "garment" signifies truth, therefore the Lord compares the truths of the former church, which was a church representative of spiritual things, to the *piece of an old garment*, and the truths of the New Church, which were spiritual truths themselves, to *the piece of a new garment;* in like manner He compared those truths to *bottles of wine*, because by "wine" in like manner is signified truth, and "bottles" are the knowledges which contain it. *A. E.* 193.

Verse 22. *And no one putteth new wine into old bottles*, &c.—Inasmuch as all comparisons in the Word are grounded in correspondences, so likewise is this comparison, and by "wine" is signified truth: by "old wine," the truth of the old or Jewish Church, and by "bottles" are signified those things which contain, by "old bottles" the statutes and judgments of the Jewish Church, and by "new bottles" the precepts and commandments of the Lord. That the statutes and judgments of the Jewish Church, which related principally to sacrifices and representative worship, do not accord with the truths of the Christian Church, is meant by the words, "No one putteth new wine into old bottles, else the new wine doth burst the bottles and the wine is spilled; but new wine must be put into new bottles." That they who were born and educated in the external things of the Jewish Church, could not be brought immediately into the internal things of the Christian Church, is signified by what is said in another place—"No one having drunk old wine immediately desireth new, for he saith the old is better." *A. E.* 376. See also *A. E.* 195.

That the New Jerusalem, that is, the New Church, cannot descend from heaven in a moment, but in proportion as the false principles of the former church are removed (for what is new cannot enter where false principles have before had birth, unless they be eradicated), the Lord teaches when He says— "No one putteth new wine into old bottles," &c. *T. C. R.* 784.

New wine is the Divine Truth of the New Testament, thus of the New Church, and *old wine* is the Divine Truth of the Old Testament, thus of the Old Church. *A. R.* 316.

Verse 23. *Corn-fields — Sabbath day.* — See chap. i. 21, Exposition; also what is meant by "plucking the ears of corn and eating them;" that is, to be instructed and nourished in things spiritual by the Lord. See above, p. 34.

Verses 27, 28. *And He said unto them, The Sabbath was made for man, not man for the Sabbath. Therefore the Son of Man is Lord also of the Sabbath.*—He who does not know what the Sabbath represented, and hence what it signified, cannot know why it was accounted the most holy of all things; but the reason why it was so accounted was, because in the supreme sense it represented the union of the Divinity and Divine Humanity in the Lord, and in the respective sense the conjunction of the Lord's Divine Humanity with the human race. Hence the Sabbath was most holy. And whereas it represented those things, it also represented heaven as to the conjunction of good and of truth, which conjunction is called the heavenly marriage; and since the conjunction of good and of truth is from the Lord alone, and nothing of it from man, and inasmuch as it is effected in a state of peace, therefore man was forbidden under the most severe penalty to do any work on that day, insomuch that the soul was to be cut off which did it, according to what is thus written in Moses,— " Ye shall keep the Sabbath, because it is holy unto you; he who profaneth it, dying shall die, because the soul of every one who doeth work on it shall be cut off from the midst of his people :" (Exod. xxxi. 14.) on this account the man was stoned who only *gathered sticks on that day :* (Numb. xv. 32—37.) therefore also the precept concerning the Sabbath is the fourth commandment in the Decalogue, immediately following the former commandments respecting the holy worship of Jehovah: (Exod. xx. 8.) and therefore the Sabbath is called an *eternal covenant,* (Exod. xxxi. 16.) for by covenant is signified conjunction. From these considerations it is evident that the Lord is the Lord of the Sabbath, according to His words in Matthew, xii. 1—9; and in Mark ii. 28: and why the Lord performed so many cures on the Sabbath days: (Matt. xii. 10—14; Mark iii. 1—9; Luke iv. 6—12.) for the diseases which were cured by the Lord, involved spiritual diseases, which are from evil. *A. C.* 8495.

The celestial man is the seventh day, and since the Lord operated during six days, it is called His work; and whereas in such case combat ceases, the Lord is said to rest from all His work; wherefore the seventh day was sanctified, and was called the Sabbath, from rest. This is manifest from what the Lord said,—" The Son of Man is Lord also of the Sabbath," (Mark ii. 27.) which words involve, that the Lord is Very Man, and the Very Sabbath. His kingdom in the heavens and in the earth is called by Him the Sabbath, or eternal peace and rest. *A. C.* 10360.

The reason why the "Sabbath," in the supreme sense, signifies the Divine Human of the Lord is, because the Lord, when He was in the world, fought from His Human against all the hells, and subdued them, and at the same time reduced the heavens into order, and after this labour united His Human to the Divine, and also made it divine Good. Hence on this occasion He had rest, for the hells do not snarl against the Divine itself. Hence now it is that by the "Sabbath" in the supreme sense is meant the Divine Human of the Lord. *A.C.* 10367.

TRANSLATOR'S NOTES AND OBSERVATIONS.

CHAPTER II.

Verse 10. *But that ye may know that the Son of Man hath power to remit sins on the earth.*—In the common version of the New Testament, these words are thus rendered:— " But that ye may know that the Son of Man hath power on earth to forgive sins," as if the expression, *on earth*, had reference to *the Son of Man*, whereas it is evident from the original Greek, that it has reference rather to the *sins* remitted.

[What is said above, at pages 44, 45, in illustration of verse 17, plainly shews us what is meant by 1 Peter iii. 19, where the apostle speaks of the Lord, after his resurrection, " going and preaching to the spirits in prison." These spirits were denoted by those " bound in the pit," (Zech. ix. 11.) and in the " lower earth" of the world of spirits, who could be delivered after the Lord's resurrection and glorification, which deliverance is signified by His " going and preaching" to them.]

MARK.

CHAPTER III.

1. AND He entered again into the Synagogue, and there was a man there who had a withered hand.

2. And they watched Him, whether He would heal him on the Sabbath, that they might accuse Him.

3. And He saith to the man who had the withered hand, Stand up in the midst.

4. And He saith to them, Is it lawful to do good on the Sabbath days, or to do evil? to save life or to kill? But they were silent.

5. And looking round about them with anger, being grieved at the hardness of their hearts, He saith to the man, Stretch forth thy hand! And he stretched it forth; and his hand was restored whole as the other.

6. And the Pharisees went forth immediately and took counsel with the Herodians

THAT the truth of the church, which had been separated from its good, is restored to conjunction, through the union of the LORD's Divinity with His Humanity. (Verses 1—6.)

Which restoration, being effected on the Sabbath day, is thought to be contrary to the sanctity of the Sabbath by those in the representative church, who are not aware that the conjunction of good and truth is the very essence of that sanctity. (Verses 2—6.)

That the LORD initiates His Humanity into the scientifics of the church, and

7

against Him, how they might destroy Him.

7. And Jesus withdrew with His disciples to the sea; and much multitude followed Him from Galilee, and from Judea;

8. And from Jerusalem, and from Idumea, and from beyond Jordan; and they about Tyre and Zidon, much multitude, having heard how many things He did, came unto Him.

9. And He said to His disciples that a boat should wait on Him, because of the multitude, lest they should crowd Him.

10. For He had healed many, insomuch that they pressed upon Him for to touch Him, as many as had plagues.

11. And unclean spirits, when they saw Him, fell down before Him, and cried out, saying, Thou art the Son of God.

12. And He earnestly charged them, that they should not make Him manifest.

13. And He goeth up into a mountain, and calleth to Him whom He willed, and they came to Him.

14. And He ordained twelve, that they might be with Him, and that He might send them forth to preach,

15. And to have power to heal sicknesses, and to cast out devils.

16. And Simon He surnamed Peter;

His Omnipotence in the removal of evils and falses manifests itself in every direction, so that people of all descriptions seek communication with Him, and the infernals themselves confess His Divine Power. (Verses 6—12.)

Yet He refuses to accept infernal testimony. (Verse 12.)

And entering, from His Divine Love, into reciprocal conjunction with those who are principled in the goods and truths of His church, He commits to them the testimony of His Divinity, and gives them power over all infernal evils and falses. (Verses 13—16.)

The distinct qualities of these goods and truths are

17. And James the [son] of Zebedee, and John the brother of James, and He surnamed them Boanerges, which is, The sons of thunder:

18. And Andrew, and Philip, and Bartholomew, and Matthew, and Thomas, and James the [son] of Alpheus, and Thaddeus, and Simon the Canaanite,

19. And Judas Iscariot, who also betrayed Him: and they went into an house.

20. And the multitude cometh together again, so that they could not so much as eat bread.

21. And when His kinsfolk heard of it, they came forth to lay hold of Him, for they said, He is beside Himself.

22. And the Scribes who came down from Jerusalem said, He hath Beelzebub, and in the Prince of the devils He casteth out devils.

23. And calling them [to Him], He said to them in parables, How can Satan cast out Satan?

24. And if a kingdom be divided against itself, that kingdom cannot stand.

25. And if a house be divided against itself, that house cannot stand.

26. And if Satan rise up against himself, and be divided, he cannot stand, but hath an end.

enumerated, from which it appears, that truth grounded in good is the first principle of the church, and that this is succeeded by truth grounded in celestial good. (Verses 16—20.)

For no good can be appropriated to man until truths are duly arranged in him, and they cannot be arranged except from good. (Verse 20.)

But this arrangement of truths from good is regarded by the natural man as unnecessary and inconsistent. (Verse 21.)

And the consequent removal of evils and falses is imputed by those of the perverse church to infernal agency. (Verse 22.)

When nevertheless it is an eternal truth, that infernal falses have no power, and that neither truths, nor goods, nor falses, can endure, except there be unanimity. (Verses 23—27.

27. No one can enter into a strong man's house and spoil his goods, unless he first bind the strong man, and then he will spoil his house.

28. Verily I say unto you, All sins shall be remitted to the sons of men, and blasphemies, wherewith soever they shall blaspheme;

29. But he that shall blaspheme against the Holy Spirit hath never remission, but is exposed to eternal damnation:

30. Because they said, He hath an unclean spirit.

31. Then came His brethren and mother, and, standing without, sent to Him, calling Him.

32. And the multitude sat about Him; and they said to Him, Behold, Thy mother and Thy brethren without seek Thee.

33. And He answered them, saying, Who is My mother, or My brethren?

34. And looking round on those who sat about Him, He saith, Behold My mother and My brethren!

35. For whosoever shall do the will of God, the same is My brother, and My sister, and mother.

Consequently, unless Divine Power be communicated for the subjugation of infernal falses, it is impossible that evils with their concupiscences can be subdued; whereas if the dominion of infernal falses be put down, in this case the dominion of evil and its concupiscences cannot long endure. (Verse 27.)

Whosoever therefore denies the power of the Divine Truth proceeding from the LORD's DIVINE HUMANITY, that is, the Word, and adulterates its essential goods, and falsifies its essential truths, must of necessity separate himself from all conjunction with the LORD and His kingdom. (Verses 28, 29, 30.)

For in heaven all are consociated according to spiritual relationships, which are of the good of love and of faith, and hence by "brethren" are signified all who are in the good of charity from the LORD; by "sisters" those who are in truths derived from that good; and by "mother" is signified the church grounded therein. (Verse 31, to the end of the chapter.)

EXPOSITION.

CHAPTER III.

VERSE 1. *Synagogue.*—See above, Exposition, chap. i. 21.

Verses 2, 4.—The reason why healings and cures were effected on the Sabbath days, see above, Exposition, chap. i. 21.

Verse 5. *Being grieved at the hardness of their hearts.*—"Hardness" is predicated of the confirmed state of what is false derived from evil. *A. C.* 6359.

That "hardness" denotes the obduracy and obstinacy of those who are principled in the falses of evil, see *A. C.* 7272, 7305.

As to "hardness of heart," or aversion from the Lord and the divine things of His kingdom, I will here briefly explain how the case is. All those who are in externals separate from an internal principle, avert themselves from the Lord, or from the Divine Being, for they look outwards and downwards, and not inwards and upwards; for man looks inwards or upwards, when the internal is open, thus when it is in heaven; but he looks outwards or downwards, when his internal is closed and only the external open, for this latter is in the world; wherefore when the external is separated from the internal, man cannot be elevated upwards. For that principle, into which heaven should operate, is not present, because it is closed; hence it is that all things of heaven and of the church are to them thick darkness; wherefore also they are not believed by them, but are denied in heart, by some also with the mouth. When heaven operates with man, as is the case when the internal is open, it withdraws him from the loves of self and of the world, and from the falses therein originating; for when the internal is elevated, the external is also elevated, since the latter is then kept in a similar direction of its views with the former, because it is in subordination; but when the internal cannot be elevated, because it is closed, then the external looks in no other direction than to itself and the world, for the loves of self and of the world reign. This also is called looking downwards, because to hell, for those loves reign there, and the man who is in them is in consort with those who dwell there, although he is ignorant of it; as to his interiors also he

actually averts himself from the Lord, for he turns the back to
Him, and the face to hell.   This cannot be seen in man, whilst
he lives in the body; but whereas his thought and will produce
this effect, it is his spirit which thus turns itself, for the spirit
is what thinks and wills in man.   That this is the case, is
manifestly apparent in the other life, where spirits turn themselves according to their loves; they who love the Lord and
the neighbour, look continually to the Lord, yea, what is
wonderful, they have Him before the face in every turning of
their body; for in the spiritual world, there are not quarters,
as in the natural world, but the quarter is there determined
by the love of every one, which turns him.   But they who
love themselves and the world above all things, turn away the
face from the Lord, and turn themselves to hell, and every one
to those there who are in a similar love with himself, and this
also in every turning of their body; hence it may be manifest
what is meant by averting themselves from the Divine Being;
also what is properly signified by averting themselves in the
Word, as in Isaiah,—" They *avert themselves backwards,* con-
fiding in a graven thing;" (xlii. 17.) and in David,—" The
heart *hath averted itself backwards;*" (Psalm xliv. 18.) and
in Jeremiah,—" Their prevarications are multiplied, and their
aversions are made strong." (v. 6.)   Again,—" They *avert
themselves,* that they do not return; this people *have averted
themselves;* Jerusalem perpetuates *things averted,* they refuse
to return." (viii. 4, 5.)   Again,—" They have *averted themselves,* they have let themselves down into the deep to dwell;"
(xlix. 8.) and in many other passages. *A. C.* 10,420.

Verses 7, 9. *He withdrew with His disciples to the sea, and
entered into a boat or ship.*—This was done, because by the
" sea," and by the " lake of Genesareth," when spoken of the
Lord, are signified the knowledges of Truth and Good in the
aggregate, and by a " ship," doctrine; hence by " teaching
from a ship," was signified that He taught from doctrine.
A. E. 514.

Judea and Jerusalem.—See above, Exposition, chap. i. 5.

Verse 8. *Tyre and Sidon.*—Tyre and Sidon were the ultimate borders of Philistia, and were near the sea, and therefore
by " Tyre" are signified interior knowledges, and by " Sidon"
exterior knowledges, and this of things spiritual, as also appears
from the Word. *A. C.* 1201.

Verses 10, 11. *He healed as many as had plagues, and
unclean spirits, when they saw Him,* &c.—By " plagues" and
" evil spirits" are understood obsessions and calamitous states
inflicted on men, in such case by evil spirits, all which,

nevertheless, signified correspondent spiritual states; for all
the healings of diseases effected by the Lord, signified spiritual
healings, hence the Lord's miracles were divine. *A.E.* 584.

Verses 13, 14, 16. *And He goeth up into a mountain, and
calleth to Him whom He willed, and they came to Him; and
He ordained twelve, that they might be with Him, and that
He might send them forth to preach. And Simon He surnamed
Peter.*—The reason why the Lord so often went up into a
mountain, and especially to the Mount of Olives, was, because
"mountains," amongst the most ancient people, signified the
Lord, because it was their practice to worship Him on mountains. Forasmuch as mountains are the highest parts of the
earth, hence "mountains" also signified things celestial, which
they also called the highest things, consequently love and
charity, thus the good things of love and charity which are
celestial. *A.C.* 795, 2708.

In the Word of the Evangelists, by the Apostle Peter is
understood truth grounded in good, which is from the Lord,
and likewise in the opposite sense truth separate from good.
And whereas truth is of faith and good is of charity, by him
also is understood faith grounded in charity, and likewise faith
separate from charity; for the twelve apostles, like the twelve
tribes of Israel, represented the church as to all things belonging to it, thus as to truths and goods, for all things of the
church have reference to those two principles as to faith and
love; for truths are of faith, and goods are of love. In general,
Peter, James, and John, represented faith, charity, and the
works of charity; wherefore those three followed the Lord
more than the rest, and therefore it is said of them in Mark,—
" He did not permit any one to follow Him, except Peter,
James, and John." (v. 37.) And whereas truth grounded in
good which is from the Lord, is the first principle of the church,
therefore Peter was first called by Andrew his brother, afterwards James and John, as is manifest in Matthew:—"Jesus
walking at the sea of Galilee, saw two brethren, Simon, called
Peter, and Andrew, his brother, casting a net into the sea, for
they were fishers; and He said unto them, Follow Me, and I
will make you fishers of men: and immediately leaving their
nets, they followed Him." (iv. 18, 19, 20.) And in John,—
" Andrew found his brother Simon, and saith unto him, We
have found the Messiah, which is, being interpreted, the Christ;
he leads him therefore to Jesus; and Jesus, beholding him,
saith unto him, Thou art Simon the son of Jonah: thou shalt
be called Cephas, which, being interpreted, is Peter." (i. 41,
42, 43.) And in Mark,—"Jesus going up into a mountain,

calleth to Him whom He willed, first Simon, whom He surnamed Peter; afterwards James the son of Zebedee, and John
the brother of James." (iii. 13, 16, 17.) The reason why Peter
was the first of the apostles, was, because truth grounded in
good is the first principle of the church; for man acquires no
knowledge from the world concerning heaven and hell, nor
concerning a life after death, nor even concerning God; his
natural lumen teaches nothing but what enters by the eyes;
thus nothing but what relates to the world and himself; his
life likewise is thence derived, and so long as man is solely in
those principles, he is in hell: it is therefore necessary for the
purpose of his being brought out thence, and introduced into
heaven, that he learn truths which may not only teach that
there is a God, that there is a heaven and a hell, and that
there is a life after death, but may also teach the way to
heaven.   Hence it may be manifest that truth is the first
principle by which the church is implanted in man; this truth
however must be grounded in good, since truth without good
is merely the knowledge that a thing is so, and knowledge
alone has no effect but to make man capable of becoming a
church; but he does not become a church until he lives
according to knowledges, in which case truth is conjoined to
good, and man is introduced into the church.   Truths also
teach how man ought to live; and when on such occasion he
is affected with truths, for the sake of truths, as is the case
when he loves to live according to them, he is then led of the
Lord, and conjunction with heaven is granted to him, and he
becomes spiritual, and after death an angel of heaven. It is
nevertheless to be noted, that truths do not produce these
effects, but good by truths, and good is from the Lord. Inasmuch as truth grounded in good, which is from the Lord, is
the first principle of the church, therefore Peter was first
called, and was the first of the apostles; he was also named
by the Lord, Cephas, which is a rock [Petra], but that it
might be the name of a person, it is pronounced Peter
[Petrus]. By "rock," in the supreme sense, is signified the
Lord as to Divine Truth, or Divine Truth proceeding from
the Lord, hence in the respective sense by "rock" is signified
truth grounded in good which is from the Lord, and the like
by Peter. *A. E.* 820.

  Verse 17. *And James the son of Zebedee, and John the*
brother of James; and He surnamed them Boanerges, which
is, The sons of thunder.—By "sons of thunder" are signified
truths grounded in celestial good.   The reason why those
truths are signified by "thunders" in the Word, is, because

in the spiritual world are also heard thunders, which exist from truths grounded in celestial good, whilst they descend from the superior heavens into the inferior; the light of truth grounded in good, on such occasions, appears as lightning, the good itself as thunder, and the truths themselves thence derived as variations of sound.   Hence it is that in the Word throughout, mention is made of "lightnings," of "thunders," and "voices," by which those things are signified.   The reason why good is there heard as thunder, is, because good, which is of the affection or love of man, also which is of his will, does not speak, but only utters a sound, whereas truth, which is of the understanding, and thence of the thought of man, articulates that sound by expression of words; celestial good is the same thing with the good of love in the will and in the act, nor is it celestial good until this is the case, and this is what produces truths by thought and the speech thence derived.   From these considerations it is evident from what ground it is that James and John were called "sons of thunder." *A. E.* 821.

Verses 24, 25, 27. *And if a kingdom be divided against itself, that kingdom cannot stand; and if a house be divided against itself, that house cannot stand.   No one can enter into a strong man's house, and spoil his goods, unless he first bind the strong man, and then he will spoil his goods.*—"House," in the internal sense, is the natural mind, for the natural mind, as also the rational mind, is like a house, in which the husband is good, the wife is truth, the daughters and sons are affections of good and of truth, also the goods and truths which are derived from them as parents; the maid-servants and men-servants are pleasures and scientifics, which minister and confirm.   That the natural mind and the rational mind of man is called a "house," is evident from the following passage in Luke:—" When the unclean spirit is gone out of a man, he wanders through dry places, seeking rest; and finding none, he saith, I will return to my house whence I came forth; and when he cometh, he findeth it swept and garnished: then goeth he, and taketh seven other spirits worse than the first, and entering in they dwell there." (xi. 24, 25, 26.)   In this passage "house" denotes the natural mind, which is called an "empty house and swept," when there are in it no goods and truths, which are husband and wife, nor the affections of good and of truth, which are daughters and sons, nor such things as confirm, which are maid-servants and men-servants.   Man himself is the *house,* because the natural mind and the rational make the man, and without them, that is, without goods and truths, and their affections, and the ministry of these affections, he is not a man but a brute. The mind of man is also meant by a *house* in these words, in the same Evangelist,—"Every kingdom divided against itself is brought to desolation, and a house against a house falleth." (xi. 17.) And in Mark,—"If a kingdom be divided against itself, that kingdom cannot stand; and if a house be divided against itself, that house cannot stand. No one can enter into a strong man's house, and spoil his goods, unless he first bind the strong man, and then he will spoil his house." (iii. 24, 25, 27.) By "kingdom" in this passage is signified truth, n. 1672, 2547, 4601; and by "house" good, n. 2233, 2234, 3710, 4982. *A. C.* 5023.

Verses 28, 29. *Verily I say unto you, All sins shall be remitted unto men, and blasphemies wherewith soever they shall blaspheme; but he that shall blaspheme against the Holy Spirit hath never remission, but is exposed to eternal judgment.*—What is signified by "sin and blasphemy against the Holy Spirit," and by a "word against the Son of Man," has not yet been known in the church, and this by reason of its not having been known what is properly meant by the *Holy Spirit*, and what properly by the *Son of Man*. By the "Holy Spirit" is meant the Lord as to Divine Truth, such as it is in the heavens, thus the Word such as it is in the spiritual sense, for this is Divine Truth in heaven; and by the "Son of Man" is meant Divine Truth such as it is in the earths, thus the Word such as it is in the natural sense, for this is the Divine Truth in the earths. When it is known what is signified by the "Holy Spirit," and what by the "Son of Man," it is known also what is signified by "sin and blasphemy against the Holy Spirit," and what by a "word against the Son of Man;" it may also be known why the sin and blasphemy against the Holy Spirit cannot be remitted, and why a word against the Son of Man can be remitted. For "sin and blasphemy against the Holy Spirit" consist in denying the Word, also in adulterating its essential goods, and falsifying its essential truths; but a "word against the Son of Man" consists in interpreting the natural sense of the Word, which is the sense of its letter, according to appearances. The reason why a denial of the Word is a sin which cannot be remitted in this age, nor in that which is to come, or to eternity, and why it exposes to eternal judgment, is, because they who deny the Word, deny a God, deny the Lord, deny a heaven and a hell, and deny the church and all things appertaining to it; and they who deny those things are Atheists, who, although they say with their lips that the creation of the universe is the work of some Highest Being, Deity, or

God, yet in heart they ascribe it to Nature; such persons, inasmuch as by denial they have loosened every bond of con_nection with the Lord, must of necessity be separated from heaven, and conjoined to hell. The reason why the adultera_tion of the essential goods of the Word, and the falsification of its essential truths, is blasphemy against the Holy Spirit, which also cannot be remitted, is, because by the Holy Spirit is meant the Lord, as to Divine Truth, such as it is in the heavens, thus the Word such as it is in the spiritual sense, as was said above. For in the spiritual sense are genuine goods and genuine truths, but in the natural sense are the same goods and truths as it were clothed, and not naked except here and there, wherefore these are called apparent goods and truths; these are what are adulterated and falsified, and they are said to be adulterated and falsified when they are explained contrary to genuine goods and truths, for in such case heaven removes itself, and man is put asunder from it, by reason that genuine goods and truths, as was said above, constitute the spiritual sense of the Word, in which the angels of heaven are principled. As for example:—If the Lord and His Divinity be denied, as was done by the Pharisees, who said that the Lord wrought miracles from Beelzebub, and had an unclean spirit, this is to commit sin and blasphemy against the Holy Spirit, because it is against the Word. Hence also it is that Socinians and Arians, who, although they do not deny the Lord, still deny His Divinity, are out of heaven, and cannot be received by any angelic society. To take another example. They who exclude the good of love and the works of charity from the means of salvation, and assume faith exclusively as the only means, and confirm themselves in this idea, not only by doctrine, but also by life, saying in their hearts,—"Goods do not save me, neither do evils condemn me, because I have faith;" these also blaspheme the Holy Spirit, for they falsify the genuine goods and truths of the Word, and this in a thousand passages, where love and charity, deeds and works, are named. Moreover, as was said above, in all and singular things of the Word, there is a marriage of good and truth, thus of charity and faith, wherefore when good or charity is taken away, that marriage perishes, and adultery is committed in its place; hence it is, that neither are such persons received into heaven. The reason also is, because in the place of heavenly love they have earthly love, and in the place of good works they have evil works, inasmuch as they proceed from earthly love, which, separate from heavenly love, is infernal love. But it is otherwise with those who indeed believe from the doctrine of the church, and from teachers, that faith is the only means of salvation, or who know, and do not interiorly affirm or deny, and still live well, under the guidance of the Word, that is, because it is commanded by the Lord in the Word: these do not blaspheme the Holy Spirit, for they do not adulterate the goods of the Word, nor falsify its truths, wherefore they have conjunction with the angels of heaven; few of them also know that faith is any thing else than to believe the Word; the doctrine of justification by faith alone without the works of the law they do not comprehend, because it transcends their understanding. These two examples are adduced to the intent that it may be known what is meant by "sin and blasphemy against the Holy Spirit," and that sin against the Holy Spirit consists in denying the Divine Truth, thus the Word, and that blasphemy against the Holy Spirit consists in adulterating the essential Goods of the Word, and in falsifying its essential Truths. The reason why a "word against the Son of Man" signifies to interpret the natural sense of the Word, which is the sense of its letter, according to appearances, is, because by the "Son of Man" is meant the Lord, as to Divine Truth, such as it is in the earths, thus such as it is in the natural sense; and the reason why this "word" is remitted to man, is, because most things in the natural sense, or in the sense of the letter of the Word, are goods and truths clothed, and only some naked, as in its spiritual sense; and goods and truths clothed are called appearances of truth. For the Word in the ultimates is as a man clad in raiment, who yet as to the face and hands is naked, and where the Word is thus naked, there its goods and truths appear naked as in heaven, thus such as they are in the spiritual sense; wherefore it can never come to pass but that the doctrine of genuine good and genuine truth, derived from the sense of the letter of the Word, may be seen by those who are enlightened of the Lord, and be confirmed by those who are not enlightened. The reason why the Word is such in the sense of the letter, is, that it may be a basis for the spiritual sense; hereby also it is accommodated to the apprehension of the simple, who can only perceive those things which are so said, and when they perceive, can believe and do them. And whereas Divine Truths, in the sense of the letter of the Word, are most of them appearances of truth, and the simple in faith and heart cannot be elevated above those appearances, hence it is not sin and blasphemy to interpret the Word according to appearances, if so be principles are not formed from them, and these confirmed even to the destruction of Divine Truth in its genuine sense. *A. E.* 778.

By "saying a word against the Holy Spirit" is meant to speak well and to think ill, and to do well and to will ill, respecting those things which relate to the Lord, His kingdom and church, and also which relate to the Word, for thereby a false principle lies concealed inwardly in the truths which are spoken, and in the goods which are done, which false principle is hidden poison, whence they are called an *offspring of vipers.* In the other life it is allowed to an evil spirit to speak what is evil and false, but not what is good and true, inasmuch as all in that life are compelled to speak from the heart, and not to divide the mind; they who do otherwise are separated from the rest, and are immersed deep in hells, from which they can never come forth. That such are they who are meant by "saying a word against the Holy Spirit," is manifest from the Lord's words on the occasion,—"Either make the tree good and the fruit good, or make the tree corrupt and the fruit corrupt; how can ye speak what is good when ye are evil?" (Matt. xii. 33, 34.) The "Holy Spirit" is the Divine Truth proceeding from the Lord, thus the Holy, Divine Principle Itself, which is thus principally and materially blasphemed. The reason why it will not be remitted to them is, because hypocrisy or deceit about holy Divine things infects the interiors of man, and destroys the all of spiritual life appertaining to him. *A. C.* 9013. See also, 882, 9264, 9818. Also, *D. P.* 98, 231. Also, *T. C. R.* 299.

"Blasphemy against the Holy Spirit" is blasphemy against the Lord's Divinity, and "blasphemy against the Son of Man" is something against the Word, by giving a wrong interpretation of its meaning; for the "Son of Man" is the Lord as to the Word, as was shewn above. *D. Lord,* 50.

Verses 31—35. *Then came His brethren and mother, and, standing without, sent to Him. And looking round on those who sat about Him, He saith, Behold My mother and My brethren! For whosoever shall do the will of God, the same is My brother, and My sister, and mother.*—That a "servant" denotes the Humanity appertaining to the Lord, before it was made Divine, may be manifest from several passages in the Prophets; the reason is, as has been occasionally observed above, that the Humanity appertaining to the Lord was nothing else but a servant, before He put it off and made it Divine. For the Humanity appertaining to Him was from the mother, thus an infirm Humanity, having with it an hereditary principle thence derived, which He conquered by temptation-combats, and altogether expelled, insomuch that there remained nothing of the infirm and hereditary principle

derived from the mother; yea, at length, nothing at all from
the mother, so that He totally put off the maternal principle,
in such a manner as to be no longer her son. To this purpose
He Himself also says in Mark,—" They said to Him, Behold,
Thy mother and Thy brethren, standing without, seek Thee;
and He answered them, saying, Who is My mother or My
brethren? And looking round about on them who sat near
Him, He said, Behold My mother and My brethren; for
whosoever shall do the will of God, the same is My brother,
and My sister, and My mother." (iii. 32—35; Matt. xii.
46—49; Luke viii. 20, 21.) And when He put off this
Humanity, He put on a Divine Humanity, from which He
called Himself the *Son of Man*, as on several occasions in
the Word of the New Testament, also the *Son of God;* and
by the " Son of Man" was signified the essential Truth, and
by the " Son of God" the essential Good, which His Human
Essence had when made Divine. The former state was that
of the Lord's humiliation, but the latter of His glorification,
concerning which, see above, n. 1999. In the former state,
viz., of humiliation, when as yet He had an infirm Humanity
appertaining to Him, He adored Jehovah as one distinct from
Himself, regarding Himself as a servant, for the Humanity
respectively is nothing but a servant. *A. C.* 2159.

It is to be noted that the Lord successively and continually,
even to the last moment of life, when He was glorified, separated from Himself, and put off what was merely Human, viz.,
what He derived from the mother, until at length He was no
longer her son, but the Son of God, not only as to conception,
but also as to nativity, and thus One with the Father; and
Himself Jehovah. That He separated from Himself, and put
off all the Humanity which He had from the mother, so that
He was no longer her son, is manifest from the Lord's words
in Matthew,—"A certain person said, Behold, Thy mother
and Thy brethren stand without, seeking to speak with Thee;
but Jesus answering, said, Who is My mother, and who My
brethren? And stretching forth His hands over His disciples,
He said, Behold My mother and My brethren! for whosoever
shall do the will of My Father who is in the heavens, the same
is My brother, and sister, and mother." *A. C.* 4649.

My brethren.—The reason why the Lord calls those His
" brethren" who do the will of His Father, is, because in
heaven no other affinities are given but such as are spiritual,
thus no other fraternities; for in heaven they do not become
brethren by virtue of any natural nativity, and they too, who
have been brethren in the world, do not there know each

other, but every one knows another from the good of love; they who are most conjoined in that good, are as brethren, and the rest, according to conjunction by good, are as relations and also as friends. Hence it is that by "brother," in the Word, is signified the good of love. That in heaven all are consociated according to spiritual relationships, which are of the good of love and of faith, and that they know each other as relations, see the "Treatise on Heaven and Hell," 205, and *A. C.* 685, 917, 2739, 3815, 4121. That hence by "brethren" in the Word are meant those who are conjoined by good, see *A. C.* 2360, 3303, 3803, 10,490. *A. E.* 46.

By the "disciples," over whom the Lord stretched forth His hand, are signified all who are of His church; by His "brethren" are signified those who are in the good of charity from Him; by "sisters" those who are in truths derived from that good; and by "mother" is signified the church consisting of such. *A. E.* 746. See also *A. C.* 685, 917, 2739, 3815. *H. D.* 9.

Verse 35. *Whosoever shall do the will of God*, &c.—By "doing the will of God," is understood to do His precepts, or to live according to them from the affection of love or charity. The "will of the Lord" is, in the Old Testament, called His good pleasure, and in like manner signifies the Divine Love; and to "do His good pleasure," or "His will," signifies to love God and our neighbour, thus to live according to the Lord's precepts. *A. E.* 295.

MARK.

CHAPTER IV.

THE WORD.

1. AND again He began to teach by the sea-side, and much multitude was gathered together to Him, so that He entered into a ship, to sit in the sea; and the whole multitude was by the sea on the land.

2. And He taught them many things in parables, and said to them in His doctrine,

3. Hearken; Behold, A sower went forth to sow.

4. And it came to pass, as He sowed, some fell by the way-side, and the fowls of the heaven came and devoured it.

5. But other fell on stony ground, where it had not much earth, and immediately it sprang up, because it had not depth of earth.

6. But when the sun arose, it was scorched, and because it had no root, it withered away.

7. And other fell among thorns, and the thorns grew up, and choked it, and it did not yield fruit.

THE INTERNAL SENSE.

FROM the knowledges of good and truth, and the doctrine thence derived, the LORD teaches, that the reception of His Word is fourfold. (Verses 1—9.)

First, as it is received by those who have no real concern about truth, being in phantasies and false persuasions which pervert it. (Verse 4.)

Secondly, as it is received by those who have a concern about truth, but not for its own sake, thus not interiorly, therefore the truth perishes, being adulterated by the lusts of self-love. (Verses 5, 6.)

Thirdly, as it is received by those who are in the concupiscences of evil, which suffocate the truth. (Verse 7.)

8. And other fell upon good earth, and yielded fruit, springing up and increasing, and brought forth, some thirty, and some sixty, and some a hundred.

9. And He said unto them, He that hath ears to hear, let him hear.

10. But when He was apart, they that were about Him with the twelve, asked of Him the parable.

11. And He said unto them, To you it is given to know the mystery of the kingdom of God, but to them that are without, all things are done in parables;

12. That seeing they may see, and not perceive; and hearing they may hear, and not understand, lest at any time they should be converted, and [their] sins should be remitted to them.

13. And He saith unto them, Know ye not this parable? and how will ye know all parables?

14. The Sower soweth the Word.

15. But these are they by the way-side, where the Word is sown; and when they have heard, Satan cometh, and taketh away the Word that was sown in their hearts.

16. And these are they likewise that are sown on stony ground, who, when they

Fourthly, as it is received by those who, from the LORD, love the truths which are in the Word, and from Him do them. (Verse 8.)

Which four-fold reception of the Word ought to be well attended to, both as to doctrine and practice, by all who are of the church. (Verse 9.)

Otherwise the Word will be understood only according to its literal or external sense, and not according to its spiritual and internal sense, which latter sense is revealed to those who are in the good of charity and the truth of faith from the LORD, but not to others, lest they should profane it. (Verses 10, 11, 12.)

And if this four-fold reception of the Word be not understood, it is impossible for the spiritual and internal sense of the Word to be seen. (Verse 13.)

Thus it cannot be seen that when the Word is received by those who have no concern about the eternal truth, it is immediately darkened and deprived of life by infernal spirits who are in falses, so that it produces no effect on the love and life. (Verses 14, 15.)

And when it is received by those who have a concern about truth, but not for its have heard the Word, immediately receive it with joy;

17. And have not root in themselves, but endure for a time; afterward when affliction or persecution ariseth because of the Word, immediately they are offended.

18. And these are they that are sown among thorns, such as hear the Word;

19. And the cares of this world, and the deceitfulness of riches, and the lusts of other things entering in, choke the Word, and it becometh unfruitful.

20. And these are they which are sown on good ground, such as hear the Word, and receive it, and bear fruit, some thirty, and some sixty, and some a hundred fold.

21. And He said to them, Is a candle brought to be put under a bushel, or under a bed? and not to be set on a candlestick?

22. For there is nothing hid which shall not be manifested; neither was any thing kept secret but that it should come to open view.

23. If any one hath ears to hear, let him hear.

24. And He said to them, Take heed what ye hear. With what measure ye mete, it shall be measured to you;

own sake, thus not interiorly, it excites indeed external delight, arising from external affection, but whereas it has no place in the will, it cannot stand the assault of evils and falses. (Verses 16, 17.)

And that when it is received by those who are in the concupiscences of evil, it is suffocated and rendered unfruitful by worldly anxieties and the lust of gain. (Verses 18, 19.)

But that when it is received by those who, from the LORD, love the truths which are in the Word, it affects first the will, and thence the understanding, and thus the life, in each according to reception. (Verse 20.)

That the light of truth therefore ought not to be subjected to the things of man's natural will, but to be exalted by affection in the intellectual mind, and thus to guide and direct the things of the will. (Verse 21.)

Inasmuch as all evils and falses must, sooner or later, be manifested to those who are in them, and likewise all goods and truths to those who are in them. (Verse 22.)

Which circumstance ought to be well attended to. (Verse 23.)

Caution also is necessary respecting the reception of truth and good in the will, since those heavenly principles and unto you that hear, more shall be added.

25. For whosoever hath, to him shall be given; and he that hath not, from him shall be taken even that which he hath.

26. And He said, So is the kingdom of God, as if a man should cast seed into the earth,

27. And should sleep, and rise, night and day, and the seed should spring and grow up, he knoweth not how.

28. For the earth bringeth forth of its own accord, first the blade, then the ear, then the full corn in the ear.

29. But when the fruit is ripe, immediately he putteth in the sickle, because the harvest is at hand.

30. And He said, To what shall I liken the kingdom of God? or with what comparison shall we compare it?

31. [It is] as a grain of mustard seed, which, when it is sown in the earth, is less than all the seeds that are sown in the earth.

are imparted to man from the LORD, in proportion as man exercises them towards others. (Verse 24.)

The same heavenly principles also are multiplied and increased, in the other life, with those who have cherished them in this life, whilst they are taken away from those who, through the love of what is evil and false, have not cherished them. (Verse 25.)

For heaven is implanted in all who receive truths and goods, not from themselves, but from the LORD, yet who coöperate in this reception as if it was from themselves, since without such coöperation there can be no reception. (Verses 26—30.)

Every man, therefore, in the course of regeneration, is alternately in a state of natural thought and spiritual thought, and his regeneration is accomplished whilst he is unconscious of its progress, being effected by scientifics, by the truths of faith, and by the goods of charity conjointly. (Verses 27, 28.)

Thus the church is implanted in man, both in general and in particular. (Verse 29.)

Beginning from a little spiritual good by truth, because at that time man thinks to do good from himself, but as truth is conjoining to love, it increases, and when it is conjoined, then things intellectual are multiplied in scientifics. (Verses 30, 31, 32.)

32. And when it is sown, it groweth up, and becometh greater than all herbs, and maketh great branches, so that the fowls of heaven may lodge under the shadow of it.

33. And with many such parables spake He the Word to them, as they were able to hear.

34. But without a parable spake He not to them; and privately He explained all things to His disciples.

35. And He saith to them in that day, when it was evening, Let us pass over to the other side.

36. And dismissing the multitude, they took Him as He was into the ship: and there were also with Him other little ships.

37. And there arose a great storm of wind; but the waves beat into the ship, so that it was now full.

38. And He was in the hinder part of the ship, sleeping on a pillow: and they awake Him, and say unto Him, Teacher, carest Thou not that we perish?

39. And awaking, He rebuked the wind, and said to the sea, Be silent, be dumb! And the wind ceased, and there was a great calm.

40. And He said unto them, Why are ye so fearful? how is it that ye have no faith?

41. And they feared with a great fear, and said one to another, Who indeed is this, that even the wind and the sea obey Him?

Which increase of truth lies concealed under the letter of the Word, and is not revealed to those who are in evils and falses, but only to those who are in goods and truths. (Verses 33, 34.)

That when the men of the church are in a natural state, and not yet in a spiritual one, the natural affections, which are the various lusts arising from self-love and the love of the world, are in uproar, and present various emotions of the mind. (Verses 35, 36, 37.)

On which occasion it appears as if the LORD was absent, but when they come from a natural state into a spiritual one, then these emotions cease, and the mind is rendered tranquil, the tempestuous emotions of the natural man being appeased by the LORD. (Verses 38, 39.)

Thus the men of the church are instructed not to be fearful, but to put their whole trust in the LORD, and adore Him, who thus subdues hell and its concupiscences. (Verses 40, 41.)

EXPOSITION.

CHAPTER IV.

VERSE 1. *He began to teach by the sea-side; and He entered into a ship,* &c.—As to the meaning of the "sea," and of a "ship," and teaching thence, see above, Exposition, chap. iii. 7, 9.

Verses 3—8. *A Sower went forth to sow,* &c.—It cannot be understood how the case is in regard to multiplication and fructification in man's rational principle, unless it be known how the case is with respect to influx, concerning which it may be observed in general, that with every individual man, there is an internal man, there is a rational man, who is an intermediate, and there is an external man. The internal man is that which is his inmost principle, by virtue of which he is a man, and by which he is distinguished from brute animals, which have not such an inmost principle; this principle too is as the gate or entrance of the Lord, that is, of the celestial or spiritual things of the Lord into man. What is transacting in this principle cannot be apprehended by man, because it is above the all of his rational principle, by which he thinks; to this inmost or internal man is subjected the rational principle, which appears as man's own or proper principle, into which, through that internal man, the celestial things of love and of faith flow in from the Lord, and through this rational principle into the scientifics, which are of the external man. But the things which flow in are received according to every one's state: unless the rational principle submits itself to the goods and truths of the Lord, then the things which flow in are either suffocated, or rejected, or perverted by the rational principle, and still more when they flow in into the sensual scientific principles of the memory. These are the things which are meant by the seed either falling on the "way-side," or on "stony ground," or "among thorns," as the Lord teaches in Matthew, xiii. 3—7; Mark iv. 3—8; Luke viii. 5—7; but when the rational principle submits itself, and believes in the Lord, that is, in His Word, then the rational principle is as *good ground,* or earth, into which the seed falls, and brings forth much fruit. *A. C.* 1940.

It is truth which is understood by "seed in a field," concerning which the Lord says—"A sower went forth to sow," &c. The "Sower" in this case is the Lord, and the "seed" is His

Word, thus truth; the "seed on the way," denotes those who have no concern about truth; the "seed on stony ground," denotes those who have a concern about truth, but not for its own sake, thus, not interiorly; the "seed in the midst of thorns," denotes those who are in the concupiscences of evil; but the "seed on the good ground," denotes those who, from the Lord, love the truths which are in the Word, and do them, thus, *bring forth fruits.* From these considerations it is evident, that the truth of the Word cannot take root with those who have no concern about truth; nor yet with those who love the truth exteriorly and not interiorly; nor yet with those who are in the concupiscences of evil; but with those with whom the concupiscences of evil are dispersed by the Lord: with these latter the seed takes root, that is, truth in their spiritual mind. *D. Life,* 90. See also *A. E.* 401.

The subject treated of in this parable is concerning a fourfold kind of earth or of ground in a field, that is, in the church. That the "seed" here spoken of is the Word of the Lord, or the truth which is said to be of faith, and that the "good earth," or "ground," is the good which is of charity, is evident, for it is the principle of good in man which receives the Word; the "way-side" denotes what is false; the "stony ground" denotes the truth, which hath no root in good; the "thorns" are evils. *A. C.* 3310.

Verse 4. *The fowls of the heaven came, and devoured it.*— By "fowls" [or birds] in general, are signified things rational, also things intellectual, which are of the internal man. That "fowls" [or birds] signify things rational and intellectual, is manifest from the prophets, as in Isaiah,—"Calling a bird from the east, a man of my council from a remote land." (xlvi. 11.) And in Jeremiah,—"I saw, and lo, no man, and every bird of the heavens was fled." (iv. 25.) And in Ezekiel,—"I will plant a twig of a high cedar, and it shall lift up its branch, and shall bear fruit, and it shall become a magnificent cedar: and under it shall dwell every bird of every wing; they shall dwell in the shade of its branches." (xvii. 23.) And in Hosea, speaking of the New Church, or of a regenerate person,—"In that day I will make a covenant for them, with the wild beast of the field, and with the fowl of the heavens, and with the creeping thing of the ground;" (ii. 18.) in which passage, it must be evident to every one that a "wild beast" does not signify a wild beast, nor "fowl," fowl, because the Lord never makes a covenant with them. *A. C.* 40.

Inasmuch as the "fowls of the heavens" signify intellectual truths, thus thoughts, they also signify things contrary, as phantasies, or false principles, which, as belonging to man's thought, are also called *fowls* or *birds*, as that "the wicked should be given for meat to the fowls of heaven, and to wild beasts," denoting phantasies and lusts. (Isaiah xviii. 6; Jer. vii. 33; xvi. 4; xix. 7; xxxiv. 20; Ezek. xxix. 5; xxxix. 4.) The Lord Himself also compares the phantasies and persuasions of what is false to *fowls* [or birds], where He says— "The seed which fell on the way-side was trodden down, and the fowls of heaven devoured it;" where the "fowls of heaven" are nothing else than false principles. *A. C.* 778.

Verses 7, 18. *And other fell among thorns, and the thorns grew up and choked it*, &c.—That "thorns" denote the false principles of concupiscence, is manifest from the following passages :—"Upon the land of my people shall come up thorns and briars;" (Isaiah xxxii. 13.) where "land" denotes the church; "thorns and briars" denote false principles and the evils thence derived. Again,—"As to your spirit, the fire shall consume you, thus the people shall be burnt to lime : as thorns cut up which are burned in the fire;" (xxxiii. 12.) where "thorns which are burned in the fire," denote the false principles which catch the flame, and consume truths and goods. And in Ezekiel,—"There shall be no longer in the house of Israel a prickly briar, and grieving thorn;" (xxviii. 24.) where a "prickly briar" denotes the false principle of the concupiscences of self-love. A "thorn" denotes the false principle of the concupiscences of worldly love. The false principles of concupiscences, which are signified by "thorns," are the false principles confirming those things which are of the world and its pleasures, for these false principles, more than others, catch fire and burn, because they are derived from concupiscences of the body, which are felt, on which account they also close the internal man, so that he has no relish for any thing which regards the salvation of the soul and eternal life. *A. C.* 9144.

There are some persons who love the world above all things, and do not admit any truth which would draw them away from any false principle of their religion, saying to themselves,— "What is this to me? it is no concern of mine;" thus they reject it instantly on hearing it, and if they hear, they suffocate it. Persons of this description are similarly affected when they hear sermons, retaining no more of what they hear than some expressions, and not any thing substantial. Inasmuch as they thus deal with truths, therefore they do not know what good is, for goods and truths act in unity, and evil is not known from the good which is not grounded in truth, unless that it also may be called good, which is effected by reasonings

from false principles.   These are they who are understood by
the "seeds which fell among thorns," of whom the Lord says—
" Other seeds fell among thorns ; and the thorns came up and
choked them.   These are they who hear the Word, but the
cares of this world and the deceitfulness of riches choke the
Word, that it becometh unfruitful."   *D. P.* 278.

Verse 8. *And other fell on good earth, and yielded fruit,
springing up and increasing, and brought forth, some thirty,
and some sixty, and some a hundred.*—The case is similar in
respect to goodness and truth [and their insemination], as it is
in respect to *seeds* and *ground.*   Interior Good is as the seed
which brings forth, but only in good ground.   Exterior Good
and Truth is as ground in which the seed brings forth, namely,
interior good and truth which cannot otherwise be rooted.
Hence it is that man's rational principle is first of all regenerated, for therein are seeds ; and afterwards the natural principle, which may serve as ground, see above, n. 3286.   And
whereas the natural principle is as ground, Good and Truth is
capable of being made fruitful and multiplying in the rational
principle, which could not be the case unless it had ground
wherein as seed to fix its root.   From this comparison, as in a
mirror, it may be seen how the case is with regeneration, and
with several arcana relating thereto.   To understand what is
Good and True, and to will them, belongs to the rational
principle ; the perceptions of Good and Truth thence derived
are as seeds ; and to know them, and to bring them into act,
belongs to the natural principle.   Scientifics and works are as
ground, and when man is affected with the scientifics which
confirm Good and Truth, and especially when he perceives
delight in bringing them into act ; in this case seeds are
therein, and grow as in their proper ground.   Hence Good is
made fruitful, and Truth is multiplied, and both continually
spring up or ascend from that ground into the rational principle, and perfect it.   The case is otherwise when man understands what is Good and True, and also inwardly perceives
somewhat of inclination of the will thereto, but yet doth not
love to know, and still less to do them ; for in this case Good
cannqt be made fruitful, nor Truth be multiplied, in the
rational principle.   *A. C.* 3671.

By " thirty," is signified something of combat, thus, a little
of combat, and the reason is, because that number, by multiplication, is compounded of " five," by which is signified some
little, and of " six," by which is signified labour or combat.
Hence also that number, wheresoever it is mentioned in the
Word, signifies something little respectively, as in Zechariah,—

" I said unto them, If it be good in your eyes, give me hire ; and if not, forbear. And they weighed out my hire, thirty pieces of silver. And Jehovah said to me, Cast it to the potter : a goodly price that I was prized at of them. And I took the thirty pieces of silver, and cast them into the house of Jehovah to the potter ;" (xi. 12, 13.) denoting the little value which they set on the Lord's merit, and on the redemption and the salvation wrought by Him. The "potter" denotes reformation and regeneration. " Thirty" also denotes what is little, in Mark, where it is written,—" The seed which fell into good earth, yielded fruit, springing up and increasing, and brought forth, some thirty, and some sixty, and some a hundred ;" where " thirty" denotes little produce, and that there was little labour. Those numbers would not have been marked, unless they had involved things significative. *A. C.* 2276.

What the number " sixty" involves, may be manifest from the simple numbers from which it is composed, viz., five and twelve, for five times twelve make *sixty ;* and what is meant by " five," may be seen, n. 649, 1686 ; and what by " twelve," n. 3272 ; also " six" and " ten," for six times ten make *sixty*, and what is meant by " six," may be seen, n. 720, 737, 900 ; and what by " ten," n. 576, 2284, 3107 ; also from " two" and " thirty," for twice thirty make *sixty*, and what is signified by " two," may be seen, n. 720, 900, 1335, 1686, and what by " thirty," n. 2276. Inasmuch as the number " sixty" is compounded of the above numbers, it involves those things in their order, which all relate to states, whether respecting the glorification of the Lord's Humanity, or the regeneration of man ; those things are presented before the angels in a clear light by the Lord, but they cannot be explained before man, especially before one who does not believe that numbers in the Word contain in them some secret mystery, and this, not only on account of incredulity, but because so many contents cannot be reduced to a series adequate to the apprehension. *A. C.* 3306.

By a " hundred" is signified a full state of the Unition of the Lord's Divinity with His Humanity, but what this state is, cannot be so well explained to the apprehension ; still however it may be illustrated by those things relating to man which are called a full state, during reformation and regeneration ; for it is a known thing that man cannot be regenerated except in adult age, because he then first acquires the powers of reason and judgment, and is thus capable of receiving good and truth from the Lord. Previous to his coming into that

10

state, he is prepared of the Lord by this, that such things are insinuated into him, as may serve him for ground to receive the seeds of truth and of good, which are several states of innocence and charity, also the knowledges of good and truth, and hence thoughts, which is effected during several years before regeneration. When man is imbued with those knowledges, and is thus prepared, his state is then said to be full, for then the interiors are so disposed as to become receptive. That the number a "hundred" signifies what is full, may also be manifest from other passages in the Word, as in Isaiah,— "There shall be no more thence an infant of days, nor an old man that hath not filled his days: for the child shall die a *hundred* years old; and the sinner, being a *hundred* years old, shall be accursed;" (lxv. 20.) where it is manifest that a "hundred" denotes what is full, for it is said—"There shall no more be an infant of days, and an old man who hath not filled his days, and a child and sinner of a hundred years," that is, when his state is full. And in Matthew,—"Every one who shall leave houses, or brethren, or sisters, or father, or mother, or wife, or children, or lands, for My name's sake, shall receive an *hundred fold*, and shall inherit eternal life;" (xix. 29.) where a "hundred fold" denotes what is full, or "good measure, pressed down, shaken together, and running over." (Luke vi. 38.) And in Mark,—"Other seed fell on good earth, and brought forth fruit a *hundred fold;*" (iv. 20; Matt. xii. 8, 23; Luke viii. 8.) where a "hundred" denotes also what is full, which number would not have been mentioned unless it had been significative. In like manner where the Lord speaks in the parable concerning debtors, that "one owed a *hundred* measures of oil, and another a *hundred* measures of wheat;" (Luke xvii. 5, 6, 7.) and so likewise in other passages where mention is made of a hundred. *A. C.* 2636.

Verse 9. *He that hath ears to hear, let him hear.*—The above words were spoken to the intent that every one who is of the church may know, that to know and understand the truths and goods of faith, or doctrinals, and likewise the Word, does not make the church, but to hearken, that is, to understand and to do, for this is signified by "having an ear to hear." *A. E.* 108.

Verse 12. *That seeing they may see, and not perceive; and hearing they may hear, and not understand: lest at any time they should be converted, and sin should be remitted to them.*— The reason why the Jews persevere in a denial of the Lord, is, because they are of such a quality that if they received and acknowledged the Divinity of the Lord, and the holy things of His church, they would profane them, wherefore the Lord says concerning them,—"He hath blinded their eyes, He hath closed their heart: that they may not see with their eyes, and understand with their heart, and be converted, and I should heal them." (John xii. 40; Matt. xiii. 15; Mark iv. 12; Luke viii. 10; Isaiah vi. 9, 10.) It is said,—"Lest they should be converted, and I should heal them," because if they had been *converted* and *healed,* they would have been guilty of profanation; and it is according to a law of Divine Providence, concerning which see above, n. 221—233, that no one shall be interiorly let into the truths of faith and the goods of charity by the Lord, only so far as he can be kept in them, even to the end of life, since if he was let in, he would profane holy things. *D. P.* 260. See also *S. S.* 60. *A. C.* 10,155.

Verse 15. *And when they have heard, Satan cometh, and taketh away the seed that was sown in their hearts.*—What is here said of *Satan,* is in Luke said of the *devil,* by reason that the "seed which fell by the way-side," signifies truth from the Word, which is only received in the memory, and not in the life; and since this is taken away both by what is evil and by what is false, therefore mention is made of the *devil* and *Satan,* because by the "devil" is signified the hell from whence come evils, and by "Satan" the hell from whence come false principles. *A. E.* 740.

Verse 17. *Afterward, when affliction or persecution ariseth because of the Word, immediately they are offended.*—That by "affliction," in the above passage, is signified temptation, may be manifest from several passages in the Word, as in Isaiah,— "I will purify thee, and not with silver; I will select thee in the furnace of *affliction;*" (xlviii. 10.) where "affliction" denotes temptation. And in Moses,—"Thou shalt remember all the way which Jehovah thy God led thee these forty years, to *afflict thee and to try thee;*" (Deut. viii. 2.) where to "afflict," manifestly denotes to tempt. Temptations are also called by the Lord, "afflictions," where He says—"Afterwards, when *affliction and persecution* ariseth because of the Word, immediately they are offended;" (Mark iv. 17.) where "affliction" manifestly denotes temptation. "Not having root in themselves," denotes the want of charity, for in charity faith is rooted, and where this root is wanting, men sink in temptations. *A. C.* 1846.

Verse 21. *Is a candle brought to be put under a bushel?* &c.—By a "candle," or a "lamp," is signified in general, Truth derived from Good, and intelligence thence. *A. E.* 223.

Verse 22. *For there is nothing hid which shall not be manifested; neither was any thing kept secret, but that it should come to open view.*—That the wicked, before they are condemned and let into hell, undergo various states of vastation, is altogether unknown to the world; it is believed that a man is instantly either condemned or saved, and that this is done without any process. But the case is otherwise, inasmuch as justice reigns in the other world, and no one is condemned until he himself knows, and is inwardly convicted, that he is in evil, and that he cannot in any wise be in heaven; his evils are likewise opened to him, according to the Lord's words in Luke,—"There is nothing hidden, which shall not be revealed; or concealed, which shall not be known. Therefore whatsoever things ye have said in darkness, shall be heard in light; and what ye have spoken into the ear in closets, shall be proclaimed upon the housetops;" (xii. 2, 3, 9; Matt. x. 26; Mark iv. 22.) and what is more, they are also admonished to desist from evil; but when they cannot do this by reason of the dominion of evil, they are then deprived of the ability to do evil by falsifications of truth, and pretences of good, which is effected successively, from one degree to another, and at length follows damnation and the letting down into hell; this is the case with every one when he comes into the evil of his life. Evil of life, is the evil of the will and of the thought thence derived; thus it is the man, such as he is interiorly, and such as he would be exteriorly, if not opposed by laws, and also by the fear of the loss of gain, of honour, of reputation, and likewise of life; that is, the life which follows every one after death; but not the external life, unless what proceeds from the internal; for man in externals assumes a contrary aspect, wherefore when he is vastated after death as to external things, it then becomes evident what his quality was, both in will and thought; to this state every wicked man is reduced by degrees of vastation; for all vastation in the other life has its progress from externals to internals. *A. C.* 7795. See *H. H.* 462.

Verse 23. *If any one hath ears to hear,* &c.—See above, verse 11, Exposition.

Verse 24. *Take heed what ye hear,* &c.—It is to be noted, that it is according to the laws of order that no one ought to be persuaded instantaneously concerning truth, that is, that truth should instantaneously be so confirmed as to leave no doubt at all concerning it; the reason is, because the truth which is so impressed, becomes persuasive truth, and is without any extension, and also without any yielding; such truth is represented in the other life as hard, and as of such a quality as

not to admit good in it, that it may become applicable; hence
it is that as soon as any truth is presented before good spirits
in the other life by manifest experience, there is presently
afterwards presented some opposite, which causes doubt; thus
it is given them to think and consider whether it be so, and to
collect reasons, and thereby to bring that truth rationally into
their mind.   Hereby the spiritual sight hath extension as to
that truth, even to opposites; hence it sees and perceives in
understanding every quality of truth, and hence can admit
influx from heaven according to the states of things, for truths
receive various forms according to circumstances.   This also is
the reason why it was allowed the magicians to do the like as
to what Aaron did; for thereby doubt was excited amongst the
sons of Israel concerning the miracle, whether it was Divine,
and thus opportunity was given them of thinking and con-
sidering whether it was Divine, and at length of confirming
themselves that it was so.   *A. C.* 7298.

Verse 24.—The truths which are called truths of faith enter
by an external way with man, and the good which is of charity
and love enters by an internal way.   The external way is by (or
through) the hearing into the memory, and from the memory
into his understanding, for the understanding is man's internal
sight; by (or through) this way the truths enter which are to
be truths of faith, to the end that they may be introduced into
the will, and thereby be appropriated to the man.   The good
which flows in from the Lord, by (or through) the internal way,
flows in into the will, for the will is the internal principle of man;
the good which is from the Lord, in the confines, there meets
the truths which have entered by (or through) the external
way, and by conjunction effects that the truths become good,
and so far as this is effected, so far the order is inverted,
that is, so far man is not led by truths but by good; consequently so far he is led of the Lord.   From these considerations
it may be manifest how man is elevated from the world into
heaven, when he is regenerating; for all things which enter by
the hearing, enter from the world, and those things which are
stored up in the memory, and in the memory appear before
the understanding, appear in the light of the world, which is
called natural lumen; but the things which enter the will, or
which become of the will, are in the light of heaven, which
light is the Truth of Good from the Lord.   When these things
come into act, they return into the light of the world, but
in this life they then appear altogether under another form,
for heretofore in singular things the world was within, but
afterwards in singular things heaven is within.   From these

considerations it is also evident why man is not in heaven until
he doeth truths from willing them, thus from the affection of
charity. *A. C.* 9227.

Verse 24. *With what measure ye mete, it shall be measured
to you; and unto you that hear, more shall be added.*—By
these words is described charity towards the neighbour, or the
spiritual affection of truth or of good, denoting, that according
to the quantity and quality of that charity in any one, or of
that affection, during man's abode in the world, in the same
degree he comes into it after death.   That this will be the
case with those who exercise charity, is meant by its being
" added to those that hear," where the " hearing" signify the
obedient and those who do.   *A. E.* 629.   See *A. C.* 6478.

Verse 25. *For whosoever hath, to him shall be given; and
he that hath not, from him shall be taken even that he hath.*—
They who come into the other life are all brought back into
a life similar to what they had in the body; and afterwards,
all evil and false principles are separated in the case of those
who are good, that by goods and truths they may be elevated
by the Lord into heaven; but with the wicked, goods and
truths are separated, that by evil and false principles they may
be brought into hell, see n. 2119, according to the words of the
Lord in Matthew,—" Whosoever hath, to him shall be given,
that he may have more abundance; but whosoever hath not,
even what he hath shall be taken away from him." (xiii. 22.)
And in another place in the same Evangelist,—"To every one
who hath shall be given, that he may abound; but from him
who hath not, what he hath shall be taken away from him."
(xxv. 29; Luke viii. 18; xix. 24, 25, 26; Mark iv. 24, 25.)
A. C. 2449.

Verse 25.—All who have procured to themselves intelligence
and wisdom in the world, are accepted into heaven and become
angels, every one according to the quality and quantity of his
intelligence and wisdom; for whatsover a man acquires to
himself in the world, this remains, and he carries it along with
him after death, and it is also increased and filled, but within
the degree of his affection and desire of truth and its good,
but not beyond it.   They who have had little of affection and
desire receive little, but still as much as they can receive
within that degree; but they who have had much of affection
and desire receive much.   The degree itself of affection and
desire is as the measure which is increased to the full, more
therefore to him whose measure is great, and less to him
whose measure is small.   This is meant by the Lord's words—
" To every one that hath, shall be given," &c.   *H. H.* 349.

The reason of the separation of evil and false principles with those who are good, is, lest they should hang between evils and goods, and that by goods they may be elevated into heaven; and the reason of the separation of goods and truths with the wicked, is, lest by any goods appertaining to them, they should seduce the well-disposed, and that by evils they may retire amongst the wicked who are in hell. For such is the communication of all ideas of thought and of affections in the other life, that goods are communicated with the good, but evils with the evil, wherefore unless they were separated, innumerable mischiefs would ensue. *A. C.* 2449). See *D. P.* 16, 17, 227, 331; and *A. C.* 4149, 7502.

That by "a man asking of his companion, and a woman of her companion, vessels of silver and vessels of gold," (see Exod. xi. 1, 2, 3.) is signified that the scientifics of *truth* and of *good*, taken from the wicked who were of the church, were to be ascribed to the good, is manifest from the signification of "vessels of silver" and "vessels of gold," as denoting the scientifics of truth and of good. That "silver" denotes truth, and "gold," good, may be seen, n. 1551, 1552, 2954, 5658, 6112; and that "vessels" denote scientifics, n. 3068, 3079. Scientifics are called vessels of truth and of good, because they contain those principles. It is believed that the scientifics of truth and of good are the very truths and goods themselves which are of faith; but this is not the case, since the affections of truth and of good are what constitute faith, which affections flow into scientifics, as into their vessels. That to "ask those things of the Egyptians," is to take them away, and appropriate them to those who ask it, is evident. How this case is, may be seen in the explication at chap. iii. 22, Exodus, from which it may be manifest, that the scientifics of truth and of good, which appertained to those of the church who were acquainted with the mysteries of faith, and yet lived evil lives, are transferred to those who are of the spiritual church, the manner of which transfer may be seen, n. 6914. These things are signified by the Lord's words in Matthew,—"Take from him the talent, and give it to him who had ten talents; for to every one that hath shall be given, that he may abound: but from him who hath not, even what he hath shall be taken away." (xxv. 25, 28, 29, 30; in like manner in Mark, iv. 24, 25.) The reason is, because the knowledges of good and of truth appertaining to the evil are applied to evil uses; and the knowledges of good and of truth appertaining to the good are applied to good uses; the knowledges are the same, but application to uses constitutes their quality with every one.

These riches are like worldly riches, which, with one, are applied to good uses, with another to evil uses; hence riches with every one have a quality, according to the uses to which they are applied. From this consideration it is also evident that the same knowledges, like the same riches, which had appertained to the wicked, may appertain to the good, and serve to promote good uses. Hence it may be manifest what is represented by the command that the sons of Israel should borrow from the Egyptians *vessels of silver* and *vessels of gold*, and should thus *plunder* and *spoil* them, which command would never have been given by Jehovah, unless it had represented such things in the spiritual world. *A. C.* 7771. See also *D. P.* 17, 227.

Verses 26—30. *And He said, So is the kingdom of God, as if a man should cast seed into the earth, and should sleep, and rise, night and day, and the seed should spring and grow up, he knoweth not how,* &c.—By the "kingdom of God," is meant the church of the Lord in the heavens and on the earth; that this church is implanted in all who receive truths and goods, not from themselves, but from the Lord, is described by the above words, each of which has a spiritual correspondence and signification, as that a man should *cast seed upon the earth,* that he should afterwards *sleep and rise, night and day;* that the *seed springeth and groweth up, whilst he is ignorant of it.* For by "seed" is signified the Divine Truth; by "casting it into the earth," is signified the operation of man; by "sleeping and rising, night and day," and at length "putting in the sickle," is signified in every state. The other parts of the parable signify the Lord's operation, and the "harvest" the implantation of the church, in particular and in general; for it is to be noted, that although the Lord operates all things, and man nothing from himself, still He wills that man, so far as it cometh to his perception, should operate as from himself, since without the coöperation of man as from himself, there would be no reception of good and of truth, thus no implantation and regeneration; for the Lord gives man to will, and whereas this appears to man as from himself, He gives him to will as from himself. Inasmuch as such things are signified by "harvest," therefore two festivals were established among the sons of Israel, one of which was called the "feast of weeks," which was of the first-fruits of the harvest, and the other the "feast of tabernacles," which was of the gathering together of the fruits of the earth, the former of which signified the implantation of truth in good, and the latter the production of good, thus regeneration; but

by the "feast of unleavened bread," or of the "passover,"
which preceded, was signified deliverance from the falses of
evils, which also is the beginning of regeneration. *A. E.* 911.

Every man who is regenerating, receives good from the Lord
as from a new father, which good is interior good, whereas the
good which he derives from parents is exterior; the former,
which he receives from the Lord, is called spiritual good, but
the latter, which he derives from parents, is called natural
good. This latter good, viz., which he derives from parents,
serves first of all for his reformation, for by it, as by something pleasant and delightful, scientifics are introduced, and
afterwards the knowledges of truth; but when it has served
as a medium for this use, it is separated thence, on which
occasion the spiritual good comes forth and manifests itself.
This may be evident from much experience, and from this
consideration alone, that when a child is first instructed, he is
affected with the desire of knowing something, at first, not for
the sake of any end manifest to himself, but for a certain pleasure and delight connate and from other sources; afterwards as
he grows up, he is affected with the desire of knowing, for the
sake of some end, viz., that he may excel others, or his rivals;
in the next place, for the sake of some end in the world. But
when he is about to be regenerated, he is affected from the
delight and pleasantness of truth; and when he is regenerating,
as is the case in adult age, he is affected from the love of truth,
and next from the love of good. In this case the ends which
had preceded, together with their delights, are by degrees separated, and are succeeded by the interior good which is from
the Lord, and which manifests itself in its affection. Hence
it is evident that the former delights, which, in an external
form, appeared as goods, have served as means [or mediums];
such succession of means [or mediums] are continual, being
comparatively like a tree, which in its first age, or first spring,
adorns its branches with leaves, afterwards, as its age or spring
advances, it decorates them with flowers, and in the next place,
about the time of summer, produces the first germinations of
fruits, which afterward become fruits, and at length it deposits
seeds in them, in which it has similar new trees, and an entire
garden, in potency, and if the seeds are sown, in act. Such
are the comparative things in nature, which likewise are representative, since universal nature is a theatre representative of
the Lord's kingdom in the heavens, hence in the Lord's kingdom
on the earth, or in the church, and hence of the Lord's kingdom
with every regenerate person. From these considerations it is
evident in what manner natural or domestic good, although a

11

mere external delight, and indeed a worldly delight, serves as a mean [or medium] of producing the good of the natural principle, which may conjoin itself with the good of the rational principle, and may thus become regenerate or spiritual good, that is, good which is from the Lord. *A. C.* 3518.

The Lord keeps man in the freedom of thinking, and so far as external bonds, which are the fear of the law, and its penalties, also the fear of the loss of reputation, of honour, and of gain, do not restrain, He keeps him in the freedom of doing; but by freedom He bends him from evil, and by freedom bends him to good, leading him so gently and tacitly, that man has no idea but that all proceeds from himself: thus the Lord, in freedom, inseminates good, and roots it, into the very life of man, which good remains to eternity. This the Lord thus teaches in Mark,—" The kingdom of God is as a man who casteth seed into the earth, which seed springs up and grows, man knoweth not how; the earth bringeth forth of its own accord." (iv. 26, 27, 28.) The "kingdom of God" is heaven appertaining to man, thus the good of love and the truth of faith. *A. C.* 9587.

What the difference is between those who are in the Lord's celestial kingdom, and those who are in His spiritual kingdom, we will here explain. The cause of the difference is, because the former turn the truths of the church immediately into goods, by living according to them, whereas the latter abide in truths, and prefer faith to life. They who turn the truths of the church immediately into goods by living according to them, thus who are of the celestial kingdom, are described by the Lord in Mark, iv. 26—29, and in several other passages. *A. C.* 10,125.

The reason why the "ears of corn" signify scientifics, is, because "corn" signifies the good of the natural principle, for scientifics are the continents of the good of the natural principle, as ears of corn are the continents of corn; for, in general, all truths are vessels of good, so likewise are scientific truths, but these are lowest truths. Lowest truths, or truths of the exterior natural principle, are called scientifics, because they are in the natural or external memory of man, and because they partake for the most part of the light of the world, and hence may be presented to view, and represented before others, by forms of expressions, or by ideas formed into expressions, by such things as are of the world and its light; but the things which are in the interior memory, are not called scientifics, but truths, so far as they partake of the light of heaven, neither are they intelligible but by that light, or utterable but by forms

of expressions, or by ideas formed into expressions, by such
things as are of heaven and its light.   A comparison with the
blade, the *ear*, and the *corn*, involves also the re-birth of man
by scientifics, by the truths of faith, and by the goods of charity,
where it is said in Mark,—" So is the kingdom of God, as if
a man should cast seed into the earth," &c.   The " kingdom
of God," which is compared to a *blade*, to an *ear*, and to *corn*,
is heaven appertaining to man by regeneration, for he who is
regenerate, has in himself the kingdom of God, and becomes in
image a kingdom of God, or heaven; the " blade" is the first
scientific principle, the " ear" is the scientific of truth thence
derived, and the " corn" is the consequent good. *A. C.* 5212.

In the Word frequent mention is made of *earth, ground,
field, seed-time, harvest, standing-corn, a barn, corn, wheat,
barley,* and by these terms such things are there signified as
relate to the establishment of the church, and to the regeneration of man, who is in the church, thus which have reference
to the truth of faith and to the good of love, from which the
church is formed.   The ground of such signification is from
correspondence, since all things which are on the earth, also
which are in its vegetable kingdom, correspond to the spiritual
things which are in heaven, as is very manifest from the appearances there; for in heaven there appear fields, grounds prepared
for seed, plains, flower-gardens, crops of corn, shrubberies, and
similar things, such as are on earth, and it is there a known
thing, that in such a manner, the things which are of heaven,
thus which are of the church, appear before their eyes.   He who
reads the Word, believes that such things in it are mere comparisons, but let him know that they are real correspondences,
as these words in Isaiah,—" Hearken, and hear my voice:
Doth a ploughman plough the whole day to sow? doth he
open and dung his ground?   When he hath made plain the
face thereof, doth he not cast abroad the fitches, and scatter
the cummin, and cast in the principal wheat, and the appointed
barley, and the determined spelt?   Thus his God doth instruct
him to judgment, and teacheth him." (xxviii. 23—26.)   These
words appear comparisons, but they are real correspondences,
by which is described the reformation and regeneration of the
man of the church, on which account also it is said—" Thus
his God instructeth him to judgment, and teacheth him;"
where to "instruct to judgment," is to give him intelligence,
for by "judgment" is signified the intelligence of truth,
n. 2235; and to " teach him," when spoken of God, is to
give him wisdom.   Hence it may be manifest what is meant
by *ploughing, dunging, casting abroad the fitches, scattering*

the cummin, casting in the wheat, the barley, and the spelt,
viz., that to "plough" is to implant truth in good; "fitches"
and "cummin" are scientifics, since these are the first things
which are learnt, that man may receive intelligence; that
"wheat" denotes the good of love of the internal man, see
n. 7605; that "barley" denotes the good of love of the
external man, see n. 7602; that "spelt" denotes its truth,
see n. 7605. *A. C.* 10,669.

Verses 30, 31, 32. *And He said, To what shall I liken the
kingdom of God? or with what comparison shall we compare
it? It is as a grain of mustard seed, which, when it is sown
in the earth, is less than all the seeds that are sown in the
earth. And when it is sown, it groweth up, and becometh
greater than all herbs, and maketh great branches, so that
the fowls of heaven may lodge under the shadow of it.*—The
"grain of mustard seed" denotes the good of man before he
is spiritual, because he thinks to do good from himself, and
what is from himself is nothing but evil; but whereas he is in
a state of regeneration, there is something of good, but "the
least of all;" at length, in proportion as faith is conjoining to
love, it becomes greater, and a "herb;" lastly, when it is conjoined, it becomes a "tree," and then the "fowls of heaven,"
which are here truths, or things intellectual, "make their nests
in its branches," which are scientifics. *A. C.* 55.

With man who is principled in good, that is, in love and
charity, *seed* from the Lord is so fructified and multiplied,
that it cannot be numbered for multitude; not so whilst he
lives in the body, but in the other life incredibly; for so long
as man lives in the body, the seed is in corporeal ground, and
amongst things therein twisted and dense, which are scientifics
and pleasures, also cares and solicitudes; but when these are
put off, as is the case when he passes into the other life, the
seed is loosened from them, and grows, as the seed of a tree is
wont to do, when it springs out of the ground to grow into a
shrub, also into a *great tree,* and next to be multiplied into
a *garden of trees.* For all science, intelligence, and wisdom,
with their delights and happinesses, thus fructify and are
multiplied, and thereby increase to eternity, and this from
the least seed, as the Lord teaches respecting the *grain of
mustard seed,* which may be sufficiently manifest from the
science, intelligence, and wisdom of the angels, which, at the
time when they were men, was to them ineffable. *A. C.* 1940.

By a "tree" from a *grain of mustard seed,* is signified a
man of the church, and also the church, beginning from a
little spiritual good, by truth, for if only a little spiritual good

has taken root in man, it grows as seed in good ground; and inasmuch as by the "tree," thence produced, is signified a man of the church, it follows, that by the "fowls of heaven," which "make their nests in its branches," are signified the knowledges of truth and the thoughts thence derived. *A. E.* 1100.

It is impossible for any one who is unacquainted with the nature and quality of the Word, to discover by any stretch of thought, that there is an infinity in all its particular parts, that is, that they all contain innumerable things, which the angels themselves cannot fathom or exhaust. Every single content of it may be compared to a seed, which has a capacity, if it be sown in the ground, of growing into a large tree, and producing an abundance of other seeds, from which again similar trees may be produced, and of these a garden formed, and from its seeds other gardens, and so on to infinity. Such is the Word of the Lord, in all its parts, and particlarly in the Decalogue, which, as it teaches love towards God, and love towards our neighbour, is a brief summary of the whole Word. That the Word is of such a nature, is evident from the following similitude which the Lord made use of:—" The kingdom of God is like unto a grain of mustard seed," &c. (Matt. xiii. 31, 32; Mark vi. 31, 32; Luke xiii. 18, 19; compare also Ezek. xvii. 2—8.) That such is the infinity of spiritual seeds, or of truths derived from the Word, is evident from the wisdom of angels, which is all from the Word, and which increaseth in them to all eternity, whilst they, in proportion as they grow wiser, see more clearly that no limit can be set to wisdom, and that they themselves are but in its outer court, and can never, in the smallest degree, attain to the Divine wisdom of the Lord, which they call an abyss. Now, since the Word is derived from this abyss, in consequence of coming from the Lord, it is plain that there is a kind of infinity in all its parts. *T. C. R.* 290. See also n. 499.

Verse 34. *But without a parable spake He not to them.*— The reason why the Lord spake by parables was, that the Jews might not understand the Word, lest they should profane it; for when the church is vastated, as it was at that time amongst the Jews, if they had understood, they would have profaned, wherefore also the Lord "spake in parables," on this account, as He Himself teaches in Matthew, xiii. 13, 14, 15; Mark iv. 11, 12; Luke viii. 10; for the Word cannot be profaned by those who are not acquainted with its mysteries, but by those who are acquainted with them, and more so by those who appear to themselves learned, than by those who appear to themselves unlearned. *A. C.* 3898.

Verses 36—39. *And dismissing the multitude, they took Him as He was into the ship: and there arose a great storm of wind, but the waves beat into the ship. And He was in the hinder part of the ship, sleeping on a pillow; and awaking, He rebuked the wind, and said to the sea, Be silent, be dumb! And the wind ceased, and there was a great calm.*—By this was represented the condition of the men of the church, when they are in a natural state, and not yet in a spiritual one,—in which state the natural affections, which are the various lusts arising from self-love and the love of the world, are in uproar, and present various commotions of the mind; in this state it appears as if the Lord was absent, which apparent absence is signified by the Lord "sleeping;" but when they come from a natural state into a spiritual one, then those commotions cease, and the mind is rendered tranquil, for the tempestuous commotions of the natural man are appeased by the Lord, when the spiritual mind is opened, and the Lord by or through it flows into the natural mind. Inasmuch as the affections which are of self-love and the love of the world, together with the thoughts and reasonings thence derived, are from hell, [for they are concupiscences of every kind, which rise up thence into the natural man,] therefore these also are signified by "the wind and the waves of the sea;" and hell itself by the "sea," in the spiritual sense. *A. E.* 514. See also *T. C. R.* 123, 614.

. By "sea," in this passage, is signified hell; and by "wind," influx thence. *A. R.* 343.

Verse 40. *How is it that ye have no faith?*—As to a true faith and its efficacy, see below, Exposition, chap. xi. 22.

Verse 41. *And they feared with a great fear,* &c.—Holy fear, which sometimes is joined with a sacred tremor of the interiors of the mind, and sometimes with horripilation, or erection of the hair, supervenes, when life enters from the Lord instead of man's proper life. The proper life of man is to look from himself to the Lord; but life from the Lord, is to look from the Lord to the Lord, and yet as if from himself; when a man is in this latter life, he sees that he himself is not any thing, but only the Lord. In this holy fear Daniel was when he saw the "man clothed with linen, and his face like lightning," &c. (Dan. x. 5—12.) In a similar fear were the disciples, when they saw the Lord transfigured. (Matt. xvii. 5, 6, 7.) *A. R.* 56.

TRANSLATOR'S NOTES AND OBSERVATIONS.

CHAPTER IV.

VERSE 8. *And other fell upon good earth, and yielded fruit, springing up and increasing.* — By "springing up," according to the spiritual idea, is to be understood *elevation to things interior*, thus ascent from merely *natural* and *external* things, to things *spiritual* and *internal;* and it is here coupled with *increasing,* for the purpose probably of inculcating the important idea of the heavenly marriage, *springing up, or ascending,* having relation to the principle of heavenly *good,* or *love,* as *increasing* has relation to the principle of heavenly *truth,* or *wisdom.*

Verse 12. *That seeing they may see, and not perceive.* — What is here rendered "seeing" and "see" is from the Greek βλεπω, but what is rendered "perceive" is from the Greek ειδω, thus proving that there are different degrees of mental light, and that the term ειδω expresses a more interior degree than the term βλεπω.

Verse 13. *And He saith unto them, Know ye not this parable? And how will ye know all parables?* — The term *know,* as applied in the former of these questions, is expressed in the original Greek by a term derived from the root οιδω, whereas the same term, as applied in the latter question, is from the Greek γινοσκω. Thus it appears that the term γινοσκω involves in it a more interior knowledge than the term οιδω.

Verse 24. *And He said to them, Take heed what ye hear.* — What is here rendered "Take heed" is expressed in the original Greek by the term βλεπετε, which properly signifies "See ye," thus, according to the spiritual idea, "understand ye," consequently denoting that what is *heard,* or allowed to affect the *will,* should first be well considered and digested in the *understanding.*

MARK.

CHAPTER V.

1. AND they came to the other side of the sea, to the country of the Gadarenes.

2. And when He was come out of the ship, immediately there met Him out of the tombs, a man with an unclean spirit;

3. Who had his dwelling in the tombs, and no one could bind him with chains;

4. Because that he had been often bound with fetters and with chains, and the chains had been plucked asunder by him, and the fetters broken in pieces; and no one could tame him.

5. And always night and day he was in the mountains and in the tombs, crying, and cutting himself with stones.

6. But having seen Jesus afar off, he ran and worshipped Him.

7. And having cried with a great voice he said, What have I to do with Thee, Jesus thou Son of God Most High? I adjure Thee by God, torment me not.

THAT man is subject to the infestation of infernal spirits, who are principled in falses derived from evil, by which they would destroy the genuine goods and truths of the church. (Verses 1, 2.)

Which infestation cannot be checked by any power merely human, but for a time infuses into man defiled affections and false persuasions. (Verses 3—6.)

Nevertheless it is constrained to submit to the Divine presence and power of the LORD, which the infernals cannot endure, because it adds to their torment. (Verses 6, 7, 8.)

8. For He said unto him, Come out, thou unclean spirit, out of the man.

9. And He asked him, What is thy name? And he answered, saying, My name is Legion; for we are many.

On the exploration too of the quality of such infesting spirits, it is discovered that the false principles by which they are governed, are manifold, and that thus the infesting spirits do not operate singly, but in societies. (Verse 9.)

10. And he entreated Him much that He would not send them away out of the country.

11. Now there was there near to the mountains a great herd of swine feeding.

12. And all the devils entreated Him, saying, Send us into the swine, that we may enter into them.

13. And immediately Jesus allowed them; and the unclean spirits having gone out, entered into the swine; and the herd ran violently down a steep place into the sea (but they were about two thousand), and they were choked in the sea.

They are also unwilling to be separated from man, and when they are so separated, their unclean lusts, especially of avarice, plunge them into their infernal abodes. (Verses 10—14.)

14. But they who fed the swine fled, and told in the city and in the country; and they went out to see what was done.

15. And they come to Jesus, and behold him who was possessed with the devil, and had the legion, sitting, and clothed, and in his right mind: and they were afraid.

16. And they that saw told them how it befel him that was possessed with the devil, and about the swine.

Nevertheless the information respecting the separation of the powers of darkness from man, which ought to prove the Divine power of the LORD, has no other effect on the thoughtless and impenitent, than to lead them to reject all Divine influence. (Verses 14—18.)

12

17. And they began to entreat Him to depart out of their coasts.

18. And when He was come into the ship, he that was possessed with the devil entreated that he might be with Him.

19. Yet Jesus did not allow him, but saith unto him, Go to thy house, to thy own, and tell them how great things the Lord hath done for thee, and hath had mercy on thee.

20. And he departed, and began to preach in Decapolis how great things Jesus had done for him: and all wondered.

21. And when Jesus had passed over again by ship unto the other side, much people gathered unto Him: and He was nigh unto the sea.

22. And, behold, there cometh one of the rulers of the Synagogue, Jairus by name; and having seen Him, he fell at His feet,

23. And entreated Him much, saying, My little daughter lieth at the point of death: come, lay Thy hands on her, that she may be healed; and she shall live.

24. And He went with him: and much people followed Him, and crowded Him.

25. And a certain woman, who had an issue of blood twelve years,

But it is otherwise with those who have experienced the separation in themselves, since these are led to declare unto others the effects of that Divine mercy and power which have been shown to themselves. (Verses 18—21.)

That supplication is made for the affection of truth, that through communication with the LORD's Humanity, it might no longer be immersed in unclean loves, but might be exalted to heavenly love. (Verses 21—23.)

Which supplication is heard by the LORD. (Verse 24.)

Spiritual love also is communicated to those who were in natural love, separate from spiritual, and thus in the profanation of good, which communication is effected through the ultimates of the Word. (Verses 25—35.)

26. And had suffered many things of many physicians, and had spent all that she had, and was nothing better, but rather grew worse,

27. When she had heard of Jesus, she came in the crowd behind, and touched His garment.

28. For she said, If I may touch but His garments, I shall be whole.

29. And immediately the fountain of her blood was dried up, and she perceived in her body that she was healed of the plague.

30. And Jesus perceived immediately in Himself that virtue had gone out of Him, turned about in the crowd, and said, Who touched My garments?

31. And His disciples said unto Him, Thou seest the multitude thronging Thee, and sayest Thou, Who touched Me?

32. And He looked round to see her that had done this thing.

33. But the woman, fearing and trembling, knowing what was done in her, came and fell down before Him, and told Him all the truth.

34. But He said unto her, Daughter, thy faith hath saved thee; go into peace, and be made whole of thy plague.

35. While He yet spake, there came [some] from the ruler of the Synagogue, saying, Thy daughter is dead; why dost thou yet trouble the Teacher?

And could not be effected by any other means, though often attempted, but by faith in those ultimates, and conjunction thus wrought with the Lord's Humanity. (Verses 26—29.)

This faith too being imparted by and from the Lord, is perceived in its return to the Lord, and excites His tender regard and compassion. (Verses 30—32.)

And this regard and compassion produces deep humiliation in those who are delivered from the profanation of good, and through humiliation conducts to the blessing of peace. (Verses 33, 34.)

The affection of truth also, which was immersed in unclean loves, is delivered from its uncleanness through faith in the Lord. (Verses 35—43.)

Though this was thought impossible by the unbelieving. (Verse 35.)

36. But Jesus, as soon as He heard the word that was spoken, saith to the ruler of the Synagogue, Be not afraid, only believe.

37. And He allowed no one to follow Him, except Peter, and James, and John the brother of James.

38. And He cometh to the house of the ruler of the Synagogue, and seeth the tumult,—them that wept and wailed much.

39. And entering in, He saith unto them, Why are you thus tumultuous, and weep? the damsel is not dead, but sleepeth.

40. And they laughed at Him; but He, putting them all out, taketh the father and mother of the damsel, and them that were with Him, and entereth in where the damsel was lying.

41. And having taken the damsel by the hand, He saith to her, Talitha cumi; which is, being interpreted, Damsel, I say unto thee, arise.

42. And immediately the damsel arose, and walked, for she was twelve years old; and they were astonished with a great astonishment.

43. And He charged them straitly that no one should know this; and He said that something should be given her to eat.

Who are therefore instructed that all things are possible, provided the LORD be approached in the spirit of faith, of charity, and the works of charity. (Verses 36, 37.)

Otherwise the mind is disturbed by mere natural affections, which make light of the Divine operation, so that no deliverance from unclean loves can be wrought until those affections are removed. (Verses 38—40.)

But on their removal, communication is opened with the Divine Omnipotence, and the affection of truth is elevated out of all impure loves to newness of life, so that the Divine Omnipotence is acknowledged. (Verses 41, 42.)

Yet all are not in a state to make this acknowledgment, until the affection of truth is united with the affection of good. (Verse 43.)

EXPOSITION.

CHAPTER V.

VERSES 2—14. *And when He was come out of the ship, immediately there met Him out of the tombs a man with an unclean spirit, who had his dwelling in the tombs,* &c.—By "tombs" are signified things unclean, consequently also infernal, and hence it is evident why the possessed by devils were in the tombs, viz., because they who possessed them during their abode in the world, had been in false principles derived from evil, or in knowledges derived from the Word, which they made dead by applying them to confirm evil, also to destroy the genuine truths of the church, especially the truths concerning the Lord, concerning the Word, and concerning the life after death, which dead knowledges are in the Word called traditions; hence it was that they who were possessed by such, were in the tombs, and the devils were afterwards cast out into the swine, who ran headlong into the sea. The reason why they were "cast out into the swine" was, because, whilst they lived in the world, they were in sordid avarice, for such avarice corresponds to *swine;* the reason why they "ran headlong into the sea" was, because the *sea* there signifies hell. *A. E.* 659.

The life which evil spirits have, and which they love excessively, is the life of the lusts of self-love and the love of the world, whence comes the life of hatred, of revenge, and cruelty of various kinds, whilst they suppose that no delight is given in any other life; they are as men, for they have been men, and from the life which they had as men, they retain this principle. But what the quality is of the life which they love, is manifest from such spirits in the other life, where it is turned into what is filthy and excrementitious, and what is wonderful, they perceive the greatest delight in that filth, as may be manifest from the facts related, n. 820, 954; in like manner as the devils, who, when they were cast out by the Lord from the man who was possessed, through fear of destruction requested to be sent into the swine. (Mark v. 7—13.) That they were such as in the life of the body had been addicted to filthy avarice, may be manifest from this consideration, that spirits of such a quality, in the other life, seem to themselves

to dwell amongst swine, inasmuch as the life of swine corresponds to avarice, and is therefore delightful to them, as is
evident from what is related from experience, n. 939. *A. C.*
1742.

The removal of sins, which is called their remission, may be
compared with the casting out of all unclean things from the
camp of the children of Israel into the wilderness that lay
around it, for their *camp* represented heaven, and the *wilderness* hell. It may also be compared with the removal of the
nations from the children of Israel in the land of Canaan, and
of the Jebusites from Jerusalem, who were not cast out, but
separated. It may be compared too with a legion of devils,
permitted by the Lord to enter into the herd of swine, which
afterwards were drowned in the sea, where, by the sea is
signified hell. *T. C. R.* 614.

Verse 13. *And the herd ran violently down a steep place
into the sea, and they were choked in the sea.*—By the "sea"
is here signified hell, where and whence are the false principles
of evil, by reason that the spirits, who were there during
their lives in the world, were in those false principles; they
appear to dwell in the bottom, as of seas, and at a greater
depth there, in proportion as the evil was more grievous, from
which the false principle was derived. *A. E.* 538.

Verses 15, 16, 18. *Possessed with the devil,* &c.—"Devils"
[or demons] signify concupiscences or lusts of evil, and also
the lusts of falsifying truths. But devils, like lusts, are of
many kinds. The worst are those who are lusts of exercising
dominion from the burning incitement of self-love over the
holy things of the church, and over heaven. And inasmuch
as this love of dominion reigns in their hearts, they are also
lusts of profaning the truths of heaven from the spurious zeal
of that love. And whereas they, when they become devils,
as is the case after death, know that the Lord only rules over
heaven and earth, they become hatreds against Him, insomuch
that after the lapse of an age they cannot endure to hear Him
named. Hence it is evident that by Babylon being become
"the habitation of devils," is signified that their hells are the
hells of the lust of dominion originating in the burning
incitement of self-love and of the lust of profaning the truths
of heaven originating in the spurious zeal of that love. It
is not known in the world that all after death become affections of the love which reigns within them. Those who have
looked up to the Lord and to heaven, and at the same time
have shunned evils as sins, become good affections, but they
who have looked only to themselves and the world, and have

shunned evils not because they were sins, but because they were injurious to their honour and reputation, become evil affections, which are lusts or concupiscences. These affections appear to the life, and are perceived in the spiritual world, whereas only the thoughts which proceed from the affections appear in the natural world. Hence it is that man does not know that hell is in the affections of the love of evil, and heaven in the affections of the love of good; and the reason why he does not know this is, because the lusts of the love of evil possess this property in consequence of being hereditary, that in the will they are delightful, and hence pleasant to the understanding, and that which is delightful and pleasant man does not reflect upon, because this delight carries his mind along, just as the current of a river carries along a ship. Wherefore those who have plunged themselves into those delights and pleasures, can no otherwise arrive at the delights and pleasures of the affections of the love of good and truth, than after the manner of those who with a strong arm ply their oars against the tide; but it is otherwise with those who have not plunged themselves in so deeply. *A. R.* 756.

Verses 25—35. *And a certain woman, who had an issue of blood twelve years, when she had heard of Jesus, coming in the crowd behind, touched His garment, for she said, if I may touch but His garments, I shall be whole,* &c.—By an "issue of blood" is signified the profanation of the good of love; by a "leprosy" the profanation of the truth of faith. *A. C.* 9014.

What is meant by *touching the hem* or *border* of the Lord's garment, see below, Exposition, chap. vi. 56.

That by "touching" is signified communication, translation, and reception, is manifest from several passages in the Word, of which it is allowed to adduce the following:— "Thou shalt anoint the tent of assembly, and the ark of the testimony, and the table and all its vessels, and the candlestick and its vessels, and the altar of incense, and the altar of burnt-offering and all its vessels, and the laver and its basis, and thou shalt sanctify them, that they may be the Holy of Holies: every one who *toucheth* them shall be sanctified." (Exod. xxx. 26—29.) Again,— "Every thing which shall *touch* the residue of the meat-offering, and the residue of the flesh of the sacrifices, which are for Aaron and his sons, shall be sanctified." (Lev. vi. 18 and 27.) And in Daniel,—"The angel *touched* Daniel, and set him on his station, and lifted him up on his knees, and *touched* his lips, and opened his mouth, and again *touched* him, and strengthened him."

(x. 10, 16, 18.) And in Isaiah,—"One of the Seraphim *touched* my mouth with a coal, saying, Lo! this hath *touched* thy lips, therefore thine iniquity is departed, and thy sin is expiated." (vi. 7.) And in Matthew,—"Jesus stretching out His hand to the leper, *touched* him, saying, I will: be thou clean. And immediately his leprosy was cleansed." (viii. 3.) And in Luke,—"A woman who had an issue of blood, *touched* the hem of Jesus' garment, and immediately the issue of blood was staunched. Jesus said, Who is it that hath *touched* Me? I perceive that virtue is gone out of Me." (viii. 44—48.) *A. C.* 10,130.

Verse 23. *My daughter lieth at the point of death.*—Inasmuch as death is from no other source than from sin, and sin is all that which is contrary to divine order, it is from this ground that evil closes the smallest and altogether invisible vessels of the human body, of which the next greater vessels, which are also invisible, are composed. For the smallest and altogether invisible vessels are continued to man's interiors; hence comes the first and inmost obstruction, and hence the first and inmost vitiation of the blood; this vitiation, when it increases, causes disease, and at length death. But if man had lived the life of good, in this case his interiors would be open to heaven, and through heaven to the Lord; thus also the smallest and invisible vascula (it is allowable to call the delineaments of the first stamina vascula, or little vessels, by reason of correspondence) would be open also, and hence man would be without disease, and would only decrease to ultimate old age, until he became altogether an infant; and when in such case the body could no longer minister to its internal man or spirit, he would pass without disease out of his earthly body into a body such as the angels have, thus out of the world immediately into heaven. *A. C.* 5726.

Verse 36. *Be not afraid.*—By being "afraid," or timid, is signified to be in no faith. *A. E.* 1300.

Be not afraid, only believe [*or have faith*].—It was often said by the Lord, when the sick were healed, that they should have faith, and that it should be done unto them according to their faith, as in Matt. viii. 10—13, ix. 2, 22, 27, 28, 29, and in many other passages. The reason why He so said, was because the first of all things is to acknowledge that the Lord is the Saviour of the world, and to have faith in Him, for without that acknowledgment and faith, no one can receive anything of Truth and Good from heaven, thus no faith, and because this is the first and most essential of all things, therefore that the Lord might be acknowledged when

He came into the world, and when He healed the sick, He asked them about faith, and they who had faith were healed; the faith was that He was the Son of God, and that He had the power of healing and saving. All the healing of diseases by the Lord, when He was in the world, signified the healings of the spiritual life, thus the things which belong to salvation. Because the acknowledgment of the Lord is the first principle of the spiritual life, and the most essential principle of the church, and because without that no one can receive any thing of the truth of faith and of the good of love from heaven, therefore the Lord also often said, that he who believes in Him hath eternal life, and that he who does not believe hath not eternal life, as in John i. I, 4, 12, 13; iii. 14, 15, 16, 36, and in many other passages. At the same time He also teaches that they only have faith in Him who live according to His precepts, so that life thus enters into their faith. These things are said to illustrate and confirm the fact, that the acknowledgment of the Lord, and that from Him is all salvation, is the first principle of life from the Divine Being with man. *A. C.* 10,083.

Verse 37. *And He allowed no one to follow Him, except Peter, and James, and John the brother of James.*—By Peter, in the Word of the Evangelists, is meant truth grounded in good which is from the Lord, and likewise in the opposite sense, [as when he denied the Lord, Mark xiv. 70.] truth separate from good; and since truth is of faith and good is of charity, by Peter is also meant faith grounded in charity, and likewise faith separate from charity; for the "twelve apostles," like the "twelve tribes of Israel," represented the church, as to all things proper to it, thus as to truths and goods, for all things of the church have reference to those two principles, as to faith and love, for truths are of faith, and goods are of love. In general, Peter, James, and John, represented faith, charity, and the works of charity, on which account they three followed the Lord more than the rest; of whom therefore it is said in Mark,—"He suffered no man to follow Him, except Peter, James, and John." *A. E.* 820.

Verse 40. *And they laughed at Him.* —"Laughing," or laughter, arises from an affection of the rational principle, and indeed from an affection of what is true or of what is false in the rational principle; hence comes all laughter. So long as such an affection is in the rational principle, which puts itself forth in laughter, so long there is something corporeal or worldly, consequently somewhat merely human therein. Celestial and spiritual good does not laugh, but expresses its delight and cheerfulness in the countenance, in the speech, and in the gesture, after another manner. For in *laughter* there are many principles contained, as for the most part something of contempt, which, although it does not appear, still lies concealed under that outward expression, and is easily distinguished from cheerfulness of mind, which also produces somewhat similar to laughter. *A. C.* 2216.

Verse 41. *And taking the damsel by the hand*, &c.—A "damsel," or virgin, signifies the affection of good, or of truth. For there are, in general, two affections which constitute the church. The affection of good constitutes the celestial church, and is called in the Word, "the daughter of Zion," and also "the daughter, the virgin of Zion;" but the affection of truth constitutes the spiritual church, and is called in the Word, "the daughter of Jerusalem," as in Isaiah,—"The daughter, the virgin of Zion, hath despised thee, and laughed thee to scorn; the daughter of Jerusalem hath shaken her head behind thee;" (xxxvii. 22.) and in many other passages. *A. C.* 2362.

Verse 42. *She was twelve years old.*—The number "twelve" signifies fulness of instruction as to the knowledges of truth and good, and also as to remains. *A. C.* 2089. See also 1925, 3129, 3354.

TRANSLATOR'S NOTES AND OBSERVATIONS.

CHAPTER V.

VERSE 34. *Go into peace.*—In the common version of the New Testament, what is here rendered "into," is expressed by the preposition "in," so that the passage is rendered, "Go in peace;" but the original Greek is υπαγε εις ειρηνην, which literally means *go into peace*, and thus implies an entrance *into a new state of life*, in consequence of the faith she had manifested towards the Lord.

MARK.

CHAPTER VI.

1. And He went out from thence, and came into His own country; and His disciples follow Him.

2. And when it was the Sabbath, He began to teach in the Synagogue; and many hearing were astonished, saying, From whence hath this man these things? and what wisdom is this which is given unto Him, that even such mighty works are wrought by His hands?

3. Is not this the carpenter, the son of Mary, the brother of James, and Joses, and of Judah, and Simon? and are not His sisters here with us? And they were offended at Him.

4. But Jesus said unto them, A prophet is not without honour, except in his own country, and among kinsfolk, and in his own house.

5. And He could there do no mighty work, except that laying hands on a few sick people, He healed [them].

That doubt is excited in the church respecting the origin of the Lord's wisdom and power. (Verses 1—3.)

The reason of which is shown to be this, that the Lord, and the Divine Truth which is from Him, is less in heart received and loved within the church than out of it, so that the Divine Omnipotence is limited in its operation. (Verses 4, 5.)

6. And He marvelled because of their unbelief. And He went round about the villages, teaching.

7. And He called the twelve, and began to send them out by two and two, and gave them power over unclean spirits;

8. And exhorted them that they should take nothing for their journey, except a staff only; no scrip, no bread, no money in the purse;

9. But be shod with sandals, and not put on two coats.

10. And He said unto them, Wheresoever ye enter into a house, there remain until ye depart thence.

11. And whosoever will not receive you, nor hear you, when ye depart thence, shake off the dust from under your feet for a testimony against them. Verily I say unto you, It shall be more tolerable for Sodom and Gomorrah in the day of judgment, than for that city.

12. And having departed, they preached that men should repent,

13. And they cast out many devils, and anointed with oil many that were sick, and healed them.

14. And Herod the king heard, for His name was made public: and he said that John the Baptist was risen from the

Nevertheless it is necessary that Divine Truth should be made known in the church, for which purpose all who are principled in goods and truths are gifted with power from the LORD's Divine Human principle over all opposing evils and falses. (Verses 6, 7.)

And are instructed that all goods and truths are not from themselves, but from the LORD alone; and since Divine Truth is only one, viz., what is from the Divine Good, therefore they are to procure from that source both interior and exterior truth, and not to ascribe it partly to the LORD and partly to themselves. (Verses 8, 9.)

And if the truths which they teach be not received in the will-principle, the loss of eternal life must be announced as the necessary consequence, since they who are in evil of life, and at the same time in ignorance of truth, are more excusable than those who know the truth, and yet cherish evil. (Verses 10, 11.)

For the essential life of truth consists in renouncing evil love, and thus in rejecting infernal influence, and admitting the good of heavenly love in the place of that which is disorderly. (Verses 12, 13.)

That they who are principled in what is evil and false, are instructed concerning the LORD, and externally confess dead, and therefore mighty works are accomplished by him.

15. Others said, that it is Elias. But others said, that it is a prophet, or as one of the prophets.

16. But when Herod heard, he said, It is John whom I beheaded: he is risen from the dead.

Him to be the Word, and to be endowed with Omnipotence. (Verses 14, 15, 16.)

17. For Herod himself having sent forth, had laid hold upon John, and bound him in prison, on account of Herodias, his brother Philip's wife: because he had married her.

18. For John said to Herod, It is not lawful for thee to have thy brother's wife.

19. Therefore Herodias bare him spite, and was desirous to kill him; and was not able:

When yet they had before done violence to the Word, because it reproved their evil concupiscences. (Verses 17, 18, 19.)

20. For Herod feared John, knowing that he was a just man and holy, and protected him; and hearing him, he did many things, and heard him gladly.

Nevertheless in their understandings they acknowledged the sanctity of the Word, and had an external delight in its precepts. (Verse 20.)

21. And when a festive day was come, that Herod on his birthday made a supper to his grandees, and chief captains, and principal people of Galilee;

22. And when the daughter of the said Herodias came in, and danced, and pleased Herod and them that sat with him, the king said to the damsel, Ask of me whatsoever thou wilt, and I will give thee.

23. And he sware unto her, Whatsoever thou shalt ask of me, I will give thee, to the half of my kingdom.

Until the affection of what is false, operating on natural delights, leads them astray, and thus tempts them to deny the Word, and thereby destroy it. (Verses 21—29.)

24. But she departing, said to her mother, What shall I ask? And she said, The head of John the Baptist.

25. And having come in immediately with haste to the king, she asked, saying, I will that thou give me by and by in a charger the head of John the Baptist.

26. And the king being very sorry, on account of his oath, and them that sat with him, was unwilling to reject her.

27. And the king sending immediately one of his guards, he ordered his head to be brought: and he went and beheaded him in the prison.

28. And he brought his head in a charger, and gave it to the damsel: and the damsel gave it to her mother.

29. And when his disciples heard it, they came and took up his corpse, and laid it in a tomb.

30. And the apostles gathered themselves together unto Jesus, and told Him all things which they had done, and which they had taught.

31. And He said to them, Come ye apart into a desert place, and rest awhile: for there were many coming and going, and they had no leisure to eat.

32. And they departed into a desert place by ship privately.

33. And the multitude saw them departing; and many knew Him, and ran thither on foot out of all cities, and outwent them, and came together to Him.

But they, on the contrary, who are principled in what is good and true, apply the Word to the regeneration of their hearts and lives, and thus have approach to and communication with the LORD. (Verses 29, 30.)

Yet these are instructed that the heavenly good of love and charity cannot be appropriated but by the apparent desolation of truth. (Verses 31, 32.)

On which occasion the affection of truth is excited anew, and with it the Divine mercy towards all who are in that affection. (Verses 33, 34.)

34. And Jesus coming out, saw much multitude, and was moved with compassion towards them, because they were as sheep not having a shepherd: and He began to teach them many things.

35. And when the day was now far spent, His disciples coming to Him, said, This is a desert place, and the hour is now far advanced:

36. Send them away, that going into the country and villages round about, they may buy themselves bread: for they have nothing to eat.

37. But He answering said unto them, Give ye them to eat. And they say to Him, Shall we go and buy two hundred pennyworth of bread, and give them to eat?

38. But He saith to them, How many loaves have ye? go and see. And when they knew, they said, Five, and two fishes.

39. And He commanded them to make all sit down by companies on the green grass.

40. And they sat down in ranks, by hundreds, and by fifties.

41. And taking the five loaves and the two fishes, He looked up to heaven, and He blessed and brake the loaves, and gave them to His disciples to set before them: and the two fishes He divided amongst them all.

42. And they did all eat, and were satisfied.

So that in states of spiritual obscurity and desolation the LORD provides for their support by the communication of truth and good from Himself. (Verses 35, 36, and part of 37.)

Which to the natural man appears impossible. (Verse 37, latter part.)

Nevertheless through exploration of himself, operating to the right arrangement of interior goods and truths, and through benediction at the same time from the Divine Good, communication is opened with the natural man. (Verses 38—43.)

43. And they took up twelve baskets full of the fragments, and of the fishes.

44. And they that did eat of the loaves were about five thousand men.

45. And immediately He constrained His disciples to get into the ship, and to go before to the other side to Bethsaïda, while He dismissed the multitude.

46. And when He had bid them adieu, He departed into a mountain to pray.

47. And when evening had come, the ship was in the midst of the sea, and He alone on the land.

48. And He saw them toiling in rowing: for the wind was contrary to them: and about the fourth watch of the night He cometh to them, walking upon the sea, and would have passed by them.

49. But when they saw Him walking on the sea, they supposed it to be a phantom, and cried out:

50. For they all saw Him, and were troubled. And immediately He spake with them, and saith to them, Take courage: it is I; be not afraid.

51. And He went up unto them into the ship; and the wind ceased: and they were above measure amazed in themselves, and wondered.

52. For they were not attentive to [the miracle of] the loaves: for their heart was hardened.

And heavenly good and truth are appropriated in all fulness to all those who are in truths derived from good. (Verses 43, 44.)

Who are instructed to acquire the knowledges of truth and good for the better restoration of order from the LORD'S Divine Human [principle] in inferior principles. (Verse 45.)

Since when this is effected, a fuller communication and conjunction with the Divine Good has place. (Verse 46.)

So that the presence and influx of the LORD are imparted to those who are in the ultimates of the church, and thereby in an unpacific state. (Verses 47—51.)

Thus they who are in the knowledges of truth and good, have conjunction with the LORD, and are restored to tranquillity, notwithstanding the weakness of their faith. (Verses 51, 52.)

53. And when they had passed over, they came to the land of Gennesaret, and drew to the shore.

54. And when they came out of the ship, they immediately knew Him,

55. [And] ran through that whole region round about, and began to carry about on couches those that were sick, where they heard He was.

56. And wheresoever He entered, into villages, or cities, or country, they laid the sick in the streets, and besought Him that they might touch if it were but the border of His garment: and as many as touched Him [or it], were made whole.

So that evils and falses are more wrought upon, and purification is effected by communication with the LORD in lowest principles. (Verse 53, to the end of the chapter.)

EXPOSITION.

CHAPTER VI.

VERSE 2. *It was the Sabbath,* &c.—As to the meaning of the *Sabbath,* see above, Exposition, chap. i. 21.

Verse 4. *But Jesus said unto them, A prophet is not without honour, except in his own country, and among his kinsfolk, and in his own house.*—By these words is signified that the Lord, and the Divine Truth which is from Him, is less in heart received and loved within the church, than out of it. *He* spake to the Jews, amongst whom the church then was; and that He was there less received than by the Gentiles who were out of the church, is a known thing. The case is the same at this day in the church, which from Him is called Christian; in this church, indeed, the Lord is received in

14

doctrine, but still by few in acknowledgment of the heart, and by still fewer from affection of love.   It is otherwise with the converted Gentiles out of the church; these worship and adore Him as their one only God, and say with the mouth aud think with the heart, that they acknowledge Him to be God, because He appeared in a human form, n. 5256.   The contrary is the case within the church, where, because He was born a man, the men of the church hardly acknowledge Him from the heart to be God;—making His Humanity like their own, although they know that His Father was Jehovah, and not a man.   From these considerations it is evident what is meant in the internal sense by "no prophet being accepted in his own country."   In that sense a "prophet" is the Lord as to Divine Truth, thus as to the doctrine of the church.   That a "prophet" is one who teaches, and in the abstract sense, what is taught, and when spoken of the Lord, that it means the Divine Truth, or the Word, may be seen above, n. 9188. *A. C.* 9198.

Verse 5. *Laying hands on a few sick people.*—By the Lord "laying His hands on the sick," and also by the "touch," is meant the communication and reception of His divine virtue, as is evident from chap. v. 27. See Exposition. *A. C.* 10,023.

Verses 7, 8, 9. *And He called the twelve, and began to send them out by two and two, and gave them power over unclean spirits; and exhorted them that they should take nothing for their journey, except a staff only; no scrip, no bread, no money in their purse; but be shod with sandals, and not put on two coats.*—Inasmuch as Divine Truth is only One, viz., what is from the Divine Good, command was also given to the twelve disciples, when they were sent to preach the Gospel of the kingdom, that they should not have *two coats;* concerning which it is thus written in Luke:—"Jesus sent the twelve disciples to preach the Gospel of the kingdom, and said to them, Take nothing for the journey, neither staves, nor a purse, nor bread, nor silver; neither have two coats apiece." (ix. 2, 3.) And in Mark,—"He commanded them that they should take nothing for the journey, except a staff only; no purse, no bread, no money in their purse; but be shod with sandals, and not put on two coats." (vi. 8, 9.)   And in Matthew,— "Provide neither gold, nor silver, nor brass in your purses, nor scrip for your journey; neither two coats, neither shoes, nor staves." (x. 9, 10.)   In the above passages singular things are representative of the celestial and spiritual things of the Lord's kingdom, to preach which they were sent. The reason why they were not to take with them *gold, silver, brass, a*

scrip, and bread, was, because those things signified goods
and truths, which are from the Lord alone; "gold" signifying good, n. 113, 1551, 1552; but "silver" the truth thence
derived, n. 1551, 2954; "brass," natural good, n. 425, 1551;
"bread," the good of love, or celestial good, n. 276, 680, 2165,
2177, 3478; but the "coat" and the "shoes" signified the
truths with which they were to be clothed, and the "staff"
the power of truth grounded in good; that a "staff" is that
power, may be seen, n. 4013, 4015. That a "shoe" denotes
the lowest natural principle, see n. 1748; on that occasion, as
to truth; a "coat" denotes interior natural truth; and since
these things were not two-fold, but single one, it was forbidden
to take *two* staves, *two* pairs of shoes, and *two* coats. These
are the arcana contained in the above command of the Lord,
which cannot in anywise be known except from the internal
sense. All and singular the things which the Lord spake were
representative of divine things, consequently of the celestial
and spiritual things of His kingdom, and were thus adequate
to the comprehension of men, and at the same time to the
understanding of spirits and angels; wherefore the things
which the Lord spake filled and do fill the universal heaven.
Hence also it is evident of what importance and concern it is
to be acquainted with the internal sense of the Word; without
that sense, also, every one may confirm from the Word whatsoever dogma he pleases, and since the Word appears of such
a quality to those who are in evil, they therefore make a mock
of the Word, and think it incredible that it should be Divine.
A. C. 4677.

By the above words was represented that they who are
principled in goods and truths from the Lord, possess nothing
of goods and truths from themselves, but that all the Good
and Truth which they have, is from the Lord. For by the
"twelve disciples" were represented all who are principled in
goods and truths from the Lord; in the abstract sense, all the
goods of love and the truths of faith from the Lord, n. 3488,
3858, 6397; goods and truths from self, and not from the
Lord, are signified by possessing "gold, silver, brass in their
girdles," and by a "scrip;" but truths and goods from the
Lord are signified by a "coat," a "shoe," and a "staff;" by a
"coat," interior truth, or truth from a celestial principle; by
a "shoe," exterior truth, or truth in the natural principle,
n. 1748, 6844; by a "staff," the power of truth, n. 4876,
4936; but by "*two* coats, *two* shoes, and *two* staves," truths
and their powers both from the Lord and from self. That
the disciples were allowed to have *one* coat, *one* pair of shoes,

and *one* staff, is manifest from Mark vi. 8, 9, and from Luke ix. 2, 3.   *A. C.* 9942.

A *shoe* is what invests the sole of the foot and the heel, wherefore a "shoe" signifies the lowest natural principle, thus the very corporeal principle; the signification of a "shoe" is according to the subjects of which it is predicated; when it is predicated of the good, it is taken in a good sense, but when of the evil, in a bad sense.   *A. C.* 1748.

Verse 10. *Wheresoever ye enter into a house,* &c.—A "house" signifies various things, as the church, good therein, also a man, and likewise his mind, both natural and rational.   *A. C.* 9150.

Good belonging to a man is, in the Word, compared to a *house,* and on this account a man who is principled in good is called the "house of God."   *A. C.* 3128.

Verse 11. *And whosoever will not receive you, nor hear you, when ye depart thence, shake off the dust from under your feet, for a testimony against them.*—By the "dust of the feet," is here signified the same as by a "shoe," viz., what is unclean, grounded in what is evil and false, because the sole of the foot denotes the ultimate natural principle; and whereas at that time they were in representatives, and supposed heavenly mysteries to be stored up in them alone, not in naked truths, therefore they were commanded so to do.   *A. C.* 1748.

By "dust" is signified what is damned, and the reason is, because the places where evil spirits are, sideways beneath the soles of the feet, appear as earth, and indeed, as uncultivated and dry earth, beneath which are certain hells; that *earth* is what is called damned earth, and the *dust* there signifies what is damned.   It has occasionally been given me to see that evil spirits shook off the dust from their feet there, when they were desirous to deliver up any one to damnation.   Hence now it is that by "dust" is signified what is damned, and by "shaking off the dust," damnation.   It was by reason of this signification that the Lord commanded the disciples to "shake off the dust of their feet, if they were not received." (See Matt. x. 14, 15; Mark vi. 11; Luke ix. 5; x. 10, 11, 12.) For by "disciples" in those passages are not meant disciples, but all things of the church, thus all things of faith and charity, n. 2089, 2129; by "not receiving" and "not hearing," is signified to reject the truths which are of faith and the goods which are of charity; by "shaking off the dust of the feet," is signified damnation.   The reason why it would be "more tolerable for Sodom and Gomorrah than for that city," is, because by "Sodom and Gomorrah" are meant those who are in evil of life, but who have known nothing of the Lord and of the Word, thus, could not receive them. Hence it may be manifest that it is not a *house* or a *city* which is here meant, but that they are understood who are within the church, and do not live the life of faith; every one may see that a whole city could not be damned on that account, because they did not receive the disciples, and instantly acknowledge the new doctrine which they preached. By "dust" is also signified what is damned, in the following passages:—"Jehovah God said to the serpent, On thy belly shalt thou go, and *dust* shalt thou eat all the days of thy life." (Gen. iii. 14.) And in Micah,—"Feed Thy people according to the days of eternity; the nations shall see, and shall blush at all Thy power: they shall lick the *dust* as a serpent." (vii. 14, 16, 17.) And in Isaiah,—"*Dust* shall be the serpent's bread." (lxv. 25.) And again in the same prophet,—"Come down, and sit on the *dust*, O virgin daughter of Babylon." (xlvii. 1.) And in David,—"Our soul is bowed down to the *dust*: our belly cleaveth to the earth." (Psalm xliv. 25.) In the Word, also, "dust" signifies a sepulchre, also what is lowly, and likewise what is numerous. *A. C.* 7418.

Verse 12. *They preached that men should repent.*—For the true doctrine of *repentance*, see above, Exposition, chap. i. 4, 5.

Verse 13. *And they cast out many devils, and anointed with oil many that were sick, and healed them.*—Inasmuch as "oil" signified the good of love and charity, and by it all are healed who are spiritually sick, therefore it is said of the Lord's disciples, that "they anointed many with *oil*, and healed them." *A. E.* 375.

Verse 14. *John the Baptist.*—See above, chap. i. 4. Exposition of the object and meaning of John the Baptist, and of his mission.

Verse 20. *Herod feared John, knowing that he was a just man and holy.*—That the term "holy" is predicated of Truth, and the term "just" of Good, is evident from these passages in the Word:—"Just and true are Thy ways, Thou King of saints." (Apoc. xv. 3.) And in Mark vi. 20. See also *A. C.* 4167, 9119, 9283.

Verse 30. *And the apostles gathered themselves unto Jesus.*—By the "twelve apostles," as by the twelve tribes, are signified all things of the church, and especially all who are in truths of doctrine from the good of love from the Lord. *A. R.* 348.

Verses 35—45. *On the miracle of the five loaves and two small fishes.*—This miracle was wrought because the Lord had before taught His disciples, and because they received His doctrine, and appropriated it to themselves; this was what they did eat spiritually, whence natural eating followed, viz., flowed in from heaven with them, as manna with the sons of Israel, whilst they were ignorant; for when the Lord wills, spiritual food, which is also real food, but only for spirits and angels, is turned into natural, in like manner as into manna every morning. *A. E.* 617.

Singular the things in this miracle, with the numbers themselves also, mentioned in it, are significative. "Five thousand men, besides women and children," signify all who are of the church, in truths derived from good; "men," those who are in truths; "women and children," those who are in goods; "loaves of bread" the goods, and "fishes" the truths of the natural man; "feeding" signifies spiritual nourishment from the Lord; "twelve baskets of fragments," signify thence the knowledges of truths and good, in all abundance and fulness. *A. E.* 430.

Verse 39. *And He commanded to make all sit down by companies on the green grass.*—By "green grass" in the Word is signified that goodness and truth which first springs up in the natural man; the same is also signified by the "herb of the field." *A. R.* 401.

Verse 41. *And taking the five loaves and two fishes, looking up to heaven, He blessed them.*—By "blessing" is here signified the communication of His divine principle, and thereby conjunction with His disciples and the people, by the goods and truths, which were signified by the "loaves," and also by the "fishes." *A. E.* 340.

Verse 43. *And they took up twelve baskets full of the fragments, and of the fishes.*—The "twelve baskets of fragments," which were *taken up*, signify what is full, thus full instruction and full benediction. *A. E.* 548.

Verses 47—52. *On the miracle of* JESUS *walking on the sea.*—Singular the things related in this miracle, signify Divine spiritual things, which yet do not appear in the letter, as the *sea,* the Lord's *walking upon it,* the *fourth watch,* in which He came to His disciples, also the *ship,* into which Jesus entered, and that He thence *restrained the winds, and the waves of the sea,* besides the rest of the things mentioned. But the spiritual things which are signified, it is unnecessary to explain here singly, only that the "sea" signifies the ultimate of heaven and of the church, inasmuch as in the ultimate borders of the heavens there are seas. The Lord "walking upon the sea," signified the presence and influx of the Lord into those seas; and hence life from the Divine Being to those

who are in the ultimates of heaven; their life from the Divine
Being was represented by the Lord's "walking on the sea;"
and their obscure and wavering faith was represented by Peter
"walking on the sea, and beginning to sink," but being caught
hold of by the Lord, he was saved. To "walk" also, in the
Word, signifies to live; this being done in the "fourth watch,"
signified the first state of the church, when it is twilight, and
the morning is at hand, for then good begins to act by truth,
and then is the Lord's coming. The "sea" in the mean time
being put in commotion by the wind, and the Lord's restrain-
ing it, signifies the natural state of life which precedes, which
state is unpacific, and as it were tempestuous; but when the
state is nearest to the morning, which is the first state of the
church with man, because then the Lord is present with the
good of love, tranquillity of mind is effected. *A. E.* 514.

Verse 56. *And wheresoever He entered, into villages, or
cities, or country, they laid the sick in the streets, and besought
Him that they might touch if it were but the border of His
garment: and as many as touched Him [or it], were made
whole.*—That the "borders of a garment" denote the most
external things where the natural principle is, is manifest from
the passages in the Word where such borders are mentioned,
as in Isaiah,—" I saw the Lord sitting on a throne, high and
lofty, and the *borders of His garment* filling the temple;"
(vi. 1.) where, by the "throne on which the Lord sat," is
signified heaven, and specifically the spiritual heaven, n. 5313,
8625; by the "borders of His garment," are there signified
Divine Truths in ultimates, or in outermost principles, such
as are the truths of the Word in the sense of the letter, which
are said to "fill the temple" when they fill the church. By
the woman being healed of an issue of blood, when "she
touched the hem of the Lord's garment," and in general, by all
being healed, "as many as touched the hem of His garment,"
was signified, that from the Divine Being or Principle in the
most external or ultimate things, went forth salvation; for
that they had strength and power in the ultimates of good,
which are from the Divine Being or Principle, may be seen,
n. 9836. *A. C.* 9917.

TRANSLATOR'S NOTES AND OBSERVATIONS.

CHAPTER VI.

VERSES 45, 46. *And immediately He constrained His disciples to get into the ship, while He dismissed the multitude. And when He had bid them adieu, He departed into a mountain to pray.*—In the common version of the New Testament, what is here rendered "dismissed," and "bid adieu to," is comprised in *one* expression, "sent away," as if both terms were synonymous, and expressive of the same idea, and as if also they were applied to the same persons, whereas the terms in the original Greek are perfectly *distinct*, expressive too of distinct ideas, and likewise applied to different persons; the first term απολυσε being applied to the *multitude*, and denoting their *dismissal*, whilst the second term [αποταξαμενος] is manifestly applied to the *disciples*, to denote that the Lord *bid them adieu*, on His departure into a mountain to pray.

MARK.

CHAPTER VII.

1. AND there gathered together to Him the Pharisees, and some of the Scribes, who came from Jerusalem.

2. And having seen some of His disciples eating bread with defiled, that is to say, with unwashen, hands, they found fault.

3. For the Pharisees, and all the Jews, except they wash [their] hands up to the wrist, eat not, holding the tradition of the elders.

4. And [when they come] from the market, except they wash, they eat not; and many other things there are which they have received to hold, [as] the washing of cups and pots, brazen vessels, and couches.

5. Then the Pharisees and Scribes asked Him, Why walk not Thy disciples according to the tradition of the elders, but eat bread with unwashen hands?

6. But He answering said unto them, Well did Esaias prophesy of you hypocrites, as it is written, This people

THE INTERNAL SENSE.

THAT they who are of the perverse church, are scrupulous about the doctrines of men and external purification, but at the same time careless about internal purification and fulfilling the requirements of GOD. (Verses 1—6.)

Hence their worship becomes merely external and hypocritical, as had been predicted. (Verses 6—9.)

15

honoureth Me with their lips, but their heart is far from Me.

7. But in vain do they worship Me, teaching doctrines the commandments of men.

8. For laying aside the commandment of God, ye hold the tradition of men, the washing of pots and cups : and many other such like things ye do.

9. And He said unto them, Full well ye reject the commandment of God, that ye may keep your tradition.

10. For Moses said, Honour thy father and thy mother, and he that speaketh evil of father or mother, let him die the death.

11. But ye say, If a man shall say to father or mother, Corban, that is to say, [it is] a gift, by whatsoever thou mightest be profited by me; [it is sufficient].

12. And ye suffer him to do nothing more for his father or his mother;

13. Making the Word of God of none effect by your tradition which ye have delivered : and many such like things do ye.

14. And when He had called [to Him] all the multitude, He said unto them, Hearken to Me all of you, and understand :

15. There is nothing from without a man, which entering into him can defile him : but the things which come

For whereas the Divine Love and Wisdom ought to be exalted above all other things, they of the perverse church exalt themselves above those Divine principles, which is contrary to the commandment of GOD. (Verses 10—14.)

Who forms His judgment of every one, not from the doctrine which he professes with his lips, but from the out of him, those are they which defile the man.

16. If any man have ears to hear, let him hear.

17. And when He was entered into a house from the multitude, His disciples asked Him concerning the parable.

18. And He saith unto them, Are ye so without understanding also? Do ye not consider that every thing from without which entereth into a man, cannot defile him;

19. Because it entereth not into his heart, but into the belly, and goeth out into the draught, purging all meats?

20. And He said, That which cometh out of a man, that defileth the man.

21. For from within, out of the heart of men, proceed evil thoughts, adulteries, fornications, murders,

22. Thefts, covetousnesses, wickednesses, deceit, lasciviousness, an evil eye, blasphemy, pride, foolishness.

23. All these evil things come from within, and defile the man.

24. And rising thence, He went into the borders of Tyre

intention and purpose of his heart and life. (Verse 15.)

Which judgment ought to be well attended to. (Verse 16.)

Since nothing either of good or evil is appropriated to man, whilst it is only in the thought of his understanding, until it gains a place in his will or love, and thence comes into the thought and act. (Verses 17—20.)

For from the will or love comes all opposition to heavenly good and truth, whence comes perversion of the rational faculty, the adulteration of good, the falsification of truth, the destruction of charity, selfish appropriation of divine gifts, the lust of possessing what is another's, all kinds of sin against GOD, hypocritical dealing, concupiscence, perversion of the understanding, opposition to the truth, exaltation of self above GOD, with separation from all heavenly light. (Verses 20—23.)

These evils therefore render man impure in the sight of GOD, because they proceed from the love. (Verse 23.)

That they who are out of the church, and yet have faith

and Sidon, and entering into a house, would have no one know it, but He could not be hid.

25. For a woman hearing of Him, whose daughter had an unclean spirit, came and fell at His feet:

26. The woman was a Greek, a Syrophenician by nation, and she besought Him that He would cast forth the devil out of her daughter.

27. But Jesus said unto her, Let the children first be satisfied: for it is not meet to take the children's bread, and to cast it to the dogs.

28. But she answered and said to Him, Yes, Lord: yet the dogs under the table eat of the children's crumbs.

29. And He said unto her, For this saying go away: the devil is gone out of thy daughter.

30. And when she was come to her house, she found the devil gone out, and her daughter laid upon the bed.

31. And again departing from the coasts of Tyre and Sidon, He came unto the sea of Galilee, through the midst of the coasts of Decapolis.

32. And they bring to Him one that was deaf, having an impediment in his speech; and they beseech Him to put His hand upon him.

33. And taking him aside from the multitude, He put His fingers into his ears, and having spat, He touched his tongue;

in the LORD, apply to Him for deliverance from infernal falses. (Verses 24, 25, 26.)

But their application seems at first to be disregarded, because they are not of the church; nevertheless it is finally granted, and they are liberated from infernal falses, because they are found to be principled in faith grounded in charity. (Verses 27—31.)

They also who are not in the understanding of truth, and consequently not in obedience, and who on that account can hardly make confession of the LORD and of the truth of the church, are restored by the LORD to the perception of truth, and to the power of confessing the LORD and the truth of the church. (Verses 31—36.)

34. And looking up to heaven, He sighed, and saith to him, Ephphatha, that is, Be opened.

35. And immediately his ears were opened, and the string of his tongue was loosened, and he spake plainly.

36. And He charged them that they should tell no one: but the more He charged them, so much the more they published [it];

So that the Divine Mercy and Omnipotence excite adoration in all. (Verses 36, 37.)

37. And were beyond measure astonished, saying, He hath done all things well: He maketh both the deaf to hear, and the dumb to speak.

EXPOSITION.

CHAPTER VII.

VERSES 1—23. *For the Pharisees, and all the Jews, except they wash their hands,* &c.—That " washings" were enjoined the children of Israel, is known from the statutes enacted by Moses; as that Aaron should *wash* himself before he put on the garments of his ministration, (Lev. xvi. 4, 24.) and before he approached the altar to minister; (Exod. xxx. 18—21; xl. 30, 31.) in like manner the Levites, (Numb. viii. 6, 7.) and also others who became unclean by sins: and that they are said to be " sanctified by washings." (Exod. xix. 14; xl. 12; Lev. viii. 6.) Wherefore, for the purpose of washing, a molten sea and several basins were placed near the temple; (1 Kings vii. 23—39.) nay, they were enjoined to wash vessels and utensils, as tables, chairs, beds, dishes, and cups. (Lev. xi. 32; xiv. 8, 9; xv. 5—12; xvii. 15, 16; Mark vii. 4.) But " washings," and several ordinances of a like nature, were enjoined and commanded the children of Israel, because the church established among them was a representative church, which was of such a nature as to prefigure the Christian church that was to come; on which account, when the Lord came into the world, He abrogated the representatives, which were all external, and instituted a church in which all things were to be internal. Thus the Lord put away figures, and revealed their true antetypes, just as when a person removes a veil, or opens a door, and thus affords the means not only of seeing the things within, but of approaching them. Of all those representatives the Lord retained but two, which were to contain in one complex whatever related to the internal church; these two are Baptism instead of washings, and the Holy Supper instead of the lamb which was sacrificed every day, and particularly at the feast of the passover.

That the above-mentioned "washings" figured and shadowed forth, that is, represented, spiritual washings, consisting in purifications from evils and falses, is very evident from the following passages:—"When the Lord shall have *washed* away the filth of the daughters of Zion, and shall have purged the blood of Jerusalem from the midst thereof, by the spirit of judgment, and by the spirit of expurgation." (Isaiah iv. 4.) "Though thou *wash* thee with nitre, and take thee much soap, still thine iniquity will retain its spots." (Jer. ii. 22; Job. ix. 30, 31.) "*Wash* me from mine iniquity, and I shall be whiter than snow." (Psalm li. 2, 7.) "O Jerusalem, *wash* thine heart from wickedness, that thou mayest be saved." (Jer. iv. 14.) "*Wash* ye, make you clean: put away the evil of your doings from before Mine eyes; cease to do evil." (Isaiah i. 16.) That the washing of man's spirit is meant by the washing of his body, and that the internal things of the church were represented by such external rites as belonged to the Israelitish church, is very clear from these words of the Lord,—"The Pharisees and Scribes seeing that His disciples ate bread with unwashed hands, found fault; for the Pharisees, and all the Jews, except they *wash* their hands, eat not. And many other things there are which they have received to hold, as the *washing* of cups and pots, brazen vessels, and tables. To whom and to the multitude the Lord said, Hearken unto Me every one of you, and understand: there is nothing from without a man, that entering into him can defile him; but the things which come out of him, those are they which defile the man." (Mark vii. 1, 2, 3, 4, 14, 15.)

What man of sound reason cannot discern that the washing of the face, of the hands and feet, and of all the limbs, nay of the whole body in a bath, effects nothing more than to wash

away the dirt, so that the outward form may appear clean
in the sight of men? And who cannot understand that it
is impossible for any such washing to enter into the spirit of
man, and in like manner render that clean? For a thief, a
robber, or an assassin have it in their power to wash themselves, even till their skin shine; but will that wash away
their thieving, pillaging, and murderous disposition? Does
not the internal enter by influx into the external, and operate
the effects of its will and understanding? But for the external
to enter by influx into the internal is utterly impossible, being
contrary to nature, because it is contrary to order.

Hence it follows that "washings," and baptism also, unless
the internal of man be purified from evils and falses, are of
no more avail than the washing of cups and platters by the
Jews, or than the whitening of the sepulchres mentioned in the
same passage, which "appear beautiful without, but within are
full of dead men's bones, and all uncleanness." (Matt. xxiii.
25—28.) This is further evident from this circumstance, that
the hells are full of satans, who were once men, some baptized,
and some not baptized. *T. C. R.* 670—673.

Verse 4. *The washing of cups, pots,* &c.—Amongst the
Israelites *external* things [such as cups, pots, vessels, &c.]
represented *internal*, and things internal were the holy things
themselves of the church pertaining to them, and not the
external things without the internal. Nevertheless, that that
nation still placed all sanctity in things external, and not in
things internal, is manifest from the Lord's words in Matt.
xxiii. 25—27,—"Woe to you, Scribes and Pharisees, hypocrites! ye cleanse the outside of the *cup* and *platter*, but the
interiors are full of rapine and excess," &c. *A. C.* 10,234.

They who are in *external* things alone, [or who make religion consist only in external acts and ceremonies of worship,
as signified by the "washing of cups, pots," &c.] do not even
know what it is to be in internal things, for they do not know
what an internal principle is. If any one makes mention
before them of an internal principle, they either affirm that
it is, because they know from doctrine that it is (but in such
case they affirm from fraud), or they deny it with the mouth
also as with the heart; for they do not go beyond the sensual
principles which belong to the external man. Hence it is that
they do not believe any life after death, and think resurrection
impossible unless the body is to rise again, on which account
it has been permitted that they should have such an opinion
of the resurrection, otherwise they would have no opinion
at all, for they place the all of life in the body, not knowing

that the life of their body is from the life of their spirit, which liveth after death. They who are in external things alone, cannot have any other belief, for the external things appertaining to them extinguish the all of thought, consequently the all of faith concerning internal things. Inasmuch as great ignorance prevails at this day as to what it is to be in *external things without internal*, it shall be here explained. They who are without conscience are all in external things alone, for the internal man manifests himself by conscience; and all they have no conscience who think and do what is true and good, not for the sake of what is true and good, but for the sake of themselves, on account of their own honour and gain, and also on account of the fear of the law and of life; for if their reputation, honour, gain, and life were not endangered, they would rush headlong without conscience into all iniquities. This appears manifest from the case of such in another life, who in the life of the body had been such, where, inasmuch as the interiors are opened, they are in a perpetual endeavour to destroy others, wherefore they are in hell, and are kept bound there in a spiritual manner.

In order that it may be further known what it is to be in *external things*, and what in *internal*, and that they who are in external things alone, cannot comprehend what internal things are, consequently cannot be affected by them (for no one is affected by those things which he does not comprehend), let us take this truth for an example,—that to be the least is to be the greatest in heaven, and that to be low is to be high, also that to be poor and needy is to be rich and abounding. They who are in external things alone, cannot comprehend these things, for they think that the least cannot in anywise be the greatest, nor the low high, nor the poor rich, nor the needy abundant; when yet this is altogether the case in heaven; and because they cannot comprehend, therefore they cannot be affected by those things, and when they reflect upon them from the corporeal and worldly things in which they are, they hold them in aversion. That the case is so in heaven, they are altogether ignorant, and so long as they are in external things alone, are not willing to know, yea, neither are they able to know; for in heaven he who knows, acknowledges, and believes from the heart, that is, from the affection, that nothing of ability is from self, but that all of ability he has is from the Lord,—he is called least, and yet is greatest, because he has ability from the Lord. The case is similar with him who is low (or humble), that he is high, for he who is low, acknowledging and believing from affection, that he has nothing of ability from himself, nothing of intelligence or wisdom from himself, and nothing of good and truth from himself,—he is gifted with ability, with the intelligence of truth, and the wisdom of good, above others, from the Lord. In like manner the poor and needy are rich and abounding, for he is called poor and needy who believes from the heart and affection that he possesses nothing of himself, knows nothing, and is nothing wise of himself; and of himself has no ability, and he in heaven is rich and abounds, for the Lord gives him all opulence, inasmuch as he is wiser than others, richer than others, dwells in most magnificent palaces, n. 1116, 1626, 1627, and is in the treasures of all the riches of heaven. To take another example,—he who is in external things alone, cannot in anywise comprehend that heavenly joy consists in loving his neighbour better than himself, and the Lord above all things, and that happiness is according to the quantity and quality of that love; for he who is in external things alone, loves himself better than his neighbour, and if he love others, it is because they favour himself, and thus he loves them for the sake of himself, consequently he loves himself in them and them in himself. He who is such, cannot know what it is to love others better than himself, yea, he is not willing to know it, neither is he able, wherefore when he is told that heaven consists in such love, n. 548, he holds it in aversion; hence it is, that they who have been such in the life of the body, cannot come near to any heavenly society, and when they do come near, by reason of their aversion they cast themselves down headlong into hell.

Inasmuch as few know at this day what it is to be in *external things,* and what in *internal,* and whereas the generality believe that they who are in internal things cannot be in external, and *vice vesrâ,* it is allowed for the sake of illustration to adduce one further example, for instance, the nourishment of the body and the nourishment of the soul. He who is in pleasures merely external, is nice about his person, pampers his appetite, loves to live sumptuously, and places his chief pleasure in the dainties of the table; but he who is in internal things, although he also has satisfaction in the above gratifications, yet his ruling affection is, that the body may be nourished by meats with pleasure for the sake of its health, to the end that there may be a sound mind in a sound body, thus principally for the sake of the mind's health, to which the health of the body serves as a means; he who is a spiritual man does not rest here, but regards the health of the mind or soul as a means

16

of intelligence and wisdom, not for the sake of reputation, honours, or gain, but for the sake of the life after death; he who is spiritual in an interior degree, regards intelligence and wisdom as a mediate end, that he may serve as a useful member in the Lord's kingdom; and he who is a celestial man, that he may serve the Lord; to this latter, corporeal food is a means to enjoy spiritual food, and spiritual food is a means to enjoy celestial food; and because they ought so to serve, therefore also those foods correspond: hence also they are called foods. From these considerations it may appear what it is to be in external things alone, and what in internal. The Jewish and Israelitish nation (treated of in this chapter, Gen. xxxiv., in the internal historical sense), except those who have died infants, are for the most part of the above description, for they are in external things above all other nations, inasmuch as they are in avarice; they who love lucre and gain, not for the sake of any other use, but for the sake of gold and silver, and place all the delight of their lives in the possession thereof, are in the outermost or lowest things, for the things which they love are altogether earthly; but they who love gold and silver for the sake of some use, elevate themselves according to the use out of earthly things; the use itself, which man loves, determines his life, and distinguishes him from others; an evil use makes him infernal, a good use makes him heavenly; not indeed the use itself, but the love of the use, for the life of every one is in the love. *A. C.* 4459.

Verse 9. *And He said unto them, Full well ye reject the commandment of God, that ye may keep your tradition.*—This "rejection" is pointed at in the Prophet Isaiah, where it is written:—"Ye have seen the breaches of the city of David, that they are very many: and ye have gathered together the waters of the lower fish-pool;" (xxii. 9.) where "the breaches of the city of David" denote false principles of doctrine, and "the waters of the lower fish-pool" denote the *traditions*, by which the Jews made breaches into the truths that are in the Word. *A. C.* 4926.

The reason why they who were obsessed by devils [Luke viii. 27—32.] did not abide in the house, but in the tombs, was, because during their abode in the world they were in false principles grounded in evil, or, in knowledges from the Word, which they rendered lifeless by applying them to confirm evils, and also to destroy the genuine truths of the church, especially to destroy the truths relating to the Lord, to the Word, and to a life after death, which dead knowledges in the Word are called *traditions*. *A. E.* 659.

By a " dead worship" [such as that of those who only care about external things, and not internal] is understood worship alone, which consists in going to church, hearing sermons, taking the Holy Supper, reading the Word and books of piety, speaking about God, heaven and hell, the life after death, and especially concerning piety, praying morning and evening, and still not desiring to know any truths of faith, nor willing to do any goods of charity, believing that they have salvation by worship alone; when nevertheless worship without truths, and without a life according to them, is only an external sign of charity and faith, within which, if there be not charity and faith, there may lie hidden evils and falsities of all kinds. For genuine worship consists in charity and faith, without which, worship is like the skin or surface of any fruit, which within is rotten and worm-eaten, and is consequently a dead fruit.   That such a worship prevails at the present day in the church is known. *A. R.* 154.

Verse 14. *He said unto them, Hearken to Me all of you, and understand.*—That the understanding is to be kept captive under obedience to faith, [or to be kept in darkness as to the understanding of divine truths,] is a dogma which the New Church rejects; and in the place of such a dogma, it maintains that the truth of the church must be seen in rational light, in order to be believed. For the Truth can no otherwise be seen than rationally. How can any man be led by the Lord, and conjoined with heaven, who shuts up his understanding against such things as belong to salvation and eternal life? For is it not the understanding which must be illustrated and taught? And what is the understanding when shut up by religion but thick darkness, and indeed such darkness as rejects from itself all light which illustrates? Who can acknowledge any truth, and retain it, except he sees it? What is a truth not seen but a word not understood? which by sensual corporeal men may be retained in the memory, but not by wise men; yea, wise men reject all empty words from their memory, that is, such words as have not entered into the memory from the understanding, as that the One God is three as to Persons, and that the Lord born from eternity is not one and the same with the Lord born in time, that is, that the one Lord is God, and no other. And likewise that the life of charity, which consists in good works, and also in repentance from evil works, contributes nothing to salvation. A wise man does not understand this; wherefore from his rationality he says—" Does therefore religion contribute nothing to salvation? Does not religion consist in shunning evil and in doing good? and does not the

doctrine of the church teach this, and also how man should
believe, in order that he may do from God the good which
religion enjoins him to do?"   *A. R.* 564.

Verses 15—24. *There is nothing from without a man, which
entering into him can defile him: but the things which come
out of him, those are the things which defile a man.*—By those
"things which come from without," in the sense of the letter,
are meant foods of every kind, which, after use in the body,
pass out into the draught; but in the spiritual sense, by those
"things which come from without," are signified all things
which from the memory, and also from the world, enter into
the thought. These things also correspond to foods, and those
which enter into the thought, and not at the same time into
the will, do not render a man unclean, for the memory, and
hence the thought, are to man only as an entrance to him,
inasmuch as the will is the man himself; those things which
only enter into the thought and no further, are rejected, as it
were, through the belly [or stomach] into the draught; the
"belly" from correspondence signifying the world of spirits,
whence the thoughts appertaining to man flow in; and the
"draught" signifying hell. It is to be noted that man cannot
be purified from evils, and the false principles thence derived,
unless the unclean things which are in him emerge even into
the thought, and be there seen, acknowledged, discerned, and
rejected. From these considerations it is evident that by that
which "comes from without," in the spiritual sense, is signified what enters into the thought from the memory and from
the world; but by that which "comes forth from him," in the
spiritual sense, is signified thought derived from the will, or
from the love, for by the "heart," from which it goes forth
into the mouth and out of the mouth, is signified the will and
love of man; and inasmuch as the love and the will constitute
the whole man, (for man is such as his love is,) hence those
things which go forth from man render him unclean, for that
these are evils of every kind, is manifest from the things there
enumerated. Thus is the Word of the Lord understood in
the heavens. *A. E.* 580.

The words of the above parable are thus to be understood.
All things, whether they be false or evil, which flow in from
what is seen, or from what is heard, into the thought or the
understanding, and not into the affection of man's will, do not
affect and infect the man, inasmuch as the thought of man's
understanding, so far as it does not proceed from the affection
of his will, is not in the man, but out of him, wherefore it is
not appropriated to him; the case is the same in regard to

Truth and Good. These things the Lord teaches by correspondences, saying, that "that which entereth by the mouth
into the belly, doth not render man unclean," inasmuch as it
doth not enter into the heart, for "that which entereth into
the belly is cast out into the draught," by which is meant, that
that which from without, or extrinsically, whether it be from
the objects of sight, or from the objects of speech, or from the
objects of memory, enters into the thought of man's understanding, does not render him unclean, but, so far as it is out
of his affection or will, is separated and ejected, as what is
taken into the belly is ejected into the draught. These spiritual things the Lord expounded by natural things, since the
foods which are taken by the mouth, and are let down into
the belly, signify such things as man spiritually swallows, and
by which he nourishes the soul; hence it is that the "belly"
corresponds to the thought of the understanding, and also
signifies it; that the "heart" signifies the affection of the
will of man, has been shewn above; also, that that alone is
appropriated to man, which becomes the property of his affection or will. That spiritual things are meant, and not natural,
is evident, for the Lord says, that "out of the heart go forth
evil thoughts, murders, adulteries," &c. Inasmuch as the false
and evil principles which enter from without into the thoughts,
enter from the hells, and if they are not received by man with
affection of the will, are ejected into the hells, therefore it is
said that they are "cast out into the draught;" for by the
"draught" is signified hell, by reason that in the hells all
things are unclean, and they who are there have been cast out
from heaven, which in form is as a man, and is hence called
the Grand Man, and also corresponds to all things of man,
whereas the hells thence correspond to ejections from the belly
of the Grand Man, or heaven, from which ground it is that
hell is meant by the "draught" in the spiritual sense. The
reason why the belly is said to "purge all meats," is, because
by the "belly" is signified the thought of the understanding,
as was said above; and by "meats" are signified all spiritual
nourishments, and the thought of the understanding is what
separates unclean things from clean, and thereby "purges."
A. E. 622.

See also *A. C.* 6204, 8910; where it is further observed on
the subject, that man cannot desist from thinking evil, but
from doing it, and as soon as he receives evil from the thought
into the will, in this case it does not go forth, but enters into
him, and this is said to enter into the heart; the things which
thence go forth render him unclean, because what a man wills,

this goes forth into speech and into act, so far as external restraints do not forbid, which restraints are the fear of the law, of the loss of reputation, of honour, of gain, and of life. See also *D. P.* 30.

The order of influx is such, that evil spirits first flow in, and that the angels dissipate the things which flow in: that such is the nature of influx, is not perceived by man, because his thought is kept in freedom by equilibrium between those two influxes, and because he does not attend to them; neither could the evil know, in case they attended, because with them there is no equilibrium between evil and good; but they who are principled in good are capable of knowing this. They also know from the Word, that there is something within which fights against what is evil and false in them, and that the spiritual man fights against the natural, thus the angels who are in man's interiors and in his spiritual principles, against the evil spirits who are in his exterior and natural principles; hence also the church is called *militant*. But the evil which flows into the thought from evil spirits does not at all hurt man, if he does not receive it; but if he receives it, and transfers it from the thought into the will, in this case he makes it his own, and in this case takes part with infernal spirits, and recedes from the angels in heaven. This is what the Lord teaches in Mark,—" Not that which entereth into a man, makes him unclean: but the things which go forth from him, because these things are from the heart or from the will." (vii. 15—23.) *A. C.* 6308.

Verse 21. *Fornications, murders.*—" Murders" denote the evils which destroy goods; "fornications" denote truths falsified. *A. C.* 3535.

What the *falsification of Truth* is, shall be illustrated by some examples. Truth is falsified when from reasonings it is concluded and said, that because no one can do good from himself, therefore good is of no effect to salvation. Truth is also falsified when it is said, that every good which man doeth, respects himself, and is done for the sake of recompense, and this being the case, that works of charity are not to be done. Truth is also falsified when it is said, that because all good is from the Lord, therefore man ought to do nothing of good, but to expect or await influx. Truth is falsified when it is said, that Truth can be given with man without the Good which is of charity, thus faith without charity. Truth is falsified when it is said, that no one can enter into heaven but he who is miserable and poor, when it is also said unless he gives his all to the poor and plunges himself into distress.

Truth is falsified when it is said, that every one, howsoever he has lived, may be let into heaven from mercy. Truth is still more falsified when it is said, that there has been given to a man [such as the pope], the power of letting into heaven whom he pleases. Truth is falsified when it is said, that sins are wiped and washed away like filth by water; and truth is still more falsified when it is said, that a man has the power of remitting sins, and that when they are remitted, they are altogether wiped away, and man becomes pure. Truth is falsified when it is said, that the Lord has taken all sins unto Himself, and thus has taken them away, and that man thereby can be saved, whatsoever his life be. Truth is falsified when it is said, that no one is saved but he who is within the church. The reasonings by which falsification is effected are, that they who are within the church are baptized, have the Word, have knowledge concerning the Lord, concerning the resurrection, concerning life eternal, heaven and hell, and thus that they know what faith is by which they may be purified. There are innumerable cases like these, for there is not a single truth which cannot be falsified, and the falsification be confirmed by reasonings from fallacies. *A. C.* 7318.

Verse 27. *But Jesus said unto her, Let the children first be filled: for it is not meet to take the children's bread, and to cast it to the dogs.*—All beasts in the Word signify affections and inclinations, such as those are which appertain to man; the tame and useful beasts, good affections and inclinations, but the wild and useless beasts, evil affections and inclinations. The reason why such things are signified by beasts, is, because the external or natural man enjoys similar affections and inclinations, and likewise similar appetites and similar senses with the beasts; but the difference is, that man has an internal principle, which is called the internal man, which in man is so distinct from the external, that he can see the things which exist in the latter, and can also rule and restrain them, and likewise be elevated into heaven, even to the Lord, and thus be conjoined to Him in thought and in affection, consequently in faith and love; this man is also so distinct from the external, that he is separated from him after death, and afterwards lives to eternity. By these things man is distinguished from beasts; but they who are merely natural and sensual, do not see these things, for their internal man is closed towards heaven; wherefore neither do they know of any other distinction between man and beast, than that man can speak, which also mere sensual men make light of. By "dogs" are signified those who render the good of faith unclean by falsifications, the ground of which signification is, because dogs eat unclean things, and likewise bark at and bite men; hence also it is, that the Gentiles out of the church, who were in false principles grounded in evil, were by the Jews called *dogs,* which were accounted the vilest of animals.   That they were called *dogs,* is evident from the Lord's words to the Greek woman, a Syrophenician, whose daughter had an unclean spirit,—" It is not good to take the children's bread, and cast it to *dogs.* But she answered and said to Him, Yes, Lord: yet the dogs eat of the crumbs which fall from their master's table." (Matt. xv. 26, 27; Mark vii. 26, 27.)   In this passage by " dogs" are signified those who were out of the church, and by " children," those who were within the church. In like manner in Luke,—" There was a certain rich man, who was clothed in purple and fine linen, and fared sumptuously every day: but there was a poor man named Lazarus, who lay at his gate, full of sores, and desiring to be fed with the crumbs which fell from the rich man's table: moreover the *dogs* came and licked his sores;" (xvi. 19, 20, 21.) where, by " a rich man clothed in purple and fine linen," are signified those who are within the church; " purple and fine linen," with which he was clothed, being the knowledges of good and truth derived from the Word.   By the " poor man," are signified those within the church who, by reason of ignorance of the truth, are in a small degree of good, and yet desire to be instructed; the reason why he was called Lazarus, was from the Lazarus who was raised up by the Lord, of whom it is said, that " the Lord loved him," (John xi. 1, 2, 3, 36.) and that he was His " friend," (xi. 11.) and that " he sat down at table with the Lord;" (xii. 2.) that he was willing to be fed with the " crumbs which fell from the rich man's table," signified his desire of learning a few truths from those within the church who are principled in good, although not the genuine good of faith; to " lick sores," is to be healed by them in any possible method.   That good falsified, and thus rendered unclean, is signified by " dogs," is also evident from these words in Matthew,—" Give not that which is holy unto *dogs,* neither cast ye your pearls before swine." (vii. 6.) *A.C.* 9231.

Verses 32—36. *And they bring to Him one that was deaf, having an impediment in his speech; and they beseech Him to put His hand upon him.   And taking him aside from the multitude, He put His fingers into his ears, and having spat, He touched his tongue ; and looking up to heaven, He sighed, and saith to him, Ephphatha, that is, Be opened.   And immediately his ears were opened, and the string of his tongue was loosened, and he spake plainly.*—That all the Lord's miracles, as being Divine, involved and signified such things as are of heaven and the church, and that on this account they were the healings of diseases, by which were signified the various healings of spiritual life, may be seen in the "Arcana Cœlestia," n. 7337, 8364, 9031. By a "deaf person," are signified those who are not in the understanding of truth, and consequently not in obedience; and by one who had an "impediment in his speech," are signified those who, on that account, can hardly make confession of the Lord and of the truths of the church; by the "ears being opened" by the Lord, is signified perception of truth and obedience; and by the "tongue being loosened" by the Lord, is signified confession of the Lord and of the truths of the church. That the apostles and others after the Lord's resurrection, spake with "new tongues," signified also confession of the Lord and of the truths of the New Church, on which subject it is thus written in Mark:—"Jesus said, These signs shall follow them that believe: in My name they shall cast out devils; and shall speak with *new tongues;*" (xvi. 17.) where, by "casting out devils," is signified to remove and to reject the false principles of evil; and by "speaking with new tongues," is signified to confess the Lord and the truths of the church from Him; wherefore "there appeared to the apostles *cloven tongues* as of fire, which sat upon them; and being then filled with the Holy Spirit, they began to speak with other *tongues;*" (Acts of the Apostles, ii. 3, 4.) where by "fire" was signified the love of truth; and by being "filled with the Holy Spirit," was signified the reception of Divine Truth from the Lord; and by "new tongues," confessions grounded in the love of truths or zeal. For, as was said above, all Divine miracles, consequently all miracles mentioned in the Word, involved and signified spiritual and celestial things, that is, such things as are of the church and heaven, by which circumstance Divine miracles are distinguished from miracles not divine. *A. E.* 455. See also *A. C.* 6989.

Verse 31. *Tyre and Sidon.*—For the spiritual signification of "Tyre and Sidon," see above, Exposition, chap. iii. 8.

Verses 35 and 37. *And immediately his ears were opened.*— To "hear," in the Word, signifies not only simply to hear, but also to receive in the memory and to be instructed, also to receive in the understanding and to believe, likewise to receive in obedience and to do; the reason why these things are signified by "hearing" is, because the speech which is heard presents itself before the internal sight or understanding,

and is thus inwardly received, and there, according to the
efficacy of rational argument, or according to the powers of
persuasion from other sources, is either retained, or believed,
or obeyed.   Hence it is, that there is a correspondence of the
ear and of *hearing* with such things in the spiritual world,
concerning which correspondence, see n. 4652—4660, 5017,
7216, 8361, 8990.   That to "hear," denotes to receive in the
memory and to be instructed, also to receive in the understanding and to believe, likewise to receive in obedience and
to do, is evident from the following passages, as in Matthew,—
"I speak by parables, because seeing they do not see; and
hearing they do not *hear*, neither understand; that in them
may be fulfilled the prophecy of Isaiah, which saith, *Hearing*
ye shall *hear*, and shall not understand; and seeing ye shall
see, and shall not perceive: for the heart of this people is
waxed gross, and their *ears are dull of hearing*, and their eyes
have they closed; lest possibly they may see with their eyes,
and *hear* with their *ears*, and understand with their heart.
Blessed are your eyes, because they see: and your *ears*,
because they *hear*.   Many prophets and just men have desired
to see the things which ye see, but have not seen them; and
to *hear* the things which ye *hear*, but have not *heard* them."
(xiii. 13—17.)   In which passage to "hear" is applied in every
sense, as denoting both to be instructed, to believe, and to
obey; "hearing, they do not hear," denotes to be taught and
yet not to believe, also to be instructed and yet not to obey;
to be "dull of hearing," denotes to refuse instruction, faith,
and obedience; "blessed are your ears, for they hear," denotes
blessedness from the reception of the doctrine of faith concerning the Lord, and by the Word from the Lord.   So in
John,—"He that entereth in by the door is the shepherd of
the sheep, and the sheep *hear* his voice: all who have been
before Me were thieves and robbers, but the sheep did not
hear them.   Other sheep I have, which are not of this fold:
them also I must bring, and they shall *hear* My voice; and
there shall be one flock and one Shepherd.   My sheep *hear*
My voice, and I know them, and they follow Me;" (x. 2, 3,
8, 16, 27.) where, to "hear a voice," denotes to be instructed
concerning the precepts of faith, and to receive them in faith
and obedience.   Similar things are signified by what the Lord
so often said,—"He that hath an *ear* to *hear*, let him
hear;" also by these words in Mark,—"They said of Jesus,
He hath done all things well: for He maketh the *deaf* to *hear*,
and the dumb to speak;" (vii. 37.) where the "deaf" denote
those who are not acquainted with the truths of faith, and

on that account cannot live according to them, see n. 6989; to "hear" denotes to be instructed, to receive, and to obey. *A. C.* 9311.

TRANSLATOR'S NOTES AND OBSERVATIONS.

CHAPTER VII.

VERSE 3. *For the Pharisees, and all the Jews, except they wash their hands up to the wrist,* &c.—In the common version of the New Testament, what is here rendered "up to the wrist," is expressed by the adverb "oft," but the original Greek is πυγμη, which properly means *the fist,* and has accordingly been interpreted by some writers as denoting, in the present instance, *washing with the fist.* The learned Lightfoot, however, explains the phrase by *washing the hands as far as the fist extended,* that is, *up to the wrist.*

Verse 9. *Full well ye reject the commandment of God.*— What is here rendered "full well," is expressed in the original Greek by the adverb καλως, which means *well,* and which some writers, as Grotius and Parkhurst, have interpreted as being here applied *ironically,* or in the way of reproof. But probably the term is here adopted by the Lord, merely as expressive of the prudence of the Pharisees and Scribes in *securing their own tradition,* since, had they not first *rejected the commandment of God,* the tradition could not have been secured.

Verse 19. *Purging all meats.*—From the Lord's spiritual interpretation of the parable, of which these words make a part, it is evident, that a *rejected* or *ejected* thought, so far from defiling a man, rather tends to his purification, or, as it is here expressed, "purgeth all meats." It is not therefore the entrance of a thought *into the understanding* which ought to excite man's alarm, be it ever so evil and filthy, provided he be on his guard to prevent its admission into the *will* or *love.* For if this caution be used, the thought, in such case, operates like a *medicine,* which, by increasing the powers of digestion, has a tendency at the same time to cleanse and strengthen the constitution.

MARK.

CHAPTER VIII.

1. In those days there being much multitude, and they having nothing to eat, Jesus calling His disciples, saith unto them,

2. I have compassion on the multitude, because they have now been with Me three days, and have nothing to eat;

3. And if I send them away fasting to their own house, they will faint by the way: for some of them came from far.

4. And His disciples answered Him, From whence can any one satisfy these [men] with bread here in the wilderness?

5. And He asked them, How many loaves have ye? And they said, Seven.

6. And He commanded the multitude to sit down on the earth: and taking the seven loaves, when He had given thanks, He brake them, and gave them to His disciples to set before them; and they set them before the multitude.

That the communication of good and truth, and conjunction thereby, is effected between the Lord and His church. (Verses 1—10.)

And this of the Divine Mercy. (Verses 2, 3.)

Although it seemed impossible to those who were before destitute of good and truth. (Verse 4.)

Nevertheless it is necessary that inquiry should first be made by them concerning those heavenly principles and their origin. (Verse 5.)

And that they should enter into a state of internal rest by separation from concupiscences, and also should receive those principles with thanksgiving, through the medium of the Word. (Verse 6.)

7. And they had a few small fishes: and He blessed, and commanded to set them also before them.

8. And they did eat, and were satisfied: and they took up the overplus of the fragments, seven baskets.

9. But they that had eaten were about four thousand: and He dismissed them.

10. And immediately entering into a ship with His disciples, He came to the parts of Dalmanutha.

11. And the Pharisees came forth, and began to question with Him, asking of Him a sign from heaven, tempting Him.

12. And sighing deeply in His spirit, He saith, Why doth this generation seek a sign? Verily I say unto you, There shall no sign be given to this generation.

13. And having left them, He entered again into the ship, and departed to the other side.

14. And they had forgotten to take bread, and had in the ship with them only one loaf.

15. And He charged them, saying, Take heed, beware of the leaven of the Pharisees, and of the leaven of Herod.

16. And they reasoned among themselves, saying, [It is] because we have no bread.

17. And Jesus knowing, saith unto them, Why reason ye, because ye have no bread? Perceive ye not yet, neither understand? Have ye your heart yet hardened?

In which case the scientifics of good and truth would also be appropriated. (Verse 7.)

And full reception be enjoyed of all heavenly good. (Verses 8, 9.)

But it is otherwise with those of the perverse church, who therefore seek to be convinced in their understandings respecting truth, without any regard to heavenly good of love and charity in their wills. (Verses 10, 11.)

Which is a thing impossible, and therefore highly offensive to the Lord, and the cause of disjunction, and of inattention to the good of the Divine Mercy. (Verses 12, 13, 14.)

Which inattention ought more especially to be noted and guarded against. (Verse 15.)

Since the evil of all evils consists in possessing the light of truth in the understanding, and separating it from the good of love and charity in the will. (Verses 16—22.)

18. Having eyes, see ye not? And having ears, hear ye not? And do ye not remember?

19. When I brake the five loaves among five thousand, how many baskets full of fragments took ye up? They say unto Him, Twelve.

20. And when the seven among four thousand, how many baskets full of fragments took ye up? And they said, Seven.

21. And He said unto them, How is it that ye do not understand?

22. And He cometh to Bethsaida; and they bring to Him one that was blind, and besought Him to touch him.

23. And having taken the blind [man] by the hand, He led him out of the town; and having spit into his eyes, and laid hands upon him, He asked him if he saw anything.

24. And looking up, he said, I see men, for as trees I see them walking.

25. Then again He put [His] hands upon his eyes, and made him look up: and he was restored, and saw all men clearly.

26. And He sent him away to his house, saying, Neither go into the town, nor tell it to any one in the town.

X 27. And Jesus went out, and His disciples, to the towns of Cesarea Philippi: and in the way He asked His

Therefore the good of love and charity, and its increase by distribution, ought never to be lost sight of. (Verses 19, 20.)

That through communication with the LORD's Humanity, the intelligence of truth is restored in the church, to those who were in want of it. (Verses 22—26.)

First, by separating them from false principles; and next, by the communication of interior truth. (Verse 23.)

On which occasion intellectual sight is by degrees restored, consisting first in the perception of truth, and next in the affection of good. (Verses 24, 25.)

Which perception and affection cannot be imparted to those who are not in the desire of · truth and good. (Verse 26.)

They, therefore, who are of the church, ought to inquire concerning the LORD's Human disciples, saying unto them, Who do men say that I am?

28. And they answered, John the Baptist: and some [say], Elias; but others, One of the prophets.

29. And He saith unto them, But who say ye that I am? And Peter answering saith unto Him, Thou art the Christ.

30. And He charged them that they should tell no one of Him.

31. And He began to teach them, that the Son of Man must suffer many things, and be rejected of the elders, and the chief priests, and Scribes, and be killed, and after three days rise again.

32. And He spake the Word openly. And Peter taking Him aside, began to rebuke Him.

33. But He turning, and seeing His disciples, rebuked Peter, saying, Get thee behind Me, Satan: for thou mindest not the things that be of God, but the things that be of men.

34. And calling the people [to Him], with His disciples, He said unto them, Whosoever is willing to come after Me, let him deny himself, and take up his cross, and follow Me.

35. For whosoever is willing to save his soul, shall lose it; but whosoever shall lose his soul for My sake and the Gospel's, he shall save it.

Essence, so as not to confound it with that of other men. (Verses 27, 28.)

Because the faith of the church teaches that the LORD's Human Essence is the eternal Word, consequently Divine. (Verse 29.)

Which truth can only be received by those who are principled in good and truth. (Verse 30.)

These, therefore, are instructed concerning the LORD's temptations, and the glorification thereby of His Human Essence. (Verse 31.)

But they who profess faith alone, oppose this doctrine, and thus immerse themselves in infernal falses, by setting their own persuasions above the Divine Truth. (Verses 32, 33.)

Whereas they ought rather to acknowledge that all good and truth is from the LORD's Divine Humanity, and thus apply to Him for the removal of self-love, enduring patiently the temptations necessary for its removal. (Verse 34.)

Since in so doing they would attain conjunction of life with the LORD, which is a good of infinitely higher value than any temporal good whatsoever. (Verses 35—37.)

36. For what shall it profit a man, if he shall gain the whole world, and do hurt to his own soul?

37. Or what shall a man give in exchange for his soul?

38. For whosoever shall be ashamed of Me and of My Words in this adulterous and sinful generation; of him also shall the Son of Man be ashamed, when He cometh in the glory of His Father with the holy angels.

Whereas in rejecting the LORD and His Truth from their hearts and lives, they turn their backs at the same time on the HOLY WORD, on the Divine Humanity of the LORD, and on the angelic heaven which is in conjunction with that Humanity.

EXPOSITION.

CHAPTER VIII.

VERSES 1, 2. *The multitude having nothing to eat.*—In the Word mention is frequently made of "eating" and "drinking," and they who are unacquainted with the spiritual sense suppose that these expressions signify nothing more than natural *eating* and *drinking;* whereas they signify spiritual nourishment, consequently the appropriation of Good and Truth, "eating" signifying the appropriation of Good, and "drinking" the appropriation of Truth. Any one may know, who believes in the spirituality of the Word, that by "eating and drinking," as by bread, food, wine, and drink, is signified spiritual nourishment; for otherwise the Word would be merely natural, and not at the same time spiritual, thus only for the natural man, and not for the spiritual man, much less for the angels. To be spiritually nourished, is to be instructed and imbued, consequently it is to know, to understand, and to be wise; unless man enjoys this nourishment, together with the nourishment of the body, he is not a man but a beast, which is the reason that they who place all delight in feastings and banquetings, and daily indulge their palates, are stupid as to things spiritual, however they may be able to reason concerning the things of the world and of the body, whence, after their departure from this world, they live rather a beastly than a human life, for instead of intelligence and wisdom they have insanity and folly. In confirmation of what is here said respecting spiritual nourishment, we will adduce what the Lord says—"Man shall not live by bread only, but by every word which proceeds from the mouth of God." *A. E.* 627.

Verse 4. *In the wilderness.*—By "wilderness" in the Word is signified,—I. The church devastated, or in which all the Truths of the Word are falsified, such as it was among the Jews at the time of the Lord's advent. II. The church, in which there are not any Truths, because they are not possessed of the Word, such as it was among the well-disposed Gentiles in the Lord's time. III. A state of temptation, in which man is as it were without Truths, because he is surrounded by evil spirits who induce temptations, and then as it were take away his Truths.

I. That by "wilderness" is signified the devastated church, or the church in which all the Truths of the Word are falsified, such as it was among the Jews in the Lord's time, appears from these passages:—"Is this the man that made the earth to tremble, that did shake kingdoms; that made the world a *wilderness?*" (Isa. xiv. 16, 17.) speaking of Babel. "Thorns and thistles are come up on the land of My people; the palace shall be a *wilderness.*" (Isa. xxxii. 13, 14.) "I beheld, and lo, Carmel was a *wilderness;* the whole land shall be wasteness." (Jer. iv. 26, 27.) In which passages "earth" means the church, n. 285. "The pastors have destroyed My vineyard, they have reduced the field of My desire to a *wilderness of solitude:* the spoilers are come in the *wilderness.*" (Jer. xii. 10, 12.) "A vine is planted in the *wilderness,* in a land of dryness and thirst." (Ezek. xix. 13.) "The fire hath consumed the habitations of the *wilderness.*" (Joel i. 19, 20.) "The voice of one crying in the *wilderness,* Prepare ye the way of Jehovah; make straight in the *desert* a path for our God." (Isa. xl. 3.) Besides other places, as in Isa. xxiii. 12; xxxv. 1; Lament. v. 9; Hosea ii. 2, 3; xiii. 5, 15. That such also is the state of the church at this day, may be seen below, n. 566.

II. That by "wilderness" is meant the church in which there are not any Truths, because they are not possessed of the Word, as was the case with the well-disposed Gentiles in the Lord's time, appears from the following passages:—"The Spirit shall be poured upon you from on high; then the *wilderness* shall be a fruitful field, and judgment shall dwell

in the *wilderness*." (Isa. xxxii. 15, 16.) "I will put fountains
in the midst of the valleys: and make the *wilderness* a pool
of waters. I will give in the *wilderness* the shittim, cedar,
and the olive tree." (Isa. xli. 18, 19.) "He shall make the
wilderness a pool of waters, and the dry ground watersprings."
(Psalm cvii. 35.) "I will make a way in the *wilderness*, and
rivers in the *desert*, to give drink to My people, My chosen."
(Isa. xliii. 19, 20.) "Jehovah will make her *wilderness* like
Eden, and her *desert* like the garden of Jehovah; joy and
gladness shall be found therein." (Isa. li. 3.) "The habitations of the *wilderness* distil." (Psalm lxv. 12.) "Let the
wilderness lift up its voice: let the inhabitants of the rock
sing." (Isa. xlii. 11.)

III. That by "wilderness" is signified a state of temptation,
in which man is as it were without Truths, because he is
surrounded by evil spirits who induce temptation, and then as
it were deprive him of Truths, appears from Matt. iv. 1, 2, 3;
Mark i. 12, 13; Luke iv. 1, 2, 3; Jer. ii. 2, 6, 7; Hosea ii.
14—16; Psalm cvii. 4—7; Deut. i. 31—33; viii. 2, 3, 4, 15, 16;
xxxii. 10. *A. R.* 546.

Verses 5, 6, 8. *And He asked them, How many loaves have*
ye? And they said, Seven. And He commanded the multitude
to sit down on the earth: and taking the seven loaves, when
He had given thanks, He brake them, &c. And they took up
the overplus of their fragments, seven baskets.—Inasmuch as,
in the prophetic Book of the Apocalypse, frequent mention is
made of numbers, and no one can know the spiritual sense of
the things contained in that book, unless it be known what
each particular number signifies, for all numbers in the Word,
like all names, signify spiritual things; and whereas the number
seven is often named amongst the rest, therefore I am desirous
here to shew that the number "seven" signifies all and all things,
both what is full and the whole; for whatsoever signifies all
and all things, that also signifies what is full and the whole,
since what is full and the whole is predicated of the magni-
tude of a thing, and all, and all things of multitude. That the
number "seven" has these significations, may be manifest from
the following passages:—"The hungry have ceased, until the
barren hath borne *seven;* but she that hath many children is
waxed feeble;" (1 Sam. ii. 5.) where the "hungry who have
ceased," are those who desire the truths and goods of the church;
the "barren that have born seven," signifies those who are out
of the church, and are not acquainted with truths, because they
have not the Word; thus the Gentiles are signified, to whom
all truths will be given; "she that hath many children being
waxed feeble," signifies those who have truths, from whom

they will be taken away. And in David,—"Recompense to our neighbours *sevenfold* into their bosoms;" (Psalm lxxix. 12.) where "sevenfold" signifies fully. And in Luke,—"If thy brother shall sin against thee *seven* times in a day, and *seven* times in a day shall return to thee, saying, I repent, thou shalt forgive him;" (xvii. 4.) where, to "forgive sins seven times," if he "returned seven times," is to forgive as often as he returned, thus on all occasions. And in David,—"*Seven* times in a day do I praise Thee, because of Thy judgments of justice;" (Psalm cxix. 164.) where "seven times in a day" denotes always, or at all times. Again,—"The words of Jehovah are pure words: as silver tried in a furnace of earth, purified *seven* times;" (xii. 6.) where "silver" denotes truth from the Divine Being; "purified seven times" signifies altogether, and fully pure. From the signification of the number "seven," it may be manifest what is signified by the "*seven* days of creation;" (Gen. i.) also by "four thousand men being fed from *seven* loaves, and that *seven* baskets full remained over and above." (Matt. xv. 34—38; Mark viii. 5—9.) Hence too it is evident what is signified in the Apocalypse by "*seven* churches;" (i. 4, 11.) by "*seven* golden candlesticks, in the midst of which was the Son of Man;" (i. 13.) by "*seven* stars in His right hand;" (i. 16, 20.) by "the *seven* Spirits of God;" (iii. I.) by "the *seven* lamps of fire before the throne;" (iv. 5.) by "the book sealed with *seven* seals;" (v. 1.) by "the *seven* angels, to whom were given *seven* trumpets;" (viii. 2.) by "the *seven* thunders uttering voices;" (x. 3, 4.) by "the *seven* angels having the *seven* last plagues;" (xv. 1, 6.) and by "the *seven* vials full of the *seven* last plagues;" (xvi. 1; xxi. 9.) and in other parts of the Word where the number "seven" is named. *A. E.* 257.

Verse 11. *Asking of Him a sign from heaven, tempting Him.*—By a "sign" is understood that which declares, testifies, and persuades concerning a thing inquired after. But by a "miracle" is understood that which excites, strikes, and induces astonishment; thus a *sign* moves the understanding and faith, and a *miracle* the will and its affection. For the will and its affection is what is excited, is stricken, and amazed; and the understanding and its faith is what is persuaded, what a declaration is made to, and which admits of testification. That in the above words, by "asking and shewing a sign," is signified to testify by somewhat stupendous, or by a voice from heaven, is evident; but whereas such a testification would have condemned them rather than have saved them, therefore Jesus said—"There shall no *sign* be given to this generation." *A. E.* 706.

Verse 11. *From heaven.*—It should be known that "heaven" is not in any certain and determinate place, thus not on high, according to the vulgar opinion, but "heaven" is where the Divine Being or the Lord is, thus with every one and in every one who is in charity and faith, for charity and faith are heaven, because they are from the Divine Being; the angels also dwell there.   That heaven is where the Lord is, is evident from this consideration, that Mount Sinai, from which the Lord spake, is called heaven, which also is the reason why by "Mount Sinai" is signified heaven, whence divine Truth is.   *A. C.* 8930.

Verse 15. *Beware of the leaven of the Pharisees, and of the leaven of Herod.*—"Leaven" signifies evil and the false, whereby celestial and spiritual things are rendered impure and profane.   The conjunction of the Lord with mankind is effected by love and charity, and by faith grounded therein. Those celestial and spiritual things were represented by the *unleavened* bread which was eaten on the days of the passover, and it was to prevent the defilement of those things by any profane principles, that "leaven" was forbidden, under the severe penalty of being "cut off from Israel;" (Exod. xii. 15.) for they who profane things celestial and spiritual must needs perish.   *A. C.* 2342.

Verse 17. *Have ye your heart yet hardened?*—As to "hardness of heart," see above, Exposition, chap. iii. 5.

Verses 17, 18. *And Jesus knowing, saith unto them, Why reason ye, because ye have no bread? Perceive ye not, neither understand? Have ye your heart yet hardened? Having eyes, see ye not? And having ears, hear ye not? And do ye not remember?*—By the "eye" is signified the understanding, and the reason is, because the sight of the body corresponds to the sight of its spirit, which is the understanding; and inasmuch as it corresponds, by the "eye" in the Word, wheresoever in general it is named, is signified the understanding, even where it is believed to have another signification, as where the Lord says in Matthew,—"The lamp of the body is the *eye:* if the *eye* be simple, the whole body is lucid; if the *eye* be evil, the whole body is darkened;" (vi. 22, 23.) where the "eye" denotes the understanding, the spiritual principle of which is faith; which also may be manifest, from the explication there given,—"If therefore the light which is in thee be darkened, how great is that darkness?"   In like manner in the same Evangelist,—"If thy right *eye* scandalize, pluck it out, and cast it from thee." (v. 29; xviii. 9.)   The "left eye" is the intellectual principle, but the "right eye" is its affection; the "plucking out the right eye" denotes that the affection, if it scandalize, ought to be subdued.   And in Luke,—"Jesus said to the disciples, Blessed are the *eyes* which see the things that ye see;" (x. 23.) where, by the "eyes which see," is signified intelligence and faith; for the sight of the Lord, also of His miracles and works, did not render any one blessed, but they were blessed because they apprehended with the understanding and had faith, which is to see with the eyes; for the understanding is the spiritual principle of sight, and faith is the spiritual principle of the understanding.   The sight of the eye is from the light of the world; the sight of the understanding is from the light of heaven, flowing in to those things which are of the light of the world; but the sight of faith is from the light of heaven.   Hence mention is made of "seeing with the understanding," and of "seeing by faith." And in Mark,—"Jesus said to the disciples, How is it that ye know not, neither understand?   Is your heart still hardened? Having *eyes*, see ye not?   And having ears, hear ye not?" (viii. 17, 18.) where it is evident that not to be willing to understand and not to believe, is to "have eyes, and not to see."   *A. C.* 2701.

Verse 19. *Twelve baskets of fragments.*—See above, Exposition, chap. vi. 35—45.

Verse 22. *They bring to Him one that was blind.*—By all the "blind" whom the Lord healed, are understood those who are in ignorance and who receive Him, and are illustrated by the Word from Him.   And, in general, by all the miracles of the Lord are signified such things as appertain to heaven and the church, thus spiritual things; from which circumstance His miracles were divine, for it is divine to act from first [principles], and so to present or exhibit those things in ultimates.   *A. E.* 239.

Verses 34, 35. *And calling the people, with His disciples, He said unto them, Whosoever is willing to come after Me, let him deny himself, and take up his cross, and follow Me. For whosoever is willing to save his soul, shall lose it; but whosoever shall lose his soul, for My sake and the Gospel's, he shall save it.*—Concerning combats against evils, which are temptations, much is said in many passages in the Word; they are meant by these words of the Lord:—"I say unto you, Except a grain of wheat fall into the ground and die, it abideth alone: but if it die, it bringeth forth much fruit." (John xii. 24.)   Also by these words,—"Whosoever would come after Me, let him deny himself, and take up his *cross*, and follow Me.   Whosoever would save his life, shall lose it; but he that will lose it, for My sake and the Gospel's, the same shall save it;" (Mark viii. 34, 35.) where, by the "cross," is meant temptation, as likewise in Matthew, x. 38; xvi. 24; Mark x. 21; Luke xiv. 27.   By the "soul" is meant the life of the selfhood of man; as likewise, Matt. x. 39; xvi. 25; Luke ix. 24; and especially John xii. 25; which also is the life of the "flesh that profiteth nothing." (John vi. 63.) Concerning combats against evils, and victories over them, the Lord speaks to all the churches in the Apocalypse: to the church in Ephesus,—"To him who *overcometh*, I will give to eat of the tree of life, which is in the midst of the paradise of God." (Rev. ii. 7.)   To the church in Smyrna,—"He who *overcometh* shall not be hurt in the second death." (ii. 11.) To the church in Pergamos,—"To him who *overcometh* will I give to eat of the hidden manna; and I will give him a white stone, and on the stone a new name written, which no one knoweth but he who receiveth." (ii. 17.)   To the church in Thyatira,—"To him who *overcometh*, and keepeth My works to the end, I will give power over the nations, and the morning star." (ii. 26, 28.)   To the church in Sardis,—"Him that *overcometh* will I make a pillar in the temple of my God, and I will write upon him the name of God, and the name of the city of God, the New Jerusalem, which cometh down out of heaven from God: and [I will write upon him] My new name." (iii. 12.)   To the church in Laodicea,—"To him who *overcometh* will I give to sit with Me on My throne." (iii. 21.) Concerning those combats, which are temptations, the subject may be seen specifically treated of in the "Doctrine of the New Jerusalem," published in London in the year 1758, from n. 187 to 201: whence they are, and of what quality, n. 196, 197: how and when they take place, n. 198: what good they effect, n. 199: that the Lord fights for man, n. 200: concerning the Lord's combats or temptations, n. 201. *D. Life*, 99.

In the above passage, by "cross" are meant temptations; and by "following the Lord," is meant to acknowledge His Divinity, and to do His precepts; that this is meant by "following the Lord," may be seen above, n. 864.   The reason why temptations are meant by a "cross" is, because evils and the false principles thence derived, which adhere to man from his birth, infest and thus torment those who are natural, during the time that they become spiritual; and whereas evils and the false principles thence derived, which infest and torment, cannot be dispersed but by temptations; hence temptations are signified by a "cross."   On this account the Lord says, that His followers are to "deny themselves, and take up their *cross*," that is, that they are to reject whatever is of self, their "cross" being the selfhood of man, against which they are to engage in combats.   So in another place,—"Jesus said to the rich man, who asked Him what he ought to do that he might inherit eternal life, Thou knowest the commandments; thou shalt not commit adultery, thou shalt not kill, thou shalt not steal, thou shalt not bear false witness, thou shalt not defraud, honour thy father and mother. He answering, said, All these things have I kept from my youth.   Jesus looked at him and loved him, yet He said unto him, One thing thou lackest: go thy way, sell what thou hast, and give to the poor, so shalt thou have treasure in the heavens; nevertheless, *follow Me*, taking up the *cross*." (Mark x. 17, 19, 20, 21.)   Here also by "following the Lord," and "taking up the cross," similar things are signified as above, viz., to acknowledge the Divinity of the Lord, and the Lord to be the God of heaven and earth, for without that acknowledgment no one can abstain from evils and do good, except from himself, and except it be meritorious; the good, which is good in itself, and good not meritorious, is only from the Lord, wherefore unless the Lord be acknowledged, and that all good is from Him, man cannot be saved; but before any one can do good from the Lord, he must undergo temptation.   The reason is, because by temptation the internal of man is opened, by which man is conjoined to heaven.   Now since no one can do the precepts without the Lord, therefore the Lord said—"Yet lackest thou one thing: sell all that thou hast, and follow Me, taking up the cross;" that is, that he ought to acknowledge the Lord, and undergo temptations. That he should "sell all that he had, and give to the poor,' in the spiritual sense, signifies that he should alienate and reject from himself the things of self, thus it signifies the same as above, that he should *deny himself;* and by "giving to the poor," in the spiritual sense, is signified the doing works of charity.   The reason why the Lord so spake to the rich man was, because he was rich; and by "riches," in the spiritual sense, are signified the knowledges of what is good and true, and with him who was a Jew, the knowledges of what is evil and false, because they were traditions; hence it may be manifest that the Lord spake here, as in other places, by correspondences. *A. E.* 893.

Verse 34. *Whosoever is willing to come after Me, let him deny himself, and take up his cross, and follow Me.*—That to "go after the Lord," and to "follow Him," is to deny self, is evident, and to "deny self," is not to be led of self, but of the Lord; and he denies himself who shuns and holds in aversion all evils because they are sins, which, when man holds in aversion, he is led of the Lord, for he does His precepts not from himself, but from the Lord. Similar things are signified in other passages also by "following the Lord," as Matt. xix. 21, 28; Mark ii. 14, 15; iii. 7, 8; x. 21, 28, 29; Luke xviii. 22, 28; John xii. 26; xiii. 36, 37; xxi. 19—22. From these considerations it may be manifest, that to "follow the Lord," is to be led by Him, and not by self; and no other person can be led by the Lord, except him who is not led by himself, and every one is led by himself who does not shun evils because they are contrary to the Word, and thus are contrary to God, consequently, because they are sins and from hell; every one who does not thus shun evils and hold them in aversion, is led by himself. The reason is, because the evil which is hereditarily in man, makes his life, inasmuch as it is his selfhood, and man, before those evils are removed, does all things from them, thus from himself. But it is otherwise when evils are removed, as is the case when they are shunned because they are infernal; for in this case the Lord enters with truths and goods out of heaven, and leads man. The primary cause is, because every man is his own love, and man, as to his spirit, which lives after death, is nothing but the affection which is of his love, and every evil is from his love, thus it is of his love. Hence it follows that the love or affection of man cannot otherwise be reformed, but by the shunning of evils and holding them in spiritual aversion, which is to shun and hold them in aversion because they are infernal. From these considerations it may now be manifest what it is to "follow the Lord." *A. E.* 864.

Verse 35. *For whosoever is willing to save his soul, shall lose it*, &c.—By "loving their soul," is signified to love self and the world, for by "soul" is signified man's proper life, which every one has by birth, which consists in loving himself and the world above all things; therefore by "not loving their soul," is signified not to love self and the world more than the Lord and the things which are of the Lord; "unto death," signifies to be willing to die rather; consequently it is to love the Lord above all things, and one's neighbour as one's self, (Matt. xxii. 35—38.) and to be willing to die rather than give up those two loves. The same is signified by these words of the Lord:—"Whosoever is willing to find *his soul*, shall lose it; and whosoever loseth *his soul* for the sake of Jesus, shall find it." (Matt. x. 39; Luke xvii. 33.) "He that loveth *his soul* shall lose it; but he that hateth *his soul* in this world, shall preserve it unto life eternal." (John xii. 25.) "Jesus said, If any man will come after Me, let him deny himself; he that is willing to save *his soul*, shall lose it; and he that loseth *his soul*, for My sake, shall find it. What is a man profited, if he shall gain the whole world, and lose *his soul?* or what price can a man give sufficient for the redemption of *his soul?*" (Matt. xvi. 24, 25; Mark viii. 35, 36, 37; Luke ix. 24, 25.) By "loving the Lord," is meant to love to do His commandments. (John xiv. 20—24.) The reason is, because He Himself is His commandments, for they are from Him, therefore He is in them, and consequently is in the man in whose life they are engraven; and they are engraven in man by willing and doing them. *A. R.* 556.

Verse 35.—Every man who is reformed, is first reformed as to his *internal* man, and afterwards as to his *external*. The internal man is not reformed by merely knowing and understanding the truths and goods by which a man is saved, but by willing and loving them; but the external man is reformed by speaking and doing the things which the internal man wills and loves, and in the degree this is done the man is regenerated. That he is not regenerated before, is, because his internal is not before this in its effect, but only in the cause, and the cause, unless it is in the effect, is dissipated, for it is like a house founded upon the ice, which falls to the ground when the ice is melted by the sun. In a word, he is like a man without feet upon which he can stand and walk. *A. R.* 510.

Verse 36. *What shall it profit a man, if he shall gain the whole world*, &c.—From these words it is manifest that worldly blessing is nothing in respect to heavenly blessing, which is eternal; but the man who is immersed in worldly and earthly things does not comprehend this, for worldly and earthly things suffocate and annihilate a belief in life eternal. *A. C.* 8939.

Verse 38. *For whosoever shall be ashamed of Me and My words in this adulterous and sinful generation, of him also shall the Son of Man be ashamed*, &c.—By "committing adultery," in a spiritual sense, is meant to adulterate the goods of the Word, and to falsify its truths. That this is meant by committing adultery, has been heretofore unknown to mankind, because the spiritual sense of the Word has remained heretofore undiscovered; but that this is signified in the Word by "committing whoredoms, adulteries, and fornications," is very evident from the following passages:—"I have seen also in the prophets of Jerusalem a horrible thing: they *commit adultery*, and walk in lies." (Jer. xxiii. 14.) "They have *committed villany* in Israel, they have *committed adultery*, and have spoken lying words in My name." (Jer. xxix. 23.)

19

" They shall *commit whoredom,* because they have left off to
take heed to the Lord." (Hosea iv. 10.) Forasmuch as the
Jewish nation had falsified the Word, therefore it is called by
the Lord an "adulterous generation;" (Matt. xii. 39; Mark
viii. 38.) and the "seed of the adulterer;" (Isa. lvii. 3.) not
to mention other passages in the Word, where by "adulteries
and whoredoms" are understood *adulterations* and *falsifications* of the Word, as in Jer. iii. 6, 8; xiii. 27; Ezek. xvi.
15, 16, 26, 28, 29, 32, 33; xxiii. 2, 3, 5, 7, 11, 14, 16, 17;
Hosea v. 3; vi. 10; Nahum iii. 4.   *T.C.R.* 314.   See also
A.R. 134.   *A.E.* 222.

Verse 38. *When He cometh in the glory of His Father with
the holy angels.*—The angels of heaven by "glory" perceive
nothing else than the divine Truth, and because all divine
Truth is from the Lord, by "giving glory to Him," (Apoc.
xiv. 7.) they perceive the acknowledgment and confession that
all Truth is from Him. For all the glory in the heavens is
from no other Source, and in the degree that a society of
heaven is in the divine Truth, all things there are splendid,
and the angels are in the splendour of glory. That by "glory"
is understood the divine Truth, is evident from the following
passages:—"The voice of one crying in the wilderness, Prepare
the way of Jehovah; the *glory* of Jehovah shall be revealed,
and all flesh shall see it." (Isa. xl. 3, 5.) "I will give Thee
for a covenant of the people, a light of the Gentiles; and My
glory I will not give to another;" (Isa. xlii. 6, 8.) and in many
other passages. *A.R.* 629.

*Of him shall the Son of Man be ashamed, when He cometh
in the glory of His Father.*—That Divine Truth is the Son,
and Divine Good the Father, may be manifest from the signification of "Son," as denoting truth, and of "Father," as
denoting good; also from the conception and nativity of truth,
as being from good. The reason why "Son" is Divine Truth,
and "Father" Divine Good, is, because the union of the Divine
Essence with the Human, and of the Human with the Divine,
is the marriage of Divine Good with Truth, and of Truth with
Good, from which comes the heavenly marriage; for in Jehovah
or the Lord there is nothing but what is infinite, and inasmuch
as it is infinite, it cannot be apprehended by any idea, only
that it is the *esse* and *existere* of all good and truth, or Good
itself and Truth itself. Good itself is the Father, and Truth
itself is the Son; but whereas there is a divine marriage, as
was said, of Good and Truth, and of Truth and Good, the
Father is in the Son, and the Son in the Father, as the Lord
Himself teaches in John,—"Now is the Son of Man glorified,

and God is glorified in Him; if God be glorified in Him, God shall also glorify Him in Himself." Hence it may be manifest what is the quality of the union of the Divinity and Humanity in the Lord, viz., that it is mutual, or reciprocal, which union is what is called the divine marriage, from which descends the heavenly marriage, which is the kingdom of the Lord in the heavens. *A. C.* 2803.

The Divine Truth in the Human Divine [principle] of the Lord, which endured temptations, is not the Divine Truth Itself, for this is above all temptation; but it is the rational truth such as angels have, consisting in appearances of truth, and is what is called the " Son of Man," but *before* glorification; but the Divine Truth in the Divine Human [principle] of the Lord glorified is above appearances, neither can it come to any understanding, still less to the apprehension of man, nor even to that of angels, thus it cannot at all be subject to temptation. Concerning this Divine Truth, or Son of Man glorified, it is thus written in John:—" Jesus said, Now is the Son of Man glorified, and God is glorified in Him; if God be glorified in Him, God shall also glorify Him in Himself, and shall straightway glorify Him." (xiii. 31, 32.) That a distinct idea may be had of this very great mystery, it is allowed to call the truth appertaining to the Lord, which was capable of being tempted, and which endured temptations, *Truth Divine in the Human Divine [principle] of the Lord,* but to call the Truth which could not be tempted or undergo any temptation, because it was glorified, *Divine Truth in the Divine Human [principle] of the Lord. A. C.* 2814. See also 9429, 10,053, 10,067; *D. Lord,* 35; and *T. C. R.* 128.

TRANSLATOR'S NOTES AND OBSERVATIONS.

CHAPTER VIII.

Verse 15. *And He charged them, saying, Take heed, beware of the leaven of the Pharisees, and of the leaven of Herod.*— What is here rendered, " Take heed, beware of," is expressed in the original Greek by the two terms ορατε, βλεπετε, both of which have relation to the sight of the eye, whilst the former, viz., ορατε, is expressive of a more interior sight, and the latter, viz., βλεπετε, of a more exterior sight. The two terms, therefore, as being here spiritually applied, have relation to the *understanding and its sight*, and evidently imply an admonition to explore attentively *the leaven of the Pharisees and the leaven of Herod*, by every power of the understanding, both *interior* and *exterior*.

Verse 24. *I see men, for as trees I see* [*them*] *walking.*— In the common version of the New Testament, these words are rendered, "I see men as trees, walking," but in the original Greek the words are thus written:—βλεπω τους ανθρωπους οτι ως δενδρα ορω περιπατουντας; where it is plain that two distinct expressions are applied to denote seeing, viz., βλεπω and ορω, and that the conjunction οτι is also added in a causal sense, as denoting the reason of this double sight. It deserves further to be noted that the *first* sight here spoken of, is expressed by the Greek βλεπω, which, as has been shewn in a foregoing note, has reference to a more *external* sight, and that the *second* sight is expressed by the Greek ορω, which has reference to a more interior sight. Perhaps it may not be easy to discover the full scope of the passage in regard both to its natural and spiritual meaning, but surely one thing is certain, viz., that the *two* terms expressive of sight ought to be preserved, together with the conjunction by which they are united.

MARK.

CHAPTER IX.

THE WORD.

1. AND He said unto them, Verily I say unto you, That there are some of them that stand here, who shall not taste of death, till they have seen the kingdom of God coming in power.

2. And after six days Jesus taketh Peter, and James, and John, and leadeth them up into a high mountain apart by themselves: and He was transformed before them.

3. And His raiment became shining, exceeding white, as snow; so as no fuller on earth can whiten it.

4. And there appeared unto them Elias with Moses: and they were talking with Jesus.

5. And Peter answering, said unto Jesus, Rabbi, it is good for us to be here: and let us make three tabernacles; one for Thee, and one for Moses, and one for Elias.

6. For he knew not what to say; for they were sore afraid.

7. And there was a cloud that overshadowed them; and

THE INTERNAL SENSE.

BUT it is otherwise with those who are principled in faith, in charity, and in works of charity, for these no longer experience any separation of life from the Divine Being, but behold heaven opened through the LORD's Divine Humanity, and see in that Humanity the All of Divinity. (Verses 1, 2.)

And that from it proceeds all Divine Truth, both historical and prophetical. (Verses 3, 4.)

Which state of interior perception affects the will of those who are in the truths of the church, so that they earnestly desire the reception of the Word in themselves, yet know not how it can be accomplished. (Verses 5, 6.)

Until they are instructed from the letter, that they

a voice came out of the cloud, saying, This is My beloved Son: hear ye Him.

8. And suddenly looking around them, they saw no one any more, but Jesus only with themselves.

9. But as they came down from the mountain, He charged them that they should tell no man what they had seen, until the Son of Man were risen from the dead.

10. And they kept the word to themselves, questioning amongst themselves what the rising from the dead should mean.

11. And they asked Him, saying, Why say the Scribes that Elias must first come?

12. But He answering, said unto them, Elias indeed cometh first, and restoreth all things; and how it is written of the Son of Man, that He must suffer many things, and be set at nought.

13. But I say unto you, That Elias has already come, and they have done unto him whatsoever they willed, as it is written of him.

14. And coming to the disciples, He saw much multitude about them, and the Scribes questioning with them.

15. And immediately all the multitude, seeing Him, were greatly amazed, and running to [Him], saluted Him.

16. And He asked the Scribes, What question ye with them?

ought to obey the LORD, who is Divine Truth, or the Word. (Verse 7.)

And who on this occasion is seen to be the All of the Word in themselves. (Verse 8.)

Which yet cannot be seen but by faith in the LORD's Divine Humanity. (Verses 9, 10.)

Agreeably to the testimony of the Word, which teaches that the LORD's Humanity was glorified, or made Divine, by temptation-combats, in which it was representative of the Word, and suffered itself to be treated as the Word itself had been treated by the church. (Verses 11, 12, 13.)

That much inquiry is made in the church concerning goods and truths, and especially concerning the LORD's Humanity. (Verses 14, 15.)

So that application is made in favour of those who, through infernal influence, are destitute

17. And one of the multitude answering, said, Teacher, [Διδασκαλε,] I have brought my son unto Thee, having a dumb spirit;

18. And wheresoever he taketh him, he teareth him: and he foameth, and gnasheth with his teeth, and pineth away: and I said to Thy disciples that they should cast him out; and they could not.

19. But He answering him, saith, O faithless generation, how long shall I be with you? How long shall I suffer you? Bring him unto Me.

20. And they brought him unto Him: and seeing Him, immediately the spirit tare him; and falling on the earth, he wallowed foaming.

21. And He asked his father, How long is it ago since this came unto him? And he said, From a child.

22. And ofttimes he casteth him into the fire, and into the waters, to destroy him: but if Thou canst do any thing, have compassion upon us, and help us.

23. But Jesus said to him, If thou canst believe, all things are possible to him that believeth.

24. And immediately the father of the child crying out, said with tears, I believe, O Lord; help Thou mine unbelief!

25. And Jesus seeing that the multitude ran together, rebuked the unclean spirit,

of the perception and understanding of truth, that they may be delivered from such influence. (Verses 16, 17, and former part of the 18th verse.)

Which yet cannot be affected by goods and truths, unless in conjunction with their Divine Source. (Verse 18, latter part.)

To accomplish which conjunction, successive changes of state are necessary, both of Divine consolation and of temptation-combats. (Verse 19.)

And these temptation-combats become extreme, in proportion as the Divine presence is near, and operative to gain the victory. (Verse 20.)

Commencing at the first period of regeneration, sometimes by the lusts of evil in the will, and sometimes by the seduction of false principles in the understanding, but in all cases tending to the manifestation of the Divine mercy, and of the Omnipotence of a right faith grounded in that mercy. (Verses 21, 22, 23, 24.)

Which faith, being directed to the Lord's Divine Humanity, draws from Him a Divine saying unto him, [Thou] dumb and deaf spirit, I charge thee, come out of him, and enter no more into him.

26. And crying out and violently rending him, he came out: and he was as one dead; insomuch that many said that he was dead.

27. But Jesus having taken him by the hand, lifted him up; and he arose.

28. And when He came into the house, His disciples asked Him privately, Why could not we cast him out?

29. And He said unto them, This kind can come out by nothing but by prayer and fasting.

30. And departing thence, they passed through Galilee; and He was not willing that any one should know [it].

31. For He taught His disciples, and said unto them, The Son of Man is delivered into the hands of men, and they shall kill Him; and after that He is killed, He shall rise the third day.

32. But they understood not the saying, and were afraid to ask Him.

33. And He came to Capernaum: and being in the house, He asked them, What was it that ye disputed about among yourselves by the way?

34. But they were silent: for by the way they had disputed among themselves who should be the greatest.

Power for the restoration of the perception and understanding of truth, and for the total removal of infernal influence. (Verses 25, 26.)

Yet not without violent opposition from the infernals, insomuch that it appears as if they prevailed to destroy all perception and understanding both of good and truth, when yet this is merely an appearance. (Verses 26, 27.)

Nevertheless this opposition can only be overcome by those whose interiors are opened, through temptation-combats, to the LORD's Divine Humanity. (Verses 28, 29.)

Therefore the LORD endured those combats, and thus glorified, or made Divine, His Human Principle. (Verses 30, 31.)

Which is a doctrine little understood, because the natural man is alarmed at it. (Verse 32.)

For the natural man is eager to exalt himself in self-love, rather than to abase himself under a sense of his own nothingness. (Verses 33, 34.)

35. And having sat down, He called the twelve, and saith unto them, If any one be willing to be first, let him be the last of all, and the servant of all.

36. And having taken a child, He set him in the midst of them: and having taken him into His arms, He said unto them,

37. Whosoever shall receive one of such children in My name, receiveth Me: and whosoever receiveth Me, receiveth not Me, but Him that sent Me.

38. But John answered Him, saying, Teacher, [Διδασκαλε,] we saw a certain one casting out devils in Thy name, who followed not us: and we forbad him, because he followed not us.

39. But Jesus said, Forbid him not: for there is no one who shall do a mighty work in My name, and can readily speak evil of Me.

40. For he that is not against us is for us.

41. For whosoever shall give you a cup of water to drink in My name, because ye are of Christ, verily I say unto you, he shall not lose his reward.

42. And whosoever shall offend one of the little ones that believe in Me, it is better for him that a millstone were hanged about his neck, and he were cast into the sea.

43. And if thy hand offend thee, cut it off: it is better

When yet the eternal Truth teaches, that man becomes great only by the humility which inclines him to promote the good of others, and that innocence therefore ought to be exalted above every other good, since all who are in innocence are in the LORD, and the LORD in them. (Verses 36, 37.)

Mankind, therefore, ought not to be judged from outward profession, or from the religious sect to which they belong, but from the sincerity with which they oppose and reject what is evil because it is sin against the LORD. (Verses 38, 39, 40.)

For all who, from a principle of obedience, do what is good and true, are the LORD's children and heirs of His kingdom. (Verse 41.)

As, on the other hand, all who reject innocence, separate themselves from the LORD, and plunge themselves into all infernal evils and falses. (Verse 42.)

Therefore every natural affection which rejects the

for thee to enter maimed into life, than having two hands to go into hell [gehenna], into the fire that never shall be quenched:

44. Where their worm dieth not, and the fire is not quenched.

45. And if thy foot offend thee, cut it off: it is better for thee to enter halt into life, than having two feet to be cast into hell [gehenna], into the fire that cannot be quenched:

46. Where their worm dieth not, and the fire is not quenched.

47. And if thine eye offend thee, pluck it out: it is better for thee to enter into the kingdom of God with one eye, than having two eyes to be cast into the hell [gehenna] of fire:

48. Where their worm dieth not, and the fire is not quenched.

49. For every one shall be salted with fire, and every sacrifice shall be salted with salt.

50. Salt is good: but if the salt become saltless, wherewith shall ye season it? Have salt in yourselves, and be at peace one with another.

goods of innocence, ought to be separated, since it is safer to be in simple good without genuine truth, than to know what is good and true, and yet oppose it. (Verses 43, 44, 45, 46.)

In like manner the natural thought of the understanding, which rejects the truths of innocence, ought to be discarded, since it is better not to know and apprehend such truths, than to know and apprehend, and still live a life of evil. (Verses 47, 48.)

For all genuine good desires truth, and all genuine truth desires good, in which case it becomes good, and therefore all ought to cherish such desire, by cherishing the spirit of mutual love, which is the source from the Lord of true peace. (Verses 49, 50.)

EXPOSITION.

CHAPTER IX.

Verses 1—11. *And after six days, Jesus taketh Peter, and James, and John, and leadeth them up into a high mountain apart by themselves: and was transformed before them,* &c.— In this "transformation" the Lord represented the Divine Truth, which is the Word, for the Lord, when He was in the world, made His Humanity Divine Truth, and when He went out of the world, He made His Humanity Divine Good, by uniting it with the essential Divine principle, which was in Himself from conception. That the Lord made His Humanity Divine Truth when He was in the world, and afterwards Divine Good, may be seen in the "Doctrine of the New Jerusalem," n. 303, 304, 305, 306; and that the Lord is the Word, n. 263; hence it is that singular the things which were seen at His "transformation," signify the Divine Truth proceeding from the Divine Good of the Lord. The Divine Good of the Divine Love which was in Him, and from which in His Humanity was Divine Truth, was represented by "His face shining as the sun;" for the "face" represents the interiors; wherefore by the *face* the interiors present themselves in lucidity, and the "sun" signifies the Divine Love, see above, n. 401, 424; the Divine Truth was represented by "raiment, which became as light." "Raiment," in the Word, signifies truths; and the Lord's "raiment," Divine Truth, see also above, n. 64, 271, 395; wherefore also they appeared as *light,* for Divine Truth makes light in the angelic heaven, and hence "light" in the Word signifies Divine Truth, on which subject see the Treatise on "Heaven and Hell," n. 126—140.

Inasmuch as the Word, which is Divine Truth, was represented, therefore "Moses and Elias were seen talking with Him;" for by Moses and Elias are signified the Word, by Moses the historical Word, and by Elias the prophetic Word. But the Word in the letter was represented by the "cloud which overshadowed the disciples, and into which they entered," for by "disciples" in the Word was represented the church, which at that time and afterwards was principled only in truths derived from the sense of the letter; and whereas revelations and responses were given by Divine Truth in ultimates, as was

said in a former article, and this truth is such as is the truth
of the sense of the letter of the Word, therefore it came to
pass that a "voice was heard out of the cloud, saying, This is
My beloved Son: hear ye Him;" that is, that He is Divine
Truth or the Word.   He who does not know that by "cloud,"
in the spiritual sense of the Word, is meant the Word in
the letter, cannot know the arcanum which is involved in the
following passages:—"That in the consummation of the age,
they should see the Son of Man coming in the *clouds* of heaven
with power and glory." (Matt. xxiv. 30; Mark xiii. 26; xiv.
61, 62; Luke xxi. 27.)   Also in the Apocalypse,—"Behold,
Jesus Christ cometh with *clouds;* and every eye shall see
Him;" (i. 7.) and in another place,—"I saw, and lo, a white
cloud, and one like to the Son of Man, sitting upon the *cloud.*"
(xiv. 14.)   And in Daniel,—"I saw in the visions of the night,
and lo, one like the Son of Man was coming with the *clouds*
of heaven." (vii. 13.)   *A. E.* 594.

Verse 2. *Jesus taketh Peter, and James, and John.*—By
Peter, James, and John were represented in this, as in other
passages wheresoever they are named in the books of the
Evangelists, *faith, charity,* and the *good of charity;* and by
their being alone present, was signified that no others can see
the glory of the Lord, which is in *His* Word, but they who
are in faith, in its charity, and in the good of charity; others
may indeed see, but still they do not see, because they do not ·
believe.   See preface to chap. xviii. of Genesis, in the *A. C.*

As to Peter, James, and John, see above, Exposition,
chap. v. 37.

*And leadeth them up into a high mountain apart by them-
selves.*—"Inasmuch as a "mountain" signified the good of
love, and when concerning the Lord, the Divine Good of the
Divine Love, and since from that Good proceeds Divine Truth,
therefore Jehovah, that is, the Lord, descended upon Mount
Sinai, and promulgated the law, for it is written that "He
descended upon that *mountain,* to the head of the *mountain;*"
(Exod. xix. 20.) and that He *promulgated the law* there.
(Exod. xx.)   Hence also by "Sinai," in the Word, is signified
Divine Truth from Divine Good; in like manner by the law
there promulgated.   On this account also the Lord "took
Peter, James, and John into a high mountain," when He was
transformed; and when He was transformed, He appeared in
Divine Truth from Divine Good, for His "face," which was
as the *sun,* represented Divine Good, and His "garment,"
which was as *light,* Divine Truth; and Moses and Elias, who
appeared, signified the Word, which is Divine Truth from
Divine Good.   *A. E.* 405.

Verse 3. *His raiment became shining, exceeding white, as snow*, &c.—By "raiment," when applied to the Lord, is signified the Divine Truth proceeding from Him; and whereas Divine Truth is signified, the Word is also signified, for the Word is Divine Truth from the Lord on earth and in the heavens. This was represented by the Lord's "raiment," when He was "transformed before Peter, James, and John." *A. E.* 195. See also *H. H.* 129. *S. S.* 98.

Verse 4. *And there appeared unto them Elias with Moses.*— The reason why Moses and Elias appeared was, because they both signify the Word. *A. E.* 64. See also *A. C.* 6752.

Verse 7. *And there was a cloud that overshadowed them; and a voice came out of the cloud, saying, This is My beloved Son: hear ye Him.*—By the "cloud that overshadowed" the disciples, and into which the disciples entered, was represented the Word in the letter, for by "disciples" in the Word was represented the church, which at that time and afterwards was only in truths derived from the sense of the letter: and whereas revelations and responses are made by Divine Truth in ultimates, and this truth is such as is the truth of the sense of the letter of the Word, therefore it came to pass that a "voice was heard from the *cloud*, saying, This is My beloved Son: hear ye Him;" that is, that He is Divine Truth or the Word. *A. E.* 594.

Verses 11, 12, 13. *Why say the Scribes that Elias must first come? But I say unto you, That Elias is already come, and they have done unto him whatsoever they willed.*—In the Word there are several who represent the Lord, as to Divine Truth, or as to the Word; but amongst them were chiefly Moses, Elias, Eliseus, and John the Baptist. That Elias should come, and that they would not acknowledge him, but "would do to him whatsoever they willed," signifies that the Word indeed taught them, but that still they would not be willing to comprehend it, interpreting it in favour of their own dominion, and thus extinguishing the divine principle within it; and that they would do this in like manner with the Divine Truth itself, is signified by the "Son of Man suffering many things of them." For the "Son of Man" is the Lord, as to the Divine Truth or Word. *A. C.* 9372.

Verse 18. *And wheresoever he taketh him, he teareth him: and he foameth, and gnasheth with his teeth, and pineth away: and I said to Thy disciples that they should cast him out; and they could not.*—He who is not acquainted with the spiritual sense of the Word, may be led to suppose that the "gnashing of teeth," here mentioned, was expressive only of anger, by reason that in cases of anger the teeth are

pressed together; but "gnashing of teeth" is here spoken of,
because the "teeth" signify false principles in the extremes,
and "gnashing," the vehemence of contending in their favour;
this endeavour and act are likewise grounded in correspondence.
Such also was the "deaf and dumb spirit" whom the Lord
cast out; for all spirits are from the human race, and this *deaf
and dumb spirit* was of that race of men who had vehemently
combated in favour of false principles against truths; hence it
is, that he who was possessed or obsessed by him *foamed and
gnashed with his teeth.*   He is called by the Lord "deaf and
dumb," because he was not willing to perceive and understand
the truth, for the "deaf" and "dumb" signify such; and
whereas he had been resolute and obstinate in opposing truths,
and had confirmed himself in false principles, he "could not
be cast out by the disciples;" for the false principles in favour
of which he had contended, could not as yet be dispersed by
them, since they were not as yet of a quality to disperse them,
wherefore also the disciples were on that account reproved by
the Lord.   That the spirit was of such a quality, and that the
obsessed by him was not of such a quality, is signified by that
spirit "tearing him," and by the obsessed "pining," and by
the Lord saying to the spirit that "he should enter no more
into him.   From these considerations also it may be manifest
what is signified by "gnashing of teeth."   (Matt. viii. 12;
xiii. 42, 50; xxii. 13; xxiv. 51; xxv. 30; Luke xiii. 18.)
By "gnashing of teeth" in the hells, is meant a continual
wrangling and combat of false principles amongst each other
and against truths, consequently of those who are in false
principles, joined with contempt of others, with enmity,
derision, mockery, blasphemy, which evils also burst forth
into blows, since every one contends in favour of his own
false principle from the love of self, of learning, and of
reputation.   These disputes and combats are heard out of
those hells like *gnashing of teeth,* and are likewise turned
into *gnashing of teeth,* when truths flow in thither out of
heaven; but on this subject see more in the Treatise concerning "Heaven and Hell," n. 575.
   Inasmuch as the "teeth," with the evil, correspond to false
principles which they cherish in the ultimates of intellectual
life, which are called sensual-corporeal, therefore the spirits
who are of this description, appear deformed in the face, a
great part of which consists of *teeth,* which stand out, as in
rows, when the jaws are opened, and this because such opening
of the "teeth" corresponds to the love and desire of combat-
ing in favour of false principles against truths.   Inasmuch as

CHAP. IX.]   TO MARK.   **159**

"teeth" correspond to the ultimates of the intellectual life of man, which ultimates are called sensual, and inasmuch as these ultimates are in the false principles of evil, when they are separated from truths of interior intellect, which are called spiritual truths, but the same correspond to the truths of good in sensual principles when not separated, hence it is that "teeth," in the Word, also signify ultimate truths, as in Job xix. 19, 20; and in Amos iv. 6; which may be seen explained above. And whereas the Lord glorified His whole Humanity, that is, made it Divine, therefore it is said of Him in Moses,— "His eyes were red from wine, and His *teeth* white from milk." (Gen. xlix. 12.) By His "eyes being red from wine," is signified that His intellectual principle was Divine Truth from Divine Good; and by His "teeth being white from milk," is signified that His sensual principle in like manner was Divine Truth from Divine Good; for by "Shiloh" is there meant the Lord. *A. E.* 556.

Verse 22. *Ofttimes he casteth him into the fire, and into the waters,* &c—Evil spirits continually endeavour to cast man into the dangers of death, and to bring injury upon him; these evils [called accidents or misfortunes] come from evil spirits, whether they are aware of it or not. But good spirits and angels from the Lord, are constantly delivering man from these dangers. *Spir. Diary,* 96, Index.

Verses 23, 24. *Jesus said unto him, If thou canst believe, all things are possible to him that believeth,* &c.—They who are born within the church ought to acknowledge the Lord, His Divinity, and His Humanity, and to believe in Him, and love Him; for from the Lord is all salvation. This the Lord teaches in John iii. 36,—"He that *believeth* on the Son hath eternal life; but he that *believeth not* the Son shall not see life." The "Son" denotes the Divine Human of the Lord. The reason why they "have not eternal life" who do not acknowledge the Lord from faith, is, because the whole heaven is in that acknowledgment. *A. C.* 10,112, 10,370.

To *believe* that there is a heaven and a hell; that there is a life after death, where the good live in happiness for ever, and the evil in unhappiness; that the particular life which any individual has formed to himself, remains with him; that faith and charity constitute spiritual life, and that this is the life which angels have in heaven; that the Lord has "all power in the heavens and the earth," as Himself says; (Matt. xxviii. 18.) that from Him we live; that the Word is the doctrine of heavenly and divine Truths, and the like;—such are the objects of faith in spiritual things as are signified by "believing." *A. C.* 6970.

Verse 29. *By prayer and fasting.*—By "prayers" are meant the things which are of faith, and at the same time the things which are of charity, with those who pour forth prayer, because prayers without such things are not prayers, but empty sounds. *A. R.* 278.

By "fasting," is signified to mourn by reason of a defect of Truth and Good. *A. E.* 1189.

Verse 34. *They disputed among themselves who should be the greatest.*—It may be manifest what is the quality of self-love [which desires to be the *greatest*], even from this consideration, that it conceals in itself hatred against all who do not submit to it as servants, and by reason of hatred that it also conceals revenge, cruelty, deceit, and several other abominations. But mutual love in man, which alone is celestial, consists in this, that he not only says, but acknowledges and believes that self-love is most unworthy, and that he of himself is something vile and filthy, which the Lord, out of infinite mercy, continually withdraws and withholds from hell, into which he continually endeavours, yea desires to plunge himself. The reason why man ought to acknowledge and believe this, is, because it is true; not that the Lord, or any angel, wills such acknowledgment and belief to the intent that he may submit himself, but lest self-love should exalt itself, when still it is of such a quality, which would be like excrement calling itself pure gold, or as if a fly on a dunghill should call itself a bird of paradise. So far, therefore, as a man acknowledges and believes that he is of such a quality as he really is, so far he recedes from self-love and its lusts, and so far he abhors himself; and in proportion as he does this he receives from the Lord celestial love, that is, mutual love, consisting in a desire to serve all. These are they who are understood by the *least*, who, in the Lord's kingdom, become the *greatest*. *A. C.* 1594.

Verse 35. *And having sat down, He called the twelve, and saith unto them, If any one be willing to be first, let him be the last of all, and the servant of all.*—There are two kingdoms into which the whole heaven is distinguished, one inhabited by the angels who are in the good of celestial love, the other inhabited by the angels who are in the good of spiritual love, or in charity; the celestial kingdom of the Lord is called His priesthood, and the spiritual kingdom is called His royalty, see the Treatise on "Heaven and Hell," n. 24, 226. The term "ministering" is applied to those who are in the celestial kingdom, but the term "serving" to those who are in the spiritual kingdom; hence it is evident what is signified by

" ministering" and a " minister," and what by " serving" and
a " servant," in the following passages:—" Jesus said to the
disciples, Whosoever is willing to be great, ought to be a
minister; and whosoever is willing to be first, ought to be
a *servant:* as the Son of Man came not to be *ministered* unto,
but to *minister.*" (Matt. xx. 26—28; xxiii. 11, 12; Mark
ix. 35; Luke xxii. 24—27.) " Jesus saith, If any one will
minister to Me, let him follow Me; in such case where I am,
there also shall My *minister* be: if any one *minister* to Me,
him shall the Father honour." (John xii. 26.) *A. E.* 155.

Verses 36, 37. *And having taken a child, He set him in the
midst of them: and having taken him into His arms, He said
unto them, Whosoever shall receive one of such children in My
name, receiveth Me: and whosoever receiveth Me, receiveth not
Me, but Him that sent Me.*—In the Word mention is made of
a " suckling," an " infant," and a " child," and by them are
signified three degrees of innocence,—the first degree by a
suckling, the second by an *infant,* and the third by a *child;*
but whereas with a *child,* innocence begins to be put off, therefore by a " child" is signified that innocent principle which is
called guiltless. Inasmuch as the three degrees of innocence
are signified by a " suckling," an " infant," and a " child,"
the three degrees of love and charity are also signified by
the same, by reason that celestial and spiritual love, that is,
love to the Lord and charity towards our neighbour, cannot
be given except in innocence. But it is to be noted, that
the innocence of *sucklings,* of *infants,* and of *children* is only
external, and that internal innocence is not given with man
until he be born anew, that is, be made anew, as it were, a
suckling, an *infant,* and a *child.* These states are what are
signified in the Word by a " suckling," an " infant," and a
" child," for in the internal sense of the Word, nothing is
meant but what is spiritual, consequently spiritual birth,
which is called re-birth, and likewise regeneration. That the
innocent principle, which is called guiltless, is signified by
a " child," is manifest from Luke,—" Jesus said, Whosoever
does not receive the kingdom of God as a *little child,* shall
not enter into it;" (xviii. 17.) where, to " receive the kingdom
of God as a little child," is to receive charity and faith,
grounded in innocence. So in Mark,—" Jesus took a *child,*
set him in the midst of them, and took him up into His arms,
saying unto them, Whosoever receiveth one of such *children*
in My name, receiveth Me;" (ix. 36, 37.) where, by a "child,"
is here represented innocence, which, " whosoever receiveth,"
receiveth the Lord, because He is the Source of all innocence.

That to "receive a child in the name of the Lord," is not to receive a child, every one may see; thus it is evident that somewhat celéstial was represented by this act. *A. C.* 5236.

Verse 37. *Receiveth Him that sent Me.*—The Lord, as to the Divine Human, is called an *Angel* or the *Sent*, for "angel" in Hebrew signifies the *sent*. This is evident from many passages, as in Mark ix. 37, &c. *A. C.* 6831.

Verse 40. *He that is not against us is for us.* — That the Lord's disciples are hated by all those who do not think of His Divinity at the same time that they think of His Humanity, cannot be known from those who are in the world, but from the same in the other life, where they burn with such hatred against those who approach the Lord alone, as cannot be described in a few words, desiring nothing more than to slay and to murder them. The reason is, because all who are in the hells are against the Lord, and all who are in the heavens are with the Lord; and they who are of the church, and do not acknowledge the Divinity of the Lord in His Humanity, act in unity with the hells, whence they derive so great hatred. *A. E.* 137.

Verse 41. *For whosoever shall give you a cup of water to drink in My name, because ye are of Christ, verily I say unto you, he shall not lose his reward.*—In the Word frequent mention is made of a "cup" or chalice, and by it is signified, in the genuine sense, spiritual truth, that is, the truth of faith which is grounded in the good of charity, the like as by "wine;" and in the opposite sense, the false principle productive of evil, and likewise the false principle derived from evil. The reason why a "cup" signifies the like as "wine," is, because a *cup* is the continent, and *wine* is what is contained, and hence they constitute one, and thus one is understood by the other. That such is the signification of a "cup" in the Word, is evident from the following passages:—"Jehovah, Thou shalt prepare before me a table in the presence of my foes: and Thou shalt make fat my head with oil; my *cup* shall overflow;" (Psalm xxiii. 5.) where to "prepare a table," and to "make fat the head with oil," denotes to be gifted with the good of charity and of love; "my cup shall overflow," denotes that the natural principle shall thence be filled with spiritual truth and good. Again,—"What shall I render to Jehovah? I will take the *cup* of salvation, and will call on the name of Jehovah;" (Psalm cxvi. 12, 13.) where to "take the cup of salvation," denotes the appropriation of the good things of faith. So in Mark,—"Whosoever shall give you to drink a *cup of water* in My name, because ye are of Christ, verily I say unto you, he shall not lose his reward;" (ix. 41.) where to "give a cup of water to drink in My name," denotes to instruct in the truths of faith, from a little charity. *A. C. 5120.*

By "giving to drink a cup of water in My name, because ye are of Christ," is signified to teach truth from the love of truth, thus from the Lord; in like manner to do it. The love of truth for the sake of truth, is meant by "giving a cup of water in the name of Christ;" by "Christ" also is meant the Lord as to Divine Truth. *A. E. 960.*

In My name.—By the "name" of Jehovah or of the Lord, in the Word, is not meant His *name,* but all by which He is worshipped; and inasmuch as He is worshipped in the church according to doctrine, by His "name" is meant the all of doctrine, and in a universal sense the all of religion. The reason why these things are meant by the "name" of Jehovah or of the Lord, is, because in heaven no other names are given, but what the quality of any one is, and the quality of God is all by which He is worshipped. Whoso does not understand this signification of "name" in the Word, can understand nothing but *name* literally, and in that alone there is nothing of worship or of religion. He therefore who keeps in mind this signification of the "name" of Jehovah, as here explained, whenever it occurs in the Word, will understand of himself what is meant by it in the following passages:—"In that day shall ye say, Praise Jehovah, call upon His *name.*" (Isa. xii. 4.) "From the rising of the sun shall My *name* be called upon." (Isa. xli. 25.) "In every place incense shall be offered unto My *name;*" (Mal. i. 11.) besides many other passages. Who cannot see that the term *name* alone is not understood. The same is signified, in the New Testament, by the "name" of the Lord, as in the following:—"Jesus said, Ye shall be hated of all men for My *name's* sake." (Matt. x. 22.) Again,—"Where two or three are gathered together in My *name,* there am I in the midst of them." (Matt. xviii. 20.) "They who believe will have life in His *name.*" (John xx. 31.) "Hallowed be Thy *name.*" (Matt. vi. 9.) That "name," with others, is the quality of their worship, appears in the following passages:—"The Shepherd of the sheep calleth His own sheep by their *name.*" (John x. 3.) "I have a few *names* in Sardis;" (Apoc. iii. 4.) and in other passages. *A. R. 81.*

He shall not lose his reward.—By these words is meant, that they will receive the delight of heaven, who "give to drink a cup of water in the name of Christ," that is, who from affection hear, receive, and teach truth; because truth

and its affection are from the Lord, thus for the sake of the
Lord,—consequently also for the sake of Truth, or " because
ye are of Christ," signifies for the sake of Divine Truth proceeding from the Lord. *A. E. 695.*

Inasmuch as few know what is properly understood by
" reward," it shall be explained. By " reward" is properly
understood that delight, satisfaction, and blessedness, which is
contained in the love or affection of good and truth, for that
love or that affection has in itself all the joy of heart which is
called heavenly joy, and also heaven. The reason is, because
the Lord is in that love or in that affection, and with the Lord
is also heaven; this joy, therefore, or this delight, satisfaction,
and blessedness, is what is properly understood by the *reward*
which they shall receive who do good and speak truth from
the love and affection of Good and Truth, thus from the Lord,
and by no means from themselves; and whereas they act and
speak from the Lord, and not from themselves, therefore the
reward is not of merit but of grace. From these considerations
it may appear, that he who knows what heavenly joy is, may
know also what *reward* is; what heavenly joy is in its essence,
may be seen in the work concerning " Heaven and Hell,"
n. 395, 414. This, therefore, is signified by the " reward"
which is given to those who are in truths from good; but the
reward of those who are in falses from evil, is joy or delight,
satisfaction and blessedness, in the world, but hell after their
departure out of the world. Hence it may appear what is
signified by " reward" in the following passages :—Thus in
Isaiah,—" Behold, the Lord Jehovah cometh in might: behold,
His *reward* is with Him, and the *recompense* of His work with
Him." (xl. 10.) And in the Apocalypse,—" Behold, I come
quickly; and My *reward* is with Me, to give to every one as
his work shall be." (xxii. 12.) And again in Isaiah,—" Say
to the daughter of Zion, Behold, thy Salvation cometh; and
His *recompense* before Him." (lxii. 11.) " Behold, the Lord
Jehovah cometh in might," " Behold, thy Salvation cometh,"
and "Behold, He cometh quickly," signify the first and second
advent of the Lord; " His reward is with Him," signifies heaven,
and all things thereto appertaining, as above, inasmuch as
where the Lord is, there is heaven, for heaven is not heaven
from the angels there, but from the Lord with the angels;
that they shall receive heaven according to the love and affection of good and truth from the Lord, is understood by " the
recompense of His work before Him," and by "giving to every
one according as his work shall be." By the " work" for which
heaven shall be given as a *reward*, nothing else is meant than

what proceeds from the love or affection of good and truth, inasmuch as nothing else can produce heaven in man; for every work derives all that it has from the love or affection whence it proceeds, as the effect derives all that it has from the efficient cause, wherefore according to the quality of the love or affection, such is the work;—and hence it may appear what is understood by the "work," according to which it "shall be given to every one," and what by "the recompense of his work." *A. E.* 695.

Verse 42. *And whosoever shall offend one of the little ones that believe in Me, it is better for him that a millstone were hanged about his neck, and he were cast into the sea.*—A "millstone" denotes truth serviceable to faith; the "neck" denotes the conjunction of interior and exterior principles; to be "hung" there, denotes the interclusion and interception of what is good and true; to be "sunk into the depths of the sea," denotes in the mere worldly and corporeal principle, thus in hell. These things which the Lord spake, like all the rest, are thus significative. *A. C.* 9755. See also *A. R.* 791.

By a "millstone" is signified the confirmation of truth from the Word, and likewise the confirmation of what is false, from the same source; and the reason is, because "wheat" signifies the principle of good, and "fine flour" its truth. Hence by a "millstone," by which *wheat* is ground into *fine flour*, or *barley* into *meal*, is signified the production of truth from good, or the production of what is false from evil, thus likewise the confirmation of what is true or false from the Word, as may be manifest from the following passages:—" I will take away from them the voice of joy, and the voice of gladness, the voice of the bridegroom, and the voice of the bride, the voice of the *millstones*, and the light of a candle." (Jer. xxv. 10.) In these words is described the joy of heaven and of the church; and by the "voice of joy," is signified exultation of heart grounded in the good of love; and by the "voice of gladness," is signified the glorification of the soul grounded in the truths of faith, for *joy* in the Word is predicated of good, and *gladness* of truth; by the "voice of millstones," is signified the like as by the *voice of joy;* and by the "light of a candle," is signified the like as by *gladness*, viz., grounded in the truth of faith. The reason why the "voice of millstones" signifies the joy of heart grounded in the good of love, is, because a *millstone* grinds wheat into fine flour, and by "wheat" is signified the good of love, and by "fine flour" the truth derived from that good. So in the Lamentations,—" They took away the young men to *grind at the mill*, and the children fell

under the wood;" (v. 13.) where to "take away the young men
to grind at the mill," signifies to drive those who might be in
the understanding of truth, to falsify truths; "children falling
under the wood," signifies to drive those who might be in
the will of good, to adulterate goods; to "grind," denotes to
falsify truths, or to confirm false principles by the Word;
"wood" denotes good.   And in Moses,—"No one shall take
for pledge a *mill* or *millstone:* for he taketh the soul for
pledge." (Deut. xxiv. 6.)   This was amongst those laws, all
of which corresponded to spiritual things.   By not "taking
for pledge a mill or a millstone," was signified, in the spiritual
sense, that no one should take from another the opportunity
of understanding truths, from a principle of good, thus that
no one should deprive another of goods and truths; inasmuch
as these things were signified, therefore it is said, "he taketh
the soul for pledge," by which is signified, that thus he spiritually perishes.   Again,—"All the firstborn in the land shall
die, even to the firstborn of the maidservant who is behind
the *mill;*" (Exod. xi. 5.) where, by the "firstborn of the
maidservant who is behind the mill," are signified the primary
things of the faith of the natural man, which are falsified.
And in Matthew,—"In the consummation of the age, two
[women] shall be grinding at the *mill;* the one shall be taken,
the other shall be left." (xxiv. 40, 41.)   The "consummation
of the age," is the last time of the church; by "two [women]
grinding at the mill," are meant those who confirm themselves
in truths, and who confirm themselves in false principles from
the Word; they who confirm themselves in truths, are meant
by "her who will be taken;" and they who confirm themselves
in false principles, by "her who shall be left."   So in the
Evangelists,—"Jesus said, Whosoever shall scandalize one of
the little ones that believe in Me, it were better for him that
an *ass-millstone* be hung about his neck, and he be cast into
the depth of the sea;" (Matt. xviii. 6; Mark ix. 42; Luke
xvii. 2.) where, by "scandalizing one of the little ones that
believe in Jesus," is signified to pervert those who acknowledge
the Lord; by its being "better that an ass-millstone be hung
about the neck," is signified that it is better for him not to
have known any good and truth, but only what is evil and
false,—this is an "ass-millstone;" and to be "hung about the
neck," denotes interception lest he should know what is good
and true; by being "cast into the depth of the sea," is signified into hell.   The reason why this is "better," is, because
to know goods and truths, and to pervert them, is to profane
them, [and thus to suffer a more direful punishment than if he
had not known them.]   *A. E.* 1182.

Inasmuch as by "millstone" is here signified the truth of
the Word adulterated, and by the "sea," hell, therefore the
Lord says—"Whosoever shall scandalize one of the little ones
that believe in Me," &c. *A. R.* 791.

Verse 43. *And if thy hand offend thee, cut it off: it is
better for thee to enter maimed into life, than having two
hands to be cast into hell [gehenna], into the fire that never
shall be quenched.*— That by the "right eye" and "right
hand," the Lord did not mean the *right eye* and the *right
hand*, must be plain to every one, from this consideration, that
it is said that "the eye is to be plucked out," and that "the
hand is to be cut off, if they should scandalize," but inasmuch
as by "eye," in the spiritual sense, is signified all that which
is of the understanding, and thence of the thought, and by the
"right hand" all that which is of the will, and thence of the
affection, it may be manifest that by "plucking out the right
eye if it should scandalize," is signified that evil should be
rejected from the thought, if it entered into the thought; and
by "cutting off the right hand if it should scandalize," is
signified that evil should be dislodged from the will, if it
entered into the will; for the *eye* itself cannot scandalize, nor
the *right hand*, but scandal comes from the thought of the
understanding, and the affection of the will which corresponds
thereto.　The reason why it is said the "right eye" and the
"right hand," and not the *left eye* and the *left hand*, is, because
by "right" is signified good, and in the opposite sense evil,
but by "left" is signified truth, and in the opposite sense what
is false; and all scandalizing comes from evil, but not from
what is false, unless grounded in evil. *A. E.* 600.

The *left eye* is the intellectual principle, but the *right eye*
is the affection of that principle; by the "right eye" therefore
being "plucked out," is denoted that the affection, if it offend,
ought to be subdued. *A. C.* 2701.

Verse 45. *And if thy foot offend thee, cut it off: it is better
for thee to enter halt into life, than having two feet to be cast
into hell [gehenna], into the fire that cannot be quenched.*—By
the "foot which is to be cut off, if it scandalize," or offend,
is meant the natural principle, which continually opposes itself
to the spiritual principle,—that it ought to be destroyed if it
attempt to infringe truths, and thus that, by reason of the
discordance and dissuasion of the natural man, it is better to
be in simple good, although in the denial of truth; this is
signified by "entering halt into life." That the "foot" denotes
the natural principle, may be seen, n. 2162, 3147, 3761, 3986,
4280. *A. C.* 4302. See also *A. R.* 49.

By being "halt" is signified to be in good, in which as yet are no genuine truths, but only common truths, into which genuine truths may be insinuated. *A. C.* 4302.

Verse 47. *And if thine eye offend thee, pluck it out: it is better for thee to enter into the kingdom of God with one eye, than having two eyes to be cast into the hell* [*gehenna*] *of fire.*—By the "eye" is signified the understanding, and the reason is, because the *eye* corresponds to the understanding; for the understanding sees from the light of heaven, but the *eye* from the light of the world. Those things which the former *eye*, or the understanding sees, are spiritual, and the field of its view is the scientific principle which is in man's memory; but the things which the external *eye* sees, are terrestrial, and the field of its view is every thing which appears in the world. That the "eye," in the spiritual sense, is understanding, and likewise faith, because this latter makes the life of the interior understanding, may be seen, n. 2701, 4402—4421, 4523—4534. He who does not know that the understanding is meant in the Word by the "eye," cannot know what is signified by what the Lord spake concerning the "eye" in the Evangelists, as thus:—" If thy *right eye* offend thee, pluck it out: it is better for thee to enter into the kingdom of God with *one eye*, than having *two eyes* to be cast into the hell of fire." (Matt. v. 29; Mark ix. 47.) Every one knows that the *eye* is not to be *plucked out*, although it scandalize or offend, and that no one enters one-eyed into the kingdom of God; but by the "right eye" is signified the false principle of faith concerning the Lord; this, therefore, is what is to be plucked out. *A. C.* 9051. See also 10,742—10,749.

Verse 48. *Where their worm dieth not, and the fire is not quenched.*—They who do not know that the vital fire appertaining to man is from another origin than elementary *fire*, cannot possibly know otherwise than that by the "fire of hell" is meant such *fire* as is in the world, when yet in the Word no such fire is meant, but the fire which is of love, thus which is of the life of man, proceeding from the Lord as a Sun, which fire, when it enters into those who are in opposite principles, is turned into the *fire of lusts*, viz., as was above said, the lusts of revenge, of hatred, of cruelty, derived from the love of self and of the world. This is the *fire* which torments those who are in the hells, for when the rein is given to their lusts, they then rush one upon another, and torment each other by direful and inexpressible methods, since every one wishes to be supereminent, and by secret and open arts to take away from another what is his. From this cupidity exist intestine hatreds, and hence the savage practices which are exercised, especially by magical arts, and phantasies, which arts are innumerable, and altogether unknown to the world. *A. C.* 6832. See also *H. H.* 401, 570, 571.

The reason why to be "burned with fire" denotes to be consumed by the evils of self-love, is, because that love consumes all the goods and truths of faith. That this is the effect of self-love, is scarcely known to any one at this day, and hence neither is it known that that love is hell with man, and that it is meant by *infernal fire*. For there are two fires of life appertaining to man, one is self-love, the other is love to God. They who are in self-love cannot be in love to God, inasmuch as the loves are opposite. The reason why they are opposite is, because self-love produces all evils, consisting in contempt of others in comparison of itself, in enmity against those who do not favour it, at length in hatred, revenge, savageness, cruelty, which evils altogether resist Divine influx, consequently extinguish the truths and goods of faith and charity, for these are what flow in from the Lord. *A. C.* 10,038.

Where the fire is not quenched.—Infernal spirits are not in any *material fire*, but in *spiritual fire*, which is their love, wherefore they do not feel any other fire; concerning which, see *H. H.* 566—575. All love in the spiritual world, when it is excited, appears at a distance like fire; within the hells, like a burning fire; and without, like the smoke of a burning fire, or like the smoke of a furnace. *A. E.* 422.

By "their worm dying not," is signified the false principles of evil which is in the good derived from man's selfhood, which false principle is compared to a *worm*, because their effects are similar; for the false principle corrodes and thereby torments. There are two things which make hell, as there are two things which make heaven;—the two things which make heaven are good and truth, and the two which make hell are evil and what is false. Consequently those two things in heaven are what make happiness there, and the two in hell are what make torment there. Torment in hell, derived from the false principle, is compared to a *worm*, and torment from evil is there compared to *fire*. Thus in Isaiah,—"As the new heavens and the new earth, which I am about to make, shall stand before Me, so shall your seed and your name stand; at length it shall come to pass from month to month, and from Sabbath to their Sabbath, and they shall stand before Me; afterwards they shall go forth, and shall see the carcases of the men that have transgressed against Me: for *their worm* shall not die, and *their fire* shall not be quenched; and they shall be an abhorring unto all flesh." (lxvi. 22, 23, 24.) In like manner it is said by the Lord in Mark,—"Where *their worm* dieth not, and *their fire* shall not be quenched;" (ix. 44, 46, 48.) speaking of Gehenna or hell. *A. C.* 8481.

Verses 49, 50. *For every one shall be salted with fire, and every sacrifice shall be salted with salt. Salt is good: but if the salt become saltless, wherewith shall ye season it? Have salt in yourselves, and be at peace one with another.*—To be "salted with fire," denotes the desire of good to truth; and to be "salted with salt," denotes the desire of truth to good; "saltless salt" is truth without a desire to good; to "have salt in themselves" is that desire. So in Luke,—"Every one of you who doth not renounce all that he hath, cannot be My disciple. *Salt* is good: but if the *salt* have lost its savour, wherewith shall it be seasoned? It is neither serviceable for the earth, nor for the dunghill; but men cast it out." (xiv. 33, 34, 35.) In this passage, in like manner, "salt" denotes truth desiring good; and "salt which hath lost its savour," denotes truth which is without a desire for good; "not serviceable for the earth, nor for the dunghill," denotes that it is altogether unprofitable for any use whether good or evil; they who are in such truth, are what are called *lukewarm*, which is evident from what goes before, where it is said—"That he cannot be the Lord's disciple, who doth not renounce all that he hath;" that is, who does not love the Lord above all things, for they who love the Lord, and likewise themselves, in the same degree, are those who are called *lukewarm*, and who are not serviceable for any use either good or evil. So in Moses,— "Every oblation of thy meat-offering shall be *salted* with *salt;* neither shalt thou suffer the *salt* of the covenant of thy God to be lacking from thy meat-offering: on all thine offering thou shalt offer *salt*." (Lev. ii. 13.) By "salt being in every offering," was signified that the desire of truth to good and of good to truth should be in all worship; hence also that "salt" is called the *salt of the covenant of God;* for "covenant" is conjunction, n. 665, 666, &c.; and "salt" is the desire of conjunction. When the one desires to be conjoined to the other, reciprocally, that is, good to truth and truth to good, then they mutually respect each other; but when truth severs itself from good, then they avert themselves from each other, and look backward or behind themselves. This is signified by Lot's wife becoming a statue of salt, as in Luke,—"Whosoever shall be on the housetop, and his vessels in the house, let him not go down to take them: and whosoever is in the field, in like manner, let him not return to the things behind him. Remember Lot's wife." (xvii. 31, 32.) That this is to "look behind him," or backwards, may be seen, n. 3652, 5895, 5897, &c. The reason why "salt" signifies the desire of truth, is, because *salt* renders the earth fruitful, and gives relish to food, and because in *salt* there is a fiery principle and at the same time a conjunctive one, as in truth there is an ardent desire to good, and at the same time a conjunctive principle. *A. C.* 6207.

Every one being "salted with fire," denotes that every one shall desire from genuine love; "every sacrifice being salted with salt," denotes that desire, grounded in genuine love, shall be in all worship; "saltless salt," signifies desire grounded in other love than what is genuine; to "have salt in themselves," is the desire of truth to good. Who can know what is meant by being "salted with fire," and why the sacrifice should be "salted with salt," and what is signified by "having salt in themselves," unless it be known what is meant by *fire*, what by *salt*, and by being *salted*. *A. C.* 10,300.

"Fire" [in a good sense] corresponds to heavenly love, or love to God and love to the neighbour; and hence it is that "fire" signifies *love*. Hence also it was that Jehovah God was seen before Moses in *fire*, or in the burning bush, and in like manner on Mount Zion, before the sons of Israel. Hence it was commanded that *fire* should be perpetually kept upon the altar, and that the lights of the candlestick in the tabernacle should be kindled every evening. This was commanded because "fire" signifies *love*. *D. Influx*, 6.

Verse 50. *Be at peace one with another.*—By "peace" are signified all things in the complex or aggregate which come from the Lord, and consequently all things of heaven and the church, and the beatitudes of life in them; these are what belong to *peace* in a supreme or inmost sense. That "peace" is charity, spiritual security, and internal tranquillity, follows of course; for when man is in the Lord, he is in peace with his neighbour, which is charity; in protection against the hells, which is spiritual security; and when he is in peace with his neighbour, and in protection against the hells, he is in internal tranquillity from evils and falses. Keep in mind *spiritual peace*, and you will see it plainly. *A. R.* 306. See also *H. H.* 284—290. *A. E.* 365.

MARK.

CHAPTER X.

1. AND having arisen from thence, He cometh into the coasts of Judea, through the further side of Jordan: and the multitude again resort to Him; and, as He was wont, He again taught them.

2. And the Pharisees having come to Him, asked Him, Is it lawful for a man to put away his wife? tempting Him.

3. But He answering, said unto them, What did Moses command you?

4. And they said, Moses suffered to write a bill of divorcement, and to put her away.

THAT the LORD, as to His Human principle, arose out of scientifics into the goods and truths of the church, that He might restore them to order. (Verses 1, 2.)

Teaching from the Word that all marriages on earth are grounded in the heavenly marriage of good and truth, which marriage requires that every truth shall have its proper good, and every good its proper truth, and that the understanding of truth ought to be separated from what is evil and false, that it may be conjoined to the will of good, so that both together may be made one good. (Verses 3—9.)

And although the external of the Word appears to teach otherwise, yet this is merely in accommodation to the natural

5. And Jesus answering, said unto them, For the hardness of your heart he wrote you this precept.

6. But from the beginning of creation, God made them male and female.

7. On this account a man shall leave his father and mother, and shall cleave unto his wife ;

8. And they two shall be one flesh : so that they are no longer two, but one flesh.

9. What therefore God hath joined together, let not man put asunder.

10. And in the house again His disciples asked Him of this matter.

11. And He saith unto them, Whosoever shall put away his wife, and marry another, committeth adultery against her.

12. And if a woman put away her husband, and be married to another, she committeth adultery.

13. And they brought to Him little children, that He should touch them: and the disciples rebuked those that brought them.

14. But when Jesus saw it, He was much displeased, and said unto them, Suffer the little children to come unto Me, and forbid them not: for of such is the kingdom of God.

mind, which is not qualified to receive a purer law. (Verses 4, 5.)

Which purer law originates in the union of the Divine Love and Wisdom, and therefore ought to be regarded as sacred and inviolable. (Verse 9.)

For the order of GOD requires that the understanding of truth shall not in any wise separate itself from its proper will of good, so long as that will abides in good, and does not decline to evil, and that the will of good, in like manner, shall not separate itself from its proper understanding of truth. (Verses 10—12.)

The same order also requires that the goods and truths of innocence be ascribed to the LORD, because heaven consists in the acknowledgment, that those goods and truths are from the LORD, and that He is in them. (Verses 13—16.)

15. Verily I say unto you, Whosoever shall not receive the kingdom of God as a little child, he shall not enter into it.

16. And having taken them up in His arms, and put His hands upon them, He blessed them.

17. And when He was gone forth into the way, one came running, and kneeling to Him, asked Him, Good Teacher, what shall I do that I may inherit eternal life?

No one therefore can enter into heaven unless he acknowledge the LORD, even as to His Human [essence], to be the GOD of heaven, and that from Him proceeds every good which is good, and unless he also live according to the precepts of the Decalogue, by shunning as sins the evils which are there forbidden. (Verses 17—20.)

For the LORD alone is good, and the Source of good. (Verse 18.)

18. And Jesus said unto him, Why callest thou Me good? None is good but One, namely God.

19. Thou knowest the commandments, Do not commit adultery, Do not commit murder, Thou shalt not steal, Do not bear false witness, Thou shalt not defraud, Honour thy father and mother.

And His precepts teach that man ought not to adulterate the goods of the Word, nor to destroy in himself the life of love and charity, nor to ascribe that life to himself, but to the LORD alone, nor to call anything good or true but what is of the LORD, thus that he should not rob the LORD of His glory, but should rather respect and exalt in himself the Divine Love and Wisdom above every other good and truth. (Verse 19.)

20. But he answering, said to Him, Teacher, all these things have I kept from my youth.

Yet these precepts cannot be fulfilled until man removes his heart from the love of riches, acknowledges the LORD

21. Then Jesus beholding him, loved him, and said unto him, One thing thou lackest: go, sell whatsoever thou hast, and give to the poor, and thou shalt have treasure in heaven: and come, follow Me, taking up the cross.

22. But he, being sad at that saying, went away grieved, for he had many possessions.

23. And Jesus looking round about, saith to His disciples, How hardly shall they that have riches enter into the kingdom of God!

24. And the disciples were astonished at His words. But Jesus again answering, saith unto them, Children, how hard is it for those who trust in riches to enter into the kingdom of God!

25. It is easier for a camel to go through the eye of a needle, than for a rich man to enter into the kingdom of God.

26. And they were astonished out of measure, saying one to another, Who then can be saved?

27. And Jesus looking on them saith, With men it is impossible, but not with God: for with God all things are possible.

28. And Peter began to say unto Him, Lo, we have forsaken all things, and have followed Thee.

29. And Jesus answering, said, Verily I say unto you,

to be the Only GOD, and endures temptations. (Verses 20, 21.)

Which things appear grievous to those who abound in the knowledges of truth separate from the life of good. (Verses 22, 23.)

Therefore those knowledges, when so separated, are rather hindrances to the attainment of conjunction with the LORD, since it is contrary to Divine order, that sciences or knowledges of themselves, separate from the life of love and charity, should enter into heaven. (Verses 24, 25.)

Nevertheless they are not hindrances, if the Divine Truth be respected and exalted. (Verses 26, 27.)

For all who reject their hereditary evils and falses, through faith in and love to the LORD's Divine Human principle, shall receive, through temptations, spiritual and celestial things, there is no one who hath left house, or brethren, or sisters, or father, or mother, or wife, or children, or lands, for My sake and the Gospel's,

30. But he shall receive an hundred-fold now in this time, houses, and brethren, and sisters, and mothers, and children, and lands, with persecutions; and in the age to come eternal life.

31. But many that are first shall be last, and the last first.

X

32. And they were in the way going up to Jerusalem; and Jesus was going before them; and they were amazed; and as they followed, were afraid. And taking again the twelve, He began to tell them what things should happen unto Him,

33. [Saying], Behold, we go up to Jerusalem; and the Son of Man will be delivered to the chief Priests and the Scribes; and they shall condemn Him to death, and shall deliver Him to the Gentiles:

34. And they shall mock Him, and shall scourge Him, and shall spit upon Him, and shall kill Him: and the third day He shall rise again.

35. And James and John, the sons of Zebedee, came unto Him, saying, Teacher, we are willing [desirous] that Thou shouldest do for us whatsoever we ask.

together with eternal conjunction with the LORD in the good of His love. (Verses 28, 29, 30.)

But they, who place merit in their own works, instead of ascribing it to the LORD, cannot attain such conjunction. (Verse 31.)

They, too, who are principled in the goods and truths of the church, are perplexed and troubled in their own minds about the process of regeneration. (Verse 32.)

Until they are instructed that by a similar process the LORD glorified His Humanity, and therefore suffered Himself to be treated by the perverted church as His Word had been treated, through the perversion and destruction of its truth. (Verses 33, 34.)

They, also, who are principled in charity and the works of charity, cannot separate, for a time, the love of dominion from those heavenly gifts, until they are instructed that they

36. And He said unto them, What will ye that I should do for you?

37. They said unto Him, Grant unto us that we may sit, one on Thy right hand, and the other on Thy left hand, in Thy glory.

38. But Jesus said unto them, Ye know not what ye ask: can ye drink of the cup which I drink of? and be baptized with the baptism that I am baptized with?

39. And they say unto Him, We can. But Jesus said unto them, Ye shall indeed drink of the cup that I drink of; and with the baptism that I am baptized with shall ye be baptized:

40. But to sit on My right hand and on My left hand, is not Mine to give, except to those for whom it is prepared.

41. And when the ten heard, they began to be much displeased with James and John.

42. But Jesus calling them unto Him, saith unto them, Ye know that they who are appointed to rule over the Gentiles exercise lordship over them; and their great ones exercise authority upon them.

43. But it shall not be so among you: but whosoever willeth to be great among you, shall be your minister:

44. And whosoever of you willeth to be the first, shall be the servant of all.

45. For even the Son of Man came not to be ministered

ought to prepare themselves to follow the LORD in the regeneration by temptation-combats, that so they may be fitted for conjunction with Him, since none can be great in heaven but through such preparation. (Verses 35—41.)

For they who are unprepared reject heavenly good, by seeking to be greatest in the kingdom of heaven. (Verses 41, 42.)

Whereas they ought rather to make themselves the least, since heavenly joy consisteth in serving others from love, or in doing good for the sake of good, after the LORD's example. (Verses 43, 44, 45.)

unto, but to minister, and to give His soul a ransom for many.

46. And they came to Jericho: and as He went out' of Jericho with His disciples and a considerable multitude, blind Bartimeus, the son of Timeus, sat by the way, begging.

47. And having heard that it was Jesus of Nazareth, he began to cry out, and say, Jesus, Thou Son of David, have mercy on me!

48. And many charged him that he should be silent: but he cried out much more, Thou Son of David, have mercy on me!

49. And Jesus standing, commanded him to be called. And they call the blind man, saying unto him, Be of good courage, arise; He calleth thee.

50. But he, casting away his garment, and arising, came to Jesus.

51. And Jesus answering, saith unto him, What wilt thou that I should do unto thee? The blind man said unto him, Rabboni, that I might receive my sight.

52. And Jesus said unto him, Go, thy faith hath saved thee. And immediately he received his sight, and followed Jesus in the way.

Who, out of pure mercy, imparts spiritual understanding to the ignorant. (Verse 46, to the end of the chapter.)

If they ask it of Him from a right faith in the Divinity of His Humanity. (Verse 47.)

And are the more urgent to receive in proportion as they meet with opposition to their desires. (Verse 48.)

For in such case the Divine Mercy is the more excited, and with it the consolation of hope, inclining all who wish to understand the truth to lay aside their natural prejudices, and elevate their minds to the LORD's Divine Humanity. (Verses 49, 50.)

They are taught also to explore the end or intention they have in view, when they seek the knowledge of the truth. (Verse 51.)

Thus their understandings are opened to the light of truth by communication with the LORD's Divine Humanity. (Verse 52.)

EXPOSITION.

CHAPTER X.

VERSES 2—10. *And the Pharisees having come to Him, asked Him, Is it lawful for a man to put away his wife? tempting Him*, &c.—All the laws of what is true and right flow from celestial principles, or from the order of life from the celestial man, for the whole heaven is a celestial Man, inasmuch as the Lord alone is the Celestial Man, and is the All in all, even to the minutest things, of heaven and of the celestial Man, whence they are called celestial. Inasmuch as every law of what is true and right descends from celestial principles, or from the order of life in the celestial man, the law of marriages principally descends from that source; the celestial marriage is that from which, and according to which, all marriages on earth ought to be contracted, its quality being such, that there is one Lord and one heaven, or one church, the head of which is the Lord; hence comes the law of marriages, that there should be one man and one wife, and when this is the case, they represent the celestial marriage, and are a type of the celestial man. This law was not only revealed to the men of the most ancient church, but was also inscribed on their internal man, wherefore a man at that time had only one wife, and constituted one house; but when their posterity ceased to be internal men, and became external, they then married more wives than one. Inasmuch as the men of the most ancient church, in their marriages, represented the celestial marriage, conjugial love was to them a kind of heaven and heavenly happiness; but when the church declined, they no longer perceived happiness in conjugial love, but in gratification derived from more wives than one, which is of the external man; this is called by the Lord "hardness of heart," on account of which it was allowed them by Moses to marry several wives, as the Lord Himself teaches, where He says,—"For the *hardness of your hearts* Moses wrote for you this precept, but from the beginning of creation God made them male and female; on this account shall a man leave his father and mother, and shall cleave to his wife; and they two shall be one flesh: wherefore they are no longer two, but one flesh. What therefore God hath joined together, let not man put asunder." (Mark x. 5—9.) *A. C.* 162.

That the Jewish nation had not any conjugial principle, whether understood in a spiritual or in a natural sense, is very manifest from this consideration, that they were permitted to marry several wives; for where there is a conjugial principle, understood in a spiritual sense, that is, where the Good and the Truth of the church are, consequently where the church is, this is in no wise permitted; for a genuine conjugial principle is in no case given except with those with whom the church or kingdom of the Lord is, and with these only between two, n. 1907, 2740, 3246. Marriage between two, who are in genuine conjugial love, corresponds to the heavenly marriage, that is, to the conjunction of Good and Truth, the husband corresponding to good, and the wife to the truth of that good; also when they are in genuine conjugial love, they are in that marriage; therefore where the church is, there it is never permitted to marry more wives than one; but whereas there was no church amongst the posterity of Jacob, but only the *representative* or *type* of a church, or the external of the church without its internal, n. 4307, 4500, therefore with that posterity it was permitted. And, moreover, the marriage of one husband with several wives would present in heaven the idea, or image, as if one Good might be conjoined with several Truths which are not in accord with each other, and thus that Good was none, for good becomes none in consequence of truths not agreeing together, since Good derives its quality from truths, and their agreement with each other. It would also present an image as if the church was not one, but several, and these distinct amongst themselves, according to the truths of faith, or according to doctrinals, when yet it is one where Good is its essential, and this essential is qualified and as it were modified by truths. The church is an image of heaven, for it is the Lord's kingdom on earth; heaven is distinguished into many general societies, and into lesser ones subordinate to the general ones, but still they are one by virtue of Good, the Truths of faith being there according to good congruously; for they regard Good, and are derived from it. If heaven was distinct according to the *truths* of faith, and not according to *good*, there would be no heaven, since there would be nothing of unanimity, for one principle of life, or one soul, could not be in its inhabitants from the Lord; this is only given in the principle of Good, that is, in love to the Lord, and in love towards the neighbour; for love conjoins all, and when the love of what is good and true is in each, then there is a common principle which is from the Lord, thus the Lord, who conjoins all. The love of what is good and true, is what is called "love towards the neighbour," for the *neighbour* is one who is principled in good, and the truth thence derived, and in the abstract sense Good itself and its Truth. From these considerations, it may be manifest why marriage within the church must be between *one* husband and *one* wife; and why it was permitted to the posterity of Jacob to marry *several* wives; and that the reason of this was, because there was no church among them, and consequently the representative of a church could not be instituted by marriages, because they were in principles contrary to conjugial love. *A. C.* 4837.

Good and Truth, conjoined with an angel and a man, are not two but one, since in this case good is of truth and truth of good. This conjunction is as when man thinks what he wills and wills what he thinks, in which case thought and will make one, thus one mind; for thought forms, or exhibits in form, that which the will wills, and the will gives it delight. Hence also it is, that two conjugial partners in heaven are not called *two,* but *one* angel. This likewise is what is meant by these words of the Lord:—"Have ye not read, that He who made [them] from the beginning, made them male and female, and said, For this reason a man shall leave father and mother, and shall cleave to his wife : and they *two* shall be *one flesh ?* wherefore they are no longer *two,* but *one* flesh. Wherefore what God hath *joined together, let not man separate;* all do not comprehend this word, but they to whom it is given." (Matt. xix. 4, 5, 6, 11; Mark x. 6—9; Gen. ii. 24.) In this passage is described the heavenly marriage in which the angels are, and at the same time the marriage of Good and Truth; and by "man not separating what God hath joined together," is meant that good ought not to be separated from truth. *H. H.* 372.

X That the verses from 2 to 10 of this chapter contain interior arcana, may be manifest from what the Lord says, that "all do not apprehend these words, but they to whom it is given." The interior arcana, contained in what is here said by the Lord, is little apprehended by men, but is apprehended by all the angels in heaven. The reason is, because the latter perceive those words of the Lord spiritually, and the arcana contained in them are spiritual, being to this effect,—in the heavens there are marriages equally as on earth, but in the heavens marriages are made of like with like, for the man [vir] is born to act from understanding, but the woman from affection; and understanding with men is the understanding of Truth and Good, and affection with women is the affection of Truth and Good; and whereas all understanding derives life

from affection, therefore they are there united together, as the
affection, which is of the will, is united with correspondent
thought, which is of the understanding; for understanding
with every one is various, as the truths are various from which
it is formed.   In general there are celestial truths, there are
spiritual truths, there are moral truths, there are civil truths,
yea, there are natural truths, and of every truth there are
innumerable species and varieties; and whereas it hence
comes to pass that the understanding of one person is in no
case like that of another, nor the affection of one like the
affection of another, therefore to the intent that understanding
and affection may nevertheless act in unity, they are so united
in heaven, that the correspondent affection, which is of the
woman, is conjoined with a correspondent understanding,
which is of the man; hence it is that each has life from the
correspondence, full of love.   Inasmuch as two various affections cannot correspond to one understanding, hence in heaven
it is in no case given, nor can be given, that one man shall
have more wives than one.   From these considerations it may
be seen and concluded, what is also spiritually meant by the
above words of the Lord, as what by a " man leaving father
and mother, and cleaving to his wife," and becoming " one
flesh," viz., that a man shall leave what is evil and false, which
appertains to him in a religious view, and which defiles his
understanding, thus which he has from his father and mother,
and that his understanding, separated from them, shall be
conjoined with a correspondent affection, which is of the wife,
whence *two* become *one* affection of Truth and of Good.   This
is meant by the *one flesh*, in which the two shall be, for
" flesh" in the spiritual sense signifies the good which is of
love or affection.   " Wherefore they are no longer two, but
one flesh," signifies that thus the understanding of good and
truth, and the affection of good and truth, are not *two*, but
one, in like manner as will and understanding indeed are
two, but still one,—in like manner also as truth and good,—
likewise faith and charity, which indeed are two, but still one,
viz., when truth is of good and good is of truth, also when
faith is of charity and charity is of faith; hence likewise
conjugial love is derived.   The reason why Moses, on account
of " hardness of heart, permitted them to put away a wife for
every cause," was, because the Israelites and Jews were natural
and not spiritual, and they who are merely natural, are *hard
of heart*, because they are not in any conjugial love, but in
lascivious love, such as is that of adultery.   The reason why
" whosoever shall put away a wife except for fornication,

and shall marry another, committeth adultery;" is, because
"fornication" signifies what is false; and with the woman,
the affection of what is evil and false, thus an affection which
in no sort agrees with the understanding of truth and good;
and hence heaven and the church altogether perish with man,
for when interior conjunction, which is that of minds [mentes]
and of minds [animi], is annulled, marriage is dissolved. The
reason why he who "marrieth her who is put away," also
"committeth adultery," is, because by her that is put away,
on account of *fornication*, is meant the affection of what is
evil and false, as above, which is not to be united with any
understanding of Truth and Good; for hence the understanding is perverted, and also becomes an understanding of what
is false and evil, and the conjunction of what is false and evil
is *spiritual adultery*, as the conjunction of what is True and
Good is *spiritual marriage*. *A. E.* 710.

Verse 5. *And Jesus answering, said unto them, For the
hardness of your heart, he [Moses] wrote you this precept.*—It
appears from this passage, and especially from Divine command
to Moses, to "hew him out two tables like unto the former,"
(Exod. xxxiv. 1.) that the external of the Word, of the church,
and of worship, was accommodated to the Jewish nation, and
would therefore have been different if that nation had been of
a different quality. For the sake of that nation, therefore,
it was permitted to marry several wives, which was a thing
altogether unknown in ancient times; and also to put away
their wives for various causes. Hence laws were enacted concerning such marriages and divorces, which otherwise would
not have entered the external of the Word; therefore this
external is called by the Lord [the external] of Moses, and is
said to be granted on account of the "hardness of their
heart." *A. C.* 10,603.

As to "hardness of heart," what it is, see above, chap. iii. 5,
Exposition.

Verses 6, 7, 8. *But from the beginning of creation, God
made them male and female. On this account a man shall
leave his father and mother, and shall cleave unto his wife;
and they two shall be one flesh; so that they are no longer
two, but one flesh.*—These words are not only to be understood
naturally, but also spiritually, and if they are not also understood spiritually, no one knows what is signified by the "male
and female," or the husband and wife, being "no longer two,
but one flesh," as is likewise said. (Gen. ii. 24.) By "male
and female," in the spiritual sense, is here signified, as above,
Truth and Good, consequently also the doctrine of Truth,

which is the doctrine of life, and the life of truth, which is the life of doctrine. These must not be two but one, since truth does not become truth with man without the good of life, nor does good become good with any one without the truth of doctrine, for good does not become spiritual good except by truths, and spiritual good is real good, but not natural good without it. When they are one, then truth is of good, and good is of truth; this *one* is meant by "one flesh." The case is similar with doctrine and life; these likewise make one man of the church, when doctrine is conjoined to life, and life to doctrine in him, for doctrine teaches how he ought to live, and to do or act, and life liveth the latter and doeth it. *A. E.* 725.

Verses 11, 12. *And He saith unto them, Whosoever shall put away his wife, and marry another, committeth adultery,* &c.—Marriages are most holy, but adulteries are most profane. Those who take pleasures in *adulteries* and *fornications* no longer believe those things which belong to heaven and the church, because the love of adultery is derived from the marriage of the evil and false, which is infernal, n. 9961, 10,175. The delights of *marriage* flow in from heaven, but the pleasures of *adultery* ascend from hell, n. 10,174. When any one commits adultery on earth, heaven is closed against him, and he becomes, as to his spirit, infernal, and his life after death, is in hell. *A. C.* 2750.

What "adultery," in a spiritual sense, means, see above, chap. viii. 38, Exposition.

Verses 13—17. *And they brought to Him little children, that He should touch them.*—The selfhood [proprium] of man, as was said, is nothing but evil, and when it is presented to the sight it is most deformed; but when charity and innocence from the Lord are insinuated into this selfhood, it appears good and beautiful, according to what was said above, n. 154. Charity and innocence are the virtues, which not only excuse this selfhood, or what is evil and false in man, but as it were abolish it, as every one may see in the case of infants, who, whilst they love each other and their parents, and whilst at the same time the infantile principle of innocence shines forth, in this case their evil and false principles not only disappear, but are even pleasing; hence it may be known that no one can be admitted into heaven unless he has somewhat of innocence, agreeably to what the Lord said,—" Suffer the *little children* to come to Me, and forbid them not; for of such is the kingdom of God. Verily I say unto you, Whosoever shall not receive the kingdom of God *as a little child,* he shall not enter into it. And, taking them up in His arms, putting His hands upon them, He blessed them." (Mark x. 14—16.) *A. C.* 164.

That he should touch them.—For the signification of "touching," see above, chap. i. 41, Exposition.

The reason why interior principles are signified by "infants," and likewise by "little children," is, because by the former and the latter is signified innocence, and innocence is the inmost principle. For in the heavens the case is this,—the inmost or third heaven consists of those who are in innocence, for they are principled in love to the Lord; and since the Lord is innocence itself, therefore they, who are in heaven, inasmuch as they are principled in love to Him, are in innocence, and although they are the wisest of all in heaven, still they appear to others as infants; hence it is, and likewise from this consideration that infants are in innocence, that by "infants" in the Word is signified innocence.

Inasmuch as the inmost principle of the heavens is *innocence,* therefore the interior principle, appertaining to all who are in the heavens, must be innocence; the case herein is like that of things successive, in regard to things co-existing, or of those things which are distinct from others by degrees, in regard to those things which exist from them; for every thing which exists in connection with other things, originates in things successive. When the former exist from the latter, they place themselves in the same order in which they were before they were distinguished by degrees; as, for the sake of illustration,—end, cause, and effect, are things successive and distinct from each other, and when these exist together they place themselves in the same order, viz., the end the inmost, next the cause, and lastly the effect. The effect is co-existing, and unless the cause be in it, and in the cause the end, it is not an effect, for if you remove the cause from the effect, you destroy the effect, and more so, if you remove the end from the cause; for from the end the cause derives that quality which makes it a cause, and from the cause the effect derives that quality which makes it an effect. So likewise it is in the spiritual world; as end, cause, and effect are distinct from each other, in like manner in the spiritual world, love to the Lord, charity towards a neighbour, and works of charity are distinct; when these three become one, or exist together, the first must be in the second, and the second in the third. As in works of charity, unless charity grounded in affection or the heart, be interiorly in them, they are not works of charity, and unless love to God be interiorly in charity, it is not

24

charity; wherefore if you take away that which is interior, what is exterior perishes, for what is exterior exists and subsists from its interior principles in order. This is the case with innocence, since innocence makes one with love to the Lord, so that unless it be interiorly in charity, it is not charity; consequently, unless charity, in which there is innocence, be inwardly in works of charity, they are not works of charity; hence it is, that with all who are in the heavens there must interiorly be innocence. That this is the case, and that by "infants" is signified *innocence* is manifest in Mark,—"Jesus said to the disciples, Suffer *little children* to come to Me, and forbid-them not; for of such is the kingdom of God. Verily I say unto you, Whosoever shall not receive the kingdom of God as a *little child*, he shall not enter into it; and taking them up into His arms, He laid His hand upon them, and blessed them." (x. 14, 15, 16; Luke xviii. 15, 16, 17; Matt. xviii. 3.) That by "little children" is here signified innocence may be manifest, because with *little children* there is innocence, and because innocencies in heaven appear as *little children;* that no one can enter into heaven unless he have something of innocence may be seen, n. 4797; and, moreover, *little children* suffer themselves to be governed by angels, who are innocencies, and are not as yet under the influence of selfhood, like adults, who govern themselves from their own judgment and their own will. That infants suffer themselves to be governed by those angels is manifest from the Lord's words in Matthew,—"See that ye despise not one of these *little ones;* for I say unto you, That *their angels* in the heavens do always behold the face of My Father." (xviii. 10.) No one can see the *face of God* except from innocence. In the following passages also, by "infants" is signified innocence, as in Matthew,— "Out of the mouth of *infants* and *sucklings* Thou hast perfected praise." (xxi. 16; Psalm viii. 3.) Again in the same Evangelist,—"Thou hast hid these things from the wise and intelligent, and hast revealed them unto *infants;*" (xi. 25; Luke x. 21.) for innocence, which is signified by "infants," is essential wisdom, inasmuch as genuine innocence dwells in wisdom, n. 2305, 2306, 4797; hence it is said, that "out of the mouth of infants and sucklings there was perfected praise;" also that such things are "revealed to infants." But in regard to the innocence of infants, it is only external, but not internal, and since it is not internal, it cannot be conjoined with any wisdom; whereas the innocence of angels, especially of those of the third heaven, is internal innocence, and thus is conjoined with wisdom, n. 2305, 2306. Man also is so created, that, when he grows old, and becomes as an infant, in this case the innocence of wisdom conjoins itself with the innocence of ignorance, which he had in infancy, and thus as a true infant he passes into the other life. *A. C.* 56.08. See also 3519, 9301.

Verse 15. *Verily I say unto you, Whosoever shall not receive the kingdom of God as a little child, he shall not enter into it.*—Innocence is the essence of every good, for good is only so far good as innocence is in it; whereas wisdom is of life, and thence of good, it follows that wisdom is only so far wisdom as it partakes of innocence. The like is true of love, charity, and faith. Hence it is that no one can enter heaven unless he has *innocence*, which is meant by these words of the Lord :—" Verily I say unto you, Whosoever shall not receive the kingdom of God as an *infant* or *little child*, he shall not enter therein." (Mark x. 14, 15; Luke xviii. 16, 17.) By "infants" or "little children," in these passages, as also in other parts of the Word, are meant those who are in innocence. The reason why good is [really] good only so far as *innocence* is in it, is, because all good is from the Lord, and *innocence* is to be led of the Lord. *C. S. L.* 414. See also *A. C.* 1453, 6013.

Verses 17—24. *And when He was gone forth into the way, one came running, and kneeling to Him, asked Him, Good Teacher, what shall I do that I may inherit eternal life?* &c. It is said that " Jesus loved him," and this because he said that he " had kept the commandments from his youth;" but whereas three things were wanting, viz., that he had not removed his heart from riches, that he had not fought against concupiscences, and that he had not yet acknowledged the Lord to be God, therefore the Lord said that he should " sell all that he had," by which is meant, that he should remove his heart from riches; that he should " take up his cross," by which is meant, that he should fight against concupiscences; and that he should " follow Him," by which is meant, that he should acknowledge the Lord to be God. The Lord spake these words, as all others, by correspondences, see the " Doctrine concerning the Sacred Scripture," n. 17; for no one can shun evils as sins unless he acknowledge the Lord, and come to Him, and unless he fights against evils, and thus removes concupiscences. *D. Life,* 66.

Verse 19. *Thou knowest the commandments, Do not commit adultery,* &c.—There are two tables upon which the precepts of the Decalogue are written, one for the Lord, the other for man. What the first table contains, is, that a plurality of

gods is not to be worshipped, but only One. What the
second table contains, is, that evils are not to be committed;
wherefore when a man worships the One God, and does not
commit evils, a conjunction with God is effected. For in
proportion as a man desists from evils, that is, does the work
of repentance, in the same proportion he is accepted of God,
and does good from Him. But who now is this one God?
[For on a right idea of this one God, as said in the preface to
this work, the "Apocalypse Revealed," is founded both heaven
and the church.] A trine or triune God is not one God, when
by trinity or triunity three Persons are understood. But He
whose trinity or triunity is one Person, the same is the One
God, and this God is the Lord [Jesus Christ]. Enter into
whatever intricacies of thought you will, yet you will never
be able to extricate yourself, and make out that God is one,
unless He is also one Person. That this is the case, the
whole Word teaches, as well the Old Testament and Prophets
as the New Testament and Evangelists, as may be clearly seen
in the "Doctrine of the New Jerusalem concerning the Lord."
A. R. 490. See also *A. E.* 894, 934. *A. C.* 2634, 7089.

Verses 20, 22. *All these things have I kept from my youth.
But he, being sad at that saying, went away grieved,* &c.—
If the commandments are not kept, or if evils are not removed
because they are sins, all things which man thinks, speaks,
wills, and does, are not good nor true before God, however
they may appear as good and true before the world. The
reason is, because they are not from the Lord, but from man,
for it is the love of man, and of the world, from which they
are derived, and which is in them. Most people at this day
believe that they shall come into heaven if they have faith,
live piously, and do some good works; and yet they do not
hold evils in aversion on account of their being sins, whence
they either commit them, or believe them to be allowable, and
they that believe them to be allowable, commit them when
opportunity is given; but let them know that their faith is not
faith, that their piety is not piety, and their good works are
not good, for they flow from the impurities which lie inwardly
concealed in man, the externals deriving all their quality from
the internals; for the Lord says—"Thou blind Pharisee,
cleanse first the inside of the cup and platter, that the outside
may be clean also." (Matt. xxiii. 26.)

From these considerations it may now appear, that if a man
could fulfil all things of the law, if he should give much to the
poor, if he should do good to the fatherless and the widow,
nay, if he should also give bread to the hungry and drink to the
thirsty, gather the sojourners and clothe the naked, visit the

sick and them that are bound in prison, if he should preach the Gospel strenuously and convert the Gentiles, frequent temples and hear preachings with devotion, attend the sacrament of the Supper frequently and be instant in prayer, with other things of a like nature, and his internal is not purified from hatred and revenge, from craftiness and malice, from insincerity and injustice, from the filthy delight of adultery, from the love of self and the love of rule thence derived, and the pride of self-derived intelligence, from contempt of others in comparison with himself, and from all other evils and the falses thence derived, still all those works are hypocritical, and are from the man himself, and not from the Lord. But, on the other hand, those same works, when the internal is purified, are all good, because they are from the Lord with man, who cannot do otherwise than perform such things, because he is in the love and faith of doing them.

In the above words, by "following the Lord," and "taking up the cross," similar things are signified as above, viz., to acknowledge the Divinity of the Lord, and the Lord to be God of heaven and earth, for without that acknowledgment no one can abstain from evils, and do good, unless from himself, and unless it be meritorious. The good, which is good in itself, and not meritorious good, is only from the Lord, wherefore unless the Lord be acknowledged, and that all good is from Him, no one can be saved. But before any one can do what is good from the Lord, he must undergo temptations; the reason is, because by temptations the internal of man is opened, by which man is conjoined to heaven. Now, whereas no one can do the commandments without the Lord, therefore the Lord said—"Yet lackest thou one thing: sell all that thou hast, and follow Me, taking up the cross;" that is, that he should acknowledge the Lord, and undergo temptations. By "selling all that he had, and giving to the poor," is signified, in the spiritual sense, that he should alienate from himself and reject the things of self, thus that he should *deny himself*; and by "giving to the poor," in the spiritual sense, is signified the doing works of charity. *A. E.* 893.

Verse 21. *One thing thou lackest: go, sell whatsoever thou hast*, &c.—Hereby is understood, in a spiritual sense, that he should reject the falses which were of the Jewish doctrines [and traditions], and should receive the doctrine of Truth from the Lord, and that he should undergo assault and temptations from falsities; wherefore they are mistaken who believe that they who desire to follow the Lord should sell all their [earthly] goods or property, and suffer [literally] the "cross." *A. E.* 122.

Verses 23, 24. *And Jesus looking round about, saith to His disciples, How hardly shall they that have riches enter into the kingdom of God! And the disciples were astonished at His words,* &c.—Some have supposed from what is said in these verses that the "rich" find a difficulty in entering into heaven, and that the "poor" enter easily, because they are poor, inasmuch as it is said,—"Blessed are the *poor*, because theirs is the kingdom of the heavens;" (Luke vi. 20, 21.) but they who know anything concerning the spiritual sense of the Word think otherwise, for they know that heaven is appointed for all who live the life of faith and of love, whether they be *rich* or *poor*. From much discourse and life with the angels, it has been given to know for certain that the rich come into heaven as easily as the poor, and that man is not excluded from heaven because he abounds in many things, neither is he received into heaven because he is in poverty. There are in heaven both rich and poor, and more *rich* than *poor* in its greater glory and happiness. *H. H.* 357. See the subject more fully discussed, *H. H.* 358—365.

Verse 25. *It is easier for a camel to go through the eye of a needle, than for a rich man to enter into the kingdom of God.*—By the "rich man" spoken of in this verse are meant the *rich*, in each sense, both natural and spiritual; the "rich" in a natural sense are they who abound in wealth, and place their hearts in wealth; but in a spiritual sense, the "rich" are they who abound in knowledges and sciences, for these are spiritual riches, and who are willing to introduce themselves thereby, from their own proper intelligence, into the things of heaven and the church; and since this is contrary to Divine order, it is said, that "it is easier for a camel to pass through the eye of a needle;" for, in the spiritual sense, by a "camel" are signified the principles of knowledge and of science in general; and by "the eye of a needle," spiritual truth. That such things are meant by a *camel* and *the eye of a needle* is not known at this day, because heretofore the science has not been opened which teaches what is signified in the spiritual sense by those things which are said in the literal sense in the Word; for in singular the things of the Word, there is a spiritual sense, and also a natural sense, since the Word, to the intent that there might be conjunction of heaven with the world, or of angels with men, after that immediate conjunction had ceased, was written by mere correspondences of natural things with spiritual. *H. H.* 365.

That "camels" signify common [or general] scientifics, is manifest from other passages in the Word where they are

named, as in Isaiah,—" What is prophetic of the beasts of the
south : in the land of trouble and anguish, the young lion and
the old lion from them, the viper and fiery flying serpent; they
carry their riches upon the shoulders of young asses, and their
treasures on the back of *camels,* they are not profitable to the
people : and Egypt shall help in vain, and to no purpose;"
(xxx. 6, 7.) where " the beasts of the south" denote those
who are in the light of knowledges, or in knowledges, but in
the life of evil; to " carry their riches on the shoulders of
young asses," denotes the knowledges appertaining to the
natural principle : that a young ass denotes rational truth, see
n. 2781 ; " their treasures on the back of camels," denotes the
knowledges appertaining to the natural principle ; the " back
of camels" is the natural principle ; the " camels" themselves
denote the common [or general] scientifics which are in that
principle; the " treasures" are the knowledges which they hold
precious.　The reason why " Egypt will help in vain, and to no
purpose," is, because the sciences are of no use to them ; that
" Egypt" denotes science, may be seen, n. 1164, 1165, 1186.
That by " camels" here are not meant camels, is evident, for
it is said, that " the young lion and the old lion carry their
treasures on the back of camels;" every one may see that
some arcanum of the church is hereby signified.　Again in
the same Prophet,—" What is prophetic of the wilderness
of the sea.　Thus saith the Lord, Go, set a watchman, he
shall declare what he has seen ; and he saw a chariot, a pair
of horses, a chariot of an ass, a chariot of a *camel,* and he
hearkened a hearkening : he answered and said, Babylon is
fallen, is fallen ;" (xxi. 6, 7, 9.) where the " wilderness of the
sea " denotes the vanity of sciences which are not for use; the
" chariot of an ass" denotes a heap of particular scientifics ;
the " chariot of a camel" denotes a heap of common [or
general] scientifics, which are in the natural man ; the vain
reasonings appertaining to those who are signified by "Babylon," are what are thus described.　Again in the same Prophet,—" Thy heart shall dilate itself, because the multitude of
the sea shall be converted to thee ; the riches of the Gentiles
shall come to thee ; the abundance of *camels* shall cover thee ;
the dromedaries of Media and Epha, all these shall come from
Sheba, they shall carry gold and frankincense, and shall pro-
claim the praises of Jehovah ;" (lx. 5, 6.) speaking of the
Lord, and of the Divine celestial and spiritual things, in His
natural principle; the " multitude of the sea" denotes an
immense store of natural truths; the "riches of the Gentiles,"
an immense store of natural good; the "abundance of camels,"

an abundance of common [or general] scientifics; " gold " and
" frankincense " denote goods and truths, which are " the
praises of Johovah;" "from Sheba" denotes from the celestial
things of love and faith, see n. 113, 117, 1171. By " the
queen of Sheba coming to Solomon at Jerusalem with exceeding great wealth, with camels carrying spices, and very much
gold, and precious stones," (1 Kings x. 1, 2.) was represented
the wisdom and intelligence which were added to the Lord,
who in the internal sense is here Solomon; the " camels
bearing spices, gold, and precious stones," denote those things
which are of wisdom and intelligence in the natural man.
From these passages it may be manifest that by " camels," in
the internal sense of the Word, are signified common [or
general] scientifics, which are of the natural man. Scientifics
are common [or general] which comprehend in them several
particulars, and in these singular ones, and form in general the
natural man, as to his intellectual part. *A. C.* 3048.

Verses 28—31. *And Peter began to say unto Him, Lo, we
have forsaken all things, and have followed Thee. And Jesus
answering said, Verily I say unto you, there is no one who hath
left house, or brethren, or sisters, or father, or mother, or wife,
or children, or lands, for My sake and the Gospel's, but he
shall receive an hundred-fold now in this time, houses, and
brethren, and sisters, and mothers, and children, and lands,
with persecutions; and in the age to come eternal life,* &c.—
Who cannot see, that *father, mother, wife, children, brethren,
and sisters,* together with *house* and *lands,* are not here meant,
but only such things as are of man himself, and are called his
own, for these a man must leave and hate, if he is willing to
worship the Lord, and to be His disciple, and to receive a
hundred-fold, and to inherit eternal life. The things belonging to man [or proper to him], are the things of his love, and
thence of this life into which he was born, and consequently
they are evil and false principles of every kind; and since they
are of his love and life, therefore it is said, that he ought also
to "hate his own soul;" these evil and false principles are signified by " father and mother, wife, children, brothers, and
sisters;" for all things which are of man's love and life, or
which are of the affection and thence of the thought, or which
are of the will and thence of his understanding, are formed
and joined together, like generations descending from one
father and mother, and are likewise distinguished as into
families and houses; the love of self, and the consequent love
of the world, are their *father* and *mother,* and the lusts thence
derived, together with their evil and false principles, are the

children, who are *brethren and sisters.* That these things are meant may be very manifest from this consideration, that the Lord does not will that any one should hate *father* and *mother,* or *wife,* or *children,* or *brothers,* or *sisters,* because this would be to act contrary to the spiritual love implanted in every one from heaven, which is the love of parents towards their children, and of children towards their parents; also contrary to conjugial love, which is that of a husband towards a wife, and of a wife, towards a husband; likewise contrary to mutual love, which is that of brothers and sisters amongst each other; yea, the Lord teaches that even enemies are not to be hated, but loved. From these considerations it is evident, that by the names of those who are related by consanguinity, affinity, and kindred, in the Word, are meant those who are related by consanguinity, affinity, and kindred in a spiritual sense. *A. E.* 724.

He who is not acquainted with the internal sense of the Word, will believe that by "house, brethren, sisters, father, mother, wife, children, lands," are signified *house, brethren, sisters, father, mother, wife, children,* and *lands;* but they are such things as appertain to man, being proper to him, which he must leave, and in the place thereof will receive spiritual and celestial things, which are of the Lord; and this by temptations, which are meant by "persecutions." Every one may see, that if he "leaves a mother," he is not to receive *mothers,* in like manner neither is he to receive *brothers* and *sisters. A. C.* 4843.

Verse 30. *Brethren and sisters,* &c.—All in the other life are consociated together according to affections, and those who are thus consociated, constitute a fraternity; not that they call each other *brethren,* but that they are brethren by conjunction. Essential Goodness and Truth, in the other life, make that which on earth is called consanguinity and relationship, or affinity, wherefore they correspond. For goods and truths, considered in themselves, do not acknowledge any other Father than the Lord, inasmuch as they are from Him alone. Hence all are in a *brotherhood,* or fraternity, who are in goods and truths. Nevertheless, there are degrees according to the quality of goods and truths; these degrees are signified in the Word by *brethren, sisters, sons-in-law, daughters-in-law, grandsons, granddaughters,* and by several names of families. But on earth they are so named in respect to common parents, howsoever they differ as to affections; whereas, in the other life that brotherhood and relationship are dissipated, and every one comes into other brotherhoods, unless on earth they have been principled in like good. In the beginning, indeed, they generally meet together, but in a short time they are disjoined, for [worldly] gain in that life does not consociate, but, as was said, affection, the quality whereof then appears as in clear day, even the quality of the affection which one has had towards another. And as this is the case, and as affection draws every one to his own society, therefore they are dissociated who have been of different inclinations. Then also all brotherhood and all friendship, which was grounded merely in the external man, is obliterated with both parties, and only the brotherhood and friendship of the internal man remains. *A. C.* 4121.

Works done by [or from] man are not good, but only those which are done by [or from] the Lord, attendant on man; but to the intent that works may be done by [or from] the Lord, and not by [or from] man, two things are necessary,—*First,* That the Lord's Divinity be acknowledged, and likewise that He is God of heaven and earth, even as to His Humanity, and that all good, which is good, is from Him. *Secondly,* That man should live according to the precepts of the Decalogue, by abstaining from the evils which are there forbidden, as from the worship of other gods, from profaning the name of God, from theft, from adultery, from murder, from false witness, from coveting the possessions and property of others. These two things are requisite, to the intent that the works which are done by man may be good. The reason is, because all good comes from the Lord alone, and because the Lord cannot enter so as to abide with man and lead him, so long as those evils are not removed as sins, since they are infernal,— yea, are hell with man; and unless hell be removed, the Lord cannot enter and open heaven. These things are also meant by the Lord's words to the rich man, (Matt. xix. 16—22; Mark x. 17—22; Luke xviii. 18—25.) who questioned Him concerning eternal life, and said that "from his youth he had kept the commandments," [or precepts of the Decalogue] whom the Lord is said to have loved, and to have taught, that "one thing was wanting to him," that he should "sell all that he had, taking up the cross." By "selling all that he had," is signified that he should quit his religious tenets, which were tradi- tions, for he was a Jew, and likewise, that he should quit the things proper to himself, consisting in the love of himself and the world more than God, thus in leading himself; and by "following the Lord," is signified to acknowledge Him only, and to be led by Him; wherefore also the Lord said—" Why callest thou Me good? there is none good but God alone."

By " taking up his cross," is signified to fight against evils and false principles, which are from selfhood. *A. E.* 934.

Verse 31. *But many that are first shall be last, and the last first.*—The faith of charity does not belong to those who place merit in their actions, for thus they are willing to be saved, not from the Lord's justice, but from their own. That in them there is no faith of charity, that is, no charity, is manifest from these considerations, that they prefer themselves to others; thus they regard themselves, not others, only so far as others are serviceable to them, and such as are not willing to be serviceable, they either despise or hate; thus by self-love they dissociate, and never join in society, in consequence of which they destroy what is celestial, viz., mutual love, which is the support of heaven, for in it heaven itself, and all its consociation and unanimity, subsist and consist. For whatsoever destroys unanimity in the other life, this is contrary to the order of heaven itself, and thus conspires to the destruction of the whole; such are they who place merit in their actions, and claim to themselves justice. Of these there are multitudes in the other life, whose faces occasionally shine like torches, but from false fire, which proceeds from self-justification, yet they are cold; they seem occasionally to run about and confirm self-merit from the literal sense of the Word, hating the truths which are of the internal sense, n. 1877; their sphere is full of self-respect, thus destructive of all ideas which do not regard them as a kind of deity;—the combined sphere of several of them is so distracting, that there is nothing in it but what is unfriendly and hostile, for every one when he is desiring the same thing, viz., that he may be served, murders another [who stands in his way] in his heart. Some of them are amongst those who say that they have laboured in the Lord's vineyard, when yet at the same time they have continually had in view their own preëminence, glory, and honours, also their gain, and thus that they might become "greatest in heaven,"—yea, that they might be served by the angels, in heart despising others in comparison with themselves; thus void of mutual love, in which heaven consists, but full of self-love, in which they make heaven to consist, not knowing what heaven is, concerning whom, see n. 450, 451, 452, 1594, 1679. These are amongst those who wish to be " the first," but who become " the last;" (Matt. xix. 30; xxi. 16; Mark x. 31.) and who say that they have " prophesied in the Lord's name," and have done many virtuous actions, but of whom it is said,—" I know you not." (Matt. vii. 22, 23.) It is otherwise with those who, from simplicity of heart, have conceived that they merited heaven, and have lived in charity. These have regarded the meriting heaven as a promise of heaven, and easily acknowledge it to be of the Divine Mercy; for a life of charity has this along with it, charity itself loving all that is true. *A. C.* 2027.

Verses 33, 34. *The Son of Man will be delivered to the chief Priests and the Scribes,* &c.—He who knows in what respect the Lord is called the "Son of God," and in what the "Son of Man," possesses a key to many arcana of the Word; for the Lord at one time calls Himself the *Son,* at another, the *Son of God,* and again, at another, the *Son of Man;* always using the epithet which is appropriate to the subject of His discourse. When His Divinity, His unity with the Father, His divine power, faith in Him, and life from Him, are treated of, He then calls Himself "the Son," and "the Son of God;" as in John v. 17—26, and elsewhere. But where His passion, the judgment, His coming, and, in general, redemption, salvation, reformation, and regeneration, are treated of, He calls Himself "the Son of Man;" the reason is, because He is then spoken of as the Word. The Lord is designated by various names in the Word of the Old Testament, being there named Jehovah, Jah, the Lord, God, the Lord Jehovih, Zebaoth, the God of Israel, the Holy One of Israel, the Mighty One of Jacob, Shaddai,* the Rock; as also the Creator, Former, Saviour, and Redeemer; that name being always applied which is appropriate to the occasions on which it is used. Similar distinctions are made in the Word of the New Testament, where the Lord is called Jesus, Christ, the Lord, God, the Son of God, the Son of Man, the Prophet, and the Lamb, with other names: which are never applied indiscriminately, but that is adopted which is suitable to the subject.

Having shewn in what respect the Lord is called the *Son of God,* we will now explain in what respect He is called the *Son of Man.* He is called the "Son of Man" when His passion, the judgment, or His coming is treated of; and, in general, where it relates to redemption, salvation, reformation, or regeneration. The reason is, because the Lord is the *Son of Man* as to the Word; and it is as to the Word that He suffers, judges, comes into the world, redeems, saves, reforms, and regenerates. This shall be now shewn in what follows:—

I. *That the Lord is called the Son of Man when the Passion is treated of,* is evident from the following passages:—Jesus said unto the disciples, "Behold, we go up to Jerusalem; and *the Son of Man* shall be delivered unto the chief Priests and unto the Scribes; and they shall condemn Him to death, and

---

* This name does not occur in the authorized version of the English Bible, being there always translated *the Almighty;* the learned, however, are much divided about its exact meaning.

shall deliver Him to the Gentiles: and they shall mock Him, and shall scourge Him, and shall spit upon Him, and shall kill Him: and the third day He shall rise again." (Mark x. 33, 34.) So, likewise, in other places where He foretels His passion, as Matt. xx. 18, 19; Mark viii. 31; Luke ix. 22. Jesus said,— "Behold, the hour is at hand, and *the Son of Man* is betrayed into the hands of sinners." (Matt. xxvi. 45.)

II. *That the Lord is called the Son of Man when Judgment is treated of*, is clear from these passages:—"When *the Son of Man* shall come in His glory, then shall He sit on the throne of His glory; and He shall set the sheep on His right hand, but the goats on the left." (Matt. xxv. 31, 33.) "When *the Son of Man* shall sit on the throne of His glory, ye shall also sit upon twelve thrones, judging the twelve tribes of Israel." (Matt. xix. 28.) "The *Son of Man* shall come in the glory of His Father, and He shall reward every man according to his works." (Matt. xvi. 27.) "Watch ye, therefore, that ye may be accounted worthy to stand before *the Son of Man*." (Luke xxi. 36.) "In such an hour as ye think not, *the Son of Man* cometh." (Matt. xxiv. 44; Luke xii. 40.) "For the Father judgeth no man, but hath committed all judgment unto the Son; because He is *the Son of Man*." (John v. 22, 27.) The reason why the Lord thus calls Himself the "Son of Man" when judgment is treated of, is, because all judgment is executed according to the Divine Truth, which is in the Word. That it is this which judges every one, the Lord Himself declares in John,—"If any man hear My words, and believe not, I judge him not; for I came not to judge the world: *the Word that I have spoken*, the same shall judge him in the last day." (xii. 47, 48.)

III. *That the Lord is called the Son of Man where His coming is treated of*, is plain from the following passages:— The disciples said unto Jesus,—"What shall be the sign of Thy coming, and of the consummation of the age?" in answer to which inquiry, the Lord foretold the successive states of the church down to the period of its end; of which He says— "Then shall appear the sign of *the Son of Man*. And they shall see *the Son of Man* coming in the clouds of heaven, with power and great glory." (Matt. xxiv. 3, 30; Mark xiii. 26; Luke xxi. 27.) By the "consummation of the age," is meant the last time of the church; by the "coming of the Son of Man in the clouds of heaven with glory," is signified the opening of the Word, with a manifestation that it treats of the Lord alone.

IV. *That the Lord is called the Son of Man where Redemption, Salvation, Reformation, and Regeneration are treated of*, appears from the following passages:—"The *Son of Man* came

to give His life a ransom for many." (Matt. xx. 28; Mark
x. 45.) "The *Son of Man* is not come to destroy men's lives,
but to save them." (Luke ix. 56.) "The *Son of Man* is come
to seek and to save that which was lost." (Luke xix. 10.)
"He that soweth the good seed is the *Son of Man.*" (Matt.
xiii. 37.) Salvation and redemption are here treated of; and,
as the Lord effects these by means of the Word, therefore He
calls Himself the "Son of Man." The Lord says, that "the
Son of Man hath power to forgive sins;" (Mark ii. 10; Luke
v. 24.) that is, to save. Also, that "the *Son of Man* is Lord
even of the Sabbath;" (Matt. xii. 8; Mark ii. 28; Luke vi. 5.)
because He is the Word, which is what He there teaches.

*That because the Son of Man signifies the Lord as to the
Word, the same title was also given to the Prophets.*—The
title, "Son of Man," was given to the prophets, because they
represented the Lord as to the Word, and thence signified the
doctrine of the church derived from the Word.

From all that has been advanced, then, it is evident that
the Lord is called the "Son of God" with respect to the
Divine Human, and the "Son of Man" with respect to the
Word. *D. Lord,* 22—28. See chap. viii. 38, Exposition.

Verses 35—37. *And James and John, the sons of Zebedee,
came unto Him, saying, Teacher, we are willing [desirous] that
Thou shouldest do for us whatsoever we ask. And He said
unto them, What will ye that I should do for you? They said
unto Him, Grant unto us that we may sit, one on Thy right
hand, and the other on Thy left hand, in Thy glory.*—The
doctrinals of the ancient church, which was after the flood,
were for the most part external representatives and significatives, in which were stored up internal truths; the members
of that church, for the most part, were in holy worship when
in externals, and if any one in the beginning had said to
them that those representatives and significatives were not the
essentials of Divine worship, but that those essentials were the
spiritual and celestial things which were represented and signified, they would altogether have rejected the idea, and would
thus have become no church. This would have been still more
the case with the Jewish church, so that if any one had told
them that rituals derived their sanctity from the Divine things
of the Lord which are in them, they would not have acknowledged it. Such also was man when the Lord came into the
world, and still more corporeal, especially they who were of
the church; this is very evident from the disciples themselves,
who were continually attendant on the Lord, and heard so
many things concerning His kingdom; nevertheless they could
not as yet perceive interior truths, for they could not form any

notion of the Lord, than (as the Jews at this day conceive regarding the Messiah whom they expect), that He would exalt that people to dominion and glory above all nations in the universe; and although they heard so many things from the Lord concerning the heavenly kingdom, still they could not but think that the heavenly kingdom would be like an earthly kingdom, and that God the Father would be supreme there, and after Him the Son, and next to them the twelve, and thus they should reign in order; wherefore also James and John asked that "one might sit on His right hand, and the other on the left," (Mark x. 35—37.) and the rest of the disciples were indignant because these two were desirous to be greater than they; (Mark x. 41; Matt. xx. 24.) wherefore also the Lord, after having taught them what it was to be "greatest in heaven," (Matt. xx. 25—28; Mark x. 42—45.) still spake to them according to their conceit, viz., that they should "sit upon twelve thrones, and judge the twelve tribes of Israel." (Luke xxii. 24, 30; Matt. xix. 28.) If they had been told that by *disciples* are not meant disciples, but all those who are in the good of love and of faith, n. 3354, 3488; also that in the kingdom of the Lord there are not *thrones*, nor *principalities*, nor *governments*, as in the world, and that they could not even *judge* the smallest particular respecting any man, n. 2129, 2553, they would have rejected the Word, and leaving the Lord, would have gone every one about his business. The reason why the Lord so spake was, that they might receive what He said, and thereby be introduced into internal truths; for in those external truths which the Lord spake, were stored up and concealed internal truths, which are opened in time, and when they are opened, the former external truths are dissipated, and serve only as objects or mediums of thinking about internal truths. *A. C.* 3857.

As to what further concerns those who seek *recompense* for the works they perform, it is to be noted, that they are never contented, but that they are indignant if they are not rewarded more than others, and they mourn and find fault if they see others more blessed than themselves; neither do they make blessedness to consist in internal blessedness, but in external, viz., that they may become eminent, and have dominion, and be served by the angels, so as to be above the angels, consequently princes and great ones in heaven, when yet heavenly blessedness consists, not in being willing to have dominion, nor in being served by others, but in being willing to "serve others," and in being "the least," as the Lord teaches where He says,—"Ye know that they who are appointed to rule over the Gentiles exercise lordship over them; and their great ones exercise authority upon them. But it shall not be so amongst you: but whosoever willeth to be *great* among you, shall be your *minister:* and whosoever of you willeth to be *the first,* shall be the *servant* of all. For even the Son of Man came not to be ministered unto, but to *minister.*" (Mark x. 42—46.) And that heaven is the portion of those who do good without a view to "recompense," the Lord thus teaches in Luke,—"For whosoever *exalteth* himself shall be *abased,* and he that *humbleth* himself shall be *exalted.* When thou makest a dinner or supper, call not thy friends, nor thy brethren, neither thy kinsmen nor rich neighbours; lest they also bid thee again, and a *recompense* be made thee. But when thou makest a feast, call the poor, the halt, the lame, the blind: and thou shalt be blessed; for they cannot *recompense* thee, but thou shalt be *recompensed* at the resurrection of the just." (xiv. 11—14.) "Recompense at the resurrection of the just," is internal happiness, resulting from doing good without remuneration, which they receive from the Lord when they perform uses; and they who love to serve without recompense, are given to preside over more noble uses, and actually become greater and more powerful than others, in proportion as they have a greater love to serve. They who do good works for the sake of recompense, say also, because they have learnt it from the Word, that they are "willing to be the least" in heaven; but in this case they think, by so saying, to become great, thus they have still the same end in view. But they who do good without a view to recompense, do not actually think of eminence, but only of serving. See what has been said and shewn above concerning merit grounded in works; also of what quality they are in another life, who seek to establish such merit, and that they appear to cut wood, and to mow grass, n. 1110, 1111, 4943; in what manner they are represented, n. 1774, 2027; that they who have done good with a view to themselves and from a love of the world, receive nothing of recompense for that good in the other life, n. 1835; that they who place merit in works, interpret the Word according to the letter in favour of themselves, and that they ridicule its interior contents, n. 1774, 1877; that true charity is void of every idea of merit, n. 2340, 2373, 2400, 3816; that they who separate faith from charity, make the works which they do meritorious, n. 2373; that all who enter into heaven, strip themselves of selfhood and merit, n. 4007; that in the beginning of reformation an idea is cherished with many persons that they do good of themselves, and that by that good they merit heaven, but in proportion as they are regenerated, they put off this idea, n. 4175. *A. C. 6393.*

From the love by which any one is influenced in spiritual combat, it may be known what his faith is, since if this be any other love than love towards his neighbour, and towards the Lord's kingdom, he does not fight from a principle of faith, that is, he does not believe in Jehovah, but in that which he loves; for the love itself, in favour of which he fights, is his faith; as for example,—he who fights from the love that he may become greatest in heaven, does not believe in Jehovah, but rather in himself, for to desire to " become greatest" is to desire to rule others; thus he fights for rule in like manner in other cases; wherefore from the love itself, by which he is influenced in spiritual combat, it may be known what his faith is; but the Lord, in all His temptation-combats, never fought from the love of self, or for Himself, but for all in the universe; consequently, not that He might be greatest in heaven, for this is contrary to Divine Love, hardly that He might be least, only that all others might become something and be saved, as He Himself likewise says in Mark,—" Whosoever will be *great* among you, shall be your minister; and whosoever of you will be *the first,* shall be your servant. For even the Son of Man came not to be ministered unto, but to minister, and give His soul a ransom for many;" (x. 43—45.) this love, or this faith, is that from which the Lord fought. *A. C.* 1812.

Verses 38, 39. *But Jesus said unto them, Ye know not what ye ask: can ye drink of the cup which I drink of? and be baptized with the baptism that I am baptized with?* &c.—By " drinking of the cup which the Lord drinks of," the like is signified as by the cross above spoken of, viz., the undergoing temptations; and by " the baptism by which the Lord was baptized," is signified to be regenerated by temptations; but the difference between " the cup which the Lord drank of," and " the cup which they were to drink of," is like the difference between the Lord's temptations and the temptations of men; for the Lord's temptations were most grievous, and against all the hells, since the Lord brought into subjection all the hells by temptations admitted into Himself, whereas the temptations of men are against the evil and false principles which appertain to them from the hells, in which temptations the Lord fights, and not man, except against some sorrows. The like is the difference between " the baptism with which the Lord is baptized," and " the baptism with which men will be baptized," being like the difference between glorification and regeneration; for the Lord by temptations glorified His Humanity through His own proper power, whereas men are

regenerated, not from their own proper power, but by the
Lord; for by "baptism" is signified to be regenerated by temptations, but by "the Lord's baptism," to glorify His Humanity
by temptation. That by "baptism" is signified regeneration
and likewise temptation, may be seen in the "Doctrine of the
New Jerusalem," n. 187—193. And that the Lord glorified
His Humanity and made it Divine, as He regenerates man,
and makes him spiritual, see "Arcana Cœlestia," n. 1725,
1729, 1733, 3318, 3381, 3382, 4286. *A. E.* 893.

Verse 40. *But to sit on My right hand and on My left
hand, is not Mine to give, except to those for whom it is prepared.*—By the "right hand" of the Lord is signified the
good of celestial love, which is the good of love to the Lord;
and by the "left hand" is signified the good of spiritual love,
which is the good of neighbourly love; hence likewise all
things which are on the right side of man correspond to
celestial good, and those on the left to spiritual good; for all
things appertaining to man correspond to heaven. They who
are principled in those goods are meant by "sitting on the right
and left hand" of the Lord, in Mark,—"To sit on My *right
hand* and on My *left hand,* is not Mine to give, but [or except]
to those for whom it is prepared." (x. 40.) To "give to those
for whom it is prepared," signifies to give, from mercy, to those
who are in the good of life and of faith, n. 9305; thus who are
in celestial good and in spiritual good. *A. C.* 9511.

Verse 45. *For even the Son of Man came not to be ministered unto, but to minister, and to give His soul a ransom for
many.*—The celestial principle of love consists in not being
willing to be its own, but the property of all, so that it is
willing to give to others all things which it has, this being the
very essence of celestial love; the Lord, inasmuch as He is
love itself, or the essence and life of the love of all in the
heavens, is willing to give to mankind all things which He has,
which is signified by the Lord's words,—"The Son of Man
came to give His soul a ransom for many." Hence it is
manifest that *name* and *glory,* in the internal sense, have a
meaning altogether different from what they have in the
external sense; wherefore all in heaven who are desirous to
become great and greatest are rejected, because it is contrary
to the essence and life of celestial love, which is from the
Lord; hence also it is that nothing is more contrary to
celestial love than the love of self. *A. C.* 1419.

By "giving His soul a ransom for many," is signified that
they might be vindicated and delivered from hell; for the
passion of the cross was the last combat and plenary victory

by which the Lord subdued the hells, and by which He glorified His Humanity, see "Doctrine of the New Jerusalem,"
n. 293—297, and 300—306. *A. E. 328.*

TRANSLATOR'S NOTES AND OBSERVATIONS.

CHAPTER X.

VERSE 40. *But to sit on My right hand and on My left
hand, is not Mine to give, but* [*or except to those*] *for whom it
is prepared.*—In the common version of the New Testament
there is an interpolation in this passage, which is not to be
found in the original Greek, and which, on that account, is
properly enough printed in italics, viz., "*It shall be given to
them,*" so that the whole verse runs thus:—"To sit on My
right hand and on My left hand, is not Mine to give, but
it shall be given to them for whom it is prepared." But it
deserves to be considered, that, according to this interpolation,
the Lord is made to say what He does not say, viz., that
"to sit on His right hand and on His left hand, is not His to
give," whereas He only declares that it "is not His to give,
but [*or except*] *to the prepared.*" The power, therefore, of
dispensing future rewards belongs of right to Him, in agreement with His own declaration; (John xvii. 2.) but then He
dispenses only according to the laws of His own order, which
laws require that there be a *suitable preparation* on the part
of those who are to receive.

Verse 42. *But JESUS calling them unto Him, saith unto
them, Ye know that they who are appointed to rule over the
Gentiles exercise lordship over them; and their great ones
exercise authority upon them.*—The Lord here speaks in
reference to the heavenly marriage, when He distinguishes
between "those who are appointed to rule over the Gentiles,"
and those whom He calls "their great ones," ascribing to the
former the *exercise of lordship,* and to the latter the *exercise
of authority.* A similar distinction is made in the subsequent
verses (43, 44), between him that is *willing to be great,* and
him that is *willing to be first,* also between being a *minister*
and a *servant,* which distinction cannot be understood, unless
it be interpreted according to the eternal distinction existing
between the two principles, the GOOD and the TRUE, and
also between the recipients of those principles, the *will* and
the *understanding.*

M.A R K.

CHAPTER XI.

THE WORD.

1. AND when they came nigh to Jerusalem, to Bethphage and Bethany, at the Mount of Olives, He sendeth forth two of His disciples,

2. And saith unto them, Go into the village over against you : and immediately on entering into it, ye shall find a colt tied, on which never man sat; having loosed him, bring him.

3. And if any one say to you, Why do ye this? say ye, That the Lord hath need of him; and immediately he will send him hither.

4. And they went, and found the colt tied at the door without, where two ways met; and they loose him.

5. And some of them that stood there said unto them, What do ye, loosing the colt?

6. And they said unto them as Jesus had commanded; and they let them go.

7. And they led the colt to Jesus, and cast their garments on him; and He sat upon him.

THE INTERNAL SENSE.

THAT the LORD, from His Divine Love, and by His Divine Truth, explores the principles of the rational man, requiring them to be separated from what is evil and false, and to receive influx of life from Himself. (Verses 1, 2.)

And if the persuasions of the natural man oppose, they are to be overcome by teaching the necessity of such influx to restore Divine order. (Verse 3.)

Accordingly those persuasions are overcome, and the rational man is set at liberty to receive Divine influx. (Verses 4, 5, 6.)

So that goods and truths in every complex, together with the perceptions of good and truth, are acknowledged

8. And many spread their garments in the way: and others cut down branches from the trees, and strewed them in the way.

9. And they who went before, and they who followed, cried, saying, Hosanna! Blessed is He that cometh in the name of the Lord!

10. Blessed is the kingdom of our father David, that cometh in the name of the Lord: Hosanna in the highest!

11. And Jesus entered into Jerusalem, and into the temple: and when He had looked round about upon all things, and now the eventide was come, He went out unto Bethany with the twelve.

12. And on the morrow, when they were coming from Bethany, He was hungry:

13. And seeing a fig-tree afar off having leaves, He came, if perhaps He might find any thing thereon: and when He came to it, He found nothing but leaves; for it was not the time of figs.

14. And Jesus answering, said unto it, Let no man eat fruit of thee hereafter for an age. And His disciples heard.

15. And they came to Jerusalem: and Jesus having entered into the temple, began to cast out them that sold and bought in the temple, and overthrew the tables of the money-changers, and the seats of them that sold doves;

16. And would not suffer that any man should carry a vessel through the temple.

to be from the LORD, and to be His. (Verses 7, 8.)

And all lower principles, both interior and exterior, exalt the Divine Humanity of the LORD, and whatsoever proceeds from it. (Verses 9, 10.)

Since the church, and all things therein, are under the inspection of that Humanity, even at the last time of the church, when the LORD can no longer dwell in it, with His goods and truths. (Verse 11.)

For the LORD is ever in the desire of good in the church, and therefore if there be no such good, as was the case in the Jewish church, there can be nothing but truth falsified, which is incapable of producing any natural good from a spiritual origin. (Verses 12—14.)

On which occasion the LORD effects a work of judgment, by separating from the church those who make gain of holy things, whether by truths or goods, and who defile the truths of the church by natural scientifics. (Verses 15, 16.)

17. And He taught, saying unto them, Is it not written, My house shall be called the house of prayer for [or by] all nations? but ye have made it a den of thieves.

18. And the Scribes and chief Priests heard, and sought how they might destroy Him: for they feared Him, because all the multitude were astonished at His doctrine.

19. And when it was evening, He went out of the city.

20. And in the morning, as they passed by, they saw the fig-tree dried up from the roots.

21. And Peter calling to remembrance saith unto Him, Rabbi, behold, the fig-tree which Thou cursedst is withered away.

22. And Jesus answering, saith unto them, Have the faith of God.

23. For verily I say unto you, that whosoever shall say to this mountain, Be thou removed, and be thou cast into the sea; and shall not doubt in his heart, but shall believe those things which he saith shall come to pass; he shall have whatsoever he saith.

24. Therefore I say unto you, Whatsoever things ye desire, when ye pray, believe that ye shall receive, and ye shall have [them].

25. And when ye stand praying, forgive [remit], if ye have ought against any: that your Father also who is in the heavens may forgive you [remit] your trespasses.

In which case, as the Word teaches, the purity of Divine worship in the church ceases, being supplanted by self-love. (Verse 17.)

Which is eager to destroy all the life of heavenly love and charity. (Verse 18.)

And howsoever it may be principled in the doctrines of faith, is destitute of the real life of faith. (Verses 19—21.)

Which faith is the Divine truth in man from the Lord, containing in it the Divine Omnipotence, so that whosoever is principled in this faith has power to remove self-love and the love of the world, and cast them into hell. (Verses 22, 23.)

And he also has all his desires granted, because he can desire nothing but what is in agreement with the Divine Will or Love. (Verse 24.)

Every man therefore ought to regulate his desires by the spirit of charity, under the acknowledgment that as he extends mercy to others, so mercy will be extended from

26. But if ye forgive [remit] not, neither will your Father who is in the heavens forgive [remit] your trespasses.

27. And they come again to Jerusalem: and as He was walking in the temple, there come to Him the chief Priests, and the Scribes, and the Elders,

28. And say unto Him, By what authority doest. Thou these things? and who gave Thee this authority to do these things?

29. But Jesus answering, said unto them, I will also ask you one word, and answer Me, and I will tell you by what authority I do these things.

30. The baptism of John, was it from heaven, or from men? Answer Me.

31. And they reasoned with themselves, saying, If we shall say, From heaven; He will say, Why then did ye not believe him?

32. But if we shall say, From men; they feared the people: for all held John to be a prophet indeed.

33. And they answering, said to Jesus, We do not know. And Jesus answering, saith unto them, Neither do I tell you by what authority I do these things.

the LORD to him, and *vice versâ*. (Verses 25, 26.)

That the Divine power of the LORD, manifested in His Divine Humanity, cannot be seen and acknowledged, only so far as mankind are initiated into heavenly wisdom by submitting to the process of spiritual purification and regeneration which the Word teaches. (Verse 27, to the end of the chapter.)

EXPOSITION.

CHAPTER XI.

VERSES 1—12. *And when they came nigh to Jerusalem, to Bethphage and Bethany, at the Mount of Olives, He sendeth forth two of His disciples, and saith unto them, Go into the village over against you: and immediately on entering into it, ye shall find a colt tied, on which never man sat; having loosed him, bring him, &c.*—Jesus went from the Mount of Olives to Jerusalem, and suffered; and by this was signified, that in all things He acted from Divine Love, for the "Mount of Olives" signified that love; for whatsoever the Lord did in the world was representative, and whatsoever He spake was significative. The reason why He was in representatives and significatives, when in the world, was, that He might be in the ultimates of heaven and of the church, and at the same time in their first principles, and thus might govern and arrange ultimate things from first principles, and all intermediate things from first principles by things ultimate. *A. E.* 405.

"To ride upon an ass" was a token that the natural principle was subordinate, and to "ride upon a colt the son of an ass," that the rational principle was subordinate; hence it pleased the Lord to do so, both because it was the badge of a judge and of a king to ride upon them, and at the same time that the representatives of the church might be fulfilled. From these considerations it is manifest that all and singular things in the church at that time were representative of the Lord, and hence of the celestial and spiritual things which are in His kingdom, and this even to a "she-ass," by which was represented the natural man as to good and truth; the cause of the representation was, that the natural man ought to serve the rational, and this the spiritual, and the spiritual the celestial, and the celestial the Lord: such is the order of subordination. *A. C.* 2781.

Verse 8. *And many spread their garments in the way: and others cut down branches from the trees, and strewed them in the way.*—By the disciples "putting their garments on the ass and her colt" was represented that truths in every complex should be strewed beneath the Lord, as the highest Judge and King, for the disciples represented the church of the Lord as

to truths and goods; and their "garments" the truths themselves. The like was represented by the multitude " strewing
their garments in the way," and also the " branches of trees."
The reason why they *strewed them in the way*, was, because
by " way" is signified the truth, by which the man of the
church is led. The reason why they *strewed branches of the
trees*, was, because "trees" signify perceptions, and also knowledges of truth and good; hence the " branches" denote the
truths themselves. *A. C.* 9212. See also *A. R.* 166.

Verses 9, 10. *And they who went before, and they who
followed, cried, saying, Hosanna! Blessed is He that cometh
in the name of the Lord! Blessed is the kingdom of our
father David, that cometh in the name of the Lord, &c.*—In
many passages in the Word mention is made of the name of
Jehovah, the name of the Lord, the name of Jesus Christ, and
the name of God. They who do not think beyond the sense
of the letter suppose that a name alone is meant, when yet by
name is not meant name, but all that by which the Lord is
worshipped, all which has reference to love and faith, hence
by the name of the Lord in the Word are meant all things of
love and of faith by which He is worshipped. The reason
why by the name of Jehovah or the Lord is not meant the
name itself, but all things of love and of faith, originates in
the spiritual world; for the names used on earth are not there
uttered, but the names of the persons of whom they speak are
formed from the idea of all things which are known concerning
them, which are compressed into one term; such is the utter-
ance of names in the spiritual world ; whence it is that names
also in that world, like all other things, are spiritual. The
name Lord, and the name Jesus Christ, are not there uttered
as on earth, but instead of those names, a name is formed
from the idea of all things which are known and believed
concerning Him, which idea is derived from all things of love
and of faith in Him; the reason is, because these things in
the complex are the Lord with them; for the Lord is with
every one in the goods of love and of faith, which are from
Him; this being the case, every one is there immediately
known as to his quality in regard to love and faith in the
Lord, if he only utters, with a spiritual voice or a spiritual
name, the Lord, or Jesus Christ. And hence also it is that
they who are not principled in any love, or in any faith in
Him, cannot name Him, that is, cannot form any spiritual
name concerning Him. *A. E.* 102. See also n. 340.

Verses 12—15. *And on the morrow, when they were coming
from Bethany, He was hungry : and seeing a fig-tree afar off*

27

having leaves, He came, if perhaps He might find any thing
thereon: and when He came to it, He found nothing but
leaves; for it was not the time of figs, &c.—By a "fig-tree"
is also here meant the church amongst the Jewish nation;
that with that nation there was not any natural good from a
spiritual origin, but only truth falsified, which in itself is
false, is signified by the Lord "coming to a fig-tree, but
finding nothing on it but leaves;" the "fruit," which He
did not find, signifies natural good, such as has been above
described, and "leaves" signify truths falsified, which in itself
is false; for "leaf," in the Word, signifies truth; but the
"leaf" of a fruit-tree, which is without fruit, signifies what
is false, and with that nation truth falsified, because they
have the Word, in which are truths, but which they have
falsified by application to themselves, whence came their traditions.   That that nation would never do any natural good
from a spiritual origin, which is called spiritual-natural good,
is signified by the words of the Lord concerning it,—"Let no
man eat fruit of thee hereafter for an age."   In consequence
of which it was immediately "dried up," signifying that that
nation would produce no longer either good or truth.   The
reason why the Lord saw and said this when He returned to
the city an hungered, is, because by the city "Jerusalem" is
signified the church, and by "hungering," when applied to
the Lord, is signified to desire good in the church, see above,
n. 386.   He who does not know what a "fig-tree" signifies,
and that by that "fig-tree" was understood the church
amongst that nation, has no other idea than that this was done
by the Lord out of indignation because He hungered, yet
this was not the case, but that it might be signified what was
the quality of the Jewish nation; for all the Lord's miracles
involve and signify such things as relate to heaven and the
church, whence those miracles were Divine.   *A. E.* 403.
   It is manifest from the Word throughout, that where man
is compared to a tree, or is called a tree, "fruits" signify the
good of charity, and the "leaf" the truth thence derived, as
in Ezekiel,—"Near the river came up on its bank, on this
side and that, every *tree of food,* whose *leaf* falleth not, neither
is its fruit consumed, it is re-born in its months; because its
waters go forth from the sanctuary, and its *fruits* shall be for
food, and its *leaf* for medicine;" (xlvii. 12; Rev. xxii. 2.)
where the "tree" denotes the man of the church in whom is
the kingdom of the Lord; "fruit" denotes the good of love
and charity; "leaf" denotes the truths thence derived, which
serve for the instruction of mankind, and their regeneration,

wherefore the "leaf" is said to be for *medicine*. And in Jeremiah,—" Blessed is the man who trusteth in Jehovah; he shall be like a *tree* planted near waters; his *leaf* shall be green; in the year of scarcity ₚhe shall not be anxious, and he shall not depart from bringing forth *fruit;*" (xvii. 7, 8.) where a "green leaf" denotes the truth of ₚfaith, thus essential faith which is grounded in charity. In like manner in David. (Psalm i. 3.) Similar things are understood by the "fig-tree," which Jesus saw, and whereon He found nothing but "leaves," wherefore it withered. (Matt. xxi. 19, 20; Mark xi. 13, 14.) The Jewish church specifically was here meant by the "fig-tree," in which church there was no longer anything of natural good; but the doctrinal of faith,, or the truth which was preserved in it, is the "leaf." The vastated church is such, that it knows what is true, but is not willing to understand; the case is the same with those who say that they know the truth, or the things which are of faith, and have nothing of the good of charity;—they are only the "leaves" of the fig-tree, and wither away. *A. C.* 885.

They who know what sin is, and particularly they who have much knowledge of the Word, and teach it to others, and yet do not examine themselves, and consequently do not see in themselves any sin, may be likened to such as scrape together great riches, and store them up in boxes and chests, without applying them to any other purpose than looking at and counting them;—who are like that trader that "hid his talent in the earth, and his pound in a napkin." (Matt. xxv. 25; Luke xix. 20.) They are also like "hard and stony ground, on which seed falleth;" (Matt. xiii. 4, 5.) and like "fig-trees, full of leaves but barren of fruit," (Mark xi. 12.) and like the "five virgins who had lamps and no oil." (Matt. xxv. 1—12.) *T. C. R.* 527.

Verse 13. *For it was not the time of figs.*—By these words is meant that the New Church had not yet commenced, in which natural good from a spiritual origin could be produced [which *fruit* or good can alone satisfy the Lord's hunger, or His ardent desire of saving the human race]. That the commencement of a new church is meant by a "fig-tree," is evident from the Lord's words in Matthew, xxiv. 32, 33. *A. E.* 386. See also *A. R.* 17.

As to the farther meaning of the "fig-tree," see below, chap. xiii. 28, 29, Exposition.

Verse 15. *And Jesus having entered into the temple, began to cast out them that sold and bought in the temple, and overthrew the tables of the money-changers, and the seats of them*

that sold doves.—By " those that sold and bought," are signified those who make gain to themselves of things holy; by the
"tables of the money-changers," are signified from holy truths;
and by the " seats of them who sold doves," are signified those
who do so from holy goods; wherefore it is afterwards said,
that " they made the temple into a den of thieves," for *thieves*
are those who plunder the goods and truths of the church, and
hence make to themselves gain. *A. E.* 840.

Verse 17. *And He taught, saying unto them, Is it not
written, My house shall be called the house of prayer for
[or by] all nations? but ye have made it a den of thieves.*—
By " house," in a universal sense, is signified the church; and
because worship was performed in the temple at Jerusalem,
therefore it is called " the house of prayer;" by a " den of
thieves," is signified evil of life derived from false principles
of doctrine; they are called " thieves," who steal truths from
the Word, and pervert them, and apply them to false and evil
principles, and thus extinguish them. *A. E.* 410; also n. 325.

Verses 22—24. *And Jesus answering, saith unto them, Have
the faith of God. For verily I say unto you, That whosoever
shall say to this mountain, Be thou removed, and be thou cast
into the sea; and shall not doubt in his heart, but shall believe
that those things which he saith shall come to pass; he shall
have whatsoever he saith. Therefore I say unto you, Whatsoever things ye desire, when ye pray, believe that ye shall
receive, and ye shall have [them].*—That these words are to be
understood otherwise than according to the words themselves,
may be manifest from this consideration, that it is said to the
disciples, [as in Matthew,] if they had " faith as a grain of
mustard seed, that they should be able to pluck up a mountain
and a sycamore-tree from its place, and cast it into the sea;"
also that " they should receive whatsoever they should ask,"
when yet it is not in agreement with Divine order that
every one should receive what he asks, if he only has faith;
also that they should pluck up a mountain or a tree from
its place, and cast it into the sea. But by " faith" is here
meant faith from the Lord, wherefore also it is called the
" faith of God;" and he who is in faith from the Lord, asks
nothing else but what is conducive to the Lord's kingdom,
and to his own salvation; other things do not engage the affections of his will, for he says in his heart,—" Why should
I ask for things which are not of such use?" Wherefore
he cannot have any *faith of God*, or faith from the Lord,
in asking for anything but what is given him from the
Lord to ask; yea, it is impossible for the angels to will

anything else, thus to ask anything else, since, in such case, they cannot have faith that they will receive. The reason why the Lord compared such faith to the importance and ability of *casting a mountain or sycamore-tree* into the sea, was, because on this, as on other occasions, He spake by correspondences, wherefore the above words are also to be spiritually understood. For by a " mountain" is signified the love of self and of the world, thus the love of evil; and by a " sycamore-tree" is signified the faith of that love, which is the faith of what is false grounded in evil; and by the " sea" is signified hell; wherefore by " plucking up a mountain, and casting it into the sea, by the faith of God," is signified to cast into hell those loves which in themselves are diabolical, in like manner the faith of what is false grounded in evil, which is effected by faith from the Lord. The reason why the importance and ability of faith from the Lord was compared with the *plucking up and casting into the sea a mountain and a sycamore-tree*, is grounded in what actually is done in the spiritual world; for in that world those evil loves occasionally appear as *mountains*, and the faith of what is false derived from evil as a *sycamore-tree*, and each may be *plucked up and cast into the sea*, by an angel influenced by faith from the Lord. That by a " mountain" is signified love to the Lord, and in the opposite sense the love of self, may be seen above, n. 405, 510; and that a " fig-tree" or a " sycamore-tree" signifies the natural man as to goods and truths in him; and in the opposite sense, the same man as to evil and false principles, see above, n. 403. *A. E.* 815.

He who does not know the arcana of heaven and the spiritual sense of the Word, may believe that the Lord spake the above words, not concerning saving faith, but concerning some other faith, which is called historical and miraculous, but the Lord spake them concerning saving faith, which faith makes one with charity, and is all from the Lord, wherefore the Lord calls this faith " the faith of God;" and whereas the Lord by this faith, which is the faith of charity from Himself, removes all the evils resulting from self-love and from the love of the world, and casts them down into hell from whence they come, therefore He says,—" Whosoever shall say to this mountain, Be thou removed and cast into the sea,"—what He said shall come to pass, for by a " mountain" are signified the evils of those loves, and by the " sea" is signified hell; hence by saying to a mountain, " Be thou removed," is signified the removal of those things, and by being " cast into the sea," is signified their being cast down into hell whence they originate. From this signification of a *mountain* and of the *sea*, it was usual with the ancients in their ordinary discourse, when speaking of the power of faith, thus to express themselves, not meaning that mountains on earth can by that faith be cast into hell, but the evils which are from hell.   Mountains also in the spiritual world, on which the wicked dwell, are wont to be overturned, and cast down by faith which is from the Lord; for when the evils appertaining to them are cast down, the mountains also are cast down on which they dwell, as has been occasionally said above, and likewise has been frequently seen by me.   That no other faith than the faith of charity from the Lord is here meant, is evident from the continuation of the Lord's discourse in Mark, where it is said,—" Therefore I say unto you, Whatsoever things ye desire, when ye pray, believe that ye shall receive, and ye shall have [them].   And when ye stand praying, forgive [remit], if ye have ought against any: that your Father also who is in the heavens may forgive you [remit] your trespasses.   But if ye forgive [remit] not, neither will your Father who is in the heavens forgive [remit] your trespasses." (xi. 24—26.)   From which words it is evident that the faith of God, of which the Lord there speaks, is the faith of charity, that is, the faith which makes one with charity, and hence which is all from the Lord.   *A. E.* 405.   See also *A. C.* 9230.

Verse 22. *Have the faith of God.*—As to a *true faith* which is saving, and here called the "faith of God," [or faith derived from God,] not "faith in God," as in the common version, the following extracts may be read with great advantage:—

It shall be here shewn that faith alone cannot produce any good, or that from faith alone no good fruit can be produced. It is supposed that faith consists in believing that the Lord suffered the passion of the cross for our sins, and thereby redeemed us from hell, and that the faith of these things is what principally justifies and saves; and besides these it is supposed that faith is to believe that God is triune, also to believe those things which are declared in the Word, to believe in eternal life, and the resurrection at the day of the Last Judgment, and other things which the church teaches; and inasmuch as they separate faith from the life of charity, which is to do good works, most persons at this day suppose that to know these things, to think, and to speak them, is the faith which saves, wherefore they pay no attention to the willing and doing of them, nor do they even know that they ought to will and to do them; neither does the church teach this, inasmuch as the doctrine of the church is a doctrine of faith alone, and not a doctrine of life.   The doctrine of life they call moral

theology, which they make but little account of, because they
believe that the virtues of a moral life, which in themselves
are good works, contribute nothing to salvation.   But that to
know, to think, and to speak the things above-mentioned, is
not faith, and, if they are called faith, that still they do not
produce good, as a tree its fruits, may appear from these
considerations :—

I. All things which a man knows, thinks, and speaks, in
proportion as he understands them [and approves of them], he
calls truths; and all things which he wills and does, in proportion as he loves them, he calls goods.   Hence *truths* are of the
faith of man, and *goods* are of his love; from which it is evident
that truths which are of faith are distinct from goods which are
of love, as knowing and thinking are distinct from willing and
doing.   That they are distinct, and how far they are so, may
appear from this consideration, that it is possible for man to
know, think, speak, and even to understand many things which
he does not will and do, because he does not love; but, on the
other hand, that whatsoever a man wills and does from love,
this he also thinks and speaks from faith, if not before the
world, yet with himself when he is left alone.   From these
considerations it follows,—

II. That the love and will of man enter into all things of
his faith and thought, but that faith and thought cannot enter
into his love and will; for what a man loves, this he also loves
to do, to know, to think, to speak, and to understand, thus
also to have the faith thereof.   In like manner if the will be
assumed in the place of love, what a man wills, this he also
wills to do, to know, to think, to speak, and to understand,
thus also to have the faith thereof.   The reason why the same
is predicated of the will as of the love, is, because love is of
the will, and the will is the receptacle of love; hence then it
follows that love produces faith, as the will produces thought;
and inasmuch as faith, like thought, is produced, and love,
like the will, produces, it follows that it is speaking inversely
to say that faith produces love.   From these considerations it
may appear that to believe that faith produces goods, which
are called good works, as a tree produces fruit, is contrary
to order.

III. The same things which are here said concerning faith
and love, are also to be understood concerning Truth and Good,
for truth is of faith, and faith is of truth, for what a man believes,
this he calls Truth; and good is of love, and love is of good,
for what a man loves, this he calls Good.   Truth, viewed in
itself, is nothing else but Good in form, for Good may indeed

present itself to be felt, but not to be seen, except in some form, and the form in which it presents itself to be seen in the thought, thus in the understanding and perception, is called Truth.   From these considerations also it follows that love produces faith, as good produces truth; consequently that faith does not produce the good of love, as a tree produces fruit.

IV. Moreover, to know, and thence to think and speak, are from the memory, but to will and act from love are from the life. Man can think and speak many things from the memory which are not from his life, which is love, as is the case with every hypocrite and flatterer; but he cannot think and speak anything, when left to himself, from the life, which is not from his love; for love is the life of every one, and according to the quality of the love, such is the life. But the memory is only the storehouse from which the life takes what it may think and speak, and what may be serviceable for its nourishment; wherefore to say that faith produces good as a tree does fruit, is to say that the thought and speech of man produce his life, and not the life them; when, notwithstanding, the wicked, even the very worst, can think and speak truths from the memory, but the good only can speak them from the life.

V. That faith alone, or faith separate from goods in act, which are good works, cannot be given, may appear from the essence of faith, which is charity; and charity is the affection of doing those things which are of the faith; wherefore faith without charity is like thought without affection, and thought without affection is no thought; consequently faith without charity is no faith. To speak therefore of faith without charity, is to speak of thought without affection, likewise of life without a soul, of existere without an esse, of a form without a thing forming, of a product without somewhat producing, and of an effect without a cause; wherefore faith alone is a nonentity, and from a nonentity, to produce goods in act, which are good works, as a good tree does fruit, is a contradiction,—from which that which is believed to be something turns out to be nothing.

VI. Inasmuch as faith without charity has no existence, and still thought and persuasion of a thing's being so appears as if it was faith, and also is called faith, it is evident that such faith cannot be saving, but is merely an historical faith, because from the mouth of another; for he who believes anything from another whom he supposes worthy of credit, and so receives it, stores it in his memory, and thence thinks and speaks it without seeing whether it be false or true, possesses it no otherwise than as somewhat historical.   But if he confirms it in himself, by appearances from the Word, and by reasonings, then from historical faith it becomes persuasive faith, which is like the sight of an owl, which sees objects in darkness, and nothing in the light. Such a persuasive faith exists from all confirmation of what is false, for everything false may be confirmed, until it appears as truth, and the false confirmed shines with a deceitful lumen. From these considerations also it may appear that such faith cannot possibly produce goods, which are good works, [such as the Lord speaks of in Matt. v. 16; vi. 1; and the Apostle in Eph. ii. 10; 1 Tim. ii. 10; v. 10, 25; vi. 18; Titus ii. 7, 14, &c.]

VII. Inasmuch as faith in the thought is nothing else but historical or persuasive faith, it follows also that it is merely natural. For spiritual faith is produced from spiritual love, which is charity, as light from the sun, and which does not produce the sun; wherefore a faith merely natural is produced from a love merely natural, which derives its soul from the love of self, the delight of which love is a delight of the flesh, which is called pleasure, lust, and lasciviousness, from which flow evils of every kind, and from evils, falses. Hence it may be evident that the faith thence proceeding cannot produce goods as a tree does good fruit; and if it appear to produce any, they are goods from the proprium of man, which in themselves are evils, and at the same time meritorious goods, which in themselves are iniquitous. *A. E.* 789.

Verses 24, 25. *Whatsoever things ye desire, when ye pray, believe that ye shall receive, and ye shall have [them]. And when ye stand praying, forgive [remit], if ye have ought against any,* &c.—In these words by "praying," in the spiritual sense, is meant the life of love and charity, for to those who are in the life of love and charity, it is given by the Lord what they shall ask; wherefore they ask nothing but what is good, and this is done to them. And whereas faith also is from the Lord, therefore it is said,—"Believe that ye shall receive;" and since prayers proceed from the life of charity, and are according to it, therefore, to the intent that prayers may be effectual, it is also said,—"When ye stand *praying,* forgive [remit], if ye have ought against any." *A. E.* 325.

In the spiritual world there are things existing similar to those on earth, but all derived from a spiritual origin; amongst other things there are gold and silver and precious stones of all kinds, whose spiritual origin is the literal sense of the Word; hence it is that, in the Revelations, the "foundations of the walls of the New Jerusalem" are described by *twelve*

28

precious stones, because by the "foundation of its wall" is
signified the doctrinal of the church, derived from the literal
sense of the Word.   Hence likewise it is, that in Aaron's
ephod there were twelve precious stones, called Urim and
Thummim, and that by means of these responses were given
out of heaven.   Besides these, there are still many more
wonderful phenomena resulting from the Word, which respect
the power of Truth therein, and which are so extraordinary
that the description of them would pass all belief; for the power
of Truth in the Word is such, that it *overturns mountains
and hills* in the spiritual world, and removes them to a great
distance, and *casts them into the sea*, with many other circumstances; in short, the power of the Lord, by virtue of the
Word, is infinite.   *T. C. R.* 209.

Verses 25, 26. *And when ye stand praying, forgive*, &c.—
The evidences that sins are forgiven, or remitted, that is,
removed, are the following:—They whose sins are remitted
experience a delight in worshipping God for His own sake,
and in serving the neighbour for the sake of the neighbour,
in doing good for the sake of good, and in speaking truth
for the sake of truth,—such persons disclaim all merit in the
exercise of their charity and faith; they are utterly averse to
all evils, as enmity, hatred, revenge, adultery, and not only
do they shun them, but they abhor the very thought of them
connected with any intention.   But the evidences that sins are
not remitted, or removed, are these:—They whose sins are not
remitted do not worship God for His own sake, nor serve the
neighbour for his own sake, thus they do not do good and
speak truth for the sake of good and truth, but for the sake
of themselves and the world.   They claim merit on account
of their deeds; they perceive nothing undelightful in evils,
such as enmity, hatred, revenge, and adultery, and, inflamed
with these lusts, they cherish the thought of them in all
licentiousness.   *H. D.* 167.

Verses 30—33. *The baptism of John*, &c.—See chap. i. 4,
Exposition.

TRANSLATOR'S NOTES AND OBSERVATIONS.

CHAPTER XI.

VERSE 22. *Have the faith of God.*—What is here rendered "the faith of God," is called, in the common version of the New Testament, "the faith in God." But in the original Greek the words are πιστιν Θεου, which is literally *the faith of God,* and is expressive therefore not only of *faith in* God, but of faith *derived from* God, thus that all proper and saving faith is *of* God, and not of man alone.

Verse 31. *And they reasoned with themselves, saying, If we shall say, From heaven; He will say, Why then did ye not believe him?* &c.—It deserves to be noted that, in the original Greek, three distinct terms are applied to express what is here rendered "saying" and "say;" *saying* being expressed by λεγοντες, and *say,* in the first instance, by ειπωμεν, and in the second instance by ερει. Hence it is reasonable to conclude, that as the terms λεγοντες and ειπωμεν are applied to the chief Priests, the Scribes, and Elders, and the term ερει to the Lord, therefore the latter term is expressive of more interior speech than the two former.

MARK.

CHAPTER XII.

THE WORD.

1. AND He began to say to them in parables, A man planted a vineyard, and set a hedge about it, and digged a wine vat, and built a tower, and let it out to husbandmen, and went from home.

2. And at the season He sent to the husbandmen a servant, that he might receive from the husbandmen of the fruit of the vineyard.

3. But they, having taken him, beat him, and sent him away empty.

4. And again He sent unto them another servant, and having cast stones at him, they wounded him in the head, and sent him away dishonoured.

5. And again he sent another; and him they killed, and many others; beating some, and killing some.

6. Having yet therefore one Son, His well-beloved, He sent Him also last unto them,

THE INTERNAL SENSE.

THAT spiritual truth is communicated from the LORD by the Word to man, as a security against evils and falses, and for the procuring of heavenly good, and for elevation to interior intelligence, whilst the LORD Himself appears absent. (Verse 1.)

For the LORD is continually intent on producing in man's mind the good of love and charity, and on instructing man by His Word that this good ought to be acknowledged as a Divine gift, and thus returned to Himself, the giver. (Verse 2.)

But they who are in the science of truth without its life, either pervert, or reject, or falsify the truth. (Verses 3, 4, 5.)

Insomuch that they reject the Divine Truth itself, or the Word, when manifested in the saying, They will reverence My Son.

7. But those husbandmen said among themselves, This is the Heir; come, let us kill Him, and the inheritance will be ours.

8. And having taken Him, they killed Him, and cast Him out of the vineyard.

9. What then shall the Lord of the vineyard do? He will come and destroy the husbandmen, and will give the vineyard unto others.

10. Have ye not read this Scripture; The stone which the builders rejected is become the head of the corner?

11. This was the Lord's doing, and it is marvellous in our eyes.

12. And they sought to lay hold of Him, and feared the multitude: for they knew that He had spoken the parable against them: and having left Him, they departed.

13. And they send unto Him some of the Pharisees and of the Herodians, to catch Him in [His] word.

14. But when they came, they say unto Him, Teacher, we know that Thou art True, and carest for no one: for Thou lookest not at the person [face] of men, but teachest the way of God in Truth: Is it lawful to give tribute to Cæsar, or not?

flesh, and thus appropriate all good and truth to themselves, instead of ascribing them to their Divine Source. (Verses 6, 7, 8.)

Therefore they perish in the day of judgment, being deprived of all knowledge of the truth, which is transferred to those who are principled in good. (Verse 9.)

Thus fulfilling the prediction which teaches that the LORD's Humanity, which is Divine Truth, should, by such rejection, be exalted to union with the Divinity through its own proper power, and should thus become the supreme object of worship and adoration. (Verses 10, 11.)

They therefore, who pervert and falsify the truth, reject this object, and seek to destroy it, but are withheld by external bonds. (Verse 12.)

That they who are in hypocritical worship treat the Word with outward respect, and consult it for the regulation of the external man as to things of moral and civil life. (Verses 13, 14, and part of 15.)

15. Shall we give, or shall we not give? But He, knowing their hypocrisy, said unto them, Why tempt ye Me? Bring Me a penny, that I may see it.

16. And they brought it. And He saith unto them, Whose is this image and superscription? And they said unto Him, Cæsar's.

17. And Jesus answering, said unto them, Render to Cæsar the things that are Cæsar's, and to God the things that are God's. And they marvelled at Him.

18. And the Sadducees come to Him, who say that there is no resurrection; and they asked Him, saying,

19. Teacher, Moses wrote unto us, That if the brother of anyone die, and leave a wife, and leave no children, his brother should take his wife, and raise up seed unto his brother.

20. Now there were seven brethren: and the first took the woman, and dying left no seed.

21. And the second took her, and died, neither left he any seed: and in like manner the third.

22. And the seven took her, and left no seed: last of all the woman died also.

23. In the resurrection therefore, when they shall have risen, whose wife shall she be of them? for the seven had her to wife.

But this they do without any regard to the regulation of the internal man. (Verse 15, latter part.)

Whereas the Word teaches by significatives that the external man bears the image of the world for which it was created, and therefore ought to be regulated by and submit to the laws of moral and civil life; but that the internal man bears the image of heaven for which it was created, and therefore ought to be regulated by and submit to the laws of heavenly or spiritual life. (Verses 16, 17.)

That they also who deny the Scripture doctrine of regeneration consult the Word respecting the heavenly marriage of good and truth. (Verses 18—24.)

24. And Jesus answering, said unto them, Do ye not therefore err, not having known the Scriptures, nor the power of God?

But being perplexed about it, they are instructed that their perplexity is the effect of their ignorance, in consequence of not admitting into their minds and lives the Divine Truth and Good of the Word by regeneration. (Verse 24.)

25. For when they shall have risen from the dead, they neither marry, nor are given in marriage; but are as the angels who are in the heavens.

Which heavenly principles must be admitted during man's abode in this world, otherwise they cannot be admitted after death; and which, if admitted, form angelic life. (Verse 25.)

26. But respecting the dead, that they are [already] risen, Have ye not read in the Book of Moses, how in the bush God said unto him, saying, I am the God of Abraham, and the God of Isaac, and the God of Jacob?

27. He is not the God of the dead, but the God of the living: ye therefore do greatly err.

Therefore the Word teaches that all celestial, spiritual, and natural good and truth are from the LORD, and that none can attain such good and truth but in the degree in which they renounce self-love, and cherish heavenly love. (Verses 26, 27.)

28. And one of the Scribes came, and having heard them questioning together, seeing that He had answered them well, asked Him, Which is the first commandment of all?

29. And Jesus answered him, The first of all the commandments is, Hear, O Israel: The Lord our God is one Lord:

30. And thou shalt love the Lord thy God from thy whole heart, and from thy whole soul, and from thy whole thought, and from thy whole strength: this is the first commandment.

The Word further teaches that the LORD, in His Divine Humanity, is Divine Love and Divine Wisdom United, and is thus the Only GOD; and that He ought to be loved by man with the whole of his will, and of his understanding, also with those things which are of the will and of the understanding in the external man. (Verses 28—30.)

31. And the second is like it, namely this, Thou shalt love thy neighbour as thyself. There is none other commandment greater than these.

32. And the Scribe said unto Him, Well, Teacher, Thou hast said the truth: for there is One God; and there is none other but He:

33. And to love Him from the whole heart, and from the whole understanding, and from the whole soul, and from the whole strength, and to love [his] neighbour as himself, is more than all whole burnt-offerings and sacrifices.

34. And Jesus seeing him, that he answered discreetly, said unto him, Thou art not far from the kingdom of God. And no one durst question Him any longer.

35. And Jesus answering said, teaching in the temple, How say the Scribes that Christ is the Son of David?

36. For David himself said in the Holy Spirit, The Lord said unto my Lord, Sit Thou on My right hand, till I make Thine enemies Thy footstool.

37. David therefore himself calleth Him Lord; and whence is He his Son? And the numerous multitude heard Him gladly.

38. And He said unto them in His doctrine, Beware of the Scribes, who desire to go in long clothing, and [desire] salutations in the market-places,

In like manner man ought to love the good and truth which are from the LORD in others as in himself. (Verse 31.)

Which doctrine is assented to even by those who are of the perverted church, and who, on that account, are pronounced by the LORD to be in the way of advancement towards heaven. (Verses 32—34.)

The Word further teaches that man ought to consider well the quality of the LORD's Humanity, so as to discern clearly, that although before glorification it was the Son of Mary and of David, yet after glorification it ceased to be so, being then one with the Eternal FATHER, and thus having Omnipotence and Omniscience. (Verses 35—37.)

Caution also is necessary respecting those in the perverted church, who seek pre-eminence in the communication of good and of truth, and to be thought better and wiser

39. And the chief seats in synagogues, and the uppermost couches at feasts:

40. Who devour widows' houses, and for a pretence make long prayers: these shall receive greater damnation.

41. And Jesus sat over against the treasury, and saw how the multitude cast money into the treasury: and many that were rich cast in much.

42. And there came one poor widow, and cast in two mites, which make a farthing.

43. And having called His disciples, He saith unto them, Verily I say unto you, That this poor widow hath cast more in, than all they who have cast into the treasury:

44. For they all did cast in of their abundance; but she of her penury did cast in all that she had, even her whole living.

than others, whilst under a pretence of piety they deprive those of truth who are in the desire of truth, and thus increase their own condemnation. (Verses 38—40.)

For the LORD, from His Divine Love, perceives the quality of everyone's worship, as proceeding either from the knowledges of truth in the understanding, or from the desire of truth in the will. (Verses 41, 42.)

But the worship proceeding from the latter source is more acceptable to Him than the worship proceeding from the former source. (Verses 43, 44.)

EXPOSITION.

CHAPTER XII.

VERSES 1—9. *And He began to say to them in parables, A man planted a vineyard, and set a hedge about it, and digged a winevat, and built a tower, and let it out to husbandmen, and went from home,* &c.—What was the quality of the Jewish nation, is very manifest from several things, which the Lord Himself spake in parables, and which, in the internal, historical sense relate to that nation; as what is said in the parable concerning a king, who called his servant to account, in whom there was nothing of mercy towards another; (Matt. xviii. 23, to the end.)

29

in the parable too concerning the householder, who let out a
vineyard to husbandmen and went abroad, and the husbandmen laid hold of the servants whom he sent, and beat them
with rods, killed, and stoned them; at length he sent his son,
whom they cast out of the vineyard, and slew him; on hearing
which parable, the Scribes and Pharisees knew that it related
to themselves. (Matt. xxi. 33—45; Mark xii. 1—9; Luke
xx. 9, and following verses.)   And in the parable concerning
the man who gave talents to his servants, and how he, who
received one talent, went and hid it in the earth; (Matt. xxv.
14—30; Luke xix. 13—26.) and in the parable concerning
those who came to the man wounded by thieves; (Luke x.
30—37.) and in the parable concerning those who were invited
to a great supper, and they all excused themselves, of whom
the Lord declared,—"I say unto you, That none of those men
who were called shall taste of my supper;" (Luke xiv. 16—24.)
and in the parable concerning the rich man and Lazarus;
(Luke xvi. 19, to the end.) and in the parable concerning those
who despise others in comparison with themselves; (Luke xviii.
10—14.) and in the parable concerning two sons, one of whom
said,—"I will go into the vineyard," but did not go; and
Jesus said,—"Verily I say unto you, That the publicans and
harlots shall enter into the kingdom of the heavens before
you." (Matt. xxi. 28—32.)   From these considerations it may
be manifest that goods and truths were altogether destroyed
with that nation.   *A. C.* 4314.

In the Word, churches are everywhere described by *gardens*,
also by the *trees* of a garden, and they are likewise so named,
and this from the "fruits," which signify those things which
are of love and charity; wherefore it is said that "man is
known from the fruit."   The comparison of churches with
gardens, trees, and *fruits*, originates in representations in
heaven, where also gardens of inexpressible beauty are occasionally presented to view, according to spheres of faith;
hence likewise the celestial church was described by the
garden of paradise, in which were *trees* of every kind; and
by the "trees of the garden" were signified the perceptions
of that church; and by the "fruits," goods of every kind,
which are of love.   But the ancient church, as being spiritual,
is described by a *vineyard*, which description is grounded in
the "fruits," which are grapes, representing and signifying
works of charity, which is manifest from several passages from
the Word, as in Isaiah,—"I will sing to my Beloved a song
of my Beloved, touching His *vineyard*. My Beloved had a
vineyard in the horn of a son of oil: and He hedged it round

about, and encompassed it with stones, and planted it with
a noble *vine*, and built a tower in the midst of it, and also
cut out a wine-press in it: and waited that it should bring
forth *grapes*, and it brought forth *wild grapes*. And now,
O inhabitants of Jerusalem, and men of Judah, judge, I pray,
between Me and My *vineyard*. The *vineyard* of Jehovah of
Hosts is the *house of Israel*." (v. 1, 2, 3, 7.) In this passage
a "vineyard" signifies the ancient church, thus the spiritual
church, and it is plainly said that it is the "house of Israel;"
for by "Israel," in the Word, is spiritually signified the
spiritual church; but by "Judah," the celestial church. So
in Jeremiah,—"Again I will build thee, and thou shalt be
built, O virgin of Israel! thou shalt again be adorned with
thy tabrets, and shalt go forth into the dances of them that
sport; again thou shalt plant *vineyards* in the mountains of
Samaria;" (xxxi. 4, 5.) where "vineyard" denotes the spiritual church, and the subject treated of is "Israel," by whom, as
was said, is signified the spiritual church. And in Ezekiel,—
"When I shall gather together the *house of Israel* from
amongst the people, they shall dwell on the land in confidence, and shall build houses and *plant vineyards*;" (xxviii.
25, 26.) where "vineyard" denotes the spiritual church, or
Israel; to "plant vineyards" denotes to be instructed in the
truths and goods of faith. And as "vineyard" signifies the
spiritual church, so also does a "vine," for a *vine* is of a
vineyard; the case being like that of a church and a man of
the church, wherefore it is the same thing; as in Ezekiel,—
"Take up a lamentation over the princes of Israel; thy mother
was as a *vine in thy likeness*, planted near the waters, bearing
fruit, and bearing leaves from many waters;" (xix. 1, 10.)
where "vine" denotes the ancient spiritual church, which was
a mother, thus it denotes Israel; wherefore also it is said, "in
thy likeness." The parables of the Lord concerning "labourers
in vineyards," in like manner, signified spiritual churches.
(Matt. xx. 1—16; Mark xii. 1—12; Luke xx. 9—18; Matt.
xxi. 33—44.) Inasmuch as a "vine" signifies the spiritual
church, and the primary principle of that church is charity, in
which the Lord is present, and by which He conjoins Himself
to man, and by which He operates all good, therefore the
Lord compares Himself to a *vine*, and describes the man of
the church, or the spiritual church, in these words in John,—
"I am the true *vine*, and My Father is the *vine-dresser;* every
branch in Me that beareth not *fruit*, He taketh away; but
every one that beareth *fruit*, He purgeth it, that it may
bring forth more *fruit*. Abide in Me, and I in you; as the

branch cannot bear *fruit* from itself, unless it abide in the *vine*, so neither can ye, unless ye abide in Me. I am the *vine*, ye are the *branches;* he that abideth in Me, and I in him, the same bringeth forth much *fruit:* for without Me ye cannot do any thing. This is My commandment, That ye love one another, as I have loved you." (xv. 1, 2, 3, 4, 5, 12.) Hence it is manifest what the spiritual church is. *A. C.* 1069.

By the "vineyard" which the householder planted, is signified the church established amongst the sons of Israel; by the "hedge" which he set about it, is signified a guard from the false principles of evils which are from hell; by his "digging a wine-press in it," is signified that it had spiritual good; and by "building a tower," are signified interior truths from that good, which looked to heaven; by "letting it out to husbandmen," is signified to that people; by "their killing the servants sent to them," are signified the prophets; and by their finally "killing the Son," is signified the Lord. *A. E.* 922.

By a "wine-press" is signified exploration, the reason of which signification is, because in wine-presses the new wine is pressed out from the clusters of grapes, and the oil from the olives, and by the new wine and oil pressed out it is perceived what was the quality of the grapes and olives; and whereas by a "vineyard" is signified the Christian church, and by its "clusters of grapes" are signified works, therefore the exploration of these amongst the men of the Christian church is signified by casting into a "wine-press." This exploration of works is also signified by a "wine-press" in the following passages:—"My Beloved had a *vineyard* in the horn of a son of oil: He planted it with a noble *vine*, also He cut out a *wine-press* in it." (Isaiah v. 1, 2.) "Put ye in the sickle, for the harvest is ripe: get ye down, for the *wine-press* is full, the *vats* overflow; for their wickedness is great." (Joel iii. 13.) "The floor and the *wine-press* shall not feed them, and the *new wine* shall deceive them." (Hosea ix. 1, 2.) The "wine-press" is also applied to the goods of charity, from which are the truths of faith, in these words in Joel,—"Rejoice, ye daughters of Zion; the floors are full of corn, and the *wine-presses* overflow with *new wine* and *oil.*" (ii. 23, 24.) *A. R.* 651.

Cities in old times were fortified with *towers*, in which were guards; *towers* were also in the boundaries, and were therefore called "guard towers," (2 Kings ix. 17; xvii. 9; xviii. 8.) and "watch towers." (Isaiah xxiii. 13.) Moreover also, when the church of the Lord is compared to a *vineyard*, the things which regard worship, and also its preservation, are compared to a *wine-press*, and to a *tower* in the *vineyard*, as is manifest in Isaiah, v. 1, 2; Matt. xxi. 33; Mark xii. 1. *A. C.* 1306.

Verses 2—9. *And at the season He sent to the husbandmen a servant, that He might receive from the husbandmen of the fruits of the vineyard. But they, having taken him, beat him, and sent him away empty*, &c.—These words were spoken concerning the church established amongst the Jews, and by them is described the perversion and falsification of every truth, derived to them from the Word by traditions and applications to themselves; every single expression contains a spiritual sense, for whatsoever the Lord spake, He spake also spiritually, because from the Divinity. By the "vineyard which the man planted," is signified the church which is principled in truths; by the "servant whom He sent three times," is meant the Word given them by Moses and the prophets. It is said *three times*, because "three" signifies what is full and complete. By the "husbandmen smiting them, wounding, and sending them empty out of the vineyard," is signified that they falsified and perverted the truths contained in the Word. To "send away empty out of the vineyard," signifies that they deprived the Word of its goods and truths; by the "beloved Son" is meant the Lord, as to Divine Truth, who hence is also called the Word; by "casting Him out of the vineyard, and slaying Him," is signified, not only that they so dealt with Himself, but also with every divine truth which is from Him. *A. E.* 315.

Verse 7. *But those husbandmen said among themselves, This is the Heir; come, let us kill Him, and the inheritance will be ours.*—That to "inherit," in the internal sense, when it is predicated of the Lord, is to have the life of the Father, thus in Himself; and when it is predicated of men, that it is to have the life of the Lord, that is, to receive life from the Lord, is manifest from several passages of the Word; to have life in Himself is the very esse of life, that is, Jehovah; but to have the life of the Lord, or to receive life from the Lord, is to receive the Lord by love and faith; and since they who so receive are in the Lord, and are the Lord's, they are called His heirs and sons. In the Word of the Old Testament, *inheritance* is predicated both of what is celestial or good, and of what is spiritual or true, but still it is expressed by different terms; in the former case by *possessing hereditarily*, but in the latter case by *inheriting;* the former expression also in the original tongue involves possession, but the latter derivation thence, as is the case with what is celestial in regard to what is spiritual, or as what is good in regard to what is true; in this verse, where by Isaac is represented the rational principle or Divine Human principle of the Lord, it is an expression of possession grounded in hereditary right, because the Divine Human principle of the Lord is the ONLY POSSESSING HEIR,

as He Himself likewise teaches in the parable; (Matt. xxi.
33, 37, 38; Mark xii. 7; Luke xx. 14.) and everywhere
declares, that all things of the Father are His; that to
"possess hereditarily" and to "inherit," when predicated of
men in the Word, signifies to receive life from the Lord,
consequently eternal life or heaven (for they alone receive
heaven who receive the Lord's life), is manifest from the
Revelations,—"He that overcometh shall *inherit* all things,
and I will be to him a God, and he shall be to Me a son;
(xxi. 7.) and in Matthew,—"Every one who has left houses,
or brethren, or sisters, for My name's sake, shall receive a
hundred-fold, and shall *inherit* eternal life." (xix. 29; xxv.
34; Mark x. 17; Luke xviii. 18.) Heaven is here called
"eternal life," in other places simply "life," as Matt. xviii.
8, 9; xix. 17; John iii. 36; v. 24, 29; by reason that the
Lord is life itself, and he who receives His life is in heaven.
A. C. 2658.

Verse 9. *And will give the vineyard to others.*—Those who
are within the church, and who have confirmed themselves
against divine Truths, especially against these Truths,—that
the Humanity of the Lord is divine, and that the works of
charity contribute nothing to salvation; if they have confirmed
themselves against these Truths, not only in doctrine but in
life, they have reduced themselves, as to their interiors, to
such a state, that they cannot afterwards be led to receive
them. For the things which have been once confirmed, both
in doctrine and in life, remain to eternity. Those who do not
know the interior state of man, may think that every one,
howsoever he may have confirmed himself against these Truths,
may nevertheless easily receive them, if [after death] he is only
convinced that they are Truths. But that this is impossible,
has been given me to know by much experience, from such
spirits in the other life. For that which is confirmed by
doctrine imbues the intellectual faculty, and that which is confirmed in life imbues the will faculty; that which is enrooted in
each life of man, that is, both in the life of his understanding
and in the life of his will, cannot be rooted out. The very
soul of man, which lives after death, being formed by these
things, and is such as in nowise to recede therefrom. This
also is the reason why the lot of those who are within the
church, with whom this is the case, is worse than the lot of
those who are out of the church. For those who are out
of the church, and are called Gentiles, have not confirmed
themselves against those Truths, because they have not known
them; wherefore those of them who have lived in mutual

charity easily receive divine Truths, if not in the world, never-theless in the other life, as may be seen from the state of the Gentiles and peoples, and from their lot in the other life, as described from experience, see n. 2589—2604. Hence it is, that when a new church is being established by the Lord, it is not established amongst those who are within the church, but amongst those who are without, that is, amongst the Gentiles; [this is meant by "giving the vineyard to others." Mark xii. 9.] *A. C.* 4747.

Verse 15. *But He, knowing their hypocrisy,* &c.—To will evil, and yet to speak what is true and good, is from *hypocrisy,* using truth and good as means; and when these means are with-drawn in the other life, the man rushes into all the evils of his will, and defends them by his understanding. *A. C.* 10,122.

Evils effected by deceit are the worst of all, for deceit is like a poison which infects the whole mind, penetrating even to its interiors, and destroying all that is human. Hence "poison," in the Word, denotes deceit or hypocrisy; and "venomous serpents" denote the deceitful or hypocrites. *A. C.* 9013.

Verse 18. *And the Sadducees come to Him, who say that there is no resurrection* [*or life after death*], &c.—By "Canaan being cursed," in Gen. ix. 25, and also by "Canaan" in Gen. x. 15, is signified external worship, in which there is nothing *internal.* This worship is such as pertained to the Jews before the Lord's advent, and also since, as at the present day. For the Jews had an external worship which they strictly observed, but still they knew nothing of an internal principle, and were so utterly ignorant that they thought that they lived only as to the body. What the soul is, what faith is, what the Lord is, what spiritual and celestial life is, what the life after death is, they were entirely ignorant; wherefore also at the time the Lord was in the world, many denied the resurrection, as is evident from Matt. xxii. 23—33; Mark xii. 18—28; Luke xx. 27—38. When a man is of such a quality that he does not believe that he shall live after death, he also does not believe that there is anything of an internal which is spiritual and celestial; such persons also are of this nature, who live in mere cupidities, because they live the mere life of the body and of the world, especially such as are immersed in filthy avarice. They nevertheless have a worship, for they frequent synagogues and temples, and observe the rites, and some of them indeed do this very strictly; but because they do not believe in a life after death, their worship can be nothing else than external, in which there is nothing internal, like a shell without a kernel, or like a tree on which there is no fruit, and not even leaves. *A. C.* 1200.

Verses 18—28. *On the Resurrection, and on Marriages in heaven.*—There are two things which the Lord taught on this occasion,—*first*, that man rises again after death; and *secondly*, that they are not given in marriage in heaven. That man rises again after death, is taught by these words, that " God is not the God of the dead, but of the living;" secondly, that they are not given in marriage in heaven, by these words,—"In the resurrection, they neither marry, nor are given in marriage." That no other marriages are here meant but *spiritual marriages*, is manifest from the words which immediately follow,—"They are as the angels of God in heaven." By "spiritual marriage," conjunction with the Lord is meant, and this is effected on the earth, and when it is effected on the earth, it is also effected in the heavens; wherefore in the heavens *marriage* [or this spiritual conjunction with the Lord, which is salvation], is not again effected, neither are they *given in marriage*. This is also meant by these words in Luke,—" The sons of this age *marry* and are *given in marriage*, but they who are accounted worthy to attain the other age, neither *marry*, nor are *given in marriage;*" the latter also are called by the Lord " sons of the marriage;" (Matt. ix. 15; Mark ii. 19.) and sometimes "angels," "sons of God," and "sons of the resurrection." That to "marry" denotes to be conjoined to the Lord, and that to "enter into the marriage" denotes to be received into heaven by the Lord, is evident from the following passages:— " The kingdom of the heavens is like to a man, a king, who made a *marriage* for his son, and sent forth servants, and invited to the *marriage*." (Matt. xxii. 1—14.) "The kingdom of the heavens is like to ten virgins, who went forth to meet the bridegroom, of whom five, being prepared, *entered into the marriage*." (Matt. xxv. 1, and following verses.) That the Lord here meant Himself, is evident from verse 13 of the same chapter, where it is said,—"Watch, because ye know not the day nor the hour in which the Son of Man is about to come;" also from the Revelations,—"The time of the *marriage* of the Lamb is come, and His wife hath prepared herself. Blessed are they who are called to the *marriage supper* of the Lamb." (xix. 7, 9.) *C. L.* 41.

Marriages [or the union of one male with one female angel] are given in the heavens as on the earth, but to no others there, except to those who are regenerated, or who are in the marriage of Good and Truth, neither are any others angels; wherefore spiritual marriages, which are those of Good and Truth, are meant by the Lord, when He 'says,—"In the resurrection, they neither marry nor are given in marriage."

These spiritual marriages are effected on the earth, and not after man's decease, thus not in the heavens; as it is said of the foolish virgins, who were even invited to the marriage, that "they could not enter," because they had not the marriage of Good and Truth, for they had no *oil*, but only *lamps*. By "oil" is meant good, and by "lamps," truth; and to be "given in marriage," is to enter into heaven, where is the marriage of Good and Truth. *C. L.* 44.

It is said in Scripture that "there shall be no marriages in heaven," in the same manner as it is said,—1. That "you shall not call any man father upon earth, nor any one teacher, or master." 2. That "it is as difficult for a rich man to enter into heaven, as it is for a camel to go through the eye of a needle." 3. That "friends are to be made of the unrighteous mammon." 4. That "when one cheek is smitten, the other cheek is to be turned to the smiter;" that "the coat also is to be surrendered to him who would take the cloak;" and that "we are to go two miles with him who would compel us to go one." 5. That the adulteress was liberated by "writing on the ground." 6. That "the eye is to be plucked out."—(From Swedenborg's MSS. found at the end of the Index to the Scripture passages in *Apocalypse Explained*.)

Verse 26. *I am the God of Abraham, and the God of Isaac, and the God of Jacob.*—That hereby is signified the Divine [principle] Itself, and the Divine Human, is manifest from the representation of Abraham, Isaac, and Jacob, as denoting the Divine [principle] Itself, and the Divine Human of the Lord. That Abraham represents the Lord as to the Divine [principle] Itself, Isaac as to the Divine rational, and Jacob as to the Divine natural, see n. 1893, 2011, 2066, 2072, 2089, 2245, 2251, 2630, 3144, 3210, 3305, 3439, 3704, 4180, 4286, 4536, 4570, 4615, 6098, 6185, 6276, 6424, 6804. By "God" is signified the Divine Being; and by their "names" what is representative. Hence those things in the Lord are what are meant by "the God of Abraham, the God of Isaac, and the God of Jacob." *A. C.* 6847.

Verse 27. *He is not the God of the dead, but the God of the living.*—It is manifest from these words that heaven and hell are from the human race; and the church might have known this, if she had admitted illustration from heaven, and attended to these words of the Lord, and what was said to the thief on the cross,—"To-day shalt thou be with Me in paradise;" (Luke xxiii. 43.) and to what was also said concerning the rich man and Lazarus, that "the former went into hell, and thence discoursed with Abraham; and that the latter went into heaven." (Luke xvi. 19—31.) *L. J.* 19.

As to the *resurrection,* or life after death, man is so created
that, as to his internal, he cannot die; for he is capable of
believing in and of loving God, and thus of being conjoined
to God by faith and love; and to be thus conjoined to God
is to live to eternity.

This internal exists in every man who is born; his external
is that by which he brings into effect the things which belong
to his faith and love. The internal of man is the spirit, and
the external is the body. The external, or the body, is suited
to the performance of uses in the natural world, and is rejected
or put off at death; but the internal, which is called the spirit,
and which is suited to the performance of uses in the spiritual
world, never dies. After death, this internal exists as a good
spirit and an angel, if the man had been good during his abode
in the world, but if during that time he had lived in evil, he
is, after death, an evil spirit.

The spirit of man, after the dissolution of the body, appears
in the spiritual world in a human form, in every respect as in
the natural world. He enjoys the faculty of sight, of hearing,
of speaking, and of feeling, as he did in the world; and he is
endowed with every faculty of thought, of will, and of action,
as when he was in the world; in a word, he is a man in all
respects, even to the most minute particular, except that
he is not encompassed with the gross body which he had in
the world. This he leaves when he dies, nor does he ever
resume it.

This continuation of life is meant by the *resurrection.* The
reason why men believe that they shall not rise again before
the Last Judgment, when, as they suppose, the whole visible
creation will be destroyed, is, because they do not understand
the Word, and because sensual men place all their life in the
body, and imagine that unless the body be re-animated, the
man can be no more.

The life of man after death is the life of his love and of his
faith; hence the nature of his life to eternity is determined
by the quality which had belonged to these during his life in
the world. With those who loved themselves and the world
supremely, this life is the life of hell; and with those who had
loved God supremely, and the neighbour as themselves, it is
the life of heaven. The latter are they who have faith; but
the former are they who have no faith. The life of heaven
is called *eternal life,* and the life of hell is called *spiritual
death.*

That man continues to live after the death of the body is
plainly taught in the Word; as when it is said, that "God is not
the God of the dead, but of the living;" (Matt. **xxii.** 32.) that

Lazarus after death was "carried into heaven," and that the rich man "lifted up his eyes in hell;" (Luke xvi. 22, 23, and the following verses.) that "Abraham, Isaac, and Jacob," are in heaven; (Matt. viii. 11; xxii. 31, 32; Luke xx. 37, 38.) and when Jesus said to the thief on the cross,—"To-day shalt thou be with Me in paradise." (Luke xxiii. 43.) *H. D.* *223—228.*

Verse 30. *And thou shalt love the Lord thy God from thy whole heart, and from thy whole soul, and from thy whole thought, and from thy whole strength: this is the first commandment.*—By "loving Jehovah God, with the whole heart and the whole soul," is meant with all the will and all the understanding, likewise with all the love and all the faith; for "heart" signifies the love and the will, and "soul" signifies the faith and understanding. The reason why "heart" signifies those two principles, viz., the love and the will, is, because man's love is of his will; and the reason why "soul" signifies also two principles, viz., faith and understanding, is, because faith is of the understanding. The reason why "heart" and "soul" have such signification, is, because the *heart* of man corresponds to the good of love which is of his will, and the *soul* [*anima,* or breath] of the lungs corresponds to the truth of faith, which is of the understanding. *A. E.* 750.

By "heart" is meant the life of love, and by "soul" the life of faith, and by "thought" those things which proceed from the life of faith, thus which proceed from the soul, or from the understanding enlightened. That these things are signified in the Word by "heart" and "soul" is known to few at this day within the church, by reason that it has not been considered that man has two faculties, distinct from each other, viz., a will and an understanding, and that those two faculties must constitute one mind, that man may be truly a man. Neither has it been considered that all things in the universe, both in heaven and in the world, have reference to Good and Truth, and that these principles must be joined together before they can be anything and produce anything; in consequence of ignorance on these subjects, man has separated faith from love, for he who is ignorant of those universal laws, cannot know that faith has reference to truth, and love to good, and that unless they be joined together they are not anything, since faith without love is not faith, and love without faith is not love, for love has its quality from faith, and faith its life from love; hence faith without love is dead, and faith with love is alive. *A. C.* 9050.

It is said that "God should be loved from the whole heart, from the whole soul, and from all the strength," by which words is signified, that He should be loved from all things appertaining to man. "From the heart," denotes from the will where the good of love is; "from the soul," denotes from the understanding where the truth of faith is, thus it denotes from faith; which two principles are of the internal man; "from all the strength," denotes from those things which are of the understanding and of the will in the external man. *A. C.* 9936.

That love to the Lord and love towards the neighbour comprehend in them all divine Truths, may be manifest from what the Lord spake concerning those two loves, saying,—" Thou shalt love the Lord thy God from thy whole heart, and from thy whole soul, and from thy whole thought. This is the first and great commandment. But the second is like unto it, Thou shalt love thy neighbour as thyself. On these two commandments hang the whole law and the prophets." (Matt. xxii. 37—41.) The "law and the prophets" are the whole Word, thus every divine Truth. *H. H.* 19.

In the beginning, when any church is established, the Word is at first closed to them, but afterwards it is unclosed, the Lord so providing, and hence it is learnt that all doctrine is founded on these two precepts, that the Lord is to be loved above all things, and a man's neighbour as himself. When these two precepts are regarded as an end, then the Word is unclosed, for "all the law and all the prophets," that is, the whole Word, depend upon them; insomuch that all things are thence derived, and all things have reference to them; and whereas in such case the members of the church are in the principle of Truth and Good, they are enlightened in singular things which they see in the Word, for the Lord is then present with them by the angels and teaches them, although they are ignorant of it, and also leads them into the life of Truth and Good. *A. C.* 3773.

It is said by the Lord in the Old Testament, and confirmed in the New, that "all the law and all the prophets are founded in love to God, and in love towards the neighbour," thus in the very life, but not in faith without life, therefore in nowise in faith alone, consequently neither in confidence, for this cannot exist without charity towards the neighbour. *A. C.* 5826.

That all things of heaven and of the church are from the good of love, and that the good of love is from the Lord, cannot be seen, and hence cannot be known, unless it be demonstrated. The reason why it is not known because it is not seen, is, because good does not enter the thought of man like truth, for truth is seen in the thought, because it is from the light of heaven, whereas good is only felt because it is from the heat of heaven, and it rarely happens that any one, whilst he reflects on those things which he thinks, attends to those which he feels. This is the reason why the learned have attributed all things to thought, and not to affection, and why the church has attributed all things to faith and not to love, when yet the truth, which at this day in the church is said to be of faith, or is called faith, is only the form of good which is of love. Now, whereas man does not see good in his thought, for good, as was said, is only felt, and is felt under various species of delight, and whereas man does not attend to those things which he feels in thought, but which he sees there, therefore he calls all that good which he feels from delight, and from delight he feels evil, because this is in-born from nativity, and proceeds from the love of self and of the world; this is the reason why it is unknown that the good of love is the all of heaven and of the church, and that this good is not in man, but from the Lord, and that it does not flow in from the Lord with any others but those who shun evils with their delights as sins. This is what is meant by the Lord's words,—"The law and the prophets hang on these two commandments, *Thou shalt love God above all things, and thy Neighbour as thyself.*" And I can assert that there is not a grain of truth given, which in itself is truth, with man, only so far as it is from the good of love from the Lord; and hence not a grain of faith, which in itself is faith, that is, living, saving, and spiritual faith, unless so far as it is grounded in charity, which is from the Lord. *A. R.* 908.

When love to the Lord becomes the ruling love, it is present in singular the things of man's life; as he who loves his king, or his parents, manifests this love in their presence by its shining forth from singular the parts of his face, by its being heard in singular the things of his speech, and by its appearing in singular the things of his gesture. This is meant by "having God continually before the eyes," and by "loving Him above all things, with the whole soul and with the whole heart." *A. C.* 8857.

Verse 32. *There is One God, and there is none other but He.*—God is ONE both in Person and in Essence, in whom there is a Trinity, and that God is the Lord Jesus Christ. Upon a just idea of God, the whole heaven and the whole church, and all things of religion are founded, because thereby conjunction is effected with God, and by conjunction heaven and eternal life. *A. R.* 42. See also Preface to that work, and n. 469.

The Scriptures throughout teach that God is One. There is a universal influx into the souls of men to the effect that

there is a God, and that He is one.   Human reason may
perceive, if it will, that there is a God, and that He is one;
for the existence and unity of God are evident from the
phenomena of the universe.   God is Substance itself and
Form itself; He is *Esse* itself and *Existere* itself.   He is
infinite, because He is and exists in Himself, and all things
in the universe are and exist from Him.   He is Love itself
and Wisdom itself, consequently He is Good itself and Truth
itself; thus He is the verimost Life, which is Life in itself.   He
is Omnipotent, Omniscient, and Omnipresent by the Wisdom
of His Love.   His power and will are one, and since He wills
nothing but what is good, therefore He can do nothing but
what is good.   He is in His Omnipotence in the order of the
universe, according to which He acts.   He sees, perceives,
and knows all things that are done according to order, and by
that means also whatsoever is done contrary to order.   He is
Omnipresent from first to last in His own order.   The one
God descended and was made Man, for the purpose of effect-
ing redemption.   Being in inmost or in purest principles, He
could not by any other means descend to ultimates, or to
lowest principles.   Although He descended as the Word, or
as the Divine Truth, He did not separate the Divine Good.
He is never angry with any one; He never avenges, tempts,
punishes, casts into hell, or condemns; such things are as
far from God as hell is from heaven, and infinitely farther.
Every one has a place in heaven according to his idea of God.
This idea, like a touchstone, by which gold and silver are
tried, is the true test for examining the quality of what is
good and true in a man.   The Humanity of the Lord is
Divine, and consequently in Him God is Man and Man is
God.   He is the same from eternity to eternity, though His
identity is not simple identity, but infinite; and all variation
is from the subject in which He abides.   Unless God be
approached in thought as a Man, [that is, as a Divine Man,
such as He manifested Himself when transfigured, Matt. xvii.]
all idea of God is lost, and becomes like bodily vision when
directed to the wide universe, so that it either fixes itself on
an empty nothing or on nature.   *T. C. R.*, see Index, under
the term *God*.

The thought only of God as a MAN, in whom is the divine
Trinity of Father, Son, and Holy Spirit, *opens heaven;* but
on the contrary, the thought concerning God as being not a
MAN (which appears in the spiritual world as a little cloud, or
as nature in its least principles), *shuts heaven.*   For God is
a MAN [*Homo*], even as the universal angelic heaven in its

aggregate is a *Man* [*homo*], and every angel and spirit is thence a man. *A. E.* 1097.

Verse 33. *To love God with the whole heart, &c., and his neighbour as himself.*—To "love the Lord," is to live according to His precepts, as He Himself teaches in John,— "If ye love Me, keep My commandments." *A. C.* 10,829.

It is in the power of every one to see that no kind of life exists without love, and that there is no kind of joy but what flows from love : such however as the love is, such is the life and such is the joy. If you remove loves, or, what is the same thing, desires which have relation to love, thought would instantly cease, and you would become like a dead person, of which I have often been convinced by lively experience. Self-love and the love of the world have in them some resemblance of life, and some resemblance of joy, but inasmuch as they are altogether contrary to true love, which consists in a man loving the Lord above all things, and his neighbour as himself, it must be evident that they are not loves but hatreds; for in proportion as any one loves himself and the world, in the same proportion he hates his neighbour, and thereby the Lord; wherefore true love is love towards the Lord; and true life is the life of love from Him; and true joy is the joy of that life. There cannot exist more than one single true love, nor more than one single true life, whence flow true joys and true happinesses, such as are enjoyed by the angels in the heavens. *A. E.* 33.

So far as man recedes from self-love and the lusts thereof, so far he receives from the Lord celestial love, that is, mutual love, which consists in a desire to serve all others; these are understood by the *least* who become the *greatest* in the kingdom of God. (Matt. xx. 26—28.) Hence it may appear that what principally disjoins the external man from the internal, is self-love; and that mutual love is what principally tends to unite them, which mutual love cannot exist before self-love recedes, for they are altogether contrary to each other. The Lord gives to angels and to men, whilst they live in mutual love, a celestial *proprium,* so that it appears to them as if they did good of or from themselves; hence the internal man is predicated of man as if it was his own. But whosoever is principled in mutual love, acknowledges and believes that all goodness and truth are not his, but the Lord's, and that the ability to love another as himself, and especially as the angels, to love another *more* than himself, is the gift of the Lord, from which gift and its happiness he recedes, in proportion as he recedes from the acknowledgment that it is the Lord's. *A. C.* 1594.

Verse *33. To love God and the neighbour is more than whole burnt-offerings and sacrifices.* — "Burnt-offerings and sacrifices" were nothing else than the *types* or *representatives* of internal worship, and when separated from internal worship they became idolatrous. Sacrifices were indeed commanded by Moses to the children of Israel; but they of the most ancient church, which was before the flood, were altogether unacquainted with sacrifices, nor did it ever enter their minds to worship the Lord by the slaying of animals. The ancient church which was after the flood was likewise unacquainted with sacrifices; that church was indeed in representative worship, but not in that of sacrifice. Sacrifices were first instituted in the succeeding church, which was called the Hebraic church, and thence spread among the Gentiles; thence also such worship descended to Abraham, Isaac, and Jacob, and thus to their posterity. That the posterity of Jacob were principled in sacrificial worship before they departed from Egypt, thus before sacrifices were enjoined by Moses on Mount Sinai, may appear from Exodus v. 3; x. 25, 26; xviii. 12; xxiv. 4, 5; and especially from the "golden calf." (xxxii. 5, 6.) This was done before the command was brought to them concerning the altar and sacrifices; which command, therefore, was given because sacrificial worship with them, as with the Gentiles, had become idolatrous; from which worship they could not be withdrawn, because they esteemed it to be of especial sanctity, and because what is once implanted from infancy with an idea of sanctity, particularly if it be implanted into children by their fathers, and thereby rooted in them, the Lord never breaks, but bends, unless it be contrary to essential order. Hence appears the reason why it was prescribed that sacrifices should be under such particular rules and regulations, as written in the law of Moses. That sacrifices were never acceptable to Jehovah, but were only permitted and tolerated for the reason just mentioned, plainly appears in the Prophets, as in Jer. vii. 21—23. *A. C.* 922, 2180.

"Burnt-offerings" denote worship grounded in the good of love, and "sacrifices" worship grounded in the truth of faith. *A. C.* 8680.

Verse *34. Kingdom of God.* — See above, chap. i. 14, 15, Exposition.

Verses *35—38. And Jesus answering, said, teaching in the temple, How say the Scribes that Christ is the Son of David?* &c. — That David might represent the Lord as to Divine Truth, the Lord was willing to be born of the house of David, and also to be called the *Son*, the *stem*, and the *offspring of David*, likewise the *root of Jesse;* but when the Lord put off the Human principle derived from the mother, and put on the Human principle derived from the Father, which is the Divine Human, He was then no longer the Son of David; this is meant by the Lord's words in the above verses. Hence it is, that He was not the Son of David, as neither the Son of Mary, whom therefore He did not call His mother, but woman. (Matt. xii. 46—49; Mark iii. 31, to the end; Luke viii. 19—21; John ii. 4.) *A. E.* 205.

That the Lord had a Divine Principle and a Human one, the Divine one from Jehovah the Father, and the Human one from the Virgin Mary, is a known thing; hence it is that He was God and Man, and thus He had a Divine Essence and a Human Nature, the Divine Essence from the Father, the Human Nature from the Mother, and hence He was equal to the Father as to the Divine Principle, and inferior to the Father as to the Human; also that He did not transmute this Human Nature from the Mother into the Divine Essence, nor mixed the former with the latter, as the Doctrine of Faith, which is called the Athanasian Creed, teaches; for the Human Nature cannot be transmuted into the Divine Essence, nor be commixed with it. And yet, from the same doctrine, it is to be understood that the Divine Principle took to itself a Human Principle, that is, united itself to it, as the soul to its body, until they were not two, but one Person; from this consideration it follows, that He put off the Human Principle derived from the Mother, which in itself was like the Human Principle in another man, and thus material, and put on a Human Principle from the Father, which in itself is like to its Divine Principle, and thus substantial, by virtue of which the Human Principle was also made Divine. Hence it is that the Lord, in the Word of the Prophets, is called Jehovah and God even as to the Human Principle; and in the Word of the Evangelists, the Lord, God, Messiah or Christ, and the Son of God, in whom mankind are to believe, and by whom they are to be saved. Now, whereas the Lord had from the beginning a Human Principle from the Mother, and this He successively put off, therefore, whilst He was in the world, He passed through two states, which are called a state of humiliation or exinanition, and a state of glorification or unition with the Divine Principle which is called the Father; a state of humiliation, so far and so long as He was in the Human Principle from the Mother, and a state of glorification, so far and so long as He was in the Human Principle derived

31

from the Father. In the state of humiliation He prayed to
the Father as to another distinct from Himself; but in the
state of glorification, He discoursed with the Father as with
Himself. In this latter state He said, that the Father was in
Him and He in the Father, and that the Father and He were
one; but in the state of humiliation He underwent temptations, and endured the cross, and prayed to the Father not to
forsake Him; for the Divine Principle could not be tempted,
and still less suffer the cross. From these considerations it is
now evident, that by temptations and continual victories at the
time, and by the passion of the cross, which was the last
temptation, He fully overcame the hells, and fully glorified
the Human Principle, as was shewn above. That the Lord
put off the Human Principle derived from the Mother, and
put on the Human Principle derived from the Divine Principle
in Himself, which is called the Father, is evident also from
this consideration, that the Lord, as often as He spake from
His own mouth to the Mother, did not call her Mother, but
woman. In the Evangelists we read only three times that
from His own mouth He spake to the Mother and concerning
her, and that on these occasions He twice called her woman,
and that once He did not acknowledge her as His Mother.
That He twice called her woman, we read in John,—"The
Mother of Jesus said to Him, They have no wine. Jesus
saith to her, What [is it] to Me and thee, *Woman?* My hour
is not yet come;" (ii. 4.) and in the same Evangelist,—"Jesus
from the cross seeth the Mother and the disciple standing by,
whom He loved; He saith to His Mother, *Woman,* behold
thy son! Then saith He to the disciple, Behold thy mother!"
(xix. 26, 27.) That on one occasion He did not acknowledge
her, we read in Luke: Jesus was told, "Thy mother and Thy
brethren stand without, and are desirous to see Thee." Jesus
answering, said unto them,—"My mother and My brethren
are those, who hear the word of God and do it." (viii. 20, 21;
Matt. 46—49; Mark iii. 31—35.) In other passages Mary is
called His Mother, but not from His own mouth. This is
also confirmed by the circumstance that He did not acknowledge Himself to be the Son of David, for we read in the
Evangelists,—"Jesus asked the Pharisees, saying, What think
ye of Christ? whose Son is He? They say unto Him, The
Son of David. He saith unto them, How then doth David
in spirit call Him Lord, saying, The Lord said unto my Lord,
Sit Thou on My right hand, until I make Thy foes Thy
footstool? If David then call Him Lord, how is He his Son?
And no one could answer Him a word." (Matt. xxii. 41—46;
Mark xii. 35—37; Luke xx. 41—44; Psalm cx. 1.) From

these considerations it is evident that the Lord, as to the glorified Human Principle, was not the Son of Mary, nor of David. What was the nature of His glorified Human Principle, He shewed to Peter, James, and John, when He was transfigured before them;—that "His face did shine as the sun, and His raiment was as light; and then a voice from a cloud said, This is My beloved Son, in whom I am well pleased: hear ye Him." (Matt. xvii. 1—8; Mark ix. 2—8; Luke ix. 28—36.) The Lord also was seen by John, "as the sun shining in his strength." (Rev. i. 16.) *D. L.* 35.

It is believed that the Lord, as to His Human Principle, not only was, but also is the Son of Mary; but in this the Christian world is mistaken. That He was the Son of Mary, is true; but that He still is the Son of Mary, is not true; for by acts of redemption He put off the Human Principle derived from the Mother, and put on the Human Principle derived from the Father. Hence it is that the Human Principle of the Lord is Divine, and that in Him God is Man, and Man, God. This is also confirmed by the consideration that He did not acknowledge Himself to be the Son of David; for we read in the Evangelist,—"Jesus asked the Pharisees, saying, What think you of the Christ? whose Son is He?" &c. *T. C. R.* 102. *A. C.* 2649.

Verse 36. *The Lord said unto my Lord, Sit Thou on My right hand, until I make Thine enemies Thy footstool.*—By "right hand," when applied to the Lord, is signified both Omnipotence and Omniscience. The reason is, because to the *right* in heaven is the south, and to the *left* the north; and by the "south" is signified Divine Truth in the light, and by the "north," Divine Truth in the shade; and whereas all power appertains to Divine Good by Divine Truth, therefore by the "right hand," when applied to the Lord, is signified Omnipotence; and whereas all intelligence and wisdom appertain to Divine Good by Divine Truth, and to the *right* in heaven is Divine Truth in the light, as was said, therefore by the "right hand," when applied to the Lord, is also signified Omniscience. By the above words is described the Lord's combat in the world against the hells, and their subjugation, which was effected from the Divine Good by the Divine Truth. The "right hand" signifies the Divine Truth, wherefore it is said, "until I make Thine enemies Thy footstool;" where, by "enemies," are signified the hells; and by "making them a footstool," is signified altogether to subdue. *A. E.* 298.

By "footstool" are here signified things natural, both sensual things and scientific, and hence the rational things of man, which are called "enemies," when they pervert worship, and this from the literal sense of the Word; so that there is worship only in things external, and no internal worship but what is filthy. *A. C.* 3162. See also 2162.

Verse 36. *The Lord said unto my Lord,* &c.—By these words is signified the Divine Principle itself, which is called *Father,* to the Divine Human Principle, which is called *Son.* "Sit Thou on My right hand," signifies Divine Power or Omnipotence by Divine Truth; "until I make Thine enemies Thy footstool," signifies until the hells are conquered and subdued, and the wicked cast down thither; "enemies" denote the hells, consequently the wicked; and "footstool" signifies the lowest region beneath the heavens, under which are the hells. For the Lord, whilst He was in the world, was Divine Truth, which has Omnipotence, and by which He conquered and subdued the hells. *A. E.* 687.

Verse 39. *Chief seats in synagogues.*—For the signification of "synagogue," see chap. i. 21, Exposition.

Verse 41. *Jesus saw how the multitude cast money into the treasury,* &c.—That good done from a selfish motive, or when the heart is not purified, is of no avail, see above, chap. x. 20, 22, Exposition.

Verse 42. *One poor widow coming, cast in two mites,* &c.— By a "widow" is signified one who is in good without truth, and still desires truth. The reason why this is signified by a *widow,* is, because by a "man" [*vir*] is signified truth, and by his "wife," good; wherefore the wife of a man, when made a "widow," signifies good without truth. *A. C.* 9198.

TRANSLATOR'S NOTES AND OBSERVATIONS.

CHAPTER XII.

Verse 11. *This was the Lord's doing, and it is marvellous in our eyes.*—The pronoun "this," as it here occurs, is in the feminine gender, and so likewise is the adjective "marvellous;" from which circumstance it is evident that both the pronoun and the adjective have reference to *the head of the corner,* which "head," in the original Greek, is also expressed by a feminine substantive.

MARK.

CHAPTER XIII.

THE WORD.

1. AND as He went out of the temple, one of His disciples saith unto Him, Teacher, behold what manner of stones and what buildings [are here]!

2. And Jesus answering, said unto him, Seest thou these great buildings? there shall not be left stone upon stone, which shall not be thrown down.

3. And as He sat upon the Mount of Olives over against the temple, Peter and James and John and Andrew asked Him privately,

4. Tell us, when shall these things be? and what shall be the sign when all these things shall be fulfilled?

5. And Jesus answering them, began to say, Take heed [see] lest any one deceive you:

6. For many shall come in My name, saying, I am [Christ]; and shall deceive many.

7. But when ye hear of wars and rumours of wars, be ye not troubled: for it

THE INTERNAL SENSE.

THAT the state of the church is not to be judged of from the external aspect of the truths, which the members of the church profess to believe, since if these truths be separated from the good of charity, the church itself must come to vastation and destruction. (Verses 1, 2.)

For which reason the understandings of the members of the church ought to be opened to the light of truth, to prevent their being misled by falses, since those are about to come, who will say that this is of faith, or that this is truth, when yet it is neither of faith, nor is it truth, but what is false. (Verses 3—6.)

Debates also and disputes will exist concerning truths. (Verse 7.)

must needs be so; but the end is not yet.

8. For nation shall rise against nation, and kingdom against kingdom: and there shall be earthquakes in divers places, and there shall be famines and disturbances: these are the beginnings of sorrows.

And evil is about to fight against evil, and the false against the false, so that the state of the church will be changed, and there will no longer be any knowledge of what is good and true, but infection from falses. (Verse 8.)

9. But take ye heed [see] to yourselves: for they shall deliver you up to councils and to synagogues; ye shall be beaten: and shall be brought before rulers and kings for My sake, for a testimony against them.

They, therefore, who are principled in what is good and true, will be in danger, first, from the perversion of truth; next, from its captivity by falses; and all on account of the goods of love and the truths of faith from the Lord. (Verse 9.)

10. And the Gospel must first be preached amongst all nations.

Which goods and truths must first be made known to all who are principled in good. (Verse 10.)

11. But when they shall lead you, and deliver you up, take no thought beforehand what ye shall speak, neither do ye premeditate: but what-soever shall be given you in that same hour, that speak ye: for it is not you who speak, but the Holy Spirit.

To whom instruction is given, under all infestation by falses, to consult Divine Truth for security, rather than depend on their own prudence. (Verse 11.)

12. Now the brother shall deliver the brother to death, and the father the son; and children shall rise up against parents, and shall cause them to be put to death.

13. And ye shall be hated of all for My name's sake: but he that shall endure unto the end, the same shall be saved.

For evil will destroy good, and what is false will destroy what is true, by bringing those heavenly principles into con-tempt and aversion. (Verse 12, and former part of 13.)

Nevertheless no injury can be done to those who abide patiently in the Lord. (Verse 13, latter part.)

14. But when ye shall see the abomination of desolation, spoken of by Daniel the prophet, standing where it ought not, (let him that readeth understand,) then let them who are in Judea flee to the mountains:

15. And let him who is on the house-top not go down into the house, neither enter to take anything out of his house:

16. And let him who is in the field not turn back again to take his garment.

17. But woe to them that are with child, and to them that give suck in those days!

18. And pray ye that your flight be not in the winter.

19. For in those days shall be affliction, such as was not from the beginning of the creation which God created unto this time, neither shall be.

20. And unless the Lord had shortened those days, no flesh could be saved: but for the elect's sake, whom He hath chosen, He hath shortened the days.

And who therefore are forewarned, when they observe the predicted vastation of good and truth, not to look elsewhere than to the LORD, thus to the love of Him and neighbourly love. (Verse 14.)

And they who are in the good of charity, ought not to betake themselves to those things which relate to the doctrinals of faith. (Verse 15.)

And they who are in the good of truth, ought not to betake themselves to the doctrinals of truth. (Verse 16.)

For they who are imbued with the good of love to the LORD, and with the good of innocence, will then be in danger of profaning those goods, and thus of eternal damnation. (Verse 17.)

They, therefore, who are principled in good and truth, ought to take heed lest a removal from those principles should be made precipitately, in a state of too much cold arising from self-love. (Verse 18.)

For on that occasion will be the highest degree of perversion and vastation of the church as to good and truth, which is profanation. (Verse 19.)

So that for the salvation of those who are in the life of good, it will be necessary that they who are of the church should be removed from interior goods and truths to exterior. (Verse 20.)

21. And then if any one shall say unto you, Lo, here is Christ! or, Lo, He is there! believe not:

22. For false Christs and false prophets shall arise, and shall shew signs and wonders, to seduce, if possible, even the elect.

23. But take ye heed [see ye]: behold, I have foretold you all things.

24. But in those days, after that tribulation, the sun shall be darkened, and the moon shall not give her light,

25. And the stars of heaven shall be falling, and the powers which [are] in the heavens shall be shaken.

26. And then shall they see the Son of Man coming in the clouds with much power and glory.

27. And then shall He send His angels, and shall gather together His elect from the four winds, from the extreme of the earth to the extreme of heaven.

28. But learn a parable from the fig-tree: When its branch is yet tender, and putteth forth leaves, ye know that summer is near:

29. So ye in like manner, when ye shall see these things come to pass, know ye that it is nigh at the doors.

And the doctrine of those who are in a holy external principle, but in a profane internal, is to be guarded against, because abounding with falses. (Verses 21—23.)

And when there is no longer any faith remaining, all love to the LORD and neighbourly love will disappear, and the knowledges of good and truth will perish, and thus the foundations of the church will be removed. (Verses 24, 25.)

And then shall be the appearing of Truth Divine through the revelation of the Word as to its internal sense. (Verse 26.)

Then too shall be election through the influx of holy good and truth from the LORD by the angels, and thus the establishment of a New Church. (Verse 27.)

And when this New Church is erecting by the LORD, then first of all appears the good of the natural principle, with its affections and truths. (Verse 28.)

And when all the things above spoken of appear, then will be the consummation of the church, that is, the last judgment and coming of the LORD, consequently then the Old Church will be rejected, and the New established. (Verse 29.)

30. Verily I say unto you, That this generation shall not pass away, until all these things be done.

31. The heaven and the earth shall pass away: but My words shall not pass away.

32. But of that day and hour knoweth no one, neither the angels who [are] in heaven, nor the Son, except the Father.

33. See ye, Watch and pray: for ye know not when the time is;

34. [For it is] as a man taking a far journey, leaving his house, and giving authority to his servants, and to every one his work, and he commanded the porter to watch.   '

35. Watch ye therefore: for ye know not when the Lord of the house cometh, at even, or at midnight, or at the cock-crowing, or in the morning:

36. Lest coming suddenly [or unawares] He find you sleeping.

37. But what I say unto you, I say unto all, Watch ye.

In the meantime the Jewish nation, together with their worship, will not be extirpated like other nations. (Verse 30.)

And the internals and externals of the former church will perish, but the Word of the LORD will remain. (Verse 31.)

And the state of the church at that time, as to goods and truths, will not appear to any one, either in earth or in heaven, but to the LORD alone. (Verse 32.)

Therefore man ought to procure to himself spiritual life, which is life from the LORD, because he is in ignorance what the state of his life is, which is to remain to eternity. (Verse 33.)

For the LORD gives to all who are in the church the knowledges of truth and good from the Word, with the faculty of perceiving them, and of securing them from injury. (Verse 34.)

Wherefore all ought to keep their minds open to the light of truth, to preserve them from the darkness of evil and error. (Verses 35—37.)

EXPOSITION.

CHAPTER XIII.

On the general Contents of this Chapter.

THAT the " consummation of the age" signifies the last time
of the church, was shewn in the foregoing articles, whence it
is evident what is meant by the " consummation of the age,"
spoken of by the Lord in the Gospels, (Matt. xxiv.; Mark xiii.;
Luke xxi.) for it is written,—"As Jesus sat upon the Mount
of Olives, His disciples came to Him privately, saying, Tell
us, when shall these things be? and what is the sign of Thy
coming, and of the *consummation of the age?*" (Matt. xxiv. 3.)
and immediately the Lord began to foretel and describe the
consummation in all its successive states, even to His advent,
and that then He would " come in the clouds of heaven with
power and great glory, and would gather together His elect,"
with many other particulars, (verses 30, 31.) which in no sort
came to pass at the destruction of Jerusalem.   These things
the Lord described on that occasion in a prophetic discourse,
every word of which was weighty and significant; the spiritual
import of every particular expression may be seen explained in
the " Arcana Coelestia," n. 3353—3356, 3486—3489, 3650—
3655, 3751—3757, 3898—3801, 4057—4060, 4229—4231.
T. C. R. 757.   See also Matthew, chap. xxiv., Exposition.

Verse 2. *And Jesus answering, said unto him, Seest thou
these great buildings? there shall not be left stone upon stone,
which shall not be thrown down.*—By " a stone of the temple
not being left upon a stone which should not be thrown down,"
is signified the destruction and total vastation of the church;
a " stone" also signifies the truth of the church; and whereas
that destruction and vastation was signified, therefore in Matt.
xxiv., Mark xiii., and Luke xxi., the subject treated of is
concerning the successive vastation of the church. *A. E.* 220.

From the time of the Council of Nice, dreadful heresies
began to be propagated concerning God, and concerning the
Person of Christ, whereby the head of Antichrist was lifted
up, and God was divided into three, and the Lord the Saviour
into two, and thus the temple erected of the Lord by the
apostles was destroyed, and this to such a degree, until " stone
was not left upon stone, which was not thrown down," according

to the Lord's words in Matt. xxiv. 2; Mark xiii. 2; where, by the "temple," is not only meant the temple of Jerusalem, but also the church, the consummation, or end of which, is treated of in those chapters throughout. *T. C. R.* 174.

The greatest part of mankind believe that, when the Last Judgment comes, all things in the visible world are to perish, that the earth is to be burned up, the sun and the moon be dissipated, and the stars vanish away; and that afterwards a new heaven and a new earth shall be formed. This opinion has been conceived from the prophetic revelations, which are so expressed; but that the case is otherwise, may be manifest from what has been shewn concerning the Last Judgment, n. 900, 931, 1850, 2117—2133. Hence it is evident that the Last Judgment is nothing else but the end of the church with one nation, and its beginning with another, which end and which beginning then have place, when there is no longer any acknowledgment of the Lord, or, what is the same thing, when there is no faith; no acknowledgment or no faith comes to pass when there is no charity, for faith cannot be given but with those who are principled in charity. That in such case there is an end of the church, and a translation of it to others, evidently appears from all those things which the Lord Himself taught and predicted concerning that last day, or concerning the "consummation of the age," in the Evangelists, viz., in Matt. xxiv., in Mark xiii., and in Luke xxi. But whereas those things cannot be comprehended by any one without a key, which is the internal sense, it is allowed to unfold them, and first the things contained in chap. xxiv. of Matthew, 3—9. They who abide in the sense of the letter, cannot know whether the contents of these verses, and those things which follow in that chapter, have relation to the destruction of Jerusalem, and the dispersion of the Jewish nation, or to the end of days, which is called the Last Judgment; but they who are in the internal sense, see clearly that the subject here treated of is concerning the end of the church, which end is what is here and in other passages called the "coming of the Lord," and the "consummation of the age." And since that end is meant, it may be known that all those things signify such things as relate to the church; but what they signify may be manifest from each in the internal sense, as where it is said,—"Many shall come in My name, saying, I am Christ; and shall seduce many;" where *name* does not signify name, nor *Christ*, Christ, but "name" signifies that by which the Lord is worshipped, and "Christ," the very Truth; thus it signifies that they will come who will say that "this is of faith," or that "this is the truth," when yet it is neither of faith, nor the truth, but what is false. Again, where it is said,—"That they shall hear of wars and rumours of wars," it denotes that debates and disputes, which are *wars* in the spiritual sense, will exist concerning truths. Again,—"That nation shall be stirred up against nation, and kingdom against kingdom," signifies that evil is about to fight with evil, and what is false with what is false. And again,—"There shall be famines, and pestilences, and earthquakes, in divers places," denotes there shall be no longer any knowledge of goods and truths, and thus that the state of the church will be changed, which is an *earthquake*. From these considerations it is evident what is meant by the above words of the Lord, viz., that they describe the first state of the perversion of the church, which is when they begin no longer to know what is good and what is true, but dispute with each other on those subjects, from which disputes come falsities. Inasmuch as this is the first state, therefore it is said that "the end is not yet," and that "those things are the beginning of sorrows;" and this state is called "earthquakes in divers places," which, in the internal sense, signify a change in the state of the church in part, or the first state. This being "said to the disciples," signifies that it is said to all who are of the church, for the twelve disciples represent the church; wherefore it is said,—"See lest any one seduce you;" also, "Ye are about to hear of wars and rumours of wars, see that ye be not troubled." *A. C. 3353, 3354.*

By "a stone not being left upon a stone which should not be thrown down," is signified that the Lord would be altogether denied amongst them, wherefore also the temple was utterly destroyed. *A. E. 391.*

Verse 3. *And as He sat upon the Mount of Olives,* &c.— The "Mount of Olives" signifies the Divine Love, on which account the Lord was accustomed to tarry upon that mountain, as is evident in Luke,—"Jesus was in the day teaching in the temple, but going forth at night, He passed the night in the mount, which is called [the Mount] of Olives;" (xxi. 37; xxii. 39; John viii. 1.) and there "discoursed with His disciples concerning His coming and the consummation of the age," that is, concerning the Last Judgment; and also thence went to Jerusalem, and suffered, by which was signified that He did all things from Divine Love, for the "Mount of Olives" signified that love; for whatsoever the Lord did in the world was representative, and whatsoever He spake was signficative. The reason why He was in representatives and significatives, when in the world, was, that He might be in the ultimates of heaven and of the church, and at the same time in their first principles, and thus might govern and arrange ultimates from first principles, and all intermediate things from first principles by ultimates; representatives and significatives are in ultimates. *A. E.* 405.

Verse 4. *Tell us, when shall these things be? and what shall be the sign when all these things shall be fulfilled?*—By "the coming of the Lord and the consummation of the age," is signified the beginning of a New Church, and the end of a former one;—by "the coming of the Lord," the beginning of a New Church, and by "the consummation of the age," the end of an Old Church; wherefore the Lord, in this chapter, instructs the disciples concerning the vastation of the former church, and concerning the establishment of a New Church at the end of the former. But He instructs and teaches them by mere correspondences, which cannot be unfolded and known except by the spiritual sense; and inasmuch as they were correspondences by which the Lord spake, therefore they were all signs, thus testifications; they are likewise called "signs" by the Lord, as in Luke,—"There shall also be great *signs* from heaven; there shall be *signs* in the sun, the moon, and the stars; and on earth distress of nations." (**xx.** 11, 25.) *A. E.* 7006.

As to what concerns the Lord's coming, it is believed by some that the Lord is about to come again in Person, and indeed to execute the Last Judgment; and this because it is said in Matthew,—"The disciples came, saying to Jesus, Tell us, what is the sign of Thy coming, and of the consummation of the age?" and after that the Lord had predicted to them the states of the church, successively decreasing even to its devastation and consummation, He said,—" Then shall appear the sign of the Son of Man; and they shall see the Son of Man coming in the clouds of heaven with power and glory. Watch ye, therefore, because ye know not in what hour your Lord is about to come." (**xxiv.** 30, 39, 42; also in John **xxi.** 22.) But by His *coming* is not there meant His coming in person, but that He would then reveal Himself in the Word, that He is Jehovah, the Lord of heaven and earth, and that they all will adore Him alone, who shall be in His New Church, which is meant by the New Jerusalem; for which end also He has now opened the internal and spiritual sense of the Word, in which sense the Lord is everywhere treated of. This also is what is meant by His "coming in the clouds of heaven with glory." (Matt. **xxiv.** 30; **xxvi.** 64; Mark **xiii.** 26; **xiv.** 62; Luke **xxi.** 27.) That "the clouds of heaven" signify the Word in the letter, and "glory" its spiritual sense, see above, n. 36, 594. Inasmuch as He is the Word, as He is called in John, (i. 1, 2, 14.) therefore the revelation of Him in the Word is His coming. *A. E.* 870.

That by "consummation" is meant the devastation of the church, when there is no longer in it truth of doctrine and good of life, thus when its end is, see n. 658, 750; and whereas in this case is the coming of the Lord, and of His kingdom, therefore mention is made both of "the consummation of the age" and of "the Lord's coming," (Matt. xxiv. 3.) and each also is predicted in that chapter. *A. R.* 519.

It was predicted by the Lord, where He speaks of "the consummation of the age," (Matt. xxiv. 3, to the end; Mark xiii. 3, to the end; Luke xxi. 7, to the end.) that faith would be scarce at the last times; for whatsoever is said in those chapters, involves that in those times charity and faith will be scarce, and that at length there would be none. *A. C.* 1843.

Verse 6. *For many shall come in My name,* &c.—These things were said by the Lord to the disciples concerning "the consummation of the age," by which is signified the state of the church as to its ultimate or last time, which is described in this chapter; wherefore also the successive perversion and falsification of the truth and good of the Word is meant, until there is nothing left but what is false, and the evil thence derived. By those who shall "come in His name, and shall say that they are Christs, and shall seduce many," is signified that those are about to come, who will say that this is Divine Truth, when yet it is truth falsified, which in itself is what is false; for by "Christ" is meant the Lord as to Divine Truth, but here, in the opposite sense, truth falsified; by "hearing of wars and rumours of wars," is signified that disagreements and disputes are about to exist concerning truths, and that thence will come falsifications. By "nation being stirred up against nation," is signified that evil is about to fight with evil, and what is false with what is false, for evils never agree amongst themselves, neither do false principles, which is the reason why churches are divided amongst themselves, and so many heresies have come forth; "nation" signifies those who are in evils, and "kingdom" those who are in false principles, of which the church consists. By "famines, and pestilences, and earthquakes," is signified that there will no longer be any knowledges of truth and of good, and that by reason of the false principles that will infect, the state of the church will be changed; "famine" denotes the privation of the knowledges of truth and of good; "pestilences" denote infections from false principles; and "earthquakes" denote changes of the church. *A. E.* 734.

The above words are not to be understood as declaring that any would rise up, who would call themselves *Christ* or *Christs*, but who would falsify the Word, and would say that this or that is Divine Truth, when yet it is not. They who confirm false principles from the Word, are meant by "false Christs," and they who hatch false principles of doctrine, are meant by "false prophets;" for the subject treated of in the chapter from whence the above words are taken, is concerning the successive vastation of the church, thus concerning the falsification of the Word, and at length concerning the profanation of truth thence derived. *A. E.* 684.

Verse 7. *But when ye hear of wars and rumours of wars, be ye not troubled,* &c.—When the Lord said that "in the last times there should be wars," and that "nation should rise up against nation, and kingdom against kingdom," and that there should be "famines, pestilences, and earthquakes in divers places," it does not signify such things in the natural world, but corresponding things in the spiritual world; for the Word, in the prophetic parts, does not treat of kingdoms on earth, nor of nations there, thus neither of their *wars,* nor of *famine, pestilence,* and *earthquakes* there, but of such things as correspond thereto in the spiritual world. *L. J.* 13. See also *A. C.* 2120, 2547.

Verses 7—13.—By the words which precede, from verse 1, to verse 17, was described the first state of perversion of the church, which was, that they began no longer to know what was good and what was true, but disputed on those subjects one amongst another, from which disputes came falsities; but by these words is described another state of the perversion of the church, which is, that they were about to despise good and truth, and also to hold them in aversion; and thus that faith in the Lord would expire, according to the degrees in which charity would cease. That a second state of perversion of the church is described in the above words of the Lord in the Evangelist [as in Matthew], is evident from the internal sense of the same, which is to the following effect:—

"All these things are the beginning of sorrows," signifies those things which precede, viz., which are of the first state of the perversion of the church, consisting, as was said, in beginning no longer to know what was good and what was true, but in disputing among themselves on those subjects, from which disputes come falsities, consequently heresies. That such things have perverted the church for several ages past, is evident from this consideration, that the church in the Christian world is divided, and this according to opinions concerning what is good and true, thus that the perversion of the church has been begun for a long time back.

" Then shall they deliver you up to affliction, and shall kill you," signifies that good and truth are about to perish, first by *affliction*, which is by perversion, next by *killing them*, which is by denial.   That to " kill," when it is predicated of good and truth, denotes not to be received, thus to deny, see n. 3387, 3395; by "you," or by the apostles, are signified all things of faith in one complex, thus both its good and its truth.   That by the " twelve apostles" those things are signified, see n. 577, 2089, 2129, 2130, 3272, 3354; and is here made very manifest, for the subject treated of is not concerning the preaching of the apostles, but concerning the consummation of the age.

" And ye shall be hated of all nations for My name's sake," signifies contempt and aversion towards all things which are of good and truth, for to " hate" is to despise and to hold in aversion, these being the properties of hatred; " of all nations," denotes of those who are in evil; that " nations" denote such, see n. 1259, 1260, 1849, 1868, 2588; " for My name's sake," denotes for the sake of the Lord, thus for the sake of all things which are from Him; that the " name of the Lord" denotes everything in one complex, by which He is worshipped, thus everything which is of His church, see n. 2724, 3006.

" And then shall many be scandalized, and shall betray one another, and shall hate one another," signifies enmities on account of those things; " many being scandalized," denotes enmity in themselves, the Human Principle itself of the Lord being that against which they have enmity; that that principle was about to be an offence and scandal, is predicted in the Word throughout; " they shall betray one another," denotes enmity amongst themselves, derived from what is evil in opposition to what is good.

" And many false prophets shall arise, and shall seduce many," signifies preachings of what is false; that " false prophets" denote those who teach what is false, thus false doctrine, see n. 2534; " and shall seduce many," denotes that thence would be derivations.

" And because iniquity shall be multiplied, the charity of many shall grow cold," signifies the expiration of charity together with faith; " because of the multiplication of iniquity," denotes according to the false principles of faith; "the charity of many shall grow cold," denotes the expiration of charity together with faith, for each keeps pace with the other, since where there is no faith there is no charity, and where there is no charity there is no faith; but charity is what receives faith, and no charity is what rejects faith; hence the origin of all that is false, and of all that is evil.

"But he that endureth to the end, the same shall be saved," signifies the salvation of those who are in charity; "he that endureth to the end," denotes who does not suffer himself to be seduced, thus who does not yield in temptations.

"And this Gospel of the kingdom shall be preached in all the inhabited [earth], for a witness to all nations," signifies that this shall first be made known in the Christian world; "shall be preached," denotes that it shall be made known; "this Gospel of the kingdom' 'denotes this truth, that so it is; "Gospel" denotes annunciation; "kingdom" denotes truth, see n. 1672, 2547; "in all the inhabited [earth]," denotes the Christian world, see n. 662, 1066, 1067, 1262, 1733, 1850, 2117, 2118, 2928, 3355; the church is here called *inhabited*, from the life of faith, that is, from the good which is of truth, for "to inhabit," in the internal sense, is to live, and "inhabitants" are the goods of truth, see n. 1293, 2268, 2451, 2712, 3384. "For a witness," denotes that they may know, lest they should pretend that they were ignorant; "to all the nations," denotes to the evil, see n. 1259, 1260, 1849, 1868, 2588; for when they are in the principles of what is false and evil, they no longer know what is true and what is good, believing, in this case, what is false to be true, and what is evil to be good, and *vice versâ;* when the church is in this state, "then shall the end come." That the church is of such a quality, does not appear before those who are in the church, viz., it does not appear that they despise and hold in aversion all things which are of good and of truth, also that they cherish enmities against those things, especially against the Lord Himself; for they frequent temples, hear sermons, are in a sort of sanctity when there, attend the Holy Supper, and occasionally discourse with each other in a becoming manner on those subjects,—the evil doing these things the like as the good, yea, they even live one with another in civil charity or friendship; hence it is, that before the eyes of men there does not appear any contempt, still less aversion, and least of all enmity against the goods and truths of faith, thus neither against the Lord. But those things are external forms, by which one person seduces another, whereas the internal forms of the men of the church are altogether dissimilar, yea, altogether contrary to the external. The internal forms are what are here described, and which are of such a quality; what their quality is, appears to the life in heaven, for the angels do not attend to any other than things internal, that is, to ends, or to the intentions or wills of men, and to the thoughts thence derived; how dissimilar these are to the externals, may be manifest from those who come into the other life from the Christian world, concerning whom, see n. 2121—2126. For, in the other life, internal things alone are the things according to which they there think and speak, for external things were left with the body; it there evidently appears that howsoever such persons seem peaceable in the world, they still hated one another, and all things which are of faith, especially the Lord; for when the Lord is only named before them in the other life, a sphere, not only of contempt, but also of aversion and enmity against Him, manifestly breathes forth and diffuses itself around, even from those who, according to appearance, have spoken and have also preached holily concerning Him; in like manner when mention is made of charity and faith. Such is their quality in the internal form which is manifested in the other life, so that if during their abode in the world, external bonds had been loosened, that is, if they had not been afraid of the loss of life and of the penalties of the law, and especially of the loss of reputation for the sake of the honours which they courted and coveted, and for the sake of the wealth after which they lusted, they would have rushed one against another from intestine hatred, according to their tendencies and thoughts, and without any conscience, would have plundered the goods of others, and also without any conscience, would have murdered them, howsoever they were guiltless. Such are Christians at this day, as to their interiors, except a few who are not known; hence it is evident what is the quality of the church. *A. C.* 3486—3490.

Verses 12, 13. *Now the brother shall deliver the brother to death, and the father the son,* &c.—These words are spoken concerning the last times of the church, when there should be no longer any charity, and therefore no longer any faith. "Brother," "children," and "parents," in the internal sense, are the goods and truths of the church, and to "put to death," is to destroy those goods and truths. *A. C.* 6767.

That these words are not to be understood according to the letter, is manifest from what Jesus had before said, that " He came not to give peace upon earth, but division, for that five should be in one house divided, three against two, and two against three;" by which words is signified that false and evil principles are about to fight against truths and goods, as is the case when man comes into temptations, and is reformed; this combat is signified by *division* and *insurrection*. By "the father being divided against the son, and the son against the father," is signified that evil is about to fight against truth, and truth against evil; the "father" denoting evil, which is the selfhood of man, and the "son" denoting the truth which man has from the Lord. The lust of what is false being about to fight against the affection of truth, and the affection of truth against the lust of what is false, is signified by " the mother being divided against the daughter, and the daughter against the mother;" the "mother" denoting the lust of what is false, and the "daughter" denoting the affection of truth, and so forth. That this is the case, may also be manifest from this consideration, that the Lord says in another place, as in John, (xiv. 27; xvi. 33.) that "in Him they should have peace," thus not division. *A. E.* 724.

Verse 13. *But he that shall endure unto the end, the same shall be saved.*—The Lord teaches by these words, that, when man is once converted, he ought to continue in goodness and truth to the end of life. *D. P.* 231.

Verses 14—17. *But when ye shall see the abomination of desolation, spoken of by Daniel the prophet, standing where it ought not, (let him that readeth understand,) then let them who are in Judea flee to the mountains,* &c.—Every one may see that these words contain arcana, and that unless those arcana be discovered, it cannot be at all known what is meant by "those who are in Judea fleeing to the mountains," and by "him who is on the house-top not going down to take anything out of the house," and by "him who is in the field not turning back to take his garment." Unless the internal sense taught what these things signify and involve, the examiners and interpreters of the Word might be led astray, and fall into opinions altogether foreign to that sense; yea, also, they who in heart deny the sanctity of the Word, might thence conclude that in the above words was only described flight and escape on the approach of an enemy, consequently that nothing more holy was contained in them, when yet by those words of the Lord is fully described the state of vastation of the church as to the goods of love and the truths of faith, as may be manifest from the following explication of those words:—

"When therefore ye shall see the abomination of desolation," signifies the *vastation* of the church, which then has place, when the Lord is no longer acknowledged, consequently when there is no love to and no faith in Him; also when there is no longer any charity towards the neighbour, and consequently when there is not any faith grounded in what is good and true. When these things have place in the church, or rather in the tract of country where the Word is, viz., in the thoughts of the heart, although not in the doctrine of the mouth, then is *desolation*, and the above things are its *abomination;* hence, "when ye shall see the abomination," denotes when any one observes such things; what is then to be done, is taught in the following verses, 15, 16. "Declared by Daniel the prophet," signifies, in the internal sense, by the Prophets, for where any prophet is named by his name, in the Word, it is not that prophet who is meant, but the prophetic Word itself, because names in no case penetrate into heaven, n. 1876, 1888; but by one prophet is not signified the like as by another. What is signified by Moses, Elias, and Elisha, see in the preface to chap. xviii., Genesis, and n. 2762; but by Daniel is signified everything prophetic concerning the coming of the Lord, and concerning the state of the church,—in this case, concerning its last state. *Vastation* is much treated of in the Prophets, and by it is there signified, in the sense of the letter, the vastation of the Jewish and Israelitish church, but in the internal sense, the vastation of the church in general, thus also the vastation which is now at hand. "Standing in the holy place," signifies vastation as to all the things which are of good and truth; "holy place" is a state of love and truth, see n. 2625, 2837, 3356, 3387; the holy principle of that state is the good which is of love, and thence the truth which is of faith, nothing else being meant by *holy* in the Word, because those things are from the Lord, who is the Holy, or Sanctuary itself. "Let him that readeth understand," signifies that these things ought to be well noted by those who are in the church, especially by those who are in love and faith, who are now treated of. "Then let them who are in Judea flee to the mountains," signifies that they who are of the church ought not to look elsewhere than to the Lord, thus to love to Him, and to charity towards the neighbour; that by "Judea" is signified the church, will be shewn below; that by "mountain" is signified the Lord Himself, but by "mountains" love to Him and charity to the neighbour, see n. 795, 796, 1430, 2722. According to the sense of the letter it would mean, that when Jerusalem was besieged, as it was by the Romans, then they should not betake themselves thither, but to the *mountains,* according to what is said in Luke,—"When ye shall see Jerusalem encompassed by armies, then know ye that the devastation is near. Then let them who are in Judea flee to the mountains; and let them who are in the midst thereof go forth; but they who are in the countries, let them not enter into it." (xxi. 20, 21.) But with "Jerusalem" in this passage the case is similar, viz., that in the sense of the letter it is Jerusalem which is meant, but in the internal sense the church of the Lord, see n. 402, 2117; for all and singular the things which are mentioned in the Word concerning the people of Judah and Israel, are representative of the Lord's kingdom in the heavens, and of the Lord's kingdom on the earth, that is, of the church, as has been frequently shewn. Hence it is that by *Jerusalem,* in the internal sense, is nowhere meant Jerusalem, nor by *Judea,* Judea, but they were such places as were capable of representing the celestial and spiritual things of the Lord's kingdom; and they were also made that they might represent; thus the Word could be written, which might be according to the apprehension of the man who was to read it, and according to the understanding of the angels attendant on man. This was also the reason why the Lord spake in like manner, since if He had spoken otherwise, what He said would not have been adequate to the apprehension of those who heard, especially at that time, nor at the same time to the understanding of the angels; thus it would not have been received by man, nor understood by the angels.

"He that is on the house-top, let him not go down to take anything out of his house," signifies that they who are in the good of charity, ought not to betake themselves to those things which are of the doctrinals of faith; the "house-top," in the Word, signifies the superior state of man, thus his state as to good; but the things which are beneath signify the inferior state of man, thus his state as to truth; what is meant by "house," see n. 710, 1708, 2230, 2234, 3142, 3538. With the state of the man of the church, the case is this: whilst he is regenerating, he then learns truth for the sake of good, for the affection of truth is given him for that end; but when he is regenerated, he then acts from truth and good; when he arrives at this state, he then ought not to betake himself to the former state, for if he was to do this, he would reason from truth concerning the good in which he is, and would thus pervert his state. For all reasoning ceases and ought to cease, when man is in a state to will what is good and true; for in this case he thinks and acts from the will, consequently from conscience, and not from the understanding, as heretofore, for if he was to act again from this latter principle, he would fall into temptations, in which he would yield. Such are the things which are signified by the words, "Let not him who is on the house-top go down to take anything out of his house."

"And he who is in the field, let him not turn back to take his garment," or coat, signifies that they who are in the good of truth, should not betake themselves from its good to the doctrinal of truth; "field," in the Word, signifies that state of man as to good, see n. 368, 2971, 3196, 3310, 3317, 3500, 3508; and "garment," or coat, ·signifies that which clothes good, that is, the doctrinal of truth, for this is as a *garment* to good; that "garment" has this signification, see n. 297, 1073, 2576, 3301. Every one may see that deeper things lie concealed herein, than what appear in the letter, for the Lord Himself spake them. From these considerations it may now be manifest that a state of vastation of the church, as to the goods of love and the truths of faith, is fully described in these verses, and that at the same time an exhortation is given to those who are in those goods and truths, what they ought to do on the occasion. There are three kinds of men within the church, viz., they who are in love to the Lord, they who are in charity towards their neighbour, and they who are in the affection of truth. They who are in the first class, viz., they who are in love to the Lord, are specifically signified by the words, "Let those who are in Judea flee to the mountains." In the second class are they who are in charity towards their neighbour, and are specifically signified by these words, "He who is on the house-top, let him not go down to take anything out of his house." In the third class are they who are in the affection of truth, and are specifically signified by these words, "He who is in the field, let him not turn back to take his garment." That *Judea*, in the internal sense of the Word, does not signify Judea, as neither does *Jerusalem* signify Jerusalem, may be manifest from several passages in the Word. In the Word it is not so named Judea, but the "land of Judah," and by it, as by the "land of Canaan," is there signified the kingdom of the Lord, consequently also the church, for this is the kingdom of the Lord on the earth; and this, on this account,—because by "Judah," or by the Jewish nation, was represented the celestial kingdom of the Lord, and by "Israel," or the Israelitish people, His spiritual kingdom; and because this was represented, therefore also in the Word, when they are named, nothing else is signified in the internal sense. *A. C.* 3650—3654.

The abomination of desolation, or the devastation of the church, is described in these words in Daniel,—"Seventy weeks have been decided upon thy people, and upon thy city of holiness, to consummate prevarication, and to seal up sins, and to expiate iniquity, and to bring the justice of ages, and to seal the vision of the prophets, and to anoint the Holy of

Holies. Know therefore and perceive, from the going forth
to restore and build Jerusalem, even to Messiah the Prince,
shall be seven weeks : afterwards in sixty and two weeks,
the street and the trench shall be restored and built, but
in straitness of times. But after sixty and two weeks Messiah
shall be cut off, but not for Himself: then shall the people
of a prince about to come destroy the city and the sanctuary;
so that its end shall be with a flood, and even to the end of war
are decided desolations. Yet He shall confirm the covenant
with many in one week: but in the midst of the week, He shall
cause to cease the sacrifice and meat-offering; at length upon
the bird of *abomination* shall be *desolation,* and even to the
consummation and decision it shall drop upon the devastation."
(ix. 24—27.) The sense of these words has been investigated
and explained by many of the learned, but only as to the
literal sense, and not yet as to the spiritual sense, for this
latter sense has been heretofore unknown in the Christian
world. In this sense the following things are signified by the
above words :—

" Seventy weeks have been decided upon thy people," signifies the time and state of the church which was then amongst
the Jews, even to its end; " seven" and " seventy" signifying
what is full from beginning to end; and "people" signifying
those who were at that time of the church. "And upon thy
city of holiness," signifies the time and state of the end of the
church, as to the doctrine of truth derived from the Word;
"city" signifying the doctrine of truth, and the "city of
holiness" the Divine Truth, which is the Word. "To consummate prevarication, and to seal up sins, and to expiate
iniquity," signifies when nothing but false and evil principles
are in the church, thus when iniquity is fulfilled and consummated; for until this is the case, the end does not come,
for reasons treated of in a little work concerning " The Last
Judgment," since if it came sooner, the simply good would
perish, who, as to externals, are conjoined with those who
pretend to truths and goods, and assume hypocritical appearances in externals; wherefore it is added, "to bring the justice
of ages," by which is signified to save those who are in the
good of faith and charity; and "to seal the vision of the
prophets," signifies to fulfil all things which are in the Word;
and "to anoint the Holy of Holies," signifies to unite the
Divine Principle Itself with the Human Principle in the Lord,
for this latter is the *Holy of Holies.*

" Know therefore and perceive, from the going forth of the
Word," signifies from the end of the Word of the Old Testament, because it was to be fulfilled in the Lord; for all things

of the Word of the Old Testament, in the supreme sense,'
treat of the Lòrd, and of the glorification of His Human
Principle, and thus of His dominion over all things of heaven
and of the world. "Even to restore and to build Jerusalem,"
signifies when a New Church was about to be established;
"Jerusalem" signifying that church, and "to build" signifying
to establish anew. "Even to Messiah the Prince," signifies
even to the Lord, and the Divine Truth in Him and from
Him, for the Lord is called *Messiah* from the Divine Human
Principle, and *Prince* from the Divine Truth. "Seven weeks"
signify a full time and state. "Afterwards in sixty and two
weeks the street and trench shall be restored and built," signifies a full time and state after His coming, until the church
be established with its truths and doctrine; "sixty" signifying
a full time and state as to the implantation of truth, in like
manner as the number three or six; and "two" signifying
those things as to good,—thus, "sixty and two," together
signifying the marriage of truth with a little good; "street"
signifying the truth of doctrine, and "trench" the doctrine.
"But in straitness of times," signifies hardly and with difficulty, because amongst the nations who have little perception
of spiritual truth.   ',
    "But after sixty and two weeks," signifies after a full time
and state of the church, established as to truth and as to good.
"Messiah shall be cut off," signifies that they will recede from
the Lord, which was done principally by the Babylonians
through the translation of the Divine Power of the Lord to
the Popes, and thus by the non-acknowledgment of the Divine
in His Human Principle. "But not for Himself," signifies that
still He has Power and Divinity. "Then shall the people of
a prince about to come destroy the city and the sanctuary,"
signifies that thus doctrine and the church would perish by
false principles; "city" signifying doctrine, "sanctuary" the
church, and the "prince about to come" the ruling false
principle. "So that its end shall be with a flood, and even
to the end of the war are decided desolations," signifies the
falsification of truth, until there is not any combat between
what is true and what is false; "floods" signifying the falsification of truth, "war" the combat between what is true and
what is false, and "desolation" the last state of the church,
when there is no longer any truth, but merely what is false.
    "Yet He shall confirm the covenant with many in one week,"
signifies the time of the Reformation, when again there should
be reading of the Word, and acknowledgment of the Lord, viz.,
of the Divine in His Human Principle; this acknowledgment,

and consequent conjunction of the Lord by the Word, is signified by "covenant," and the time of the Reformation by "one week." "But in the midst of the week, He will cause to cease the sacrifice and meat-offering," signifies that still there is neither good nor truth in worship interiorly, amongst those who are reformed; "sacrifice" signifies worship from truths, and "meat-offerings" worship from good; by the "midst of the week" is not signified the midst of that time, but the inmost principle appertaining to the reformed, for "midst" signifies what is inmost, and "week" the state of the church. The reason why neither good nor truth was interiorly in worship after the Reformation, is, because they assumed faith for the essential of the church, and separated it from charity; and when faith is separated from charity, there is then neither good nor truth in the inmost of worship, for the inmost of worship is the good of charity, and from it proceeds the truth of faith. "At length upon the bird of abomination shall be desolation," signifies the extinction of all truth by the separation of faith from charity; "the bird of abomination" signifies faith alone, thus faith separate from charity, for "bird" signifies thought and understanding concerning the truths of the Word, which bird becomes a *bird of abomination* when there is not any spiritual affection of truths, which illustrates and teaches truth, but only a natural affection, which is for the sake of fame, glory, honour, and gain, which affection, inasmuch as it is infernal, is abominable, since mere false principles are thence derived. "And even to the consummation and decision it shall drop upon the devastation," signifies its extreme, when there is nothing of truth and of faith any longer, and when it is the Last Judgment. That these last things in Daniel were predicted concerning the end of the Christian church, is evident from the Lord's words in Matthew,—"When ye shall see the *abomination of desolation,*" &c.; (xxiv. 15.) for the subject treated of in that chapter is concerning "the consummation of the age," thus concerning the successive vastation of the Christian church; wherefore the devastation of this church is meant by the above words in Daniel. *A. E.* 684.

Verses 15, 16. *And let him who is on the house-top not go down into the house,* &c.—Man, before regeneration, acts from truth, but by it is acquired good; for truth then becomes good with him, when it gains place in his will, and thereby in his life; but after regeneration he acts from good, and by it are procured truths. For the better understanding of this, it is to be observed that man, before regeneration, acts from obedience, but after regeneration from affection; those two

34

states are inverted in respect to each other, for in the former
state truth has the dominion, but in the latter state good has
the dominion; or in the former state man looks downwards or
backwards, but in the latter state upwards or forwards. When
man is in the latter state, viz., when he acts from affection, it
is no longer allowed him to look back, and to do good from
truth, for then the Lord flows into good, and by good, leads
him.   In this case, were he to look back, or to do good from
truth, he would act from a principle of self, for he who acts
from truth, leads himself; but he who acts from good, is led
by the Lord.   These are the things which are meant by the
words of the Lord in Matthew,—"When ye shall see the
abomination of desolation, he that is on the house, let him
not go down to take anything out of his house; and he that
is in the field, let him not turn back to take his clothes."
A. C. 8505.   See also n. 2554, 3650, 8516, 9274, 10,184.

Verse 17. *But woe to them that are with child, and to them
that give suck in those days !*—What these words signify, it is
impossible for any one to comprehend, unless he be enlightened
by the internal sense.   That they were not said concerning the
destruction of Jerusalem, is manifest from several expressions
in the chapter, [Matt. xxiv.] as from the following:—"Except
those days should be shortened, no flesh would be saved: but
for the sake of the elect, those days shall be shortened;" and
again,—"After the affliction of those days the sun shall be
darkened, and the moon shall not give her light, and the stars
shall fall from heaven, and the powers of heaven shall be
shaken: and then shall appear the sign of the Son of Man;
and they shall see the Son of Man coming in the clouds of
heaven with power and glory;" and from other expressions.
That neither were those things said concerning the destruction
of the world, is also evident from several passages in the same
chapter, as from what goes before,—"He that is on the house-
top, let him not go down into the house, neither enter to take
anything out of his house; and let him who is in the field
not turn back again to take his garment;" also from what is
afterwards said,—"Pray ye that your flight be not in the
winter;" and from what follows,—"Then two shall be in the
field; one shall be taken, the other shall be left. Two women
shall be grinding at the mill; one shall be taken, the other
shall be left." But it is evident that they were said concerning
the last time of the church, that is, concerning its vastation,
which is then said to take place when there is no longer any
charity. Every one who thinks holily concerning the Lord,
and who believes that the Divine Being was in Him, and that

He spake from the Divine Being, may know and believe that
the above words, like the rest which the Lord taught and
spake, were not said concerning one nation, but concerning
the universal human race, and not concerning their worldly
state, but concerning their spiritual state; and also that the
Lord's words comprehended the things that were of His
kingdom, and which are of the church, for these things are
divine and eternal.   He who so believes, concludes that these
words, "Woe to them that are with child, and to them that
give suck in those days," do not signify those who are with
child and give suck; and that these words, "Pray ye that
your flight be not in the winter, neither on the Sabbath,"
do not signify any flight on account of a worldly enemy; and
so forth.

The subject treated of in what goes before was concerning
three states of the perversion of good and of truth in the
church; the subject now treated of is concerning a fourth
state, which also is the last. Respecting the first state, consisting in beginning no longer to know what is good and what
is true, but in disputing on those subjects amongst themselves,
whence come false principles, see n. 3354; respecting the
second state, consisting in despising what is good and true,
and also holding those principles in aversion, and in faith in
the Lord being thus about to expire, according to the degrees
in which charity was about to cease, see n. 3487, 3488;
respecting the third state, that it was a state of desolation of
the church as to good and truth, see n. 3651, 3653.   The
subject now treated of is concerning the fourth state, which
is that of the profanation of good and of truth; that this
state is here described, may be manifest from singular the
parts of the description in the internal sense, which is to
this effect.

"But woe to them that are with child, and to them who
give suck in those days," signifies those who are imbued with
love to the Lord, and the good of innocence.   "Woe" is
a formulary of expression, signifying the danger of eternal
damnation; to "be with child" denotes to conceive the good
of celestial love; to "give suck" denotes also a state of innocence; "those days" denote the states in which the church
then is.

"But pray ye that your flight be not in the winter, nor
on the Sabbath," signifies removal from them, lest this should
be done precipitately in a state of too much cold, and in a
state of too much heat; "flight" denotes removal from a state
of the good of love and of innocence, spoken of just above;

"flight in the winter" denotes removal from them in a state of too much cold; there is cold when those things are held in aversion, which aversion is induced by the loves of self and of the world; "flight on the Sabbath" denotes removal from them in a state of too much heat, which heat consists in a holy external, when the loves of self and of the world are within.

"For then shall be great affliction, such as was not from the beginning of the world until now, neither shall be," signifies the highest degree of the perversion and vastation of the church as to good and truth, which is profanation; for the profanation of what is holy induces eternal death, and much more grievous than all other states of evil, and so much the more grievous as the goods and truths profaned are more interior. Inasmuch as interior goods and truths are open and known in the Christian church, and are profaned, therefore it is said that "then shall be great affliction, such as was not from the beginning of the world until now, neither shall be."

"And except those days should be shortened, there would not any flesh be saved, but for the sake of the elect those days shall be shortened," signifies the removal of those who are of the church from interior goods and truths to exterior, that they may still be saved who are in the life of good and truth; by "days being shortened" is signified a state of removal; by "no flesh being saved" is signified that otherwise no one could be saved; by the "elect" are signified those who are in the life of good and truth. Few know what is meant by the profanation of what is holy, but it may be manifest by what has been said and shewn on the subject, viz., that they are capable of profaning, who know, and acknowledge, and imbue good and truth, but not they who have not acknowledged, still less they who do not know; thus that they who are within the church can profane holy things, but not they who are without; and that they who are of the celestial church can profane holy goods, and they who are of the spiritual church can profane holy truths; that on this account interior truths were not discovered to the Jews, lest they should profane them. *A. C.* 3751—3757.

Verse 17. *But woe to them that are with child*, &c.—The subject here treated of is concerning "the consummation of the age," by which is meant the end of the church, when it is the Last Judgment. Hence by "those who are with child," and by "those who give suck in those days," who are the objects of lamentation, are meant those who at that time receive the goods of love and the truths of that good; "they that are with child" denote those who receive the good of love, and " they that give suck" denote those who receive the truths of that good; for the "milk" which is sucked, signifies truth from the good of love.   The reason why a "woe" is pronounced upon them is, because they cannot keep the goods and truths which they receive, for at that time hell prevails, and takes them away, whence comes profanation.   The reason why hell prevails at that time, is, because in the end of the church the false principles of evil prevail, and take away the truths of good; for man is held in the midst between heaven and hell, and before the Last Judgment that which arises out of hell prevails over that which descends out of heaven. *A.E.* 710.   See also *A.R.* 416.

Verses 18, 19. *And pray ye that your flight be not in the winter; for in those days shall be affliction, &c.*—No faith and faith without love is by the Lord compared to "winter," where He predicts the consummation of the age. (Mark xiii. 13, 19.) "Flight" denotes the last time of the church, also of every man when he dies; "winter" denotes the life of no love; the "days of affliction" is the miserable state of such in the other life.   Love and faith can never be separated, because they constitute one and the same thing; when the great lights or luminaries, in Gen. i., are first treated of, they are reckoned as a one, and it is said,—"Let there be [*sit*, in the singular] luminaries in the expanse of heaven."   Concerning this circumstance I am permitted to relate the following particulars;—that the celestial angels, by virtue of the heavenly love with which they are influenced from the Lord, are in all the knowledges of faith, and enjoy such a life and light of intelligence as can scarcely be described.   But, on the other hand, spirits who are only skilled in the doctrinals of faith without love, are in such coldness of life, and in such obscurity of light, that they cannot approach even to the first limit of the entrance into the heavens, but fly back with all speed. Some of them profess to have believed in the Lord, but they have not lived according to His precepts, and it was of such that the Lord said in Matthew,—" Not every one that saith unto Me, Lord, Lord, shall enter into the kingdom; but he that doeth the will of My Father.   Many will say to Me in that day, Lord, Lord, have we not prophesied in Thy name," &c. (vii. 21, to the end.) Hence it is evident that such as are in love are also in faith, and thereby in the possession of celestial life; but it is otherwise with those who say they are in faith, and are not in the life of love.   The life of faith without love is like the light of the sun without heat, as in the time of winter when nothing grows, but all things are withered and dead; whereas faith proceeding from love is like the light of the sun in the time of spring, when all things grow and flourish in consequence of the sun's fructifying heat. The case is exactly similar in respect to things spiritual and celestial, which are usually represented in the Word by the things which exist in the world and on the face of the earth. *A. C.* 34.

Verses 19, 20. *For in those days shall be affliction, such as was not,* &c. *And unless the Lord had shortened those days,* &c.—In the Evangelists, (Matt. xxiv.; Mark xiii.; and Luke xxi.) are described the *successive* declensions and corruptions of the Christian church; and in those chapters, by "great affliction or tribulation, such as was not since the beginning of the world, neither shall be," is signified, as in all other passages throughout the Word, the infestation of truth by falses, to such a degree, that not a single truth remains which is not falsified, and brought to its consummation. This is understood also by the "abomination of desolation" in the same passages, and also by the "desolation upon the bird of abominations," and by the "consummation and decision," in Daniel; and, in the Revelation, by the circumstances described above. All this was a consequence of men's not acknowledging the Unity of God in Trinity, and His Trinity in Unity, in one Person,—but in three; and thence founding the church on the idea of three gods in the mind, and the confession of one God with the lips. For thus they have separated themselves from the Lord, and that, at length, to such a degree, that they have no idea left of the Divinity in His Human nature; when, nevertheless, He is God the Father Himself in the Humanity, on which account He is called the "FATHER OF ETERNITY;" (Isaiah ix. 6.) and He said to Philip,—"He that seeth Me, seeth the Father." (John xiv. 7, 9.)

But it will be asked,—"What is the source or fountain from whence such 'abomination of desolation,' as is described in Daniel, (ix. 27.) and such 'affliction as never was, nor shall be,' (Matt. xxiv. 21, 22.) has sprung?" I answer,—The faith which universally prevails throughout the Christian world, with its influx, operation, and imputation, according to the received traditions. It is a wonderful thing, that the doctrine of justification by this faith alone, although it be no faith, but a mere chimera, is accounted as everything in all Christian churches, that is, it bears sway among the clergy almost as if the whole of theology consisted in it alone. It is this faith which all young students in divinity eagerly learn, imbibe, and suck in, at the universities, and which afterwards, as if they were inspired by it with heavenly wisdom, they teach in their churches, publish in their writings, and make the ground of all the literary fame and reputation that they hope to acquire, as it is the way to all rewards, preferments, and university honours; and all this is done, notwithstanding that in consequence of such faith alone, "the sun, *at this day*, is darkened, the moon doth not give her light, the stars are fallen from heaven, and the powers of the heavens are shaken," according to the words of the Lord's prophecy in Matthew. (xxiv. 29.) That the doctrine of this faith has now blinded men's minds to such a degree, that they are unwilling, and therefore seemingly unable, to see any divine truth interiorly, either in the light of the sun, or in the light of the moon, but only exteriorly, rudely, and superficially, as by the light of a fire at night, has been proved to me by the clearest evidence; so that I can venture to affirm, that should the divine truths which relate to the genuine conjunction of charity and faith, to heaven and hell, to the Lord, to a life after death, and to eternal happiness, be dropped down from heaven, written in letters of silver, they would be rejected, as not worth reading, by those who maintain the doctrine of justification and sanctification by faith alone; whereas on the other hand, should a paper, containing the doctrines of justification by faith alone, be sent from hell, this they would receive, embrace, and carry home with them in their bosom.

The great arcanum respecting the impossibility of any flesh being saved, except a New Church be founded by the Lord, is this,—that as long as the dragon, with his crew, continues in the world of spirits, into which he was cast, so long it is impossible for any divine Truth, united with divine Good, to pass through unto men on earth, but it is either perverted, or falsified, or destroyed. This is what is signified in the Revelation by these words: "The dragon was cast out upon the earth, and his angels were cast out with him. Woe to the inhabitants of the earth and of the sea! for the devil is come down unto you, having great anger." (Rev. xii. 9, 12, 13.) But when "the dragon was cast into hell," (xx. 10.) then John "saw the new heaven and new earth, and the New Jerusalem descending from God out of heaven." (xxi. 1, 2.) By the "dragon" are signified all those who are principled in the faith of the present church. *T. C. R.* 180—182.

Verse 20. *No flesh could be saved.*—The combats of the Lord are described by Isaiah, (lxiii. 1—10.) where are these words,—"Thy garments are as of Him that treadeth in the

wine-press; I have trodden the wine-press alone," by which is
signified that He alone sustained the evil and false principles
of the church, and all violence offered to the Word, thus to
Himself.   It is said, "violence offered to the Word, thus to
Himself," because the Lord is the Word, and violence has
been offered to the Word, and to the Lord Himself, by the
Roman Catholic superstition, also by the superstition amongst
the Reformed concerning faith alone. The evil and false principles of the latter and the former, the Lord sustained when
He executed the Last Judgment, by which He again subdued
the hells, for unless they had been again subdued, " no flesh
could have been saved," as He Himself testifies in Matthew,
xxiv. 21, 22; Mark xiii. 20.   *A.R.* 829.

Man, after enduring temptation, as to the internal man, is
in heaven, and by the external in the world; wherefore by
temptations with man, is effected conjunction with heaven and
the world, and in this case the Lord with man rules His world
from heaven according to order.   The contrary is the case if
man remains natural, for then he is desirous to rule heaven
from the world; such is the case with every one who is in the
love of dominion grounded in the love of self, so that if he
be inwardly explored, he does not believe in any God, but in
himself, and after death he believes that he is God, who has
greatest power over others; such is the insanity prevalent in
hell.   Hence it is evident of what quality man becomes after
death, if the natural man be not regenerated, consequently
what he would become in phantasy unless a New Church was
established by the Lord, in which church genuine truths are
taught.   This is meant by the Lord's words, speaking of the
consummation of the age, that is, of the end of the present
church,—" Then shall be affliction, such. as was not from the
beginning of the world to this time, nor shall be ; wherefore
except those days should be shortened, no flesh would be
saved." *T.C.R.* 598.

As to what concerns the intention of subjugation, such as
prevails amongst the wicked who are in hell, it has also been
given to know, that it is such an attempt and intention of
subjugating those who are in good and truth as cannot be
described; for they are all malice, all cunning and fraud, all
deceit and cruelty, which are so great and of such a quality,
that if mentioned only in part, scarcely any one in the world
would believe.   The hells consisting of such are at this day
immensely increased ; and what is wonderful, especially from
those who are within the church, on account of the cunning,
deceit, hatred, revenge, adultery, which flourish there more

than in other places, for within the church cunning now passes for ingenuity, and adulteries are reckoned honourable; and they are laughed at who think otherwise. This being the case at this day within the church, is a proof that its last time is at hand, for unless there be an end, "no flesh would be saved," according to the Lord's words in Matthew, xxiv. 22; Mark xiii. 20; since all evil is contagious, and infects, as leaven infects dough, thus at length all. *A. C.* 6666.

Verse 21. *And then if any one shall say unto you, Lo, here is Christ! or, Lo, He is there! believe not,* &c.—What these words involve, no one can know, unless the internal sense teaches, as that "false Christs shall arise, who shall give signs and prodigies;" and "if they shall say that Christ is in the desert, they should not go forth; if they should say that He is in the closets, they should not believe;" and that "the coming of the Son of Man will be as lightning, which goeth forth from the east, and appears even to the west;" also that "where the carcase is, thither will the eagles be gathered together." These things, like those which precede and which follow in this chapter, [Matt. xxiv.] as to the sense of the letter, seem to be in no regular series, when yet, as to the internal sense, they are in the most beautiful; which series then first appears, when it is understood what is signified by *false Christs*, what by *signs* and *prodigies*, what by a *desert* and *closets*, also what by the *coming of the Son of Man*, and lastly, what by a *carcase* and *eagles*. The reason why the Lord so spake was to the intent that they might not understand the Word, lest they should profane it; for when the church is vastated, as it was at that time amongst the Jews, if they had understood, they would have profaned; wherefore also the Lord spake by parables for the same reason, as He Himself teaches in Matthew, xiii. 13—15; Mark iv. 11, 12; Luke viii. 10; for the Word cannot be profaned by those who do not know its mysteries, but by those who do know, and more so by those who appear to themselves learned, than by those who appear to themselves unlearned. But the reason why at this time the interiors of the Word are opened, is, because the church at this day is so far vastated, that is, without faith and love, that although they know and understand, still they do not acknowledge, still less believe, except a few who are in the life of good, and are called the elect, who can now be instructed, with whom a New Church is about to be instituted; but where they are is known only to the Lord;—there will be few within the church, new churches heretofore having been established amongst the Gentiles.

35

The subject treated of in what goes before in this chapter, was concerning the successive vastation of the church, viz., that at first they began no longer to know what was good and true, but disputed on the subject; next, that they despised those things; thirdly, that they did not acknowledge them; fourthly, that they profaned. The subject now treated of is concerning the state of the church, what its quality is at that time in regard to doctrine in general, and specifically with those who are in holy external worship, but in profane internal, that is, who with the mouth profess the Lord with holy veneration, but with the heart worship themselves and the world, so that the worship of the Lord is to them a medium of gaining honours and wealth; so far as these have acknowledged the Lord, heavenly life, and faith, so far they profane when they become of such a quality. This state of the church is now treated of, as may better appear from the internal sense of the Lord's words above quoted, which is to this effect.

" Then if any one shall say to you, Behold, here is Christ! or there, believe not," signifies exhortation to beware of their doctrine; "Christ" is the Lord as to Divine Truth, hence as to the Word, and as to doctrine derived from the Word; but in the present instance it is manifest that "Christ" denotes the contrary, viz., Divine Truth falsified, or the doctrine of what is false. That "Jesus" denotes Divine Good, and "Christ" Divine Truth, see n. 3004, 3005, 3008, 3009.

" For there shall arise false Christs and false prophets," signifies the false principles of that doctrine; that "false Christs" denote doctrinals falsified from the Word, or truths not divine, is evident from what was said just above; and that "false prophets" denote those who teach those false principles. They who teach false principles, in the Christian world, are principally those who regard their own distinction, also worldly opulence, as ends, for they pervert the truths of the Word to favour themselves; since when the love of self and the world is regarded as an end, nothing else is thought of; these are false Christs and false prophets. "And shall give great signs and prodigies," signifies things confirming and persuading from external appearances and fallacies, by which the simple suffer themselves to be seduced; that this is meant by "giving signs and prodigies," will be shewn elsewhere by the Divine Mercy of the Lord. "So as to seduce, if possible, even the elect," signifies those who are in the life of good and truth, and thence appertain to the Lord; these are they who in the Word are called " the elect." They seldom appear in the assembly of those who veil profane worship under what is holy, or if they appear, they are not known, for the Lord hides them and thus protects them; for before they are confirmed, they suffer themselves to be easily led away by external sanctities, but after they are confirmed, they endure, for they are kept by the Lord in consort with angels, which they themselves are ignorant of, and in this case it is impossible that they should be seduced by that wicked crew.

"Behold, I have told you before," signifies exhortation to prudence, viz., to take heed to themselves, since they are amongst "false prophets, who appear in sheep's clothing, but inwardly they are ravenous wolves." (Matt. vii. 15.) Those false prophets are "the sons of the age, who are more prudent, that is, more cunning in their generation than the sons of light;" (see Luke xvi. 8.) wherefore the Lord exhorts them in these words,—"Behold, I send you forth as sheep in the midst of wolves; be ye therefore prudent as serpents, and harmless as doves." (Matt. x. 16.)

"If therefore they shall say unto you, Behold, He is in the desert, go not forth; behold, He is in the closets, believe not," signifies that it must not be believed what they speak concerning Truth, nor what they speak concerning Good, and more besides. That these are the things which are signified, no one can see, unless he be acquainted with the internal sense; that an arcanum is contained in these words, may be known from this consideration,—that the Lord spake them, and that without another sense interiorly stored up, the literal sense is no sense at all; for to what end could be the exhortation, "not to go forth if they should say that Christ was in the desert, and not to believe if they should say that He was in the closets"? But vastated truth is what is signified by "desert," and vastated good by "closets," or inner chambers. The ground and reason why vastated truth is signified by a "desert," is, because when the church is vastated, that is, when there is no longer in it any divine truth, because there is no longer any good or love to the Lord, and charity towards the neighbour, it is then said to be a *desert*, or to be *in a desert;* for by "desert" is meant all that which is not cultivated or inhabited, also which has little of vital principle in it, as is the case at that time with Truth in the church. Hence it is evident that "desert" here denotes the church, in which there is no truth. But "closets," or inner chambers, in the internal sense, signify the church as to Good, also signify simple good,—the church which is in good being called *the house of God;* "closets" denote goods,

and those things which are in the house. That "the house
of God" denotes Divine Good, and "house," in general, the
good which is of love and charity, see n. 2233, 2234, 2559,
3142, 3652, 3720. The reason why what they speak concerning truth, and what they speak concerning good, ought
not to be believed, is, because they call what is false, true,
and what is evil, good; for they who regard themselves and
the world as an end, understand nothing else by truth and
good than that themselves are to be adored, and that good is
to be done to themselves; and if they inspire piety, it is that
they may appear in "sheep's clothing." Moreover, since the
Word which the Lord spake contains in it things innumerable,
and "desert" is a term of large signification, for all that is
called *desert* which is not cultivated and inhabited, and all
those things are called *closets* in which are things interior;
therefore also by "desert" is signified the Word of the Old
Testament, for this is thought to be abrogated, and by "closets"
the Word of the New Testament, because it teaches interior
things, or concerning the internal man. In like manner also the
whole Word is said to be a "desert," when it no longer serves
for doctrinals; and human institutions are called "closets,"
which, because they depart from the precepts and institutes
of the Word, make the Word to be a *desert*, as is also a
known thing in the Christian world. For they who are in
holy external worship and profane internal, on account of the
innovations which respect the exaltation of themselves over
all, and opulence above all, as ends, abrogate the Word, and
this to such a degree, that they do not even allow it to be
read by others; and they who are not in such profane worship,
although they hold the Word to be holy, and allow it to be
commonly read, still they bend and explain all things to their
doctrinals, which has this effect, that the remaining things in
the Word, which are not according to their doctrinals, are a
desert, as may be sufficiently manifest from those who place
salvation in faith alone, and despise works of charity; these
make all that as a *desert* which the Lord Himself spake in
the New Testament, and so often in the Old, concerning love
and charity, and as *closets*, all those things which are of faith
without works. Hence it is evident what is signified by the
words, "If they shall say to you, Behold, He is in the *desert*,
go not forth; behold, He is in the *closets*, believe not."

"For as the lightning goeth forth from the east, and
appeareth even to the west, so shall also be the coming of
the Son of Man," signifies that with the internal worship
of the Lord it was as with lightning, which is instantly

dissipated; for by "lightning" is signified that which is of celestial light, thus which is predicated of love and faith, for these are of celestial light; the "east," in the supreme sense, is the Lord,—in the internal sense, is the good of love, of charity, and of faith from the Lord; but the "west," in the internal sense, is what has set, or ceased to be, thus non-acknowledgment of the Lord, also non-acknowledgment of the good of love, of charity, and of faith. Thus "lightning which goeth forth from the east, and appears even to the west," denotes dissipation. The "coming of the Lord" is not according to the letter, that He is to appear again in the world, but is His presence in every one, which occurs as often as the Gospel is preached, and a holy principle is thought of.

"For wheresoever the carcase is, thither will the eagles be gathered together," signifies that confirmations of what is false by reasonings will be multiplied in the vastated church. The church, when it is without good and truth of faith thence derived, or when it is vastated, is then said to be dead, for its life is from good and truth; and hence, when it is dead, it is compared to a "carcase." Reasonings concerning goods and truths, that they are not, only so far as they are comprehended, and confirmations of what is evil and false by those reasonings, are those "eagles," as may be manifest from what will presently follow. That "carcase" here denotes the church void of the life of charity and faith, is evident from the Lord's words, where He treats of the consummation of the age in Luke,—"The disciples said, Where, Lord? [viz., where is the consummation of the age, or the Last Judgment?] Jesus said unto them, Where the *body* is, there will the *eagles* be gathered together." (xvii. 37.) In this passage it is called the "body" instead of the "carcase," for it is a dead body which is here meant, and signifies the church; for that "judgment is about to begin at the house of God," or the church, is manifest from the Word throughout. These are the things which the words of the Lord here quoted, and explained in the internal sense, signify; and that they are in a most beautiful series, although it does not so appear in the sense of the letter, may be manifest to every one who contemplates them in their connection, according to the explication. The reason why the last state of the church is compared to *eagles*, which are gathered together to a carcase, or a body, is, because by "eagles" are signified the rational principles of man, which, when predicated of goods, are true rationals, but when predicated of evils, are false rationals, or ratiocinations, as may be manifest from the passages in the Word where they are named. *A. C.* 3897—3901.

Truths ought not to be thought of as being from any other
source than from the Lord. Truths from another source are
in general those in which the Lord is not; and the Lord is
not in truths appertaining to man, when man denies Him and
His Divine Principle, and also when he acknowledges Him,
and still believes that Good and Truth are not from Him, but
from self, and hence claims to himself justice. Truths also,
in which the Lord is not, are those which are taken from
the Word, especially from the sense of the letter, and are
explained in favour of self-dominion and self-gain; these are
in themselves truths, because they are from the Word, but
they are not truths, because they are misinterpreted, and
thereby perverted. Such are the truths which are meant by
the Lord, where He says,—" If any one shall say, Behold,
here is the Christ! or there, believe not; for false Christs
and false prophets shall arise," &c. *A. C.* 8868.

Verses 24—28. *But in those days, after that tribulation,
the sun shall be darkened, and the moon shall not give her light,
and the stars of heaven shall be falling, and the powers which
are in the heavens shall be shaken. And then shall they see
the Son of Man coming in the clouds with much power and
glory,* &c.—What the consummation of the age, or the Last
Judgment, is, has been above explained, viz., that it is the
last time of the church; it is said to be the last time of the
church, when there is no longer any charity or faith in the
church; and it has also been shewn that such consummations
or last times have occasionally taken place. The consummation
of the first church was described by a flood; the consummation
of the second church, by the extirpation of nations in the land
of Canaan, and also by several extirpations and cuttings-off
mentioned by the prophets; the consummation of the third
church is not described in the Word, but is predicted, which
was the destruction of Jerusalem, and the dispersion of the
Jewish nation, with whom the church was, throughout the
whole globe; the fourth consummation is that of the present
Christian church, which consummation is predicted by the
Lord in the Evangelists, and also in the Revelations, and
which is now at hand.

The subject treated of in the preceding parts of this
chapter, [Matt. xxiv.] is concerning the successive vastation
of the church, viz., that at first they began not to know what
is good and true, but disputed on the subject; secondly, that
they despised what is good and true; thirdly, that in heart
they did not acknowledge what is good and true; fourthly,
that they profaned those holy principles. These subjects were

treated of in that chapter from verse 3 to 22; and because
there was still about to remain the truth of faith and the
good of charity, in the midst, or with some who are called
the *elect*, therefore the state of truth, which is of faith, is
treated of, what it shall then be, verse 20 to 24; and the state
of good, which is of charity and of love, is treated of in the
verses which are now quoted; the beginning of a New Church
is also treated of. From singular the things said in those
verses, it appears manifest that there is an internal sense, and
that unless that sense be understood, it cannot in anywise be
known what they involve, as that " the sun shall be darkened,
and also the moon ;", that " the stars shall fall from heaven ;"
and that " the powers of heaven shall be moved ;" that " the
Lord shall appear in the clouds of heaven ;" that " the angels
shall make a sound with the trumpet," and shall thus " gather
together the elect." He who does not know the internal
sense of these words, will believe that such things are about
to happen, yea, that the world is about to perish, with everything that appears in the universe; but that no destruction
of the world is meant by the Last Judgment, but the consummation and vastation of the church as to charity and faith,
may be seen, n. 3353; and is very evident from the words
which follow in the same chapter in Matthew,—" Then two
shall be in the field, one shall be taken, the other shall be
left; two [women] shall be grinding at the mill, one shall
be taken, the other shall be left." (40, 41.) That therefore
by the above words is signified a state of the church at that
time as to good, that is, as to charity towards the neighbour
and love to the Lord, is manifest from the internal sense of
those words, which is this.

" Immediately after the affliction of those days," signifies a
state of the church as to the truth which is of faith, treated of
in what immediately precedes; the desolation of truth, in the
Word throughout, is called "affliction ;" that "days" denote
states, see n. 23, 487, 488, 493, 893, 2788, 3462, 3785. Hence
it is evident that by those words is signified that there will be
no charity after that there is no longer any faith; for faith
leads to charity, because it teaches what charity is, and charity
receives its quality from the truths which are of faith, but the
truths of faith receive their essence and their life from charity,
as has been already abundantly shewn. " The sun shall be
darkened, and the moon shall not give her light," signifies
love to the Lord, who is the "sun," and charity towards the
neighbour, which is the "moon ;" to be "darkened and not to
give light," signifies that they are about not to appear, thus

that they are about to vanish away; that the "sun" is the celestial principle of love, and the "moon" the spiritual principle of love, that is, that the "sun" is love to the Lord, and the "moon" charity towards the neighbour, which is by faith, see n. 1053, 1529, 1530, 2120, 2441, 2495. The reason why this is the signification of the "sun" and of the "moon," is, because the Lord, in the other life, appears as a *sun* to those in heaven who are in love to Himself, who are called celestial, and as a *moon* to those who are in charity towards the neighbour, who are called spiritual, see n. 1053, 1521, 1529, 1531, 1631, 3636, 3643. The *sun* and *moon* in the heavens, or the Lord, is never obscured nor loses light, but perpetually shines, which is the case also with love to Him with the celestial, and with charity towards the neighbour with the spiritual in the heavens, also on the earth with those on whom those angels are attendant, that is, who are in love and charity; but in the case of those who are in no love and charity, but in the love of self and the world, and thence in hatred and revenge, they induce that obscurity on themselves. The case herein is as with the sun of this world, which perpetually shines, but when clouds interpose themselves, it does not appear, see n. 2441. "And the stars shall fall from heaven," signifies that the knowledges of good and of truth shall perish; nothing else is meant in the Word by "stars," where they are named, see n. 1808, 2849. "And the powers of the heavens shall be moved," signifies the foundations of the church, which are said to be moved, and to be shaken, when those things perish; for the church on the earth is the foundation of heaven, inasmuch as the influx of good and truth, through the heavens from the Lord, ultimately terminates in the goods and truths appertaining to the man of the church; wherefore when the man of the church is in such a perverse state that he no longer admits the influx of good and truth, then "the powers of the heavens are said to be moved." Wherefore it is always provided by the Lord that something of the church shall remain, and when an old church perishes, that a new one shall be established.

"And then shall appear the sign of the Son of Man in heaven," signifies on this occasion the appearing of Divine Truth; a "sign" denotes appearing; the "Son of Man" is the Lord as to Divine Truth, see n. 2803, 2813, 3704. This appearing, or this sign, is what the disciples inquired about, when they said to the Lord,—"Tell us, when shall those things be done? especially what is the sign of Thy coming, and of the consummation of the age?" (Matt. xxiv. 3.) for they knew from the Word, that, when the age was consummated, the

Lord would come, and they knew from the Lord that the Lord would come again, and they understood by that, that the Lord would come again into the world, not yet knowing that the Lord has come as often as the church has been vastated; not that He has come in Person, as when He assumed the Human [Principle] by nativity, and made this Divine, but by appearings, either manifest, as when He appeared to Abraham in Mamre, to Moses in the bush, to the Israelitish people on Mount Sinai, to Joshua when he entered the land of Canaan, or by appearings not so manifest, as by inspirations, by which the Word was written, and afterwards by the Word; for in the Word the Lord is present, inasmuch as all things of the Word are from Him and concerning Him, as may be manifest from what has heretofore been abundantly shewn. This latter appearing is what is here signified by the "sign of the Son of Man," and what is treated of in this verse. "And then shall all the tribes of the earth mourn," signifies that all shall be in grief, who are in the good of love and the truth of faith; that "mourning" has this signification, see Zech. xii. 10—14; and that "tribes" signify all things of good and of truth, or of love and faith, n. 3858, 3926, consequently those who are in them; they are called the "tribes of the earth," because they are signified who are within the church; that "earth" denotes the church, see n. 662, 1066, 1067, 1262, 1733, 1850, 2117, 2928, 3355. "And they shall see the Son of Man coming in the clouds of the heavens with power and much glory," signifies that then shall be revealed the Word as to its internal sense, in which the Lord is; the "Son of Man" is the Divine Truth which is therein, n. 2803, 2813, 3704; a "cloud" is the literal sense; "power" is predicated of the good, and "glory" of the truth, which are therein. That those things are signified by "seeing the Son of Man coming in the clouds of the heavens," see preface to chap. xviii., Genesis. This *coming* of the Lord is what is here meant, but not that He is to appear in the clouds according to the letter. The subject which now follows is concerning the establishment of a New Church, which is effected when the old one is vastated and rejected.

"He shall send forth the angels with a trumpet and a great voice," signifies election;—not that it will be by visible angels, still less by trumpets, and by great voices, but by an influx of holy good and holy truth from the Lord by angels; wherefore by "angels," in the Word, is signified somewhat of the Lord, in this case the things which are from the Lord, and concerning the Lord; by a "trumpet" and a "great voice" is signified evangelization [preaching the Gospel], as also in other passages of the Word. "And they shall gather together the elect from the four winds, from the extreme of the heavens, even to their extreme," signifies the establishment of a New Church; the "elect" are they who are in the good of charity and of faith; the "four winds" from which they shall be gathered together, are all states of good and of truth; the "extreme of the heavens to their extreme," are the internal and external things of the church. These now are the things which are signified by the above words of the Lord. *A. C.* 4056—4060.

He who is ignorant that the "clouds of heaven" signify the truths of the Word in the sense of the letter, cannot know otherwise than that the Lord in the consummation of the age, that is, in the end of the church, is about to *come in the clouds of heaven,* and to manifest Himself to the world; but it is a known thing, that after the Word was given, the Lord manifests Himself by it alone; for the Word, which is Divine Truth, is the Lord Himself in heaven and the church. From this consideration it may first appear, that the manifestation there predicted signifies the manifestation of Himself in the Word, which manifestation was effected by His opening and revealing the internal or spiritual sense of the Word, for in this sense is the Divine Truth itself, such as it is in heaven, and the Divine Truth in heaven is the Lord Himself there. Hence now it is evident that by the "coming of the Lord in the clouds of heaven," is signified the revelation of Himself in the sense of the letter of the Word, by virtue of its spiritual sense; for that the "clouds of heaven" signify those things which are of the sense of the letter, and "glory" those things which are of the spiritual sense, see the Treatise on "Heaven and Hell," n. 1, and the revelation itself of the spiritual sense, in the little Treatise concerning "the White Horse." The "Son of Man" also signifies the Lord as to Divine Truth. *A. E.* 594. See also *A. C.* 10,574, 10,604. *S. S.* 112. *T. C. R.* 271.

Verses 28, 29. *But learn a parable from the fig-tree,* &c.— The internal sense of all the preceding verses of this chapter, [Matt. xxiv.] in a summary, is evident from what has been explained, viz., that prediction is made concerning the successive vastation of the church, and at length concerning the establishment of a New Church, in this order:—I. That they began not to know what was good and true, but disputed on the subject. II. That they despised what was good and true. III. That in heart they did not acknowledge those principles. IV. That they profaned them. V. And whereas the truth of faith and the good of charity were yet about to remain with some, who were called the elect, the state of faith on the occasion is described.   VI. And next the state of charity. VII. And lastly, the beginning of a New Church is treated of, which is meant by these words: "And He shall send His angels with a trumpet and great voice, and they shall gather together His elect from the four winds, from the extreme of the heavens to their extreme."   When the end of an old church, and the beginning of a new one is at hand, then is the Last Judgment, and also the coming of the Son of Man. The subject now treated of is concerning the "coming" itself, respecting which the disciples asked the Lord, saying,—"Tell us, when shall these things be? especially what is the sign of Thy *coming*, and of the consummation of the age?"   Now therefore follow the things to be explained, which the Lord predicted concerning the very time of His coming, and of the consummation of the age, which is the Last Judgment. The internal sense is as follows:—

"But learn a parable from the fig-tree; when its branch is become soft and putteth forth leaves, ye know that summer is near," signifies the first principle of the New Church; "fig-tree" denotes the good of the natural principle; "branch" denotes the affection thereof, and "leaves" denote truths; the "parable" from which they should learn, denotes that those things are signified.   He who does not know the internal sense of the Word, cannot in anywise know what is involved in the comparison of the Lord's coming, with the *fig-tree*, its *branches*, and *leaves;* but whereas all comparatives in the Word are also significatives, it may hence be known what these things mean.   The "fig-tree," wheresoever it is named in the Word, in the internal sense signifies the good of the natural principle; that "branch" denotes the affection of that principle, is for this reason,—because affection buds forth from good as a branch from its trunk; that "leaves" denote truths, see n. 885. Hence now it is evident what that parable involves, viz., that when a New Church is created by the Lord, then first of all appears the good of the natural principle, that is, good in the external form with its affection and truths.   By good of the natural principle is not meant the good into which man is born, or which he derives from his parents, but the good which is spiritual as to origin; into this good no one is born, but is introduced of the Lord by the knowledges of good and of truth; wherefore before man is in this good, viz., in spiritual good, he is not a man of the church, howsoever he appears to be so from connate good.   "So also ye, when ye shall see all these things, know ye that it is near at the doors," signifies when those things appear which are signified in the internal sense by the words which were said just above, and by these concerning the "fig-tree," that then would be the consummation of the church, that is, the Last Judgment, and the coming of the Lord; consequently that then the old church would be rejected, and a new one established. It is said "at the doors," because the good of the natural principle and its truths are the first things which are insinuated into man, when he is regenerating, and is made a church. "Verily I say unto you, This generation shall not pass away, until all these things be done," signifies the Jewish nation, that it shall not be extirpated as other nations; see the reason why, n. 3479. "The heaven and the earth shall pass away, but My words shall not pass away," signifies the internals and the externals of the former church, that they shall perish, but that the Word of the Lord shall remain; that "heaven" denotes the internal of the church, and "earth" its external, see n. 82, 1411, 1733, 1850, 2117, 2118, 3355. That the "words of the Lord" denote not only those things which have been now said concerning His coming and the consummation of the age, but likewise all things which are in the Word, is evident. These things were said immediately after what was said concerning the Jewish nation, because the Jewish nation was preserved for the sake of the Word, as may be manifest from the passage cited, n. 3479. From these considerations it is now evident that prediction is here made concerning the beginning of a New Church. *A. C.* 4229—4232.

Verse 28. *Learn a parable from the fig-tree.*—This parable or similitude was spoken, because the "fig-tree" signifies the external church. *A. E.* 403.

Verse 30. *This generation shall not pass away until all these things be done.*—The residue of the worship of the Jewish people will have an end with the end or consummation of the present church in Europe, as the Lord predicts in Matt. xxiv. 34; Mark xiii. 30; for in those chapters the consummation of the age, which is the end of that church, is treated of, as is shewn at the beginnings of chapters xxvi. to xl. of Genesis. *A. C.* 10,497.

Verse 32. *But of that day and hour knoweth no one, neither the angels who are in heaven, nor the Son, except the Father.*—What is signified by these words, in the internal sense, will be manifest from the following explication, viz., that they contain a description of what will be the quality of the state at the time when the old church is rejected and a new one is established. That the rejection of the Old Church, and the establishment of a New one, is what is meant by the "consummation of the age," and by the "coming of the Son of Man," and in general by the Last Judgment, has been abundantly shewn above; also that a Last Judgment has occasionally taken place on this earth, viz., first, when the celestial church of the Lord, which was the most ancient, perished amongst the antediluvians by an inundation of evil and false principles, which, in the internal sense, is the flood. Secondly, when the spiritual church, which was after the flood, and is called the ancient, diffused over a large part of the Asiatic world, ceased of itself. Thirdly, when the representative of a church amongst the posterity of Jacob was destroyed, which was effected when the ten tribes were led away into perpetual captivity, and were scattered amongst the nations. And finally, when Jerusalem was destroyed, and the Jews were also dispersed. Inasmuch as on this occasion there was a consummation of the age after the coming of the Lord, therefore also several things which were said in the Evangelists by the Lord concerning the consummation of that age, are also applicable to that nation, and likewise are applied by several at this day; nevertheless the subject there treated of specifically and especially is concerning the consummation of the age which is now at hand, viz., concerning the end of the Christian church, which is also treated of by John in the Revelations; this will be the fourth Last Judgment on this earth. What is involved in the words which are contained in Matt. xxiv. 36—42, will be manifest from their internal sense, which is as follows:—

"But of that day and hour no one knoweth," signifies the state of the church at that time as to goods and truths, that it would not appear to any one either on earth or in heaven; for by "day and hour" in this passage is not meant *day and hour* of time, but states as to good and truth; that "times," in the Word, signify states, see n. 2625, 2788, 2837, 3254, 3356, and that "days" also, see n. 23, 487, 488, 493, 893, 2788, 3462, 3785; hence also "hour" signifies the same, but a specific state. The reason why it denotes states as to good and truth, is, because the subject treated of is concerning the church, for good and truth constitute the church. "Not even the angels of the heavens, but My Father alone," signifies that heaven does not know the state of the church as to specific good and truth, but the Lord alone, and also when that state of the church is about to be present. That the Lord Himself is He who is meant by the "Father," see n. 15, 1729, 2004, 2005, 3690; and that the Divine Good in the Lord is what is named "Father," and the Divine Truth, which is from the Divine Good, the "Son," n. 2803, 3703, 3704, 3736. They, therefore, who [from this passage] believe that the Father is one [Person], and the Son another, and who thus distinguish them, do not understand the Scriptures. *A. C.* 3704, 4333, 4334.

Verse 33. *Watch and pray, &c.*—By "watching" is understood to acquire spiritual life, wherefore "praying" is also mentioned, because *prayer* is the effect of spiritual life, which is its essence, and which is of so much avail as it proceeds from the life; for they are one like the soul and the body, and like the internal and external. As prayers are of such a nature as the heart is, and are consequently not prayers such as can be accepted in worship, if the heart is evil, therefore it is said in Psalm lxvi. 18,—"If I regard iniquity in my heart, the Lord will not hear me;" by which is signified that He will not receive the prayers and worship [proceeding from such a heart]. The heart of man is his love, and the love of man is his very life; hence it is that the prayers of a man are such as his love, or as his life is. Hence it follows that "prayers," in the spiritual sense, signify the life of his love and charity, or that this life is signified by "prayers;" moreover, man is in a continual state of prayer, when he is in the life of charity, although not with his mouth, yet in his heart. For that which is of man's love is constantly in his thoughts, although he may not be aware of it. Hence also it is evident that "prayer," in a spiritual sense, is worship from love. But these things will not be understood by those who place piety in prayers, and not in the life; yea, they will think against this fact; nor do such persons know what actual piety is. *A. E.* 325.

Verse 35. *Watch ye therefore: for ye know not when the Lord of the house cometh, at even, or at midnight, or at the cock-crowing, or in the morning.*—He who does not know the internal sense of the Word, will believe that the Last Judgment is meant by these expressions, and that every one ought to be prepared for it; but by those expressions is also meant the state of man as to love and faith when he dies, for then is also his judgment. Hence it is evident that by "watching" is meant to receive life from the Lord, which is spiritual life; and by "sleeping" is meant to lead a natural life, without spiritual. *A. E.* 187. See also *L. J.* 13.

By "not knowing at what hour your Lord cometh," is not only meant ignorance as to the time of man's death, but also as to the state of life which is to remain to eternity; for such as is the state of man's past life even to the end, such the man remains to eternity. *A. E.* 194.

TRANSLATOR'S NOTES AND OBSERVATIONS.

CHAPTER XIII.

VERSE 32. *But of that day and hour knoweth no one, neither the angels who are in heaven, nor the Son, except the Father.*— What is here rendered "except the Father," is expressed, in the common version of the New Testament, by "but the Father." In the original Greek, however, the term is ει μη, which properly signifies *except* or *unless*, and not *but*, and is therefore here applied to denote, not that the *Son* did *not* know the day and the hour, &c. *except* or *unless* He was the Father, thus in proportion as His Humanity was glorified, or made Divine.

Verse 33. *See ye, Watch and pray,* &c.—What is here rendered "See ye," is expressed, in the common version of the New Testament, by "Take ye heed," but the original Greek is βλεπετε, which literally means *See ye*, and which is here applied to denote that before a man can *watch* and *pray*, he must first open the eyes of his mind to a view of truth, which view is signified by "See you;" and when his eyes are thus opened, he must then be upon his guard against the principles of infernal evil and error, which guard is signified by "watch ye;" and in the third place he must keep his mind open to the principles of heavenly good and truth, signified by "pray ye." Thus the three terms, *seeing, watching,* and *praying,* stand in connection with each other, denoting, in the internal sense, that the first act in the regeneration is the illumination of the understanding, and the succeeding acts are to shut the door of the mind against the intrusion of infernal spirits, and to open it for the admission of angelic influence.

MARK.

CHAPTER XIV.

THE WORD.	THE INTERNAL SENSE.

1. AFTER two days was the [feast of the] passover and unleavened bread : and the chief Priests and the Scribes sought how, having taken Him by craft, they might put [Him] to death.

2. But they said, Not on the feast, lest there be an uproar of the people.

3. And when He was in Bethany in the house of Simon the leper, as He sat at meat, there came a woman having an alabaster-box of ointment of pure spikenard, very precious; and having broken the box, she poured it on His head.

4. And there were some who had indignation within themselves, and said, Why was this waste of the ointment made?

5. For it might have been sold for more than three hundred pence, and have been given to the poor; and they murmured against her.

6. But Jesus said, Let her alone; why trouble ye her? She hath wrought a good work on Me.

THAT at the very time of celebrating representatively their deliverance from damnation by the Divine Human Principle of the LORD, the Jewish nation sought to destroy that Principle. (Verse 1.)

Being withheld only by external considerations respecting themselves. (Verse 2.)

On which occasion preparation is made for the trial by a more intimate communication of Divine Good to the Human Principle. (Verse 3.)

But this process appears needless to those who are in external good and truth, and who suppose that the Divine Good is communicable to all alike, without regard to their capacity of reception. (Verses 4, 5.)

Until they are instructed that a more interior affection and communication of Divine Good is needful to prepare for final combat and victory. (Verse 6.)

7. For ye have the poor with you always, and whensoever ye will, ye may do them good: but Me ye have not always.

8. She hath done what she could: she hath beforehand anointed My body to the burying.

9. Verily I say unto you, Wheresoever this Gospel shall be preached through the whole world, what she also hath done shall be spoken of for a memorial of her.

10. And Judas Iscariot, one of the twelve, went unto the chief Priests, to betray Him unto them,

11. And when they heard, they rejoiced, and promised to give him money; and he sought how he might conveniently betray Him.

12. And on the first day of unleavened bread, when they sacrificed the passover, His disciples said unto Him, Where wilt Thou that we go and prepare that Thou mayest eat the passover?

13. And He sendeth forth two of His disciples, and saith unto them, Go ye into the city, and there shall meet you a man bearing a pitcher of water: follow him.

14. And wheresoever he shall go in, say to the master of the house, The Teacher saith, Where is the guest-chamber [or inn], where I may eat the passover with My disciples?

Especially in the case of the glorification of the LORD's Human Essence. (Verses 7, 8.)

Therefore this ought to be known and remembered in the church with affection. (Verse 9.)

That the LORD's merit, together with the redemption and salvation wrought by Him, were held in small estimation by the Jewish nation, therefore He was rejected by them. (Verses 10, 11.)

And this at the time that all things were preparing by the LORD for the glorification of His Human principle, and for their liberation from infernal falses. (Verse 12.)

To celebrate which glorification the church is conducted by Divine Truth leading to Divine Good. (Verses 13—16.)

37

15. And he will shew you a large upper room furnished and prepared : there make ready for us.

16. And His disciples went forth, and came into the city, and found as He had said unto them : and they made ready the passover.

17. And when it was evening, He cometh with the twelve.

18. And as they reclined and did eat, Jesus said, Verily I say unto you, That one of you who eateth with Me shall betray Me.

19. And they began to be sorrowful, and to say unto Him one by one, Is it I? and another [said], Is it I?

20. But He answering, said unto them, It is one of the twelve that dippeth with Me in the dish.

21. The Son of Man goeth indeed, as it is written of Him : but woe to that man by whom the Son of Man is betrayed! It were good for that man if he had never been born.

22. And as they did eat, Jesus taking bread, and having blessed it, brake it, and gave to them, and said, Take, eat: this is My body.

23. And taking the cup, when He had given thanks, He gave [it] to them : and they all drank of it.

On which occasion the LORD's rejection by the Jewish nation is predicted. (Verses 17, 18.)

Exciting thus self-examination in the minds of those who are principled in goods and truths. (Verse 19.)

Whereby they discover that the rejection of the LORD is an effect of self-love, which does not distinguish between Divine power and human. (Verse 20.)

And thus fulfils what had been predicted, and plunges itself into a total separation from all good and truth, which is rendered the more terrible by reason of the previous admission of the knowledges of what is good and true. (Verse 21.)

That the LORD taught by representatives that all saving good and truth are from Himself, and are communicated by Him to those who are in a state of reception. (Verses 22—24.)

24. And He said unto them, This is My blood of the New Testament, which is shed for many.

25. Verily I say unto you, I will drink no more of the fruit of the vine, until that day when I drink it new in the kingdom of God.

But that this truth cannot be fully received in this life, but in the other. (Verse 25.)

26. And when they had sung a hymn, they went out into the Mount of Olives.

27. And Jesus saith unto them, All ye shall be offended because of Me this night: for it is written, I will smite the shepherd, and the sheep shall be scattered.

28. But after that I am risen, I will go before you into Galilee.

That the LORD from His Divine Love predicted the last time of the Old Church, and the first of the New. (Verses 26—28.)

29. But Peter said unto Him, Although all shall be offended, yet will not I.

But that they who are in the science of truth, separate from obedience, do not believe this. (Verse 29.)

30. And Jesus saith unto him, Verily I say unto thee, That to-day, in this night, before the cock crow twice, thou shalt deny Me thrice.

Therefore they are instructed, that it is the last time of the church, when the truth of faith is indeed taught, but is not believed, and when there is no faith in the LORD, because no charity. (Verse 30.)

31. But he said the more vehemently, If I should die with Thee, I will not deny Thee. In like manner said they all.

Nevertheless, they who are in faith alone, still insist that they do believe in the LORD. (Verse 31.)

32. And they came to a place called Gethsemane: and He saith to His disciples, Sit ye here, whilst I pray.

That the LORD's Divine rational principle prepared itself to undergo the most grievous and cruel temptations, on which occasion He separated the former rational principle. (Verse 32.)

33. And He taketh with Him Peter and James and

And attached Himself to the spiritual and celestial

John, and began to be amazed and to be depressed.

34. And He saith unto them, My soul is exceeding sorrowful unto death: tarry ye here, and watch.

35. And going forward a little, He fell upon the earth, and prayed that, if it were possible, the hour might pass from Him.

36. And He said, Abba, Father, all things are possible to Thee; remove this cup from Me: yet not what ·I will, but what Thou [wilt].

37. And He cometh and findeth them sleeping, and saith unto Peter, Simon, sleepest thou? couldest thou not watch one hour?

38. Watch ye and pray, lest ye enter into temptation. The spirit truly is ready, but the flesh is weak.

39. And again going away, He prayed, saying the same word.

40. And when He returned, He found them again sleeping, (for their eyes were heavy,) and they knew not what to answer Him.

41. And He cometh the third time, and saith unto them, Sleep on now, and take rest: it is enough, the hour is come; behold, the Son of Man is betrayed into the hands of sinners.

42. Arise, let us go; behold, he that betrayeth Me is at hand.

things of the church, yet afterwards removed Himself from them also. (Verses 33, 34.)

And enters by most grievous temptations into close union with the Divine Good, through the entire surrender of His Human principle. (Verses 35, 36.)

And from that union communicates with those who are principled in the goods and truths of the church, cautioning them especially against separating faith from charity. (Verse 37.)

And teaching that charity and faith ought to be conjoined as the only security against infernal evils and falses. (Verse 38.)

Thus through a process of successive temptations, until it was complete, the LORD united His Human Essence to the Divine, and by subduing the bells, restored order to heaven and the church. (Verses 39—43.)

43. And immediately, while He yet spake, cometh Judas, being one of the twelve, and with him much multitude with swords and staves, from the chief Priests and the Scribes and the Elders.

44. But he that betrayed Him had given them a token, saying, Whomsoever I shall kiss, the same is He; take Him, and lead [Him] away safely.

45. And coming, [and] immediately going up to Him, he saith,. Rabbi, Rabbi; and kissed Him.

46. And they laid their hands on Him, and took Him.

47. And one of them that stood by, drawing a sword, smote a servant of the High Priest, and cut off his ear.

48. And Jesus answering, said unto them, Are ye come out, as against a thief, with swords and staves to take Me?

49. I was with you daily in the temple teaching, and ye laid no hold on Me; but the Scriptures must be fulfilled.

50. And forsaking Him, they all fled.

51. And there followed Him a certain young man, having a linen cloth cast about [his] naked [body]; and the young men laid hold on him:

52. But he, leaving the linen cloth, fled from them naked.

53. And they led Jesus away to the High Priest: and with him were assembled all the High Priests and the Elders and the Scribes.

Being entirely rejected by the Jewish nation, who, through falses and evils had destroyed in themselves all truth and good. (Verse 43.)

And thus had only external connection with Him, but no internal conjunction. (Verses 44, 45.)

On which account they did violence to the Word. (Verse 46.)

And no longer obeyed its truths, but perished in the falses which they believed. (Verse 47.)

Treating the Word with contumely, as if it deprived them of their natural rights and liberty. (Verse 48.)

And in so doing, fulfilling the Word. (Verses 49, 50.)

Insomuch that they divested themselves even of its external truth, so as to have no covering for their natural evils and falses. (Verses 51, 52.)

54. And Peter followed Him afar off, even into the palace of the High Priest; and he sat with the servants, and warmed himself at the fire.

55. But the High Priests and the whole council sought for witness against Jesus to put Him to death, and found none.

56. For many bare false witness against Him, but their witnesses were not alike.

57. And certain persons standing up, bare false witness against Him, saying,

58. We heard Him say, I will destroy this temple that is made with hands, and within three days I will build another made without hands.

59. But neither did their testimony agree.

60. And the High Priest standing up in the midst, asked Jesus, saying, Answerest Thou nothing? What [is it which] these witness against Thee?

61. But He was silent, and answered nothing. Again the High Priest asked Him, and saith unto Him, Art Thou the Christ, the Son of the Blessed?

62. But Jesus said, I am; and ye shall see the Son of Man sitting on the right hand of power, and coming with the clouds of heaven.

63. Then the High Priest rending his clothes, saith, What need we any further witnesses?

On which occasion they assault the Human Essence of the LORD with all manner of false charges. (Verses 54—60.)

Although He was Himself the purest Innocence, and only testified, in His defence, the union of His Human Essence with the Divine by temptation-combats, and the exaltation of His Human Essence to Omnipotence, and His manifestation of Himself in the internal sense of the Word. (Verses 60—62.)

Which testimony is declared to be false, and is derided by those who are in evils and falses. (Verses 63—66.)

64. Ye have heard the blasphemy, what think ye? And they all condemned Him to be deserving of death.

65. And some began to spit upon Him, and to cover His face, and to buffet Him, and to say unto Him, Prophesy: and the servants did strike Him with the palms of their hands.

66. And as Peter was beneath in the palace, there cometh one of the maids of the High Priest:

67. And seeing Peter warming himself, looking at him, she saith, And thou also wast with Jesus of Nazareth.

68. And he denied, saying, I know not, neither understand I what thou sayest. And he went out into the porch; and the cock crew.

69. And the maid seeing him again, began to say to those who stood by, This is one of them.

70. And he again denied; and a little after, they that stood by said again to Peter, Truly thou art [one] of them: for thou art a Galilean, and thy speech agreeth [thereto].

71. But he began to curse and to swear, saying, I know not this man of whom ye speak.

72. And the second time the cock crew. And Peter remembered the saying which Jesus said unto him, Before the cock crow twice, thou shalt deny Me thrice. And when he thought thereon, he wept.

And is even denied by those who are principled in faith alone without charity. (Verse 66, to the end of the chapter.)

EXPOSITION.

CHAPTER XIV.

VERSE 1. *After two days was the feast of the passover and unleavened bread.*—" Bread," in the Word, signifies in general all celestial and spiritual food, thus in general all celestial and spiritual things, see n. 276, 680, 1798, 2165, 2177; and that these things might be free from impurities, was represented by *unleavened bread;* for "leaven" signifies what is evil and false, by which celestial and spiritual things are rendered impure and profane; on account of this representation, commandment was given to those who were of the representative church, that in the sacrifices they should not offer any bread or cake but what was without leaven, or *unleavened,* as is manifest from Moses,—" Every cake which ye shall bring for Jehovah, shall not be made up with *leaven.*" (Lev. ii. 11.) On this account, commandment was also given that, on the seven days of the passover, they should not eat any other bread than what was without leaven, or unleavened. Hence the passover is called the " feast of unleavened things." That this " feast" represented the glorification of the Lord, and thus the conjunction of the Divine [Being or Principle] with the human race, will be shewn elsewhere by the Divine Mercy of the Lord; and whereas the conjunction of the Lord with the human race is effected by love and charity, and the faith thence derived, those celestial and spiritual things were represented by the *unleavened bread* which they were to eat on the days of the passover, on which occasion, lest they should be contaminated by anything profane, everything *leavened* was so severely forbidden, that whosoever ate it, was to be cut off; for they who profane celestial and spiritual things, must of necessity perish. Every one may see that, separate from this arcanum, this ceremonial would never have been enacted with such severe penalties. *A. C. 2342.*

By the " feast of unleavened bread" is signified the worship of the Lord and thanksgiving on account of deliverance from evil, and from the false principles of evil, as is manifest from the signification of a feast, as denoting worship and thanksgiving, see n. 7093, 9286, 9287; and from the signification of unleavened things, as denoting those things which are purified from evil and from the false principles of evil, see n. 9992; hence by the "feast of unleavened bread" is signified worship and thanksgiving on account of deliverance from evil and from false principles of evil; that this was signified by this feast, see n. 9286—9292. As to what concerns this feast, it is to be noted that it properly signifies the glorification of the Lord's Humanity, thus the remembrance of it, and thanksgiving on account of it; for by it, and by the subjugation of the hells by the Lord, man has deliverance from evils, and thus salvation. For the Lord glorified His Humanity by combats against the hells, and on this occasion by continual victories over them; the last combat and victory was on the cross, wherefore He then fully glorified Himself, as He Himself also teaches in John,—"After that Judas was gone out, Jesus said, Now is the Son of Man glorified, and God is glorified in Him. If God be glorified in Him, God shall also glorify Him in Himself, and shall straightway glorify Him." (xiii. 31, 32.) Again in the same Evangelist,—"Jesus lifted up His eyes to heaven, and said, Father, the hour is come; glorify Thy Son, that Thy Son may also glorify Thee. And now, O Father, glorify Thou Me with Thine own self, with the glory which I had with Thee before the world was." (xvii. 1, 5.) To "glorify the Son of Man," is to make the Human [Principle] Divine; that those words were spoken of the passion of the cross is evident. That by that last combat, which was the passion of the cross, the Lord fully subjugated the hells, He also teaches in John,—"Jesus said, The hour is come that the Son of Man should be glorified. Now is my soul troubled. And He said, Father, glorify Thy name. And there came forth a voice from heaven, I have both glorified it, and will glorify it again. And Jesus said, Now is the judgment of this world: now shall the prince of this world be cast out. And I, if I be lifted up from the earth, will draw all to Myself. This He said, signifying what death He should die." (xii. 23, 27, 28, 31, 32, 33.) Hell in all its complex is what is called the "prince of the world and the devil;" from which considerations it is evident that the Lord, by the passion of the cross, not only conquered and subjugated the hells, but also fully glorified His Humanity; hence the human race had salvation; for this also the Lord came into the world, as He also teaches in John xii. 27. For the sake of the remembrance of this work, the feast of unleavened bread, or of the passover, was principally instituted, wherefore He rose again on this festival. The reason why it was also for the sake of deliverance from evil and from the false principles of evil is, because

38

by the subjugation of the hells by the Lord, and by the glorification of His Human [Principle], all deliverance of evil is effected, and separate from those acts there is no deliverance; for man is ruled by spirits from hell, and by angels out of heaven from the Lord; wherefore, unless the hells had been altogether subjugated, and unless the Human [Principle] of the Lord had been altogether united to the Divine Itself, and thereby likewise made Divine, no man could have been delivered from hell and saved, for the hells would always have prevailed, since man is become of such a quality, that of himself he thinks nothing but what is of hell. *A. C.* 10,655.

Verse 3. *And when He was in Bethany, in the house of Simon the leper, as He sat at meat, there came a woman having an alabaster-box of ointment of pure spikenard, very precious; and breaking the box, she poured it on His head.*—By "ointment" is signified celestial good and spiritual good, or the good of love to the Lord, and the good of charity towards the neighbour. *A. E.* 375.

Verse 8. *She hath beforehand anointed My body to the burying.*—By "burying," or burial, whensoever it is mentioned in the Word, the angels understand resurrection, because it is a plenary putting off of what is human, and a putting on of what is heavenly. *A. C.* 3016.

Verse 14. *Where is the guest-chamber [or inn],* &c.—By an "inn" is signified a place of instruction, as also in Luke x. 34; xxii. 11; Mark xiv. 14. *A. E.* 706.

Where I may eat the passover with My disciples?—The "passover" signifies the presence of the Lord, and the deliverance of those who are of the spiritual church by the Divine Human of the Lord, when He rose again. *A. C.* 7867.

The "feast of the passover," or the paschal supper, represented consociations in heaven. *A. C.* 7836, 7997.

Verse 21. *The Son of Man,* &c.—What is meant by the "Son of Man," see chap. iii. 28, 29, Exposition.

Verse 22. *And as they did eat, Jesus taking bread, and having blessed it, brake it,* &c.—By the Lord "blessing the bread and giving it to His disciples," was signified the communication of His Divine Principle, and by it, conjunction with them by goods and truths, which are signified by "bread and wine," for by the Holy Supper instituted by the Lord, the angels understand the same thing as by the paschal supper, bread and wine being received in the former, instead of the paschal lamb of the latter; for the Lord said, in instituting the Holy Supper, that "the bread was His flesh," and "the wine was His blood;" and every one knows, or may know, that *bread* and *wine* are things which nourish the body, bread as meat, and wine as drink; and that in the Word, which in its bosom is spiritual, they are also spiritually to be understood; thus bread for all spiritual meat, and wine for all spiritual drink. Spiritual meat is every good which is communicated and given to man from the Lord, and spiritual drink is every truth which is communicated and given to man from the Lord. These two, viz., good and truth, or love and faith, constitute the spiritual man; it is said, "or love and faith," because all good is of love, and all truth is of faith; hence it may be manifest, that by bread is meant the Divine Good of the Lord's Divine Love, and, in respect to man, is meant that good received by him. Inasmuch as the Lord says that "His flesh is bread," and "His blood is wine," it may be manifest that by the "flesh of the Lord" is meant the Divine Good of His Divine Love, and by "eating it" is meant to receive it, to appropriate to one's self, and thereby to be conjoined to the Lord; and that by the "blood of the Lord" is meant the Divine Truth proceeding from the Divine Good of His Divine Love, and by "drinking it" is meant to receive it, to appropriate to one's self, and thereby to be conjoined to the Lord. Spiritual nourishment also is from the good and truth which proceed from the Lord, as all nourishment of the body is from meat and drink; hence also is their correspondence, which is of such a nature, that wheresoever in the Word anything of meat, and of what serves for meat, is named, good is understood; and wheresoever anything of drink, and of what serves for drink, is named, truth is understood. From these considerations it may be manifest that by the "blood" which the sons of Israel were ordered to sprinkle from the paschal lamb upon the two posts, and on the threshold of their houses, is meant the Divine Truth proceeding from the Lord; this also, when received in faith and life, protects man against the evils which arise out of hell, since the Lord in His Divine Truth is with man; for His Divine Truth is of the Lord Himself with man, yea, it is Himself with man. Who that thinks from sound reason, cannot see that the Lord is not in His blood with any one, but in His Divine Principle, which is the good of love and the good of faith received by man? *A. E.* 329, 340.

When the term "bread" is used in the Word, the angels do not know what material bread is, but what spiritual bread is, hu instead of bread they perceive the Lord, who, that He is "the Bread of Life," Himself teaches in John, vi. 33, 35;

and inasmuch as they perceive from the Lord, they perceive those things which are from the Lord, consequently His love towards the universal human race, and together therewith they perceive at the same time the reciprocal love of man to the Lord; for these things cohere in one idea of thought and affection. In a way not unlike to this man thinks, who is in a holy principle when he receives the bread of the Sacred Supper, for he thinks on such occasion not of bread, but of the Lord and of His mercy, and of those things which relate to love to Him and to charity towards his neighbour, because he thinks of repentance and amendment of life, but this with a variety according to the holiness in which he is principled, not only as to thought, but also as to affection. Hence it is evident that "bread," as mentioned in the Word, does not suggest the idea of any bread with the angels, but suggests the idea of love, together with things innumerable which relate to love. In like manner "wine," when it is read in the Word, and also is received in the Sacred Supper; on such occasions the angels do not think at all of wine, but of charity towards their neighbour; and this being the case, and this the ground of man's connection with heaven, and by heaven with the Lord, therefore *bread* and *wine* were made symbols, and unite man, who is principled in what is holy, with heaven, and by heaven with the Lord. The case is the same with every single thing contained in the Word, wherefore the Word is the uniting medium betwixt man and the Lord, and unless such a uniting medium existed, it would be impossible for heaven to flow in with man; for without a medium there could be no unition, but heaven would remove itself from man; and if heaven was removed, it would be impossible for any one any longer to be led to good, not even to corporeal and worldly good, but all restraints, even external ones, would be broken. For the Lord governs man, who is principled in good, by internal restraints, which are those of conscience; but if man be principled in evil, the Lord governs him only by external restraints, and if these were broken, every one would become insane, as he is insane who is without fear of the law, without fear of death, and without fear of the loss of honour and gain, and thence of reputation, for these are external restraints; thus the human race would perish. Hence it may appear why the Word is, and what is its quality. That the church of the Lord, where the Word is, is like a heart and like lungs; and that the church of the Lord, where the Word is not, is like the rest of the viscera, which live from the heart and lungs, may be seen, n. 637, 931, 2054, 2853. *A. C.* 4217.

By " breaking bread and giving it to the disciples," in the spiritual world, is signified to instruct in the good and truth of faith, by which the Lord appears; for spiritual meat is all the good of faith from which comes wisdom, and spiritual drink is all the truth of faith from which comes intelligence. *A. C.* 9112.

Verse 22. *This is my body.*—" Body," in the genuine sense, signifies the good which is of love, and the reason is, because the body, or the whole man which is meant by the body, is a receptacle of life from the Lord, thus the receptacle of good, for the good of love constitutes life itself in man; for the vital heat, which is love, is the vital heat itself, and unless this heat be in man, he is as somewhat dead. Hence now it is that by " body," in the internal sense, is meant the good of love; and although with man there is not celestial love, but infernal love, still the inmost principle of his life is from celestial love, for this love continually flows in from the Lord, and constitutes with man vital heat in its beginning, but in its progress it is perverted by man, whence comes infernal love, and from thence unclean heat; hence it may be manifest what is meant by the " body " of the Lord, viz., the Divine Love, in like manner as by His " flesh." The body itself also of the Lord, when glorified, that is, when made Divine, is nothing else; for what else can be supposed concerning the Divine Principle which is infinite? From these considerations it may be known that by " body," in the Holy Supper, nothing else is meant than the Divine Love of the Lord towards the universal human race. *A. C.* 6135. See also n. 10,033.

Verses 22, 24. *This is My Body; this is My Blood.*—When a man, in the Holy Supper, simply thinks of the Lord from His words,—" This is My Body, and this is My Blood," the angels with him are in the idea of love to the Lord, and of charity to the neighbour; for love to the Lord corresponds to the *Body* of the Lord and to *bread*, and charity towards the neighbour corresponds to *Blood* and to *wine*, n. 1798, 2165, 2177; and because such is the correspondence, there flows out of heaven through the angels into that holy principle in which the man then is, an affection which he receives according to the goodness of his life. For the angels dwell with every one in the affection of his life, thus they flow into the affection of the doctrines according to which he lives, and by no means of those doctrines with which his life disagrees; if his life disagrees, as if he be in the affection of gaining honours and wealth by doctrines, the angels then recede from him, and infernals come and dwell in that affection, who either infuse into him a

confirmation of such doctrines for the sake of self and the
world, thus a persuasive faith which is of such a nature as not
to care whether they be true or false, provided only they are
popular; or they take away from him all faith, and then the
doctrine of his mouth is only a sound excited and modified by
the fire of those selfish and worldly loves. *A. C.* 3464.

Verses 23, 24. *And taking the cup, when He had given
thanks, He gave* [it] *to them : and they all drank of it. And
He said unto them, This is My blood of the New Testament,
which is shed for many.*—Mention is here made of " cup," not
of wine, because " wine" is predicated of the spiritual church,
but " blood" of the celestial church, although each signifies
holy truth proceeding from the Lord,—in the spiritual church
the holy principle of faith grounded in charity towards the
neighbour, but in the celestial church the holy principle of
charity grounded in love to the Lord. The spiritual church
is distinguished from the celestial in this,—that the former is
in charity towards the neighbour, but the latter in love to the
Lord, and the Holy Supper was instituted that it might represent and signify the love of the Lord towards the universal
human race, and the reciprocal love of man towards Him.
A. C. 5120.

Verse 24. *This is My blood of the New Testament*, &c.—
Inasmuch as the Lord called, " His blood," by which is meant
the Divine Truth proceeding from Him, " the blood of the
New Testament" [or covenant], it may be expedient briefly
to say what is meant by the Old Testament [or covenant], and
what by the New. By the " Old Testament," [or covenant],
is meant conjunction by Divine Truth, such as was given to
the sons of Israel, which was external, and hence representative
of internal Divine Truth. The sons of Israel had no other
Divine Truth, because they could not receive any other, for
they were external and natural men, and not internal or
spiritual, as may be manifest from this consideration, that they
who knew anything concerning the Lord's coming, had no
other thought respecting Him than that He was to be a king,
who would exalt them above all people in the universe, and
thus who would establish a kingdom on earth with them, and
not in the heavens, and thence in the earths, with all who
believe in Him. Wherefore the " Old Testament" [or cove-
nant] was conjunction by such Divine Truth as is contained
in the Books of Moses, and was called precepts, judgments,
and statutes, in which nevertheless lay inwardly concealed the
Divine Truth such as it is in heaven, which is internal and
spiritual. This Divine Truth was opened by the Lord when

He was in the world, and whereas by it alone there is conjunction of the Lord with men, therefore it is meant by the
"New Testament" [or covenant], and also it is meant by His
"blood," which is hence called the "blood of the New Testament" [or covenant]; the like is also meant by "wine." This
new covenant, which was to be entered into by the Lord when
He was to come into the world, is treated of in the Word of
the Old Testament [or covenant] throughout. *A. E.* 701, 329.

Verse 25. *Verily I say unto you, I will drink no more of
the fruit of the vine, until that day when I drink it new in the
kingdom of God.*—By the "vine" is signified the new or
regenerate intellectual principle, so made by good from truth,
and by truth from good, which is signified by the product of
the vine, the appropriation of which is signified by drinking.
That this is not fully effected except in the other life, is
signified by the words, "until that day when I shall drink it
new in the kingdom of God." *A. C.* 5113.

By the "fruit of the vine" which they were to drink new
in the heavenly kingdom, nothing else is meant but the Truth
of the New Church and heaven; wherefore also the church,
in many passages of the Word, is called a "vineyard," as in
Isaiah v. 1, 2, 4; Matt. xx. 1—13; and the Lord calls Himself the "true vine," and the men who were engrafted in it
"branches." (John xv. 1, 5.) *T. C. R.* 708.

To "drink," in this passage, as applied to the Lord, denotes
to instruct to the life concerning truths, and to give perception
of good and of truth. *A. C.* 3069.

From what has been above said, it may be manifest what is
meant by the *flesh* and *blood* of the Lord, and by *bread* and
wine, in a threefold sense,—natural, spiritual, and celestial.
Every man imbued with religion in Christendom may know,
and if he does not know, may learn, that there is given both
natural nourishment and spiritual nourishment, and that
natural nourishment is for the body, but spiritual nourishment for the soul, for the Lord Jehovah says in Moses,—
"Man doth not live by bread alone, but by everything which
cometh forth from the mouth of Jehovah doth man live."
(Deut. viii. 3.) Now whereas the body dies, and the soul
lives after death, it follows that spiritual nourishment is for
eternal salvation. Who then does not see that those two
nourishments ought not to be at all confounded, and that if
any one confounds them, he must necessarily assume to himself natural and sensual ideas, which are material, corporeal,
and carnal, concerning the flesh and blood of the Lord, and
concerning the bread and wine, which ideas suffocate all

spiritual ideas concerning this most holy Sacrament. But if any one be so simple that he cannot raise his understanding to anything but what he sees with his eye, I would advise him to think with himself concerning the Holy Supper, when he takes the bread and wine, and hears the flesh and blood of the Lord named on the occasion, that it is the most holy rite of worship, and to recollect the passion of Christ, and His love for the salvation of man, for He says,—"Do this in remembrance of Me." (Luke xxii. 19.)   Also,—" The Son of Man came to give His soul a redemption for many." (Matt. xx. 28.) *T. C. R.* 709.

Verse 26. *And when they had sung a hymn.*—Gladness of heart is testified not only by musical instruments and by *singing*, but also by dances; for the joys of the heart, or interior joys, go forth in the body into various acts, as into *singing* and into dances; and whereas the states of gladness, which, in ancient times, excelled all others, were derived from the affections of spiritual loves, which were those of Good and Truth, wherefore it was at that time allowed to adjoin dances to songs, &c., and by these means to testify joy.   Hence it is that dances are named in the Word.   *A. C.* 8339.

He went out into the Mount of Olives.—See chap. xiii. 3, Exposition.

Verse 27. *And Jesus saith unto them, All ye shall be offended because of Me this night,* &c.—" Night" here signifies the last time of the old church, and the first of the New; and by the Lord being pleased to be "taken in the night," was signified, that Divine Truth was then in the obscurity of night, and that the false principle derived from evil was in its place; and by Peter in that "night" thrice denying the Lord, was represented the last time of the church, when the truth of faith is indeed taught, but is not believed, which time is *night*, because the Lord is then absolutely denied in the hearts of men.   *A. C.* 6000.

Verse 30. *And Jesus saith unto him, Verily I say unto thee, That to-day, in this night, before the cock crow twice, thou shalt deny Me thrice.*—By these words is signified, that in the last time of the church there was no faith in the Lord, because no charity, for " cock-crowing," alike with morning, signifies the last time of the church; and " three," or three times, signifies what is complete to the end.   *A. E.* 9; 250. See also *H. D. N. J.* 122.

Verses 32—42. *And they came to a place called Gethsemane,* &c.—In these verses are described the Lord's temptations, which were most direful and cruel, so that He was driven to despair; for all temptation has with it some species of desperation, otherwise it is not temptation; wherefore also consolation follows. He who is tempted is brought into anxieties which induce a state of desperation concerning the end; the combat itself of temptation is nothing else; he who is in assurance concerning victory, is not in anxiety, thus neither in temptation. *A. C.* 1787. See also n. 8164.

Verse 36. *Yet not what I will, but what Thou [wilt].*— Inasmuch as Jehovah, or the Father, was in the Lord, or He in the Father and the Father in Him, therefore by those words is meant, that the Lord united the Divine Principle to the Human by temptations, through His own proper power, which also is manifest from the Lord's words in John,—"As the Father knoweth Me, I also know the Father: and I lay down My soul for the sheep. For this the Father loveth Me, that I lay down My soul, that I may take it again. I have power to lay it down, and I have power to take it again. This commandment I have received of My Father." (x. 15, 17, 18.) That the Lord united His Divine Essence to the Human Essence by temptations, through His own proper power, see n. 1663, 1668, 1690, 1691, 1725, 1729, 1733, 1737, 1787, 1789, 1812, 1820, 2776, 3318. *A. C.* 3381.

Verse 38. *Watch and pray, lest ye enter into temptation.*— That the Lord had the most grievous and inmost temptations, which are described in the internal sense of this chapter, (Gen. xxii.) will be evident. Why, however, it is said that God tempts, is according to the sense of the letter, in which temptation and similar things are attributed to God, but according to the internal sense, God tempts no one; in that sense He is constantly in the act of delivering from temptations, as much as possible, or as much as the deliverance will not cause evil, for He is constantly regarding good, into which He leads the man who is in temptations. For God never otherwise concurs with temptations. And although it is said of God, that He permits, still it is not according to the idea which man has of permission, namely, that He concurs by permitting; for man cannot otherwise understand than that he who permits, also wills [or concurs in] the permission, but it is the evil with man which does this, also which leads into temptation,—the cause of which is, by no means in God; as there is no cause in a king or judge that a man should do evil, and on that account suffer punishment. For whosoever separates himself from the laws of Divine order, all which have relation to what is Good and True, casts himself into the laws opposite to Divine order,

39

all which have relation to the evil and the false, and hence into the laws of punishments and torments. *A. C.* 2768.

Verse 43. *And immediately, while He yet spake, cometh Judas, being one of the twelve, and with him much multitude with swords and staves,* &c.—By " swords" in this passage are signified false principles destroying truths, and by "staves" are signified evils destroying good; therefore this was done at the command of the High Priest, because all things relating to the Lord's passion were representative of the destruction of Good and of Truth by the Jews. *A. E.* 1145.

Verse 62. *And ye shall see the Son of Man sitting on the right hand of power, and coming with the clouds of heaven.*— To " sit on the right hand of power," signifies the Divine Omnipotence of the Lord over the heavens and over the earths, after that He had subdued the hells and glorified His Humanity; to " come with the clouds of heaven," signifies by Divine Truth in the heavens; for after the Lord had united the Human Principle to the Divine Itself, then the Divine Truth proceeded from Him, and He is with angels and with men in that Truth, because in the Word, in which and from which there is Divine Omnipotence. *A. E.* 687.

" The Son of Man" denotes the Divine Truth proceeding from the Lord; to " sit on the right hand of power" denotes that He has omnipotence, for Divine Good has omnipotence by Divine Truth; by its being said, that " henceforth they should see this," is signified that the Divine Truth was in its omnipotence, when the Lord in the world had conquered the hells, and had reduced all things there and in the heavens into order; and that thus they might be saved who should receive Him by faith and love, see n. 9715. That to " sit on the right hand" denotes omnipotence, see n. 3387, 4592, 4933, 7518, 8281, 9133; that all power of good is by truth, see n. 6344, 6413, 8304, 9327, 9410, 9639, 9643; that the Divine Power itself is the Divine Truth, see n. 6948. That the " cloud" in which the Son of Man, that is, the Divine Truth, was to come, denotes the Word in the letter, see preface to chapter xviii., Genesis, n. 4060, 4391, 5922, 6343, 6752, 8443, 8781; and that " glory" is the Divine Truth itself, see preface to chapter xviii., Genesis, n. 4809, 5922, 8627, 9429. *A. C.* 9807.

That the letter of the Word is signified by a " cloud," may appear strange to some, since by those who comprehend all things according to the sense of the letter of the Word, nothing else can be seen but that a " cloud" signifies a cloud, and not anything spiritual such as the Word is, because this does not appear to have any relation to or agreement with a cloud; nevertheless it is the Divine Truth in ultimates, such as the Word is in the letter, which is signified, and the reason is, because in the spiritual world the Divine Truth, flowing down from the superior heavens into the inferior, appears as a cloud. It has also been seen by me, and from it and its variegations I could conclude concerning the quality of the truth, about which the angels of the superior heavens were discoursing. By the " Son of Man coming in the clouds of heaven," in this and other passages, is meant the manifestation of the Lord in the Word, for after His coming they manifestly saw predictions concerning Him, in the propheticals of the Word, which they had not seen before, and still more manifestly at this day, when the spiritual sense of the Word is opened, which, in the supreme sense, treats throughout of the Lord, of the subjugation of the hells by Him, and of the glorification of His Humanity; this sense is meant by the "glory" in which He is about to come. *A. E.* 906.

The power of Divine Truth is principally against false and evil principles, thus against the hells, the combats against which ought to be waged by truths, derived from the sense of the letter of the Word; by truths appertaining to man the Lord also has power to save him, for man, by truths derived from the sense of the letter of the Word, is reformed and regenerated, and in such case is taken out of hell, and introduced into heaven; this power the Lord assumed even as to His Divine Human Principle, after that He had fulfilled all things of the Word, even to its ultimates; wherefore the Lord said to the High Priest,—" Henceforth ye shall see the Son of Man sitting on the right hand of power, and coming in the clouds of heaven." *S. S.* 49.

Verses 63, 64. *Then the High Priest rending his clothes, saith, What need we any further witnesses? Ye have heard the blasphemy,* &c.—By " rending the clothes" is signified mourning on account of the destruction of truth; by the High Priest therefore " rending his clothes, and saying that the Lord blasphemed, because He confessed that He was the Christ the Son of God," is signified that he believed no otherwise than that the Lord spake against the Word, and thus against Divine Truth. *A. C.* 4763.

Angels and spirits appear clothed in garments, and every one according to his truths; they who are in genuine Divine Truths appear clothed in white shining garments, and others in others. Some spirits do not know whence garments come to them, but they are put on whilst they are ignorant of it;

and also their garments vary according to the changes of 'their state as to truths. In a word, their intellectual principle is what is exhibited and represented by *garments :* for the intellectual principle of every one is formed by truths, and becomes of a quality such as the truths from which it is formed. The intellectual principle appertaining to the angels of heaven is in their internal, hence they have white shining garments,— the shining is from the Divine Good, and the whiteness is from the light of heaven, which is the Divine Truth. But the garments of those who are in things external without an internal principle, are dirty and tattered, like those of beggars in the streets and of robbers in forests. What is signified by the "garments" of Aaron and his sons, see n. 9814, 10,068. *A. C.* 10,536.

Verse 65. *And some began to spit upon Him, and to cover His face, and to buffet Him,* &c.—By this was represented and signified that the Jewish nation were in the externals of the Word, of the church, and of worship, without internals; for all things which are mentioned in the Word concerning the Lord's passion, represent and signify arcana of heaven and of the church, and specifically of what quality the Jews were as to the Word, the church, and worship. *A. E.* 412.

The Lord, when He was in the world, was the Divine Truth Itself, and whereas the Divine Truth was altogether rejected by the Jews, therefore also the Lord, who was that Truth, suffered Himself to be crucified; such things are signified by all that is related in the Evangelists concerning the Lord's Passion. Singular the things even to the most singular involve it; wherefore, where the Lord speaks of His passion, He calls Himself the Son of Man, that is, the Divine Truth; every single thing therefore concerning His passion, signifies how the Divine Truth, which was from the Word, was treated by the Jews. For being delivered unto the Gentiles, being mocked, being spit upon, being beaten with rods, being slain, are wicked methods by which they [correspondently] treated the Divine Truth; and whereas the Lord was the Divine Truth Itself, because the Word, and it was predicted in the Prophets that in the end of the church this Truth would be so affected, therefore it is said that "all things should be accomplished which were predicted by the prophets concerning the Son of Man." *A. E.* 83.

Verse 72. *Before the cock crow twice, thou shalt deny Me thrice,* &c.—That in the last times there would be no faith in the Lord, because no charity, was represented by Peter's "denying the Lord three times, before the cock crew twice;"

for Peter there, in a representative sense, is faith, see n. 6000, 6073. That "cock-crowing," as well as twilight, signifies, in the Word, the last time of the church, see n. 10,134; and that "three," or "thrice," signifies completion to the end. *A. C.* 2788, 4495.

General Observations concerning the Lord's Passion.

There are some within the church who believe that the Lord by the passion of the cross took away sins, and satisfied the Father, and thus did the work of redemption; some also that He transferred upon Himself the sins of those who have faith in Him, that He carried them, and cast them into the depth of the sea, that is, into hell. It may therefore be expedient to say, first, what is meant by "bearing or carrying iniquities;" and afterwards, what is meant by "taking them away." By "bearing or carrying iniquities," nothing else is meant but sustaining grievous temptations, also suffering the Jews to do with Him as they had done with the Word, and to treat Him in like manner, because He was the Word; for the church, which at that time was amongst the Jews, was altogether devastated, and it was devastated by this, that they perverted all things of the Word, insomuch that there was not any truth remaining among them, wherefore neither did they acknowledge the Lord. This was meant and signified by all things of the Lord's passion. In like manner it was done with the Prophets, because they represented the Lord as to the Word, and hence as to the church, and the Lord was the real Prophet Himself. His being "betrayed by Judas," therefore, signified that He was betrayed by the Jewish nation, amongst whom at that time the Word was, for Judas represented that nation. His being "seized and condemned by the chief Priests and Elders," signified that He was so treated by all that church; His being "beaten with rods," His face "spit upon," being "struck with fists," and "smitten on His head with a reed," signified that it was so done by them with the Word, as to its Divine Truths, which all treat of the Lord; by "crowning Him with thorns," was signified that they falsified and adulterated those truths; by "dividing His garments, and casting lots upon His coat," was signified that they dispersed all the truths of the Word, but not its spiritual sense, which sense was signified by the Lord's "coat;" by their "crucifying Him" was signified that they destroyed and profaned the whole Word; by their "offering Him vinegar to drink," was signified that they offered

Him merely things falsified and false, wherefore He did not drink it, and then said—"It is finished!." by their "piercing His side," was signified that they absolutely extinguished all the truth of the Word and all its good; by His being "buried," was signified the rejection of the Human Principle remaining from the Mother; by His "rising again on the third day," was signified glorification. Similar things are signified by those things in the Prophets, and in David, where they are predicted. Wherefore after that He was scourged and led forth, carrying the crown of thorns and the purple garment put on by the soldiers, He said—"Behold the Man!" (John xix. 1, 5.) This was said because by "the Man" was signified the church, for by "the Son of Man" is signified the truth of the church, thus the Word. From these considerations it is now evident that, by "bearing iniquities," is meant to represent and effigy in Himself, sins against the Divine Truths of the Word. That the Lord sustained and suffered such things as the Son of Man, and not as the Son of God, will be seen in what follows; for "the Son of Man" signifies the Lord as to the Word.

It may now be expedient to say something concerning what is meant by taking away sins. By "taking away sins," the like is meant as by redeeming man and saving him, for the Lord came into the world that man might be saved; without His coming no mortal could have been reformed and regenerated, thus saved; but this can be effected, since the Lord has taken away all power from the devil, that is, from hell, and has glorified His Human Principle, that is, has united it to the Divine Principle of His Father. Unless these things had been effected, no man could have received any Divine Truth so as to abide with him, and still less any Divine Good, for the devil, who before had superior power, would have plucked them away from the heart. From these considerations it is evident that the Lord, by the passion of the cross, did not take away sins, but that He takes them away, that is, removes them with those who believe in Him, by living according to His precepts, as also the Lord teaches in Matthew,—"Do not suppose that I am come to dissolve the Law and the Prophets. Whosoever shall loosen the least of these precepts, and teach men so, shall be called least in the kingdom of the heavens; but he who doeth and teacheth, shall be called great in the kingdom of the heavens." (v. 17, 19.) Every one may see from reason alone, if he be in any illustration, that sins cannot be taken away from man except by actual repentance, which consists in man seeing his sins, and imploring the Lord's aid, and desisting from them. To see, believe, and teach anything else, is not from the Word, neither is it from sound reason, but from lusts and a depraved will, which are the selfhood of man, by virtue whereof the understanding is infatuated. *D. Lord*, 15—18.

TRANSLATOR'S NOTES AND OBSERVATIONS.

CHAPTER XIV.

Verse 72. *And when he thought thereon, he wept.*—What is here rendered "he thought thereon," is expressed in the original Greek by the term επιβαλων, which expression is frequently applied by the best Greek writers to denote *the putting on of a mantle or covering*, and therefore, in the present instance, may be interpreted as signifying that Peter *covered his face with a garment*, which was a usual ceremony in cases of extreme and bitter grief. Thus we read in the Old Testament concerning David, that, when he wept, he "covered his head, or face," (2 Samuel xv. 30; xix. 4.) which same custom, we learn, prevailed among other nations. The reader therefore will adopt the meaning which is in most agreement with his own ideas.

MARK.

CHAPTER XV.

1. AND immediately in the morning the chief Priests having held a consultation with the Elders and with the Scribes, and the whole council, bound Jesus, and led Him away, and delivered Him to Pilate.

2. And Pilate asked Him, Art Thou the King of the Jews? And He answering said unto him, Thou sayest.

3. And the chief Priests accused Him of many things.

4. And Pilate asked Him again, saying, Answerest Thou nothing? Behold how many things they witness against Thee.

5. But Jesus yet answered nothing; so that Pilate marvelled.

6. Now according to the custom of the feast he released to them one prisoner, whomsoever they requested.

7. And there was [one] called Barabbas, bound with

THAT the perverse Jewish church, who are in the falses of evil, employ all subtlety to destroy the LORD's Divine Human Principle. (Verses 1, 2.)

They, on the contrary, who are in the falses of ignorance, are led to inquire concerning that principle. (Verse 3.) But are perplexed by the falsifications of truth amongst those who are of the perverse church. (Verses 3—5.)

And who, by reason of such falsifications, prefer self-derived intelligence to the Divine Wisdom and Life. (Verses 6—16.)

those who had made insur-
rection with him, who had
committed murder in the
insurrection.

8. And the multitude cry-
ing aloud began to ask [him
to do] as he had ever done
unto them.

9. But Pilate answered
them, saying, Will ye that
I release unto you the King
of the Jews?

10. For he knew that the
chief Priests had delivered
Him for envy.

11. But the chief Priests
urged the multitude, that he
should rather release Barabbas
unto them.

12. And Pilate answering
again said unto them, What
will ye then that I shall do
[unto Him] whom ye call
King of the Jews?

13. And they cried out
again, Crucify Him.

14. Then Pilate said unto
them, Why, what evil hath
He done? And they cried
out the more exceedingly,
Crucify Him.

15. But Pilate, willing to
content the people, released
Barabbas unto them, and
delivered Jesus, when he
had scourged [Him], to be
crucified.

16. But the soldiers led
Him away into the hall, which
is Pretorium; and they call
together the whole band.

17. And they clothed Him
with purple, and put on Him
a crown of thorns, which
they platted.

Treating the Word with
all manner of contumely, and
thus through direful evils
and falses adulterating all its
goods, and falsifying all its
truths. (Verses 16—21.)

40

18. And they began to salute Him, Hail, King of the Jews!

19. And they smote Him on the head with a reed, and did spit upon Him, and bowing the knees worshipped Him.

20. And when they had mocked Him, they took off the purple from Him, and put on Him His own garments, and led Him out to crucify Him.

21. And they compel one Simon a Cyrenian, who passed by, coming out of the country, the father of Alexander and Rufus, to bear His cross.

22. And they bring Him to the place Golgotha, which is, being interpreted, The place of a scull.

23. And they gave Him to drink wine mingled with myrrh: but He did not receive it.

24. And when they had crucified Him, they parted His garments, casting lots upon them, what every one should take.

25. And it was the third hour, and they crucified Him.

26. And the superscription of His accusation was written over, THE KING OF THE JEWS.

27. And with Him they crucified two thieves; one on His right hand, and one on His left.

28. And the Scripture was fulfilled, which saith, And

And thus doing all kind of violence to the truth of good. (Verse 21.)

Until they became mere falses of evil, and had dissipated every truth of the Word. (Verses 22—26.)

Testifying against themselves that they altogether rejected the Divine Truth. (Verse 26.)

And also all faith and charity. (Verses 27, 28.)

He was numbered with the transgressors.

29. And they that passed by blasphemed Him, wagging their heads, and saying, Ah, Thou that destroyest the temple, and buildest it in three days,

30. Save Thyself, and come down from the cross.

31. Likewise also the chief Priests, mocking, said among themselves with the Scribes, He saved others; Himself He cannot save.

32. Let Christ the King of Israel descend now from the cross, that we may see and believe. And they that were crucified with Him reviled Him.

33. And when the sixth hour was come, there was darkness over the whole earth until the ninth hour.

34. And at the ninth hour Jesus cried with a great voice, saying, Eloi, Eloi, Lama sabachthani? which is, being interpreted, My God, My God, why hast Thou forsaken Me?

35. And some of them who stood by, when they heard, said, Behold, He calleth Elias.

36. But one running, and filling a sponge with vinegar, putting it on a reed, gave Him to drink, saying, Let alone; let us see whether Elias will come to take Him down.

Even to the utmost possible degree of contempt and profanation. (Verses 29—33.)

Until nothing was left in the universal church but evil and the false thence derived, together with the false and the evil thence derived. (Verse 33.)

At the same time the LORD, by the passion of the cross, in which He was apparently left to Himself, glorified His Human Essence by uniting it fully with the Divine. (Verse 34.)

Still in the church falses prevailed in the extremes. (Verses 35, 36.)

37. But Jesus uttering a great voice, expired.

38. And the veil of the temple was rent in twain from the top to the bottom.

39. But when the centurion, who stood over against Him, saw that He so cried out, and expired, he said, Truly this Man was the Son of God!

40. But there were also women looking on afar off; among whom was Mary Magdalene, and Mary the mother of James the less and of Joses, and Salome;

41. (Who also, when He was in Galilee, followed Him, and ministered unto Him;) and many other women who came up with Him unto Jerusalem.

42. And now when even was come, because it was the preparation, that is, the day before the Sabbath,

43. Joseph of Arimathea, an honourable counsellor, who also himself waited for the kingdom of God, came, and went in boldly unto Pilate, and begged the body of Jesus.

44. But Pilate wondered whether He were already dead: and calling the centurion, he asked him whether He had been any while dead.

45. And when he knew from the centurion, he gave the body to Joseph.

And the LORD as to His Divine Human Principle was fully rejected. (Verse 37.)

When yet, through temptation-combats and victories, He fully united His Human Principle to the Divine, and by so doing unfolded the celestial and spiritual things of His kingdom. (Verse 38.)

Convincing those who are in simple good, of the Divinity of His Humanity. (Verse 39.)

And that every affection of good in the church is from Him, and is His. (Verses 40, 41.)

And also every truth leading to good. (Verses 42, 43.)

So that they who are principled in heavenly good seek regeneration through the reception of His Divine Good and Truth. (Verses 44—47.)

46. And having bought fine linen, and taken Him down, he wrapped Him in the linen, and laid Him in a sepulchre which was hewn out of a rock, and rolled a stone unto the door of the sepulchre.

47. And Mary Magdalene and Mary [the mother] of Joses beheld where He was laid.

And all who are in the affection of truth acknowledge His Divine life in the sensual principle, which is the. life proper to the body; and likewise the resurrection of His body. (Verse 47.)

EXPOSITION.

CHAPTER XV.

VERSES 1—37.—Respecting the circumstances attending the Lord's sufferings and crucifixion, see the "General Observations concerning the Lord's Passion," in the previous chapter.

Verse 2. *Art Thou the King of the Jews? And He answering, said unto him, Thou sayest.*—There are two things which are predicated of the Lord, namely, that He is a *King,* and that He is a *Priest.* "King," or what pertains to royalty, signifies *holy truth;* "Priest," or what pertains to the priesthood, signifies *holy good;* the former is the Divine-Spiritual Principle, the latter is the Divine-Celestial. The Lord as a King governs all things, yea, every particular in the universe, by virtue of Divine Truth, and as a Priest, by virtue of Divine Good. Divine Truth is the very essential order of His universal kingdom, all the laws whereof are true, or are eternal truths. Divine Good is the very essential *of* order, all things appertaining to which are of mercy; each is predicated of the Lord. If only Divine Truth was predicable of Him, no flesh could be saved, for truths condemn every one to hell; but Divine Good, which is of mercy, elevates from hell to heaven. This is what was represented by kings and priests in the Jewish church, and what was also represented by Melchizedéc as king of Salem, and priest to God Most High. *A. C.* 1728. See also n. 2015.

That by " King," in the Word, is meant the Lord as to Divine Truth, is evident from the above words of the Lord Himself to Pilate. From Pilate's question, " What is Truth?" it is evident that he understood that the Lord called Truth a king, but whereas he was a Gentile, and knew nothing of the Word, he could not be instructed that Divine Truth was from the Lord, and that He was Divine Truth; therefore after the question, he immediately went out to the Jews, saying,— " I find no fault in Him ;" and afterwards set over the cross, " This is Jesus, the King of the Jews ;" and when the chief Priests said to him,—" Write not, The King of the Jews; but that He said, I am the King of the Jews," Pilate replied,— " What I have written, I have written." *A. E.* 31.

Verse 17. *And put on Him a crown of thorns, which they platted.*—By the " head" of the Lord is meant the Divine Truth and Divine Wisdom, and by " crowning it with thorns" is signified that they so contumeliously treated the Divine Truth and Divine Wisdom; for the Word, which is the Divine Truth, and in which is Divine Wisdom, they falsified and adulterated by traditions, and by applications to themselves,—thus being willing to have a king who should exalt them over all in the universal earth; and whereas the kingdom of the Lord was not earthly, but heavenly, therefore they perverted all things of the Word which were said concerning Him, and laughed at the things which were predicted of Him. This was what was represented by their " setting a crown of thorns upon His head," and by their " smiting His head." *A. E.* 577.

Verse 19. *And they smote Him on the head with a reed.*— He who does not know the spiritual sense of the Word, may believe that these and several other things, which are related concerning the Lord's passion, involve no more than vulgar methods of mockery, as that they " put a crown of thorns upon His head," that they " parted His garment, and not His coat," that they " bended the knees before Him for the sake of mocking," and also this, that they " put a reed into His right hand, and then smote His head with it," also that they " filled a sponge with vinegar, or wine mixed with myrrh, and gave it Him to drink;" but it is to be noted that all things which are related concerning the Lord's passion, signify the mockery of Divine Truth, consequently the falsification and adulteration of the Word, inasmuch as the Lord, when He was in the world, was Divine Truth Itself, which in the church is the Word; and because the Lord was that Divine Truth in the world, He permitted the Jews to treat Himself as they treated the Divine Truth or the Word, by its falsification and adulteration. For they applied all things of the Word to favour their own loves, and laughed at all truths which disagreed with their loves, as at the Messiah Himself, because He would not be king over the whole world, according to their explication and religion, and would not exalt them to glory above all people and nations. That all things which are related concerning the Lord's passion have such a signification, see above, n. 64, 83, 195; but by "putting a reed into the Lord's hand," and then "smiting His head with it," was signified that they falsified the Divine Truth or Word, and that they altogether made a mock at the understanding of Truth and the Divine Wisdom. By a "reed" is signified the false principle in extremes, and by "smiting the head" is signified to reject and mock at the understanding of Truth and Divine Wisdom, signified by the Lord's "head;" and whereas they "gave the Lord vinegar to drink," by which is signified what is falsified, therefore also they "put a sponge filled with it on a reed," by which is signified the false principle in extremes, which is the false principle sustaining. *A.E.* 627.

Verse 23. *And they gave Him to drink wine mingled with myrrh: but He did not receive it.*—All and singular the things which are related in the Evangelists concerning the Lord's passion, in the spiritual sense signify the state of the church at that time in regard to the Lord and the Word; for the Lord was the Word, because the Divine Truth, and the Jews, as they treated the Word or Divine Truth, so they treated the Lord; on which subject see above, n. 64, 195. By their "giving the Lord wine mingled with myrrh," which is also called "vinegar mixed with gall," was signified the quality of Divine Truth from the Word, such as was with the Jewish nation, viz., that it was commixed with the false principle of evil, and thus altogether falsified and adulterated, wherefore "He would not drink it;" but by their afterwards "giving the Lord vinegar, and encompassing it with hyssop," was signified the false principle, such as prevailed among the well-disposed Gentiles, which was the false principle grounded in ignorance of truth, wherein was what is good and useful, therefore He drank it, since this false principle is accepted of the Lord; by the "hyssop" with which they encompassed it, is signified its purification. By the Lord saying, "I thirst," is signified

Divine spiritual thirst, which is that of Divine Truth and Good in the church, by which Truth and Good the salvation of the human race is effected. *A. E.* 519.

Inasmuch as the Jewish church had falsified all the truths of the Word, and the Lord, by all things of His passion, represented that church, permitting the Jews to treat Him as they had treated the Word, because He was the Word, therefore "they gave Him wine mixed with myrrh, but when He had tasted, He would not drink." *A. R.* 410.

Verse 24. *And when they had crucified Him, they parted His garments, casting lots upon them, what every one would take.*—He who reads these words, and is unacquainted with the internal sense of the Word, does not know that any arcanum lies concealed in them, when yet, in every single expression there is a Divine arcanum. The arcanum was, that Divine Truths we$_r$e dissipated by the Jews, for the Lord was the Divine Truth, whence He is called "the Word;" (John i. 1.) the Word is Divine Truth. His "garments" represented truths in the external form, and His "coat" in the internal; the "division of the garments" represented the dissipation of the truths of faith by the Jews; that "garments" denote truths in the external form, see n. 2576, 5248, 5954, 6918; and that a "coat" denotes truth in the internal form, see n. 4677. Truths in the external form are such as are of the Word in the literal sense, but truths in the internal form are such as are of the Word in the spiritual sense. The "division of the garments into four parts," (John xix. 23.) signifies total dissipation. *A. C.* 9093. See also n. 3812.

Verse 26. *And the superscription of His accusation was written over,* THE KING OF THE JEWS.—By this inscription on the cross was signified that the Divine Truth or the Word, was in such an aspect, and so treated by the Jews, with whom the church was. That all the things which were done to the Lord by the Jews, when He was crucified, signified states of their church as to the Divine Truth or the Word, see n. 9093. *A. C.* 9144.

Verse 27. *And with Him they crucified two thieves; one on His right hand, and one on His left.*—By the "two thieves" are here meant the same as by "the sheep and the goats," (Matt. xxv. 33.) wherefore it is said to the one who acknowledged the Lord, that "he should be with Him in paradise." *A. E.* 600.

Verse 33. *And when the sixth hour was come, there was darkness over the whole earth until the ninth hour.*—By the "darkness over the whole earth" was represented that, in the universal church, there was nothing but evil and the false principle thence derived, together with the false principle and the evil thence derived; "three hours," also, or "from the sixth to the ninth hour," signify what is full and altogether. For all and singular the things which are related in the Evangelists concerning the Lord's passion, contain in them the arcana of heaven, and signify Divine celestial things, which are discoverable only by the internal spiritual sense. *A. E. 526.* See also n. 401.

The falsities of the last times were represented and signified by the "darkness over the whole earth, from the sixth hour even to the ninth," at the Lord's crucifixion. *A. C.* 1839.

By being "darkened" and by "darkness" is signified not to be seen and known by reason of evils grounded in falses and falses grounded in evils. Evils grounded in falses take place with those who assume false principles of religion, and confirm them till they appear as truths, and when they live according to them they do evils from false-principles, or evils of the false. But falses grounded in evils take place with those who do not consider evils as sins, and still more with those who by reasonings from the natural man, and also from the Word, confirm in themselves that evils are not sins, which confirmations themselves are falses grounded in evils, and are called falses of evil. The reason why these are signified by "darkness," is, because "light" signifies truth, and when light is extinguished, darkness ensues. In proof of this many passages from the Word might be adduced. Darkness in spiritual things proceeds either from ignorance of the Truth, or from false doctrines, or from false principles of religion, or from a life of evil. Concerning those who are in false principles of religion and thence in evils of life, the Lord says,— "They shall be cast into outer darkness." (Matt. viii. 12; xxii. 13; xxv. 30.) *A. R.* 413.

Verse 34. *And at the ninth hour Jesus cried with a great voice, saying, Eloi, Eloi, Lama sabachthani? which is, being interpreted, My God, My God, why hast Thou forsaken Me?*— The passion of the cross was the last temptation which the Lord as the Grand Prophet sustained, and was the means of the glorification of His Human Principle, that is, of Union with the Divine Principle of the Father, and was not redemption. For there are two things, for the sake of *which* the Lord came into the world, and by which He saved men and angels, viz., redemption, and the glorification of His Human Principle; these two things are distinct from each other, but still they make one with respect to salvation. What redemption was,

has been shewn above, viz., that it was a combat with the
hells, the subjugation of them, and afterwards the arrangement
of the heavens into order; but glorification is the Unition of
the Human Principle of the Lord with the Divine of His
Father.   This was effected successively and plenarily by the
passion of the cross; for every man, on his part, ought to
accede to God, and so far as man accedes, so far God on
His part enters; the case herein is as with a temple, which
must first be built, and this is done by the hands of men, and
afterwards it must be consecrated, and lastly, prayer must be
made that God may be present, and conjoin Himself with the
church there.   The reason why real Union was fully effected by
the passion of the cross is, because it was the last temptation
which the Lord underwent in the world, and by temptations
conjunction is effected; for in temptations, man is left apparently to himself alone, although he is not left, for God is then
most present in his inmost principles, and supports; wherefore
when any one conquers in temptations, he is intimately conjoined to God, and the Lord on this occasion was intimately
united with God His Father.   That the Lord, during the
passion of the cross, was left to Himself, is manifest from this
His last exclamation at the time,—" My God, My God, why
hast Thou forsaken Me?"   From these considerations it may
now be manifest that the Lord did not suffer as to the Divine
Principle, but as to the Human, and that on this occasion an
intimate, and thereby plenary union was effected.   This may
be illustrated by this consideration,—that whilst man suffers
as to the body, his soul does not suffer, but only grieves; but
God takes away this grief after victory, and wipes it away, as
a person wipes tears from the eyes.   *T. C. R.* 126.

Verse 38. *And the veil of the temple was rent in twain from
the top to the bottom.*—By the " veil of the temple being rent
in twain," &c., was signified that the Lord made His Human
Principle Divine, for within the veil was the ark in which was
the testimony, and by the " testimony " was signified the Lord
as to His Divine Human Principle, as may be seen above,
n. 392; the " veil" signified the external of the church which
was amongst the Jews and Israelites, and which covered their
eyes, that they did not see the Lord and the Divine Truth or
Word in its light.   *A. E.* 400.

By the " veil of the temple being rent," was signified that
the Lord entered into the Divine Principle itself, having
shaken off all appearances, and that at the same time He
opened a passage to the Divine Principle itself by or through
His Human Principle made Divine.   *A. C.* 2576.

By the "veil of the temple being rent in twain," was also signified that the externals of the ancient church, and also of the Jewish, which were all representative of the Lord and of the celestial and spiritual things of His kingdom, that is, of love and charity, and thence of faith, were unfolded, and as it were unswathed, and that then the Christian church was manifested. *A. C.* 4772.

Verse 46. *And laid Him in a sepulchre,* &c.—Whereas "burial" signifies resurrection, it also signifies regeneration, for regeneration is man's first resurrection, inasmuch as he then dies as to the old man, and rises again as to the new. By regeneration man from being dead becomes alive; hence comes the signification of a "sepulchre" in the internal sense. That an idea of regeneration occurs to the angels, when an idea of a *sepulchre* is presented, is evident also from what was related concerning infants, n. 2299. The reason why "sepulchre," in an opposite sense, signifies death or hell, is, because the wicked do not rise again to life; and therefore when the subject treated of is concerning the wicked, and mention is made of a *sepulchre,* in this case there occurs to the angels no other idea than that of hell; this is the reason why hell, in the Word, is also called a "sepulchre." That "sepulchre" signifies resurrection and also regeneration, is evident from these words in Ezekiel,—"Therefore prophesy and say unto them, Thus saith the Lord Jehovah,—Behold, I will open your *sepulchres,* and will cause you to ascend out of your *sepulchres,* O my people, and will bring you to the ground of Israel. And ye shall know that I am Jehovah, in My opening your *sepulchres,* and causing you to ascend out of your *sepulchres,* O my people; and I will give My spirit unto you, and ye shall live, and I will place you on your own ground." (xxxvii. 12—14.) In this passage the prophet treats of vivified bones, and in an internal sense of regeneration; that he treats of regeneration is very evident, for it is said,—" I will give My spirit unto you, and ye shall live, and I will place you on your own ground." "Sepulchre" here denotes the old man, with his evil and false principles, which to open, and from which to ascend, is to be regenerated; thus the idea of a sepulchre perishes, and is, as it were, put off, when the idea of regeneration, or new life, succeeds. The same is implied by the "*sepulchres* being opened, and many bodies of sleeping saints *rising,* and going forth out of their *sepulchres* after the Lord's resurrection, and entering into the holy city, and appearing unto many;" (Matt. xxvii. 52, 53. denoting resurrection by virtue of the Lord's resurrection,

and, in an interior sense, every particular resurrection. By
the Lord's raising Lazarus from the dead, (John xi.) is also
implied the raising up of a New Church from amongst the
Gentiles, for all the miracles which were wrought by the
Lord, as being divine, involved states of His church. The
like is implied also by what is related of the man, who,
being "cast into the sepulchre of Elisha, came to life again
on touching the prophet's bones;" (2 Kings xiii. 20, 21.) for
by Elisha was represented the Lord. Inasmuch as "burial"
signified resurrection in general, and every particular resurrection, therefore the ancients were especially solicitous about
their burials and the places where they were buried, as appears
from the case of Abraham, in that he was buried in Hebron in
the land of Canaan, and also Isáac and Jacob with their wives;
(Gen. xlvii. 29—31; xlix. 30—32.) and from the case of Joseph,
in that his bones were carried from Egypt into the land of
Canaan; (Gen. l. 25; Exod. xiii. 19; Joshua xxiv. 32.) and
from the case of David and the kings after him, in that they
were buried in Zion. (1 Kings ii. 10; xi. 43; xiv. 31; xv.
8, 24; xxii. 50; 2 Kings viii. 24; xii. 21; xiv. 20; xv. 7, 38;
xvi. 20.) The reason was, because the "land of Canaan" and
also "Zion" represented and signified the Lord's kingdom, and
"burial" represented and signified resurrection; but that place
contributes nothing to resurrection may be obvious to every one.
That "burial" signifies resurrection to life, is manifest also
from other representatives, as where it is ordered that "the
wicked should not be bemoaned, neither buried, but should be
cast out;" (Jer. viii. 2; xiv. 16; xvi. 4, 6; xx. 6; xxii. 19;
xxv. 33; 2 Kings ix. 10; Rev. xi. 9.) and that "the wicked,
who were buried, should be cast out from their sepulchres."
(Jer. viii. 1, 2; 2 Kings xxiii. 16—18.) But that "sepulchre,"
in an opposite sense, signifies death or hell, may be seen in
Isaiah xiv. 19—21; Ezek. xxxii. 21, 22, 23, 25, 27; Psalm
lxxxviii. 5, 6, 11, 12; Numb. xix. 16, 18, 19. A. C. 2916.

TRANSLATOR'S NOTES AND OBSERVATIONS.

CHAPTER XV.

VERSE 2. *And Pilate asked Him, Art Thou the King of the Jews? And He answering, said, Thou sayest.*—The two expressions, "said" and "sayest," which are here applied, are from different expressions in the original Greek; the first, viz., "said," being from the Greek εἶπω, and the second, viz., "sayest," from the Greek λεγω. But the Greek εἶπω is expressive of a more interior speech than the Greek λεγω, and accordingly the former is applied, in this instance, to express the speech of the Lord, and the latter, to express the speech of Pilate.

MARK.

CHAPTER XVI.

1. AND when the Sabbath was past, Mary Magdalene, and Mary [the mother] of James, and Salome, had bought spices, that when they came they might anoint Him.

2. And very early the first day of the week, they come to the sepulchre as the sun was rising.

3. And they said among themselves, Who shall roll away for us the stone from the door of the sepulchre?

4. And when they looked, they saw that the stone was rolled away; for it was very great.

5. And entering into the sepulchre, they saw a young man sitting on the right side, clothed in a white garment; and they were affrighted.

6. But he said unto them, Be not affrighted: ye seek Jesus of Nazareth, who was crucified: He is risen; He is not here: behold the place where they laid Him.

THAT the LORD's resurrection early in the morning involves in it the arising of a New Church, both in general and in particular, yea, also in singular; thus that He rises again daily, yea, every moment, in the minds of the regenerate. (Verses 1, 2.)

On which occasion they who are in the affection of good and truth experience the removal of all false principles, so that celestial good and truth are made manifest. (Verses 3, 4, and former part of the 5th verse.)

By which they are led into holy adoration, and are admonished that the LORD's Humanity was made Divine, and is continually present to guide them. (Verses 6, 7.)

7. But go away, tell His disciples and Peter that He goeth before you into Galilee: there ye shall see Him, as He said unto you.

8. And going out quickly, they fled from the sepulchre, being troubled and amazed: and they said nothing to any one; for they were afraid.

9. Now when He was risen early on the first [day] of the week, He appeared first to Mary Magdalene, out of whom He had cast seven devils.

Yet they are afraid to publish this admonition, until it is further enforced by the LORD's visible manifestation of Himself to the humble and the penitent. (Verses 8, 9.)

10. She having gone forth told it to those who had been with Him, as they mourned and wept.

11. And they, when they had heard that He was alive, and was seen by her, did not believe.

12. But after these things He appeared to two of them as they walked, in another form, as they were going into the country.

13. And they going away told it to the rest: neither believed they them.

14. Afterwards He appeared to the eleven as they sat at meat, and upbraided them with their unbelief and hardness of heart, because they believed not them who had seen Him when He was risen.

Nevertheless it is still doubted, until it is further enforced by His visible manifestation to those who had been instructed in the doctrine of truth. (Verses 10—15.)

15. And He said unto them, Going forth into all the world, preach the Gospel to every creature.

16. He that believeth and is baptized shall be saved;

To whom a charge is given to announce to the humble and the penitent the manifestation of God in the flesh in the person of JESUS CHRIST, and that heaven and eternal but he that believeth not shall be condemned.

17. And these signs shall follow them that believe; In My name they shall cast out devils; they shall speak with new tongues:

18. They shall take up serpents; and if they drink any deadly thing, it shall not hurt them; they shall lay hands on the sick, and they shall recover.

19. But the Lord, after speaking to them, was taken up into heaven, and sat on the right hand of God.

20. And they going forth, preached every where, the Lord working with them, and confirming the Word with signs following.

life are opened to all those who believe in this manifestation and do the work of repentance, but are closed against those who do not believe. (Verses 15, 16.)

They are further taught that by a right belief all false principles of every kind are cast out; the doctrinals of the New Church are received; security is given against infestation from the hells, and the infection of wickedness; at the same time by communication and conjunction with heaven, thus with the Lord, spiritual diseases are healed. (Verses 17, 18.)

Thus the sum and substance of all evangelical truth is to be found in the acknowledgment that the Lord has Divine Omnipotence even as to His Humanity, and that He is continually at work in the minds of the humble and the penitent to confirm this acknowledgment. Amen.

EXPOSITION.

CHAPTER XVI.

VERSES 2, 9. *And very early the first day of the week, they come to the sepulchre as the sun was rising.*—Inasmuch as "morning" in a proper sense signifies the Lord, His coming, thus the approximation of His kingdom, it may be manifest what morning further signifies, viz., the arising of a New Church, for this is the Lord's kingdom on the earth, and this both in general and in particular, yea, also in singular; in *general,* when any New Church is raised up on this globe; in *particular,* when man is regenerating, and is made new, for on this occasion the kingdom of the Lord arises in him and he becomes a church; in *singular,* as often as the good of love and of faith is operative in him, for in this good is the Lord's advent. Hence the Lord's resurrection "on the third day in the morning," (Mark xvi. 2, 9; Luke xxiv. 1; John xx. 1.) involves all those things, even in particular and singular, that He rises again in the minds of the regenerate every day, yea, every moment. *A. C.* 2405.

Inasmuch as the Lord is the *morning,* therefore also He arose from the grave "early in the morning," being about to establish a New Church. *T. C. R.* 764.

Verses 3, 4. *And they said among themselves, Who shall roll away for us the stone from the door of the sepulchre? &c.*— By the "stone," which was placed before the door of the sepulchre, and which was rolled away by the angel, is signified the Divine Truth, thus the Word, which was closed by the Jews, but opened by the Lord; and whereas by a "sepulchre," in the spiritual sense, is signified resurrection and regeneration, and eminently by the "sepulchre," in which the Lord was laid, and by "angels," in the Word, is signified Divine Truth, therefore the angels were seen "one sitting at the head, and the other at the feet;" and by the "angel at the head" was signified the Divine Truth in first principles, and by the "angel at the feet" the Divine Truth in ultimates, each proceeding from the Lord, by which, when it is received, regeneration is effected and there is resurrection. *A. E.* 687.

Verse 5. *And entering into the sepulchre, they saw a young man sitting on the right side, clothed in a white garment.*— That rational truths are like a covering or clothing to spiritual truths, may be thus explained; the inmost principles of man are what constitute his soul, but the exterior principles are what constitute his body. The inmost principles of man are goods and truths, from which the soul has its life, otherwise the soul would not be soul; exterior principles hence derive their life, and are all like a body, or, what is the same thing, like a covering or clothing; which may especially be manifest from those which appear in the other life, as from the angels when they are presented to view, on which occasion their interior principles shine forth from the face, whilst the exterior principles are represented both in their body and in their clothing, insomuch that every one may there know from the clothing alone what is their quality, for they are real substances, thus essences in form. The case is the same with the angels who have been seen, and who have been described in the Word as to their faces and clothing, as with those who were seen in the Lord's sepulchre. (Matt. xxviii. 3; Mark xvi. 5.) *A. C.* 4576. See also n. 10,536. *H. H.* 180.

They saw a young man, &c.—That the spirit of a man is equally a man, may be seen demonstrated from much experience in the Treatise on "Heaven and Hell," n. 73—77, 311—316; and that every man is a spirit as to his interiors, n. 432—444. To which may be added, that everything spiritual is in its essence a man, thus the all of love and wisdom which proceeds from the Lord, for this is spiritual. The reason why everything spiritual, or which proceeds from the Lord, is a man, is, because the Lord Himself, who is the God of the universe, is a MAN, and from Him nothing can proceed but what is similar, for the proceeding Divine is not changeable in itself, and extended, and what is not extended is everywhere such; hence is His Omnipresence. The reason why man has conceived an idea of an angel, of a spirit, and of himself after death, as being like ether or air without a human body, is, because the sensually-learned have conceived it from the term *spirit*, which is a breath of the mouth, also from their being unseen, and not appearing before the eyes; for the sensual think only from the sensual principle of the body and from what is material, also from some passages of the Word not spiritually understood. Yet they know from the Word that the Lord, although He was a Man as to "flesh and bones," (Luke xxiv. 39.) still became invisible to the disciples, and "passed through the doors when shut."

(John xx. 19—26.)   Angels also have been seen in the Word as men (Mark xvi. 5.) before many, who did not assume a human form for the purpose, but manifested themselves in their own form before the eyes of their spirits which were then opened.   Lest, therefore, man should remain any longer in a fallacious idea concerning spirits and angels, and concerning his own soul after death, it has pleased the Lord to open the sight of my spirit, and to grant me to converse face to face with angels and deceased men, to contemplate them, to touch them, and to say many things concerning the incredulity and the delusion of men now living.—(*Div. Wisdom*, vii. 1, from the *Apocalypse Explained.*)

The difference between a man in the natural world and a man in the spiritual world, is, that the one man is clothed in a spiritual body, but the other in a natural body; and the spiritual man sees the spiritual man as clearly as the natural man sees the natural man.   But the natural man cannot see the spiritual man, and the spiritual man cannot see the natural man, on account of the difference between *natural* and *spiritual*.   What kind of difference this is, may be described, but not in a few words.—(*Continuation of Last Judgment*, 36.)

Verse 9.   *Risen early on the first day,* &c.—The "morning," in the supreme sense, signifies the Lord, and love from Him towards Him; hence it was that " He also rose early, at the rising of the sun." (Mark xvi. 2, 9.)   *A. C.* 10,134.

Verse 14.   *Hardness of heart.*—See chap. iii. 5, Exposition.

Verse 15.   *And He said unto them, Going forth into all the world, preach the Gospel to every creature.*—That " beasts" signify affections appertaining to man, evil affections with the wicked, and good affections with the good, may be abundantly manifest from the Word, as in Ezekiel,—"Behold, I will have respect to you, that ye may be cultivated and sown : and I will multiply upon you *man* and *beast;* and they shall be multiplied and made fruitful: and I will make you to dwell according to your ancient states;" (xxxvi. 9—11.) speaking of regeneration. And in Jeremiah,—"Behold, the days are coming, and I will sow the house of Israel and the house of Judah with the seed of *man,* and the seed of *beast;* and I will watch over them to build and plant;" (xxxi. 27, 28.) speaking also of regeneration. A distinction is made in the Prophets between *beasts* and *wild beasts* of the earth, and between *beasts* and *wild beasts* of the field.   Good principles are still called " beasts," so that they who are nearest to the Lord in heaven, are named " animals," both in Ezekiel and in the Revelations, in which latter book

it is written,—"All the angels stood round about the throne,
and the elders, and the four *animals;* and they fell before the
throne on their faces, and adored the Lamb." (Rev. vii. 11;
xix. 4.) They are also called "creatures," to whom the Gospel
was to be preached, because they were to be created anew.
"Go ye into all the world, and preach the Gospel to every
creature." (Mark xvi. 15.) *A. C. 46.*

Inasmuch as to be made, or "created," also signifies to be
regenerated, therefore he who is born again is said also to
be "made or created anew," as is plain from these passages:—
"*Create* in me a clean heart, O God; renew a right spirit
within me." (Psalm li. 10.) "Thou openest Thy hand, they
are filled with good; Thou sendest forth Thy spirit, they are
created." (Psalm civ. 28, 30.) "Behold, I *create* Jerusalem
a rejoicing;" (Isaiah lxv. 18.) and also in other passages, where
the Lord is called Creator, Former, and Maker. Hence it
is plain what is meant by these words of the Lord to His
disciples,—"Go ye into all the world, and preach the Gospel
to every *creature.*" (Mark xvi. 15.) By "creatures" are meant
all who are in a capacity to be regenerated; in like manner it
is applied in Rev. iii. 14; 2 Cor. v. 17. *T. C. R. 573.*

A baptized, that is, a regenerate person, is meant by
"creature;" (Mark xvi. 15; Rom. viii. 19—21.) and by a
"new creature;" (2 Cor. v. 17.) for it is called "creature"
from being created, by which also is signified to be regenerated. *T. C. R. 687.*

Verse 16. *He that believeth and is baptized shall be saved;
but he that believeth not shall be condemned.*—By these words
of the Lord is understood by the angels in heaven, that
whosoever acknowledges the Lord, and is regenerated, will be
saved. Hence also it is that baptism is called, by Christian
churches on earth, the "laver of regeneration." Be it known,
therefore, to every Christian, that whosoever does not believe
in the Lord cannot be regenerated, notwithstanding his having
been baptized, and that being baptized, without faith in the
Lord, is of no avail, as may be seen above in this chapter.
That "baptism" implies purification from evils, and thus
regeneration, must be very plain to every Christian, for at the
ceremony of baptism the priest signs the infant on the forehead
with the sign of the cross, as a memorial of Christ, inquiring
of the sponsors whether "they renounce the devil and all
his works?" and whether "they receive the faith?" to which
questions the sponsors answer in the child's name,—"Yes."
Renunciation of the devil, that is, of the evils which are from
hell, and faith in the Lord, perfect regeneration. *T. C. R. 685.*

Inasmuch as "baptism" is for a sign and for a memorial that all regeneration is effected from the Lord, by the truths of faith, and by a life according to them, therefore man may be baptized when an infant, and if not at that time, when an adult.   Let those, therefore, who have been baptized, know, that baptism itself does not give faith, neither salvation, but that it testifies that they receive faith, and that they are saved, if they be regenerated.   Hence it may be manifest what is meant by the Lord's words in Mark,—"He that *believeth* and is *baptized* shall be saved; but he that *believeth not* shall be condemned." (xvi. 16.)   "He that believeth" is he who acknowledges the Lord, and receives Divine Truths from Him by the Word; "he that is baptized" is he who is regenerated by those Truths from the Lord. *H. D. N. J. 206—208.*

Verses 17, 18. *And these signs shall follow them that believe: In My name they shall cast out devils; they shall speak with new tongues; they shall take up serpents; and if they drink any deadly thing, it shall not hurt them; they shall lay hands on the sick, and they shall recover.*—Although these things were miracles, they are still called "signs," because they testified concerning the Divine Power of the Lord thus operating, wherefore it is said at verse 20,—"The Lord working with them by those *signs*." They would have been called miracles, if applied to the wicked, for with the wicked such things only induce stupor, and strike the mind, and still do not persuade to a right faith.   It is otherwise with the good, for to them the same things are testifications which persuade to a right faith, wherefore also they are called "signs," and it is said, "these signs shall follow them who believe;" but in what manner those signs could persuade to a right faith, shall also be briefly explained.   Those miraculous signs, as the "casting out of devils," the "speaking with new tongues," the "taking up of serpents," "not being hurt if they drank any deadly thing," and "being restored to health by the laying on of hands," were spiritual in their essence and in their origin, from which spiritual things they flowed forth and were produced as effects, for they were correspondences, which derive all that they have from the spiritual world by influx from the Lord, as "casting out of devils in the name of the Lord," derives its effect from this circumstance, that the name of the Lord, spiritually understood, is the all of doctrine originating in the Word from the Lord; and that "devils" are false principles of every kind, which are thus cast out, that is, removed by doctrine originating in the Word from the Lord; "speaking with new tongues," derived its effect from this consideration, that "new tongues" are doctrinals for the New Church; "serpents were to be taken up," because "serpents" signify the hells as to wickedness, and thus they were to be safe from its infestation; "not being hurt if they drank any deadly thing," denoted that the wickedness of the hells would not infest them; the "recovery of the sick by the laying on of hands," denoted that by communication and conjunction with heaven, thus with the Lord, they should be healed of spiritual diseases, which are called iniquities and sins, the "laying on of hands" by the disciples, corresponding to conjunction and communication with the Lord, and thus to the removal of iniquities by His Divine Power. *A. E.* 706.

Deceit is called "hypocrisy," when expressions of piety are in the mouth, and impiety is in the heart, or when charity is in the mouth but hatred in the heart, or when innocence is in the countenance or gesture, but cruelty in the soul and bosom, consequently when innocence, charity, and piety are employed as the means of deceiving; such deceivers are "serpents and vipers" in the internal sense, since, as was said above, when viewed in the light of heaven by the angels, all such persons appear as serpents and as vipers, who conceal evils under truths, that is, who deceitfully bend truths to do evils, for they hide poison under the teeth, and thus destroy life. But they who are in the faith of truth, and in the life of good from the Lord, cannot be hurt by their poison, for they are in light from the Lord, in which light the deceitful appear as serpents, and their deceits as poisons. That they are in safety from the Lord, is meant by the Lord's words to the disciples,— "Behold, I give unto you power to tread on *serpents* and *scorpions;*" (Luke x. 19.) and in Mark,—"These signs shall follow them who believe: they shall take up *serpents;* though they drink any *deadly thing,* it shall not hurt them." (xvi. 18.) *A. C.* 9013.

Verse 19. *But the Lord, after speaking to them, was taken up into heaven, and sat on the right hand of God.*—Inasmuch as the Humanity of the Lord was glorified, that is, was made Divine, therefore after death He rose again on the third day with the whole Body, which is not the case with any man, for man rises again only as to the spirit, but not as to the body. To the intent that man might know, and no one might doubt, that the Lord rose again with the whole Body, He not only declared this by the angels who were in the sepulchre, but also shewed Himself in His human Body before the disciples, saying unto them, when they believed that they saw a spirit,—"Behold My hands and My feet, that it is

I Myself: handle Me, and see; for a spirit hath not flesh and bones, as ye see Me have." (Luke xxiv. 39, 40; John xx. 20.)

That the Lord might further prove that He was not a spirit but a man, He said to the disciples,—"Have ye here any meat? They gave Him part of a broiled fish, and of a honeycomb; which He took, and did eat before them." (Luke xxiv. 41—43.) Inasmuch as His Body was now not material, but a Divine substantial Body, therefore He came to the disciples "when the doors were shut;" (John xx. 19, 20.) and after that He had been seen, "He became invisible." (Luke xxiv. 31.) The Lord, being now of such a quality, was taken up and sat at the right hand of God, for it is said in Luke,—"It came to pass, when Jesus blessed the disciples, He retired from them, and was taken up into heaven;" (xxiv. 51.) and in Mark,— "After speaking to them, He was taken up into heaven, and sat on the right hand of God." (xvi. 19.) To "sit on the right hand of God" signifies Divine Omnipotence. *D. Lord*, 35. See also *S. S.* 49.

The Lord, after His resurrection, was no longer Jehovah under the form of an angel, but He was Jehovah Man, which also is meant by these words:—"See ye My hands and My feet, that it is I Myself: handle Me, and see; for a spirit hath not flesh and bones, as ye see Me have;" (Luke xxiv. 39.) and also from these words:—"I came forth from the Father, and am come into the world; again I leave the world, and go to the Father." (John xvi. 28.) For the Lord, when He was in the world, made His Human Divine. *A. C.* 9316.

In the Word mention is made of "walking before God," of "standing before God," and of "sitting before God;" what is signified by "standing before God," may be seen above, n. 414; and what by "walking before God," n. 97; but what by "sitting before God," may be manifest from the passages in the Word where mention is made of "sitting;" for, in the spiritual world, all things which regard man's motion and rest, signify those things which regard his life, because they thence proceed. "Walking" and "journeying" are motions on the part of man, and hence signify progression of life, or progression of the thought from the intention of the will; but "standing" and "sitting" relate to man's rest, and hence signify the *esse* of life, from which its *existere* is derived, thus, to make to live; wherefore to "sit upon thrones," when speaking of judgment, signifies to be in the operation of judging, consequently also to judge. Hence mention is made of "sitting in judgment," which is to do judgment; to "sit" also on a throne, when speaking of a kingdom, signifies to be a king or to reign. What is further signified by "sitting," in a spiritual sense, may be manifest from the following passages:—"Blessed is the man who *walketh not* in the counsel of the ungodly, and *standeth not* in the way of sinners, and *sitteth not* in the seat of the scornful." (Psalm i. 1.) In this passage mention is made of " walking," " standing," and " sitting," because one follows the other; for to " walk" has relation to the life of thought grounded in intention, to " stand" has relation to the life of intention grounded in the will, and to "sit" has relation to the life of the will,. thus to the *esse* of life; "counsel," also, of which *walking* is predicated, has respect to thought; "way," of which *standing* is predicated, has respect to intention, and to " sit in a seat," has respect to the will, which is the *esse* of the life of man. Inasmuch as Jehovah, that is, the Lord, is the very *Esse* of the life of all, therefore to "sit" is predicated of Him, as in David,—"Jehovah shall *sit* to eternity;" (Psalm ix. 7.) again,— " God reigneth over the nations; God *sitteth* upon the throne of His Holiness;" (Psalm xlvii. 8.) again,—"Jehovah *sitteth* at the flood, and *sitteth* a King for ever." (Psalm xxix. 10.) And in Matthew,—"When the Son of Man shall come in His glory, and all the holy angels with Him, then shall He *sit* upon the throne of His glory;" (xxv. 31.) where, to " sit upon the throne of His glory," signifies to be in His Divine Truth, from which is judgment;" again,—" When the Son of Man shall *sit* on the throne of His glory, ye also shall *sit* on twelve thrones, judging the twelve tribes of Israel." (xix. 28; Luke xxii. 30.) Inasmuch as by the " angels," also by the " twelve apostles," and likewise by the " twelve tribes of Israel," are signified the truths of the church, and, in the supreme sense, the Divine Truth, therefore by " sitting upon thrones" is not meant that themselves are to sit, but the Lord as to Divine Truth, from which is judgment; and by "judging the twelve tribes of Israel," is signified to judge all according to the truths of their own church. Hence it is evident that by " sitting on a throne," when predicated of the Lord, is signified to be judging, thus to judge; it is called a "throne of glory," because "glory" signifies Divine Truth, see above, n. 34, 288, 345, 678. And in the Evangelists,—" David said in the Book of Psalms, The Lord said unto my Lord, *Sit* Thou on My right hand, until I make Thy foes Thy footstool." (Matt. xxii. 43, 44; Luke xx. 42, 43; Psalm cx. 1.) " The Lord said unto my Lord," signifies the Divine Principle itself, which is called Father, to the Divine Human Principle, which is called Son; "Sit on My right hand," signifies Divine Power or Omnipotence by Divine Truth; "until I make Thy foes Thy footstool," signifies until the hells are conquered and subdued, and the wicked are cast in thither; "foes" are the hells, consequently the wicked; and a "footstool" signifies the lowest region beneath the heavens, under which region are the hells; for the Lord, whilst He was in the world, was Divine Truth, which has Omnipotence, and by which He conquered and subdued the hells. Again,—"The Lord, after that He had spoken with them, was taken up into heaven, and *sat* on the right hand of God;" (Mark xvi. 19.) where, to "sit on the right hand of God," has a like signification, denoting His Divine Omnipotence by Divine Truth. From which passages it is evident that to "sit," is to be; and to "sit on the right hand of God," is to be Omnipotent. *A.E.* 687.

Inasmuch as the Lord operates, in all cases, from first principles by last, and in the last is in His power and in His fulness, therefore it pleased the Lord to assume Humanity, and to become Divine Truth, that is, the Word, (John i. 14.) and thus from Himself to reduce to order all things of heaven and all things of hell, that is, to accomplish the Last Judgment. This the Lord could effect from the Divinity in Himself, which was in first principles, by [or through] His Humanity, which was in last principles, and not from His presence or abode in the men of the church, as heretofore, for these had altogether declined from the truths and goods of the Word, in which the Lord had before His dwelling with men. This was the primary cause of the Lord's coming into the world, and also that He might make His Humanity Divine; for by this He assumed the power of keeping in order to eternity all things of heaven and all things of hell. This is meant by "*sitting on the right hand of God*." (Mark xvi. 19.) The "right hand of God," is Divine Omnipotence; and to "sit on the right hand," is to be in that Omnipotence by the Humanity. *A.E.* 1087.

THE END.

INDEX

TERMS, SUBJECTS, AND CORRESPONDENCES,

Lightning Source UK Ltd.
Milton Keynes UK
UKHW012059230219
337878UK00014B/1138/P

9 781331 286738